Police Work

This book provides a highly readable account of police work. It builds upon *Introduction to Police Work* (Rogers and Lewis 2007) to provide a comprehensive, in-depth and critical understanding of policing in today's diverse society.

Police Work: principles and practice meets the need for an increasingly sophisticated and professional approach to training within the police, whether this is carried out within police forces themselves or within higher education institutions. Written in an accessible style by current and former police practitioners and a nationally recognized expert on the National Intelligence Model, this book focuses – in line with the government's agenda for workforce modernization – on three key areas of policing: community, investigation and intelligence. It introduces readers to many important areas through the use of definition boxes, scenario boxes highlighting good practice, points to note boxes, flowcharts and diagrams as well as a wide range of questions and exercises to help apply their knowledge to different situations and scenarios.

This book will be essential reading for those on probationer training programmes and a valuable resource for students taking courses in policing and criminology more generally where an advanced level of understanding of the nature of police work is required.

The authors

Colin Rogers is a former senior police officer and is a Reader in Police Sciences at the University of Glamorgan; **Rhobert Lewis** is a former police officer, now Associate Dean and Director of the Centre for Police Studies at the University of Glamorgan; **Tim John** is Senior Lecturer in the Centre for Criminology at the University of Glamorgan; and **Tim Read** is a former Senior Research Consultant for Evidence Led Solutions, a research consultancy working in the community safety field, and is currently Senior Lecturer in Police Science at Glamorgan University.

Police Work

Principles and practice

**Colin Rogers, Rhobert Lewis,
Tim John and Tim Read**

Routledge
Taylor & Francis Group

LONDON AND NEW YORK

First published 2011
by Routledge
2 Park Square, Milton Park, Abingdon, Oxon, OX14 4RN

Simultaneously published in the USA and Canada
by Routledge
711 Third Avenue, New York, NY 10017

Routledge is an imprint of the Taylor & Francis Group, an informa business

British Library Cataloguing in Publication Data
A catalogue record for this book is available from the British Library

Library of Congress Cataloging in Publication Data
Police work: principles and practice / Colin Rogers ... [et al.].
p. cm.
1. Police–Great Britain. 2. Law enforcement–Great Britain. I. Rogers,
Colin, 1955–
HV8195.A2P633 2011
363.2′30941–dc22   2010049277

ISBN: 978-1-84392-532-3 (hbk)
ISBN: 978-1-84392-531-6 (pbk)
ISBN: 978-0-203-81667-7 (ebk)

Typeset in Times New Roman
by Glyph International

Printed and bound in Great Britain by
TJ International Ltd, Padstow, Cornwall

Contents

Illustrations

Preface

This book is about the fundamentals of policing in England and Wales. It is written in an uncomplicated style in order to explain sometimes complex and complicated ideas and as such will appeal to the following reader:

- Those individuals who are interested in what the police in England and Wales do.
- Those individuals who are undergoing their initial police training within their respective police forces.
- Those individuals who are student police officers engaged on courses in Higher and Further Education establishments as part of their police training.
- Those individuals who are studying the police as part of an undergraduate or public services style course in Higher or Further Education establishments.

The United Kingdom has recently seen a change of government which has introduced new ideologies in many areas including that of policing and criminal justice. However, these new policies and approaches have not been fully developed, and will probably not be for another few years, so we appear to be in a state of transition regarding many government approaches to public service provision.

Whilst we believe that the fundamental approaches to policing will not be greatly affected by new policies we have included possible newer interpretations and future directions of policing. For example, discussions surrounding community engagement and involvement, a key issue for previous government, are explained, along with newer and linked ideas concerning the so called 'Big Society' involvement in the delivery and assessment of public services.

Thanks and acknowledgements

The editors would like to thank the following persons who assisted with the production of this book:

Ena Hoctor, lecturer at the Centre for Police Sciences, University of Glamorgan who assisted with Chapter 14, *The Nature and Investigation of Sexual Offences*.

Mike Hurley, Senior Lecturer at the Centre for Police Sciences, University of Glamorgan, who assisted with Chapter 7, *Legislation and Police Powers*.

James Gravelle, who assisted with Chapter 17, *Policing and Public Disorder*.

Principle authors

Dr Colin Rogers was the author for Chapters 1, 2, 3, 4, 5, 6, 8, 9 and 17.
Dr Rhobert Lewis was the author for Chapters 7, 14, 15 and 16.
Tim John was the author for Chapters 10 and 13.
Tim Read was the author for Chapters 11, 12 and 18.

Glossary of police terminology

ACC	Assistant Chief Constable
ACPO	The Association of Chief Police Office
APA	The Association of Police Authorities
ASBO	Anti Social Behaviour Order
ANPR	Automatic Number Plate Recognition
BAWP	British Association of Women Police
BCS	British Crime Survey
BCU	Basic Command Unit
BVPI	Best Value Performance Indicator
CC	Chief Constable
CCTV	Close Circuit Television
CDA	Crime and Disorder Act 1998
CDRP	Crime and Disorder Reduction Partnership
CJS	Criminal Justice System
COPs	Community Oriented Policing
CPIA	Criminal Procedure and Investigation Act 1996
CPS	Crown Prosecution Service
CPTED	Crime Prevention Through Environmental Design
CRAVED	Concealable, Removable, Available, Valuable, Enjoyable and Disposable
CRP	Crime Reduction Programme
CSP	Community Safety partnership (CDRP equivalent in Wales)
DAT	Drug Action Team
DCC	Deputy Chief Constable
DPP	Director of Public Prosecutions
DVLA	Driver and Vehicle Licensing Agency
ECHR	European Court of Human Rights
FPN	Fixed Penalty Notice
GCHQ	Government Communication Headquarters
GPA	Gay Police Association
HMIC	Her Majesty's Inspector of Constabulary
HVP	High Visibility Policing
IPLDP	Initial Police Learning and Development Programme

JDI	Jill Dando Institute
LSP	Local Strategic Partnership
NBPA	National Black Police Association
NCIS	National Crime Intelligence Service
NCPE	National Centre for Police Excellence (formerly CENTREX)
NCRS	National Crime Recording Standard
NIM	National Intelligence Model
NOS	National Occupational Standards
NPIA	National Policing Improvement Agency
NRPP	National Reassurance Policing Programme
ODPM	Office of the Deputy Prime Minister
PACE	Police and Criminal Evidence Act 1984
PAT	Problem Analysis Triangle
PCSO	Police Community Support Officer
PITO	Police Information Technology Organisation
PNC	Police National Computer
POA	Problem Oriented Approach
POP	Problem Oriented Policing/Partnerships
PPAF	Policing Performance Assessment Framework
PSA	Public Service Agreement
RAT	Routine Activity Theory
RCT	Rational Choice Theory
RSL	Registered Social Landlord
RV	Repeat Victimisation
SARA	Scanning, Analysis, Response, Assessment
SBD	Secured By Design
SCP	Situational Crime Prevention
SFO	Serious Fraud Office
SOCA	Serious Organised Crime Agency
STAC	Spatial and Temporal Analysis of Crime
TIC	An offence 'Taken into Consideration'
TPI	Targeted Policing Initiative
TT&CG	Tactical, Tasking and Co-ordinating Group
VIVA	Value, Inertia, Volume and Access
YI	Youth Inclusion
YIP	Youth Inclusion Programme
YJB	Youth Justice Board
YOP	Youth Offending Panel
YOT	Youth Offending Team
ZTP	Zero Tolerance Policing

Special features of the book

The book has been written from a practitioner's viewpoint in order to help both students and lecturer/trainers to access more easily the information contained within it. It was compiled after extensive research and consultation with serving police officers, trainers and those individuals involved in educating police officers. It has been written as a companion book to the previously published *Introduction to Police Work* by Rogers and Lewis and published by Willan in 2007 and builds on the ideas outlined within that work, providing a more critical and deeper knowledge base for the more advanced student of policing in England and Wales.

Each chapter is laid out in broadly the same manner and contains all or some of the features discussed below.

Chapter introduction

This highlights the main areas of the chapter and provides an indication of the scope of its content.

Exercises

A unique feature of this book is the inclusion of exercises throughout the various chapters. These exercises are linked to the information contained in the chapter and are sequenced throughout the text in a logical manner that enables you to work from a simple understanding of an idea to the more complex application of the idea in certain circumstances.

Figures

Where necessary, included in the chapter is a figure or example which includes data that supports a point made in the text.

Tables

Tables are also included where necessary to illustrate points and to engage you understanding sometimes complex ideas and on occasions are used as part of an exercise.

Case study

Where appropriate case studies are used to further illustrate work discussed within a chapter and to illustrate a particular point or learning experience.

Suggested further reading

At the end of each chapter you will find some books that have been highlighted as being useful for the student to read in support of the work contained in each chapter.

Useful websites

Also at the conclusion of each chapter there is mention of useful website(s) that are pertinent to that particular chapter. Readers are invited to explore these websites in order to reinforce the information and knowledge already laid out in the work.

1 The context for this book

Introduction

This book is written for those who want to know about policing practices and the underlying principles of that occupation. In particular it will be of use to those who have a general interest in policing, those who are undergoing their initial training as police officers and those undertaking the study of policing as part of an undergraduate or public services course in higher or further education. The police organisation has been under pressure from successive governments to change for quite some time, and this process appears to have accelerated recently due to the economic recession, with reports from the Audit Commission (2010) and HMIC (2010) suggesting that radical changes may take place in these times of austerity.

The purpose of this chapter is to briefly explain some of the reasons why and how policing has changed, and uses the debates about police training as an example of the types of discussions that are currently ongoing to set the scene for the remainder of the book.

Historical context

> The purpose of the police service is to uphold the law fairly and firmly: to prevent crime; to pursue and bring to justice those who break the law; and to keep the Queens Peace; to protect, help and reassure the community; and to be seen to do all this with integrity, 'common sense' and sound judgement'.
>
> (The ACPO Statement of Common Purpose, 1990, in Newburn 2003)

The Statement of Common Purpose was a document issued by the Association of Chief Police Officers in 1990 which set out the standards the police service should maintain in their everyday work within communities. It set forth a 'common' standard of behaviour and working practices which would be employed by all 43 police forces across England and Wales and was, in many senses, a precursor for the managerialist and performance-driven approach imposed on the police organisation since that time. Its contents were not too dissimilar to the founding principles of policing introduced during the late 1820s, known as Peel's Principles of Policing (Peak and Glensor 1996) which included such statements as 'The Public are the Police and the Police are the Public'. However, while in many senses these principles still persist, as the public, society and community expectations change, the police service in England and Wales has had to re-evaluate the way it trains and educates its staff to support a more professional approach to the delivery of its services. In particular there has been a need to consider producing a police officer who carries out his or her duties drawing on a bank of high-quality research-led information supported by an ethical approach in its application. This chapter will consider the main forces for the introduction of such an approach and examines the ways in which police officers are educated need to be altered from being a 'craft- or task-based' education to one of a profession.

Since the introduction of the ACPO Statement of Common Purpose based on Peel's Principles, society has changed, and with it the demands placed upon the police service have also changed, both in scale and complexity. The Select Committee on Home Office Affairs (Home Office 2008) points to several historical and ongoing issues that may be considered 'drivers for change' within the police service in England and Wales. For example, during the period between 1982 and 1992 recorded crime per officer rose from 26 (1982) to 42 (1992). Despite any organisational changes that the police service may have undergone, and even allowing for an increase in the ways in which the police can be contacted due to the growth in technologies such as the use of mobile phones, the increase in workload is significant, and appears to be increasing. Underpinning this, society has seen an increase in social mobility, the introduction of new technologies which have produced new types of crime such as internet fraud, child pornography, terrorism, financial investigation, organised criminality and a new national and international layer of criminal activity.

In addition, there has been an emphasis on a multi-agency approach to public protection which means greater police involvement in victim support, family liaison and management of offenders in society after prison release, safer schools and youth offending teams. Greater interaction with other agencies as outlined in the Crime and Disorder Act 1998 (Home Office 1998) has meant a need for a wider understanding of the role of the police within a diverse society. These major issues for the police organisation have occurred within the context of an unprecedented rise in the number of criminal offences that individuals can commit within society. Since 1997, some 3,605 new criminal offences have been created by the UK government which generates more work for the police service and their partners to deal with (*Independent* newspaper, 4 September 2008) coupled with the fact that since 1998, new Home Office crime classifications have been introduced resulting in the recording of 750,000 new offences in 2005/2006 alone (Home Office 2008).

The problems associated with tackling crime and disorder are not the only ones for the police to deal with. In a recent publication concerning the police and the community, Sergeant (2008) presented several persuasive arguments that the police service in England and Wales had lost the support of the public. In particular, the police appear not to have retained their good record when interacting with the public. Only 43 per cent of people thought the police could be relied upon to deal with minor crime, while only 41 per cent of victims of crime rated their local police as doing an excellent job compared with 57 per cent of those who had not experienced crime (Sergeant 2008). In support of these views, it is alleged that the police no longer work with the community to solve their problems, being instead performance driven by Home Office pressure to produce statistics relating to particular and narrowly defined crimes, thereby often ignoring the issues that may actually matter to the public. To some extent, this is echoed by the recent Select Committee on Home Affairs Seventh Report, entitled *Policing in the 21st Century'*(Home Office 2007), which noted, among other issues, that even allowing for the focus on serious and organised crime, minor crime and antisocial behaviour are of considerable and daily concern to the public and appear to attract insufficient police attention.

Bassett *et al.* (2009) appear to sum up the problems in asserting that in 1982 92 per cent of people expressed confidence in the police, while in 2004 only 47 per cent of people expressed the same sentiment. Bassett *et al.* (2009) suggest that the police service is now a 'force of robots', which employs centralised operational decision making and police officers who just act when told to and inhabit a dependency culture, unable to use their discretion and supervised by sergeants who are little more than highly paid constables. In addition, since 1995, while crime measured by the British Crime Survey has fallen by 48 per cent (Home Office 2008), 65 per cent of people thought that crime in the country had increased over the past two years and only 53 per cent thought that the police did an excellent or good job in their area in 2008/2009 (Bassett *et al.* 2009).

Clearly, attempting to police a multicultural, diverse, consumerist and technologically innovative society as exists in the UK is a complex and difficult task. Technology plays its part within the delivery of policing services, especially in terms of the use of situational crime prevention techniques such as CCTV cameras and alley-gates, but is a limited response to the complexities of tackling crime and disorder and engaging with communities placed upon the police service. An organisational attempt to meet the demands placed upon the police service may be found in the programme introduced by the government entitled *Workforce Modernisation* (Home Office 2009).

Workforce modernisation

This approach raises profound issues about the way in which the police service manages its staff. In particular, the approach highlights a need for the police to adopt a more flexible and integrated approach to the recruitment, development and training of police officers and police staff (Home Office 2004). One way of addressing the problems identified as the police struggle to achieve performance targets and also engage effectively with the community appears to lie within the training and education of police officers. The question addressing how police officers are educated appears to have much official support. For example, one Home Office document suggested that improved training, leadership and professionalism was required at every level of the police service if it is to take on the challenge of a more varied and satisfying approach to modern policing (Home Office 2007). Consequently, workforce modernisation is an ongoing strategy and can be seen in many other areas of policing including organisational restricting and professionalising the interview programme (PIP).

The influential Flanagan report (Flanagan 2008) introduced the idea of personal responsibility for individuals who wished to become police officers, suggesting that there should be greater ownership by individuals and responsibility for their professional development, including responsibility for their pre-employment training by completing relevant degree course programmes at their own expense before being eligible for active employment. Much of this approach builds upon previous official documents such as Her Majesty's Inspector of Constabulary (HMIC) report entitled *Training Matters* (HMIC 2002) which suggested that there was scope for partnerships with the further education sector to exploit the existing preparation for public services programmes to provide another source of training for potential recruits. Indeed, failing to recognise formal qualifications may be demeaning and disrespectful to the individual concerned, whilse not fully appreciating that training police officers is an expensive business, and providing it if it is not needed is wasteful. Training and education for probationer constables delivered locally, in partnership with local further or higher education, has been suggested as a way forward as well as supporting those individuals with an interest in policing to undergo relevant training before actually joining a particular police force and beginning their careers (Home Office 2004). As a consequence of the ideas from various governmental and academic sources, there has arisen the notion of the 'advanced constable' (Savage 2007) which requires detailed examination.

The advanced constable

This new type of constable as envisaged by Savage (2007) has the enhanced role and empowerment of the front-line officer, including new ways of thinking about tackling crime and disorder. While working with other agencies has exposed a vacuum of leadership, the police at the lower levels of the organisation can, it is believed, fulfil this vital role. The 'advanced constable' needs to be a social diagnostician and mobiliser of community resources. He or she must be seen as the leader in crime control and maintaining social order within the mixed economy of policing while ensuring that others complete their functions effectively. For example, neighbourhood policing teams, consisting of special constables, community support officers, volunteers, and other community members, plus other multi-agency staff will be directed by the 'advanced constable' in tackling crime and disorder issues. Mixed neighbourhood policing teams may take the police out of 'core delivery' to some extent creating space for them to sit at the core of the leadership of that delivery, but this approach requires that individual officers have additional and different sets of skills as well as being able to carry out the traditional enforcement role.

The 'advanced constable' role is therefore a move from the traditional 'sole-trader', omni-competent model in which the constable performed a wide range of functions, many of which require relatively limited skills, to one where the 'advanced constable' working within one specific policing capability concentrates on performing demanding tasks at a higher level of expertise, including problem solving, intelligence gathering, analysis of information and deploying high-level communication skills, to provide an ethically balanced long-term response to community issues and needs. Indeed, the Association of Chief Police Officers highlights the future need for two types of professional expertise within the police service, namely the advanced constable as team leader (front-line activity) and the technical expert, with specialist knowledge such as serious incident-investigating officers (ACPO 2007). Policing is becoming more complex in a changing landscape and it is only right that police staff be provided with the best methods and knowledge to enable them to carry out their duties.

Despite the social changes that have occurred, police officers have, until recently, received a training programme that has remained more or less constant for a long time.

Traditional police training

Centrex

Centrex, the common name of the Central Police Training and Development Authority (CPTDA), was established under Part 4 of the Criminal Justice and Police Act 2001 (Home Office 2001), and was the primary means of police training in England and Wales. It was based at Bramshill House, formerly known as the Police Staff College, Bramshill. Centrex had responsibility for many aspects of police training and development, and this was in the main delivered at bespoke police training centres situated across the country. It was responsible for overseeing the design and delivery of probationer training, investigators' training and other key areas. Centrex was also responsible for the evaluation of this training, setting the national police promotion exams and evaluating probationers, and it also advised on the assessment of recruits.

The agency was staffed by a mixture of non-police officers (civil servants) and seconded police officers from forces across England and Wales, and had five principal foundation training sites at Ashford, Bruche, St Dials in Cwmbran, Ryton-on-Dunsmore and Aykley Heads in Durham. However, there was a move away from operating Police Training Centres to running police trainee/initial probationer courses within police forces themselves but under the auspices of Centrex. Centrex itself was replaced by the National Policing Improvement Agency (NPIA) on 1 April 2007 which took over the functions of Centrex and several other bodies. The idea of the NPIA is to work in partnership with forces and other policing agencies to improve the way they work across all areas of policing.

However, the approach used by Centrex to educating police officers was not without criticism. It has been identified that for the most part of the history of police recruitment, entry and training has reflected an apprenticeship model which is guild-like in operation and form. Members begin as recruits to general policing and normally spend several years at this level before, in comparatively limited numbers, becoming specialists of any kind (O'Malley 2005). Within this system there appears to have been a conflict or major dilemma between learning the law and the practical side of learning to deal with people (Fielding 1988). The police might suspect that a recruit may not possess all the appropriate credentials at the time of their appointment but that many of the skills and qualities needed in police work may be acquired through the appropriate training programme. The police service was, by and large, regarded as a multi-faceted occupation and therefore there was a compromise between what should be included in the training syllabus and what should be omitted. However, with the recent move to divide the police force to response and neighbourhood policing, there is a need to be specific in both the skills and the content of the education which a police office receives.

In terms of the delivery of training and education to student police officers the police service still tends to hold a view that good police practitioners would automatically be good trainers. While there may be some merit in this broad statement, it also reflects in part the closed occupational culture of the police (Reiner 2000), and may explain why there appears to be some resistance to the use of higher education input delivered by academics. However, the danger of relying upon people from within an organisation to deliver training and education is that of insularity and promoting a suspicion of outsiders, and therefore inspecting other perspectives and engaging in wider discussions are inhibited.

Some commentators have argued that because the standards of entry and training in the police organisation have not kept pace with general educational improvements within society, there has been an erosion of the image of an efficient, disciplined bureaucracy which is the first element in undermining police legitimacy, and has led to a fall in public support for the police organisation (Reiner 2008). Ultimately, this could lead to support for inappropriate and unlawful behaviour and comments such as that witnessed in a 2003 television documentary, *The Secret Policeman*, which witnessed trainee officers at a Centrex-run training centre engaged in racial comments about a fellow officer in the police training school itself (BBC TV 2003). The way police officers are educated clearly needs to be addressed if policing is to position itself as a profession, to be compared with other professions.

Policing as a profession

The idea of policing as a profession is one that has generated some heated debate. Durkheim (1958) argued that what is distinctive about the idea of professional groups is not that such groups have high status or high skills or those that they represent have a politically supported monopoly over certain kinds of work, or that they are a distinctive structure of control over work. More importantly, he argued, such groups infuse their work and collective organisation with moral values, plus they incorporate the use of sanctions to ensure that these moral values are upheld – the challenge of ethical policing.

Professionalism may also be said to be that state of mind, that standard of behaviour, that image of competency and sensitivity, and that constellation of attitudes one equates with those people who follow a 'calling', who practise the art and science of a vocation and who perform the function of a job. This approach creates in the mind of the public the image of the agency. For example, South Wales police currently use the phrase based on Locard's forensic science principle that 'every contact counts' (Gilbert 1993) and is translated to how they need their staff to behave when dealing with members of the public.

The professional approach implies that a police officer has reached a level of expertise through:

1. Education
2. Training
3. Experience.

Importantly, this implies that this process separates him or her from others who are less qualified or less dedicated to public service, while also implying that a professional will strive to achieve the highest standards of behaviour and performance. It is this effort that distinguishes the professional from the non-professional whose attitude is one of getting by with less than optimum standards of ethics, behaviour and competence. Therefore if policing is to become profession, the challenge is to develop qualified personnel who are able and willing to assume many complex responsibilities. In line with many other professions, such as medicine, teaching and architecture, a simple knowledge base is insufficient to guarantee effectiveness or customer satisfaction. In addition, there must be an understanding of interaction and communication skills in order to be able to function in an appropriate and effective way.

Despite its public image, and also the recruitment literature, the majority of police work does not involve the chasing and arrest of criminals, but is about interacting with ordinary members of the public on a daily basis.

Traditional training and education methods would appear to be inadequate in providing individuals who meet the demanding criteria for a professional organisation such as the police. Therefore, a mechanism must be introduced that can move the training and education from being that of the 'guild-like craft' towards a publicly recognised professional status. The following is one way of considering how this may be achieved.

From craft to profession

Stinchcombe (1990) provides a useful understanding of the divisions that exist between a 'worker' and those considered to be professional. In his typology, Stinchcombe identifies three distinct types which are useful for an understanding of the evolution of the police organisation from being craft oriented into a professional organisation. These are categorised below.

1. *Craftsmen*. This individual learns his or her trade by supervised experience, often on a one-to-one basis. For example, a student police officer is allocated a tutor officer during their training in order to provide such learning. The individual learns a group of skills that connect practically to a certain job, such as dealing with a shoplifter which involves dealing with the suspect, taking a witness statement and recovering property. Training craftsmen is in the first instance ensuring that they know how to do this in the course of doing the work that the tutor assigns them according to their developing skill base. When the individual has acquired the basic routines involved in the job, their apprenticeship is deemed to be finished. For the police officer, this equates to the end of their two year 'probationary period' when they are signed off by the training department as being proficient. However, there is little intellectual content that connects the routines, and the individual then engages in practical work under supervisors who have experience in the application of routines. Consequently, the individual learns a list of routines and knowledge of indicators of when a particular routine should be applied, and the set of routines learned are connected practically to ensure that particular tasks are successfully performed.

2. *Young professionals*. For Stinchcombe (1990) people in this category, that of 'school'-taught individuals, are the ideal type for a modern organisation to employ. Here the individual is taught a set of courses that underpin their work, but these courses include not so much a list of things they need to know how to do, but more a set of principles they will find useful in doing the various tasks (which cannot be anticipated) they will have to tackle. If the knowledge of craftsmen is a set of routines unbound by intellectual principles, the knowledge of young professionals is a set of principles they can apply. Young professionals go to work with what 'school' has taught them – how to solve problems that are both anticipated and unexpected.

3. *Senior professionals*. These are individuals who have had the 'abstract' training of young professionals and the practical experience of many years, so they command the routines of working in a given field. They have the experience of the 'craft' and coursework, but they also have the experience of many years of applying abstract principles to various routine situations and, in doing so, have improved and revised the routines through the application of a deep abstract understanding of the objectives and the causal processes involved.

The process is illustrated in Table 1.1.

Conclusion

Clearly, the way in which the police educate their staff to meet the complex and increasing demands placed upon the police organisation is changing. This in

Table 1.1 The process of professionalising the police

	Craftsman	*Young professional*	*Senior professional*
Basic training	Supervised experience and minimal input. Learn 'bunch' of responses via 'apprenticeship'.	Taught principles coupled with some routines.	Own experience analysed in the light of taught principles (reflective practitioner).
Knowledge	List of routines and indicators of when to use routine.	Principles without routines; knowledge of what education has taught them.	Analysed and reflected routines.
Application	Bodies of routines connected 'practically' to each other.	All areas to which they can apply principles.	Creation of new routines, different ways of dealing with routines and higher management.
	Traditional police training.	Value-added education in police training programme.	Professional reflective police practitioner.

part reflects the changes and pressures to which the police as a whole have been and will be subject for the foreseeable future. As the economic recession bites and public agencies such as the police will be required to reduce expenditure as never seen previously, there is the possibility that the police will emerge with a completely new structure (Innes 2010). The accountability process may become more focused with the introduction of locally elected commissioners who will hold police chiefs to account for the delivery of local police services, while the community will be increasingly urged to become involved in the delivery of those services as part of the current government's views on the 'Big Society'.

Examining the way the way in which police staff are educated highlights the fact that the police organisation has been and still is subject to much change. Further changes are envisaged with a move to consider pre-entry schemes whereby individuals who wish to become police officers first obtain qualifications, skills and competencies that would mean a significantly reduced input in terms of training delivered by the police organisation. Among many benefits the economic advantages of such an approach in the current climate are particularly attractive.

This book is divided into four distinct sections: **Community, Investigation, Intelligence and Investigative practices.** While structured in such a format, the sections are not mutually exclusive and this is reinforced by the content of each chapter, which indicates how complex and interwoven police work can be. For example, the National Intelligence Model which drives much of police 'business' and reference may be found throughout several of the chapters.

References and suggested further reading

ACPO (2007) *Workforce Modernisation Programme*, at http://police.homeoffice.gov.uk/ human-resources/efficiency-and-productivity/workforce-modernisation-programm/ (accessed 22 July 2009).

Audit Commission (2010) *Sustaining Value for Money in the Police Service – a Joint Report with HMIC*, The Audit Commission, London.

Bassett, D., Haldenby, A., Thraves, L. and Truss, E. (2009) *A New Force*, Reform Publication, London.

BBC TV (2003) *Panorama: The Secret Policeman*, screened October 2003.

Durkheim, E. (1958) *Professional Ethics and Civic Morals,* The Free Press, Glencoe.

Fielding, N. (1988) *Joining Forces: Police Training, Socialisation and Occupational Competence*, Routledge, London.

Flanagan, R. (2008) *Her Majesties Inspectorate for the Constabulary: Serving Communities and Individuals*, HMIC, London, Central Office of Information.

Giddens, A. (1992) *Sociology*, Polity Press, London.

Gilbert, J.N. (1993) *Criminal Investigation,* Macmillan, New York.

HMIC (Her Majesty's Inspector of Constabulary) (2002) *Training Matters*, HMSO, London.

HMIC (Her Majesty's Inspector of Constabulary (2010) *Valuing the Police: Policing in an Age of Austerity*, HMSO, London.

Home Office (1998) *The Crime and Disorder Act 1998*, HMSO, London.

—— (2001) *Criminal Justice and Police Act*, HMSO, London.

—— (2004) *Building Communities: Beating Crime – A Better Police Service for the 21st Century,* HMSO, London.

—— (2007) *Policing a New Century: A Blueprint for Reform*, Home Office, London.

—— (2008) Select Committee on Home Affairs Seventh Report, entitled *Policing in the 21st Century*, HMSO, London.

—— (2009) *Workforce Modernisation Programme*, at http://police.homeoffice.gov.uk/ human-resources/efficiency-and-productivity/workforce-modernisation-programm/ (accessed 22 July 2009).

Independent Newspaper (2008) 'More than 3,600 offences created under labour', 4 September.

Innes, M. (2010) *Ideology Drive*, Police Review, pp. 22–23 (6 August), Jayne's Publications, Coulsdon, Survey.

Newburn, T. (2003) 'Policing since 1945', in T. Newburn (ed.) *Handbook of Policing*, Willan, Cullompton.

O'Malley, P. (2005) 'Policing, politics and postmodernity', in T. Newburn (ed.) *Policing: Key Readings*, Willan Publishing, Cullompton, Devon.

Peak, K.J. and Glensor, R.W. (1996) *Community Policing and Problem Solving-Strategies and Practices*, Prentice Hall, Upper Saddle River, New Jersey.

Reiner, R. (2000) *The Politics of the Police*, 3rd edn, Oxford University Press, Oxford.

—— (2008) 'Policing a post-modern society', in T. Newburn *Handbook of Policing*, 2nd edn, Willan, Cullompton, pp. 675–97.

Savage, S.P. (2007) *Police Reform – Forces for Change*, Oxford University Press, Oxford.

Sergeant, H. (2008) *The Public and the Police*, Civitas, London.

Stinchcombe, A.L. (1990) *Information and Organisations*, University of California Press, Oxford.

Part 1

Community

The context of community and policing

Part 1 introduces the reader to the idea of policing with and within communities. For the past 20 years or so, much has been discussed about community and policing, including the involvement of members of the community to the wider deliverance of policing services. Indeed, the idea of community and police working together appears to underpin much of the direction of the Home Office under the previous government and may be seen in many of its influential documents such as the National Community Safety Plan (accessed at http://police. homeoffice.gov.uk/publications/national-policing-plan/national-community-safety) and the neighbourhood policing team approach (accessed at http://www. neighbourhoodpolicing.co.uk/).

The new government appears to want to enhance community involvement in the delivery of public services and has called this approach 'the Big Society'. Basically, 'the Big Society' involves central government giving more power to local communities and neighbourhoods to allow them to have more say in determining the shape and style of the local services they receive. The approach involves such ideas as encouraging people to take a more active role in their communities, and supporting social enterprises such as co-ops, mutual aid societies and charities. Accountability will be more locally based, and information and data concerning local public services will be published in an easy and accessible format to help communities decide what and how services should be delivered to them.

Involving the community in policing, however, is not a new idea. Historically, we find many instances of communities policing themselves such as those found in the Anglo-Saxon laws (Melville Lee 1901) organised around kindred relationships and the 'hue-and-cry' approach, whereby everyone became involved in the hunt for miscreants and criminals, even up to medieval times when communities were expected to assist the constable in the execution of his duties. Despite the work of the Fielding brothers and other magistrates (Colquhoun 1806), the birth of modern policing is traditionally seen as the introduction of the Metropolitan Police Act of 1829, which was underpinned by the famous 'Peels Principles' of Policing (Peak and Glensor 1996) which sought to outline the functions of the police. Principle number seven of that list is worth illustrating below, since it underlines the partnership between the public or community and the police constable which was based upon historical precedence.

> The Police at all times should maintain a relationship with the public that gives reality to the historic tradition that the police are the public and that the public are the police; the police are only members of the public who are paid to give full time attention to duties which are incumbent on every citizen in the interest of the community welfare.
>
> (Melville Lee 1901)

Despite the fact that the community approach appears to fit in with a peculiarly 'British' way of thinking about policing, it has in fact been seen in various formats throughout differing countries over a long period of time. Brogden and Nijhar (2005) suggest it comes in all shapes and sizes, from being a perspective employed by individual police officers to a more sophisticated philosophy that suggests a community-sensitive and accountable approach. This highlights a peculiar problem of something called community policing, that of definition, which will be discussed more fully in the following chapters. The community approach to policing has not and probably will never be clearly defined to the satisfaction of all deliverers or users of police services, but does contain some common features.

The United States of America context

Community policing or, as it is normally referred to in the United States of America, community oriented policing (COP), appears to have become the dominant direction for the thinking about policing (Peak and Glensor 1996). The underlying factor was to introduce and reunite both the community and the police. Trojanowicz and Carter (1988) suggested the idea of community policing as the following:

> It is a philosophy and not a specific tactic; a proactive, decentralised approach, designed to reduce crime and disorder, and fear of crime, by involving the same officer in the same community for a long term basis.
>
> (Trojanowicz and Carter 1988: 7)

Clearly this concept means an interactive approach on the part of the police when dealing with the community. It involves working partnerships with institutions such as schools, clubs, families, businesses and other institutions regarded as key partners when it comes to dealing with crime and other problems to create safer communities.

Across the United States of America however, community policing is carried out in a number of ways. In some areas it is in the hands of individual or special-ist officers while in others it is a complete police departmental philosophy that has been transformed to embrace the ethos of community policing.

In some areas residents participate in the so-called watch patrols, while in others the public are just asked to be vigilant and inform the police of anything suspicious. In the United States of America therefore, the policing approach to COPs involves the community and civic engagement, which entails allowing people to enhance community safety, while strengthening the capacity of the community to fight and prevent crime on their own. However, the police are often the leaders when it comes to mobilising people and organisations to prevent crime and disorder. The approach primarily used in the country revolves around the problem-solving approach identified by Herman Goldstein (1990). Originally termed problem oriented policing (POP), this acronym is now defined as meaning problem oriented partnerships, emphasising the drive for the police to utilise many other agencies, including the community, within the COP programme. The POP approach will be discussed fully in a later chapter, but its basic principle is that of addressing the underlying conditions that surface as a problem to be dealt with by the police and others.

Transferring COPs to other countries

Despite the fact that Brogden and Nijhar (2005) claim that there has been little evidence to suggest a positive impact of this approach, the community policing idea has been imported by other countries, particularly those in Western Europe. Other parts of the world appear to have imported the community policing approach as part of a wider police package, such as those countries that are rebuilding following economic and political disruption. In India, according to Prateep (1996), the approach has been introduced in the format 'Friends of the Police', which is being used to rebuild a positive image of police officers, while variants of the community-oriented policing approach are seen in Mongolia, Rio De Janeiro and South Africa (COLPI 2001) as well as those countries considered to have a stable police tradition such as the Netherlands and Australia.

The important point to note about the community approach is that for a variety of reasons it has been introduced into a large number of countries and should therefore be considered within this international context, and not just seen as a style of policing being operated solely within the United States of America or the United Kingdom. This context and its development and transference is vital if any attempt to understand this model is undertaken.

The United Kingdom perspective

Following the rise of community-oriented schemes in the United States of America (Skolnick and Bayley 1986, 1988), the idea of involving and working with the community gained momentum in England and Wales. Following the Brixton riots of 1981, the industrial and urban riots of the mid-1980s, and latterly the 1999 report into the murder of Stephen Lawrence (Newburn 2008) there has been a greater urgency for the introduction of policing that works with and involves greater use of the community. Much of what underpins policing in

England and Wales today relies upon community involvement, cooperation and interaction if the police are to be seen as a legitimate agency that functions on behalf of people. The introduction of community support officers, the extended policing family, neighbourhood policing teams and the increase in the use of volunteers are all attempts to engage community at a high level of support, to ensure that the police operate efficiently and effectively, while also working within tight economic parameters. Further, with the rise in the global threat of terrorism there is renewed emphasis in the police gaining community trust, thereby ensuring important information and intelligence that may be used to combat potential terrorist attacks is forthcoming. It is against the background of the police and community working together that Part 1 has been written.

The remaining chapters in Part 1 will consider important elements surrounding the idea of community policing as it is delivered within England and Wales. It will consider the role of the police within communities, defining communities and inherent problems within communities, social capital, and fear of crime, the role of crime and disorder partnerships and how the police communicate with community, among other important areas. Part 1 forms the backcloth against which Part 2 (investigation), Part 3 (intelligence) and Part 4 (investigative practices) should be considered.

References and suggested further reading

Brogden, M. and Nijhar, P. (2005) *Community Policing: National and International Models and Approaches*, Willan Publishing, Cullompton, Devon.

Colquhoun, P. (1806) *A Treatise On the police of the Metropolis*, Mawman and others, London (available as a facsimile reprint published in 1969 by Patterson Smith, New Jersey).

Constitutional and Legal Policy Institute (COLPI) (2001) Newsletter, spring, 4, 1.

Goldstein, H. (1990) *Problem Oriented Policing*, McGraw Hill, New York.

Melville Lee, W.L. (1901) *A History of Police in England*, Methuen and Co, London.

Newburn, T. (2008) 'Policing since 1945', in *Handbook of Policing*, 2nd edn, Newburn, T. (ed.), Willan Publishing, Cullompton, Devon.

Peak, K.J. and Glensor, R.W. (1996) *Community Policing and Problem Solving – Strategies and Practices*, Prentice Hall, Upper Saddle River, New Jersey.

Prateep, P.V. (1996) 'Friends of the Police Movement', Conference on policing in Central and Eastern Europe, College of Police and Security Studies, Slovenia.

Skolnick, J. and Bayley, D. (1986) *The New Blue Line: police Innovations in Six American Cities*, Free Press, New York.

—— (1988) *Community Policing around the World*, National Institute of Justice, Washington, DC.

Trojanowicz, R.C. and Carter, D. (1988) *The Philosophy and Role of Community Policing*, East Lansing, Michigan State University. Available online at http://police.homeoffice. gov.uk/publications/national-policing-plan/national-community-safety National Community Safety Plan website. (accessed 18 April 2009); and http://www.neighbour-hoodpolicing.co.uk/The Neighbourhood Policing Website (accessed 18 April 2009).

2   Community issues

Introduction

This chapter will consider the idea of community, particularly communities in the United Kingdom, the underlying problems that exist within communities and which impact upon the delivery of policing and partnership services including the problem of social and economic deprivation; prejudice within communities; and a particular style of policing which is associated with community, that of community policing.

UK communities – an ageing population

The population of the UK is ageing. Over the past 25 years the percentage of the population aged 65 and over increased from 15 per cent in 1984 to 16 per cent in 2009, an increase of 1.7 million people. Over the same period, the percentage of the population aged under 16 decreased from 21 per cent to 19 per cent. This trend is projected to continue. By 2034, 23 per cent of the population is projected to be aged 65 and over compared to 18 per cent aged under 16.

The fastest population increase has been in the number of those aged 85 and over, the 'oldest old'. In 1984, there were around 660,000 people in the UK aged 85 and over. Since then the numbers have more than doubled, reaching 1.4 million in 2009. By 2034 the number of people aged 85 and over is projected to be 2.5 times larger than in 2009, reaching 3.5 million and accounting for 5 per cent of the total population. As a result of these increases in the number of older people, the median age of the UK population is increasing. Over the past 25 years the median age increased from 35 years in 1984 to 39 years in 2009. It is projected to continue to increase over the next 25 years, rising to 42 by 2034.

In 2009, the median age for women (40 years) was higher than for men (38 years). This is because, on average, women live longer than men. However, the gender gap has narrowed; in 1984 the median ages for women and men were 36 and 33 years respectively, a difference of three years. The ratio of women to men of those aged 65 and over is also falling. In 1984, there were 130 women aged 65 and over for every 100 men of the same age, compared to the current sex ratio of 129 women for every 100 men. By 2034, it is projected that the 65-and-over sex ratio will have fallen still further to 118 women for every 100 men. Issues such as the ageing population and other social and economic information are important to understand if one is to consider how communities are to be policed in the foreseeable future.

(See http://www.statistics.gov.uk/default.asp for more information on National Statistics.)

Distribution of minority ethnic population

The UK consists of many diverse communities based upon culture, religion, ethnicity, etc. This rich culture has implications for policing and it is useful to understand the spatial distribution of individuals throughout the country. For example, non-white ethnic groups are considerably more likely to live in England than in the other countries of the UK. In 2001, they made up 9 per cent of the total population in England compared with only 2 per cent in both Scotland and Wales, and less than 1 per cent in Northern Ireland. These figures have by now increased. The non-white population of the UK is concentrated in the large urban centres. Nearly half (45 per cent) lived in the London region in 2001, where they comprised 29 per cent of all residents. After London, the second largest proportion was in the West Midlands (with 13 per cent of the non-white population), followed by the South East (8 per cent), the North West (8 per cent), and Yorkshire and the Humber (7 per cent). In contrast less than 4 per cent of those from non-white groups lived in the North East and the South West. Minority ethnic groups made up only 2 per cent of each of these regions' populations. Seventy eight per cent of black Africans and 61 per cent of black Caribbeans lived in London. More than half of the Bangladeshi group (54 per cent) also lived in London. Other ethnic minority groups were more dispersed. Only 19 per cent of Pakistanis resided in London, while 21 per cent lived in the West Midlands, 20 per cent in Yorkshire and the Humber, and 16 per cent in the North West. In Great Britain the highest concentration of white Irish people was in London. Almost one-third (32 per cent) of the 691,000 white Irish people lived in London where they made up 3 per cent of the population. The English region with the lowest proportion of white Irish people was the North East, where they made up less than half a per cent of the population.

Defining community

Much of the official rhetoric surrounding the Police Reform Programme (Home Office 2002) and other official initiatives contain the word 'community'. Senior police officers talk about interacting with the community and providing a service that will satisfy community. However, what do we think of when we consider the word community? Reflect upon this for a moment and attempt the exercise given in Box 2.1

> **Box 2.1 Exercise 2A Defining community**
>
> Write down what you think this term actually means.

Sociologists and geographers would consider that a community may be a set of social relationships operating within certain boundaries, locations or territories.

This term has descriptive and prescriptive connotations in both popular and academic usage, and it may refer to social relationships which take place within geographically defined areas or neighbourhoods (Jay and Jay 1991).

Despite the considerations discussed above, it has been suggested that the term 'community' is a difficult and sometimes controversial phrase. Lowe (1986) suggests that 'community' and the term 'class' are often thought of with the same sense of problems of definition. Both are difficult to define exactly.

Generally speaking, particularly in common or popular usage, the term community denotes a positive image. This is often seen in phrases such as 'a sense of community', 'community spirit' and 'community cohesions'. Traditional communities are often portrayed as close knit, with mutual cooperation and assistance being provided by members of that community to each other. Whether or not this is true is open to debate.

Whatever the difficulties encountered with the definition of the term community, all communities, both real and symbolic, and today 'virtual', exist and operate within defined boundaries or territories. These exist to provide areas which define social membership from non-members, for example, religious communities, while in others they are more flexible.

Communities as neighbourhoods

In order for the police service to engage closer with the community and also seek to address long-term problems with their community safety partners, the idea of neighbourhood policing teams has been introduced. The concept of neighbourhood policing teams is examined in much more detail elsewhere in this book, but the basic idea is that teams of police officers, community support officers and special constables, with local volunteers and other groups and agencies, provide a service to 'neighbourhoods' based upon their wants and needs identified through close consultation. It is useful at this point therefore to consider not just the idea of communities as neighbourhoods, but how different people view what a neighbourhood is (Box 2.2).

Because of the problems of there being so many definitions of the term 'community', Hillery (1955) attempted to classify some 94 different definitions in order to achieve some form of commonality. Consequently he

Box 2.2   Exercise 2B What constitutes a neighbourhood?

Reflect upon this question and write down what the term neighbourhood means to you. Now ask a friend or a relative for their view of what a neighbourhood means.

decided that most of the definitions appear to contain the fact that communities consist of:

- people who engage in social interaction within a given geographical area and
- having at least one additional tie.

If this approach is considered, it is easy to see how the term community may be viewed as being synonymous with the term neighbourhood.

However, a neighbourhood has been defined as being a small physical area embedded within a larger area in which people live within dwellings. It has also some tradition of identity and continuity over a period of time (Burisk and Grasmick 1993). This idea of defining neighbourhoods in terms of past definitions and the memory of people has been highlighted by Keller (1982) who points to continued use of physical boundaries, such as streets, paths and railway lines that separate an area and its inhabitants from others, and creates definitive units. Phrases such as 'coming from the wrong side of the tracks' illustrate the physical, economic and cultural separation among certain neighbourhoods.

Clearly, the terms neighbourhood and community appear to be able to be used interchangeably, especially when boundaries between areas are clearly marked. However, economic, social, political and technological changes in world society now mean that communities and neighbourhoods have taken on new meanings. People may geographically live together in a defined area, but they do not interact in the same way as before. If we accept that communities can exist with limited or no physical boundaries to define them, then community may be considered in a variety of different and unexpected ways.

Worsely (1987) suggests that despite the problems of thinking about communities, there are three broad ideas that may be identified within the literature surrounding the idea of community. These are:

- Community as locality – this is the nearest idea to the picture of community in a geographical meaning, one of human settlement within a fixed boundary.
- Community as network of interrelationships – here community is seen as a means for conflict as well as for mutual support and reciprocity.
- Community as a particular type of social relationship – one that possesses certain qualities such as the existence of 'community spirit' or

'community feeling'. This usage is probably the closest to the 'common-sense' usage and does not rely on geography or neighbourhood.

Whatever definition is applied, it is apparent that the present political will is for communities to become more closely associated and involved in the planning, delivery and assessment of local public services.

Community as nostalgia

Reiner (2000) highlights the use of community and community policing stories in the media, such as television programmes entitled *Dixon of Dock Green*, *Heartbeat* and *The Bill*, as being based upon the harmonious relations within the police organisation, and in its interactions with the community. Community police officers, for example, are often portrayed as being efficient, sticking to rules and therefore achieving effective results. These programmes portray the police as dealing with all social issues, not just criminal matters, and appear to be welcomed by the television-watching public as a representation of a different age, when life perhaps appeared to be much simpler.

This positive nostalgic view generated by these television shows is often reflected in community and police liaison groups or meetings, when the public seek to persuade the police to provide services to the community as they did in the 'good old days'.

Indeed, Reiner (2000) refers to an idea of 'The Golden Age of Policing' following the Second World War up to the mid-1960s, and which people often talk about. In this mythical representation of policing, all was well as long as the village bobby was around to informally resolve minor issues within communities. Clearly, while there may have been an element of this type of policing as reality for some communities, it is not wholly representative of policing throughout the country at this time. In fact, the ideology of community policing draws on this idea of a 'golden age', with its roots firmly fixed in the notion of Anglo-Saxon-style policing and the Tythingman (Wright 2002), and also in the development of the 'professional' police introduced by Sir Robert Peel. Some of these issues are discussed later in this chapter. However, what must be understood is that the images attached to a nostalgic view of policing are quite powerful and that managing community expectations of what can be realistically provided in the face of nostalgic views of policing is a skill many police officers need to understand and learn.

Social and economic deprivation in communities

Perhaps one of the biggest influences upon communities and also what partially dictates the response from local public services is the problem of social and economic deprivation. On the face of it, this may appear to have little to do with the police service. However, these factors actually play a major part in the workload of the police and their partners, in specific localities.

Developing social economy is the process of economic growth and the transformation of poor societies. Economic development and growth is encouraged, since it allows various social objectives such as health, welfare and education to be achieved. Economic development has also been defined as the elimination or redistribution of poverty, inequality and unemployment, and also includes the idea of individuals and communities gaining self-esteem and removing dependence upon others.

It is suggested that while the police in their role of 'law enforcers' can perhaps do very little in the face of social and economic development, they can perhaps play a bigger part in helping communities if they are aware of the wider social problems that can lead to their involvement with individuals or sections of the community (Bright 1997). Using this knowledge they may be able to engage in partnership motivation and in particular the problem-oriented partnership approach (Goldstein 1990) discussed at length elsewhere in this book.

As a Home Office report (2006) illustrates, there may be particular reasons or risk factors that appear to underpin or explain why some people engage in anti-social behaviour, and many of these factors lie within the wide-ranging issues underpinning social and economic deprivation. These factors are illustrated below.

Family environment

The risk factors include:

- Poor parental discipline and supervision.
- Family conflict (between parents or between parents and children).
- Family history of problem behaviour.
- Parental involvement/attitudes condoning problem behaviour.

Schooling and educational attainment

The risk factors include:

- Aggressive behaviour (e.g. bullying).
- Lack of commitment to school.
- School disorganisation.
- School exclusion and truancy patterns.
- Low achievement at school.

Community life/accommodation/employment

Risk factors include:

- Community disorganisation and neglect.
- The availability of drugs and alcohol.

- Lack of neighbourhood attachment.
- Growing up in a deprived area within low-income families, high rates of unemployment and a high turnover of population.
- Areas where there are high levels of vandalism.

Personal and individual factors

Risk factors include:

- Alienation and lack of social commitment.
- Early involvement in problem behaviour.
- Attitudes that condone problem behaviour.
- For young people, a high proportion of unsupervised time spent with peers and friends involved in problem behaviour.
- Mental illness.
- Early involvement in the use of drugs.

Clearly, if the police and their partners work together to tackle social and economic deprivation, this may have a positive result in terms of workload and calls for service.

Two areas within the idea of social and economic deprivation are worthy of further discussion and understanding as they underpin the idea. These are poverty and deprivation within communities, and their impact.

Poverty

For the majority of people there is a belief that we live in an affluent society, being able to buy or have mobile phones, the latest computers, fast cars, large houses and expensive clothes. For many, shopping means trips to out-of-town stores, or shopping malls in big cities, where people are able to obtain or buy all sorts of goods. However, there are a substantial number of individuals to whom the idea of doing all of the above is just not possible, and who live their lives within twenty-first-century communities in poverty (Box 2.3).

Box 2.3 Exercise 2.C Defining poverty

Write down your own definition of poverty, and then compare it to the information provided later in this chapter.

Poverty defined

The official definition of poverty appears to be based upon the 'benefits' needs system, for example, income support, which is used to provide a basic income for certain people. However, a criticism of this approach is that every time benefits increase, the number of people defined as being in poverty increases. Consequently, the measurement of poverty is currently calculated around the relative income standard. This means that a figure calculated at 60 per cent of the median or average income is used to determine whether or not a person is in 'poverty'.

If this indicator is used, at the time of writing, the amount used to measure the level of poverty is illustrated in Table 2.1.

These amounts are the *total* sum of money to spend on food, clothing, travel, phones and all those things we need to put money aside for.

A recent report by the Joseph Rowntree Foundation (Lynn 2008) highlights the fact that people surveyed thought the amounts of money shown in Table 2.2 were required to maintain a minimum, socially acceptable quality of life.

Clearly there appears to be a situation where a large number of people struggle to meet even the demands of basic expenditures for living. The current world economic problems and the increased price for fuel has propelled a larger number of people into this category.

Despite the fact that there are a large number of disadvantaged communities, police perceptions of them are formed by their physical appearance and lack of investment, the police occupational subculture (Reiner 2000), and by the use of stories about the communities themselves which perpetuate myths about the people who live within these communities (see Holdaway 1984).

Table 2.1 Amounts of money per week used to measure poverty

Category	Amount of money per week
Single adult	£100.00
Two adults	£180.00
Two adults and two chiltdren	£260.00
Single adult and two children	£180.00

Source: Lynn, 2008.

Table 2.2 Perceptions of minimum amounts required for reasonable standard of living

Category	Amount of money per week
Single working age adult	£150.00
Pensioner Couple	£201.00
Couple with two children	£370.00
A lone parent with one child	£210.00

Source: Lynn, 2008.

For example, many local authority-owned housing estates may carry a negative image or reputations which may have some basis in incidents that the police have dealt with over a number of years, but bear no resemblance to the reality of people who live within them.

However, it should not be assumed that all of these communities are resistant to change and improvement. Many are keen to reduce street crime and antisocial behaviour in their neighbourhoods, but feel unrecognised and marginalised by those agencies engaged in community safety and crime and disorder reduction partnerships.

Work by Lynn (2008) suggests that there are a number of ways in which disadvantaged communities can be mobilised, including good leadership from agencies such as partnerships and the police, and an appreciation that disadvantaged communities are just seen in terms of the problems they experience, and by supporting efforts to develop a positive culture of mutual support.

Relative deprivation

The problem of defining poverty within communities is that it must be related to the society in which it may be present. For example, the luxuries and comforts which were once considered extravagant and which we now take for granted may become necessities given the change in economics and society.

Poverty needs to be related and defined against a particular society, at a particular time, and to reflect more than simple impoverishment. This is the concept of relative deprivation. Townsend (1979) provides a useful definition of the idea of relative deprivation and may be seen in Table 2.3.

So we see that relative poverty is linked to the expectations and norms and beliefs of society at a particular time, and that those people to which it applies do not have access to the same types of food or services that the majority of people have.

While this inequality reflects badly upon society, there is also the danger that those who suffer relative poverty may also suffer from something called social exclusion.

Table 2.3 Defining relative poverty

Townsend's definition of poverty...

Individuals families and group in the population can be said to be in poverty when they lack the resources to obtain the type of diet, participate in activities, and have the living conditions and amentities which are customary, or at leat widly encouraged or approved, in the societies to which they belong, Their resources are so seriously below those commanded by the average individual or family that they are, in effect excluded from the ordinary living patterns, customs and activites.

(Townsend 1979)

Social exclusion

Social exclusion compounds the problems and the nature of poverty and tends to persist over time. It appears to be resistant to change despite the best efforts of agencies that try to tackle it, and it tends to concentrate in localities and in particular groups. For individuals who experience social exclusion the experience can mean:

o   invisibility to those who are in power and control of their lives;
o   the attachment of 'stigma'.

For example, the police have used derogatory terms for certain sections of society who are excluded, such as Prigs, Dirt and Scum (Young 1991), Police Property (Reiner 2000), and have often been referred to as 'The Underclass' (see Murray 2001). Sometimes, the problem even extends to the exclusion from services such as health, welfare and even police services.

On an individual level some of the consequences of social exclusion may be seen in Table 2.4.

Unfortunately, poverty and relative deprivation are to be found in many communities within which the police and their partners work, and this may introduce social exclusion which can mean an increase in the amount of work required by the police and their partners. Police, partners and community should work together in whatever way they can to try to deal with the community problem of poverty, relative poverty and social exclusion, which is not necessarily confined to particular ethnic, religious or other groups within our society.

Prejudice in communities

British society consists of communities, and these communities may themselves consist of smaller groups. None of these communities or groups are exclusive as

Table 2.4 The consequences of social exclusion

Some further consequences of social exclusion can mean...

- Lack of aspiration
- Low confidence levels
- Low motivation
- Disengagement
- Family breakdown
- Lone parenthood
- No role models
- No work experience
- Delinquent responses
- Drug sub cultures
- High conflict communities
- Social dislocation.

it is possible for an individual to be a member of a number of various communities or groups. Some people in society may be identified as vulnerable with particular needs. In addition, there may be tensions that exist among certain groups and some of them will have different perceptions of the police. It is important to realise that the attitude and behaviour of one individual police officer may enhance or diminish community trust.

Police officers, like all people, have a 'frame of reference' or 'way of seeing the world' which is influenced by many factors, including the community or groups to which they belong, and of course the impact of police occupational subculture. Other factors that impact upon an individual's 'frame of reference' could include their education, religion, family and upbringing or cultural background. These factors are responsible for developing a person's value and their prejudices.

Prejudice may be defined as making negative prejudgements about other people or other groups. While in law a person is 'innocent until proven guilty', prejudices tend to work in the opposite direction as the individual who holds the prejudice believes them until they are proved false. Prejudice may be suppressed, but it may often come out in underlying attitudes, opinions and beliefs especially when under pressure. Most people join the police service with some prejudice, of which they may or may not be aware. Our prejudices often stem from relying on our 'frame of reference' to fill in the gaps in our knowledge of other groups in society. This is called *stereotyping* and it can be about communities or individuals. Stereotyping is about making sweeping generalisations about groups of people, where it is believed that just because people are members of a particular group or live in a particular community, they must, because of that fact, share particular traits which one thinks are characteristic of that group.

Allport (1979) identified five levels of prejudice. He related his scale particularly to the experience of the Jews in Nazi Germany. While this approach may be open to criticism, it is still a useful tool to help understand the nature of prejudice against particular communities or individuals from within particular communities (Figure 2.1).

The different scales of Allport's model are discussed below.

Anti-locution – Could be demonstrated by using phrases of colour which equate whiteness with purity and blackness with bad or evil. Other examples include stereotypical language or ethnic jokes.

Avoidance – Quite simply this means to avoid another individual or group.

Discrimination – Means unequal treatment. This unequal treatment reinforces the power of the dominant group and disadvantages the minority group. Discrimination on the grounds of religion, gender, sexual orientation, disability and age is unlawful. The processes of discrimination can include denying employment or a less professional service delivered by a public body.

Physical attacks – These may range from attacks on the property of individuals to direct physical attacks.

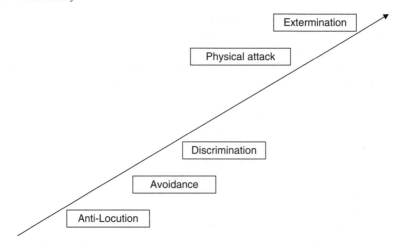

Figure 2.1 Allport's scale of prejudice.

Extermination – This is the ultimate violent expression of a prejudice. On an extreme level this could be demonstrated by the ethnic cleansing of a whole community.

Hate crimes within communities

We have seen how communities within England and Wales consist of many diverse groups and nationalities. This includes not just race, but also different sexual orientations. Hate crimes are directed against people because of some aspect of who they are, most typically because they are from an ethnic minority or visible religious minority, or because of their sexuality. Hate crime covers a wide range of behaviour, for example, verbal abuse, racist or homophobic graffiti or physical assault. A crime may be classed as a hate crime if the victim or witness sees it as being so.

The ACPO Guide to *Identifying and Combating Hate Crime* was published in 2000. It defines hate crime as 'any crime where the perpetrator's prejudice against any identifiable group of people is a factor in determining who is victimised'. Therefore, a victim of hate crime does not have to be a member of a minority or someone who is generally considered to be 'vulnerable'. Effectively anyone can be the victim of a hate crime incident.

The McPherson report defined a racist incident as 'any incident which is perceived to be racist by the victim or any other person'. The recording of racist incidents is therefore now based on the perception by *any* person that the incident is racist. 'Racist' does not simply relate to colour, but also to race, nationality, ethnic, religious or national origins.

Similarly a homophobic incident is 'any incident which is perceived to be homophobic by the victim or any other person'. 'Homophobic' does not only relate to lesbian women, gay men, bisexuals, transgender or transsexual people, but to any person perceived to be so by the perpetrator. As with racist incidents, the recording of homophobic incidents is based upon the perception by any person that the incident is homophobic. The person making the report does not need to have any evidence to show that the incident was racist or homophobic. If any person believes that the incident was so motivated, it must be recorded as such.

National research has shown that under-reporting remains a common feature of all hate crimes as victims may be reluctant to report the incident to the police. It has also been identified that many victims have suffered repeated problems before they contact the police.

The impact of a hate crime can be more traumatic on the victim due to the realisation that a normally impersonal crime is actually a personal attack. As well as affecting the individual, hate crime has been described by the ACPO Guide as a 'powerful poison to society' as it 'breeds suspicion, mistrust, alienation and fear'. In this present climate of heightened tension following the recent terrorist attacks, racists frequently exploit periods of raised anxiety and therefore there needs to be a heightened state of alert for hate crime with prompt action taken against racial harassment and strong support and reassurance for victims.

Clearly, the term community is full of contradictions and differing perceptions for people. Communities still contain social problems such as poverty and social exclusion which may have an impact upon crime, antisocial behaviour and the provision of other local partnership services. Community contains numerous diverse groups, and includes prejudices which can incite hate crime and other problems. How the police interact with these communities is vital and one approach which is seen throughout the Western world is called community or community-oriented policing.

Community or community-oriented policing

Community-oriented policing, or community policing as it is more commonly referred to in the UK, appeared in the mid-1970s as a topic of discussion among police administrators and academics. Since then it has spread worldwide as the summit of enlightened thinking. Fielding (1995) described the 1970s attempts as short-term tactics to repair police/public relations, a cosmetic exercise which masked the reluctance to make major changes when entrenched patrol and investigation methods failed. More recently, it has embraced the concepts of problem solving within the community, attempts to reduce the fear of crime and targeted foot patrols. The idea of community-oriented policing can be traced to the philosophy introduced by Sir Robert Peel in his famous 'Principles of Policing' which underpinned the introduction of the Metropolitan Police Act 1829, in particular Principle Number 7 which may be seen in Box 2.4.

Community safety and crime reduction partnerships often involve the use of community policing ideas. Therefore, the enormous influence of the community

---

Box 2.4   Important point – Peel's Principle of Policing No. 7

The police shall at all times maintain a relationship with the public that gives reality to the historic tradition that the police are the public and that the public are the police.

(Peak and Glensor 1996: 8)

---

policing approach raises the question of what it is and also why it is claimed to be successful.

The problem of definition

Herein lies the first problem with community policing. Like the problem of trying to define community discussed earlier in this chapter, it is not easy to provide a particular definition of community policing even though it is a commonly referred-to idea. In an attempt to provide a working definition, Friedmann (1992) examines community policing from three perspectives, namely the police, the community and a combination of both. For the police it is a vehicle used to improve ties with the community for the purposes of relying on community resources to assist them (e.g. neighbourhood watch), to improve intelligence gathering and to increase the acceptance of the police within the community. The community realises that it deserves and should receive improved police services with greater accountability and an increase in the power sharing in police decisions. When combined, both the police and the community assume that crime and disorder are produced by factors over which the police have little control, such as education and welfare issues, and that crime reduction needs to focus on these factors.

Policing in this style tends to assume a more pro-active stance, with greater emphasis on quality-of-life issues, with greater understanding of human rights and civil liberties, which are essential to successful democratic policing. Different and diverse tactics used by the police are seen as a way of improving quality of life and increased community satisfaction.

A working definition

In summing up this view of community policing, Friedmann (1992: 4) attempts to provide a working definition which is given in Box 2.5

Searching for a definition of community policing is quite a difficult process, but Brogden and Nijhar (2005) suggest four general propositions as guidelines of community policing. These are as follows:

- Neighbourhoods or small communities serve as the main focus of police organisations and their operations.

Box 2.5 Important point – one definition of community policing

Community policing is a policy and a strategy aimed at achieving more effective and efficient crime control, reduced fear of crime, improved quality of life, improved police services and police legitimacy, through a proactive reliance on community resources that seeks to change crime causing conditions.

(Friedmann 1992: 4)

- Communities have unique and distinctive policing problems that traditional police organisations and responses have not addressed.
- Community consensus and structures should guide police response to a community's crime and disorder problems. Policing should be both locally accountable and transparent.
- Police discretion is a fact and should be used positively to ensure community confidence in the police.

(Brogden and Nijhar 2005: 23)

It can be seen that community policing is not a single idea that can be explained easily, and it is different to rapid response and enforcement-oriented policing (Reiner 2000). Police staff are closer to the community and can represent its members, a process by which crime and disorder problems are shared with the public or as a means of developing links with the community and interest groups. The term community policing conjures up images of police and community relations in a stable and agreeable community where crime is an annoyance and disorder largely consists of minor vandalism.

In reality, of course, this is seldom the case.

Reactions to community policing

The use of community policing in crime and disorder reduction partnerships raises some problems of which police practitioners should be aware. One of the main influences in this area both in this country and in the US was Robert Trojanowicz (1983, 1986, 1990; Trojanowicz and Bucqueroux, 1990). Trojanowicz based his work upon policing experiments in Michigan, US and provides a working framework for community policing. These include the understanding that it is an idea and a strategy in one, and that it requires a new type of police officer who can work proactively and independently of police supervision yet is able to work in partnership with many other agencies. Importantly community policing rests on the idea that those law-abiding citizens deserve an input into the policing process and that solutions to problems mean allowing both police and residents to explore creative options.

So far, the idea of community policing has, in the main, been greeted as a positive step. This may be seen in Box 2.6

Box 2.6   Important point – positive view of community policing

A review of community policing evaluation studies in 12 locations portrayed the schemes in a favourable light with both police and local residents expressing more positive attitudes after programmes had been implemented.

(Lurigo and Rosenbaum 1994)

However, despite the official support and apparent success of community policing schemes it is not without its problems, and there have been some failures. Police practitioners can learn a great deal from the problems of the past.

Experiences of community policing

Brogden and Nijhar (2005) suggest that the idea of community policing is readily accepted as the 'new' face of policing in the English-speaking world, yet its meaning is often unclear in practice. The following case study (Box 2.7) illustrates some of the problems when these initiatives are introduced. Once you have read this, try the exercise immediately following it (Box 2.8).

It has been suggested that there are three main reasons that explain why community policing schemes fail in the UK. First, the level of emergency demands from the public, through 999 calls, mobile phones, etc., prevents a more pro-active style of policing. Second, sometimes the opposition of middle management, struggling to cope with the demands and who face additional

---

Box 2.7   Case study problems of community policing

A small village area was chosen for a community policing initiative which involved the local council 'paying' for more high-visibility policing and police presence. After a period of time, the initiative was evaluated and it was found that overall it had not been successful, with recorded crime and fear of crime actually increasing. The obstacles to success were:

* Insufficient consideration given to exactly what community policing would comprise and how it would assist the aims of the project.
* Ineffective management of residents' expectations.
* Removal of dedicated officers from the initiative to work elsewhere.
* Considerable turnover of staff which ensured lack of continuity.

Box 2.8   Exercise 2E Strategies

Reflecting upon the case study above, what strategies would you put in place to ensure these problems would not recur?

---

burdens and responsibilities that go hand-in-hand with consultation-style policing. Third, there may be an organisational culture that is often resistant to a community policing orientation. A slightly different explanation for failure is put forward by Sadd and Grinc (1994). They found patrol officers unwilling to implement and unenthusiastic about what they perceived as 'top-down', 'flavour-of-the-month' initiatives. In addition, the need for more effective inter-agency collaboration is not always forthcoming. Finally, a major problem to improved police community relationships can be the history of fear and suspicion by residents. This may especially be the case in minority ethnic community groups. Clearly police practitioners have to be committed to the ideals of community policing, with the understanding that crime reduction partnerships are now a permanent feature in this country. This approach also involves recognising the differences between traditional policing methods and new approaches to policing a community.

Supporters of the community policing approach point to the fact that reactive or traditional policing, with its emphasis on reactive crime fighting, has failed. Crime fighting, with its emphasis on so-called excitement, appears to have been the focus of operations, and fitted in with the idea of a war against crime. However, despite this approach, and the increase in funding for resources, the fight against crime did not appear to be winnable in the traditional format. This format tended to include the following as its basis:

- Randomised patrols, usually in vehicles, carried out by uniform officers.
- Reaction to events such as crime, with an emphasis on having a fast response time.
- A focus on minor infractions of the law, with major social problems being ignored.
- Investigation of crime being regarded as having a higher status within the police organisation rather than other types of police work.
- Contact with the public via electronic means with a reduction in face-to-face contact.
- Centralised command structures with little or no room for individual discretion.

Community-style policing appears to have, in part at least, learnt from previous research (Brogden and Nijhar 2005). These include the following:

- Doing more of the same thing does not have any effect on crime levels. Traditional crime fighting has its limits, and simply increasing this type of activity, and associated costs, is unlikely to have any measurable effect on the volume of reported crime.

- Car patrols have little effect on crime or arrest rates, with the fact that two-person car patrols are no more effective at catching criminals than one-person car patrols.
- The majority of calls to the police are not related to serious crime, and indeed, they may revolve around quality-of-life issues, which the police should acknowledge as being the staple diet of their work.
- Day-to-day contact with the public is vital if detection of crime depends upon the support from the public. Most detected crimes depend upon information from the public and this is often obtained by foot patrol officers.
- Fear of crime is often more of a problem within communities than actual crime itself. Foot patrols and high-visibility and accessible policing presence may help reduce the fear of crime within the community.
- Dealing with crime and disorder is an inter-agency problem rather than simply being the function for the police to deal with alone.
- Local knowledge is a neglected source of information within policing.
- The so-called traditional method of policing has not appeared to have had any major effect on the reduction of crime nor provided much reassurance to the public, both of major importance for policing. Therefore a smarter approach to the delivery of policing services is required. The comparison between the traditional style of policing and community policing may be seen in Table 2.5.

Table 2.5　Traditional compared to community policing

Question	Traditional approach	Community policing
Who are the police?	A government agency responsible for law enforcement.	Police are the public and the public are the police. Police officers are paid to give full attention to the duties of every citizen.
What is the relationship of the police force to other public departments?	Priorities often conflict.	Police are one of many responsible for improving quality of life.
What is the role of the police?	Focused on solving crimes.	A broader problem solving approach.
What determines the effectiveness of the police?	Response times.	Public cooperation.
What view do the police take of service calls?	Deal with them only if there is no real police work to do.	Vital function and great opportunity.
What is police professionalism?	Swift effective response to serious crime.	Keeping close to the community.
How do the police regard prosecutions?	As an important goal.	As one tool among many.

Source: Adapted from Peak and Glensor (1996: 73).

While community policing may have its problems with definition it has been adapted and applied to suit local needs across the world. It appears to work best in conjunction with the multi-agency partnership environment, using a problem-solving approach and operating in direct opposition to many of the traits underpinning traditional or reactive methods of policing.

Conclusion

The term community is one that raises many discussions and arguments. Its definition is often open to different interpretations, and it includes many diverse and competing interests. It is, in part, founded upon a nostalgic view of what it means to belong to a community, yet this, and other approaches to community, tend to ignore the fact that community includes those individuals who are defined as being in poverty, relative poverty and who may be socially excluded from community services. These issues often impact upon the delivery of policing and partnership services and should always be considered in the broad approach to tackling issues such as crime and antisocial activity. The idea of community policing as an answer to many of the policing problems generated within a community is an attractive one, but calls for a different approach from that of the traditional or reactive approach and therefore needs to be considered in the light of opposition from within the police occupational subculture. Whichever way the term community is considered, it remains an important concept in the debate concerning how policing will be delivered in England and Wales for the foreseeable future.

References and suggested further reading

ACPO (2000) *Manual of Guidance on Identifying and Combating Hate Crime*, ACPO, London.
Allport, G.W. (1979) *The Nature of Prejudice*, Perseus Books Publishing, Reading, Massachusetts.
Bright, J. (1997) *Turning the Tide: Crime, Community and Prevention*, London: Demos.
Brogden, M. and Nijhar, P. (2005) *Community Policing – National and International Models and Approaches,* Willan Publishing, Cullompton, Devon.
Burisk, R.J. and Grasmick, H.J. (1993) *Neighbourhoods and Crime*, Lexington Books, New York.
Clements, P. and Spinks, T. (1997) *The Equal Opportunities Guide*, Kogan Page, London.
Fielding, N.G. (1995) *Community Policing*, Oxford University Press, Oxford.
Friedmann, R.R. (1992) *Community Policing, Comparative Perspectives and Prospects*, St Martins Press, New York.
Goldstein, H. (1990) *Problem Oriented Policing*, McGraw-Hill, New York.
Hillery, G.A. (1955) 'Definitions of Community: Areas of Agreement', *Rural Sociology*, 20(4): 11.
Holdaway, S. (1984) *Inside the British Police: A Force at Work*, Blackwell, London.
Home Office (2002) *The Police Reform Act*, Home Office, London.
Home Office (2006) *A Guide to Anti Social Behaviour Orders*, Home Office, London.

Jay, D. and Jay, J. (1991) *The Collins Dictionary of Sociology*, Harper Collins, Glasgow.

Keller, S. (1982) 'The Neighbourhood', in R.H. Taylor (ed.) *Neighbourhoods in Urban America*, Kennikat Press, Washington, NJ.

Lowe, S. (1986) *Urban Social Movements: the City after Castles*, Macmillan, London.

Lurigo, A.J. and Rosenbaum, D.P. (1994) The Impact of Community Policing on Police Personnel: A Review of the Literature', in Rosenbaum, D.P. (ed.) *The Challenge of Community Policing: Testing the Promises*, Sage, Beverly Hills, CA, pp. 147–63.

Lynn, J. (2008) *Community Leadership Approaches to Tackling Street Crime*, Joseph Rowntree Foundation, York Publishing Services Ltd, York.

McPherson, Sir William (1999) *The Stephen Lawrence Inquiry*, HMSO, London.

Murray, C. (2001) *Underclass plus 10*, Civitas, London.

Peak, K.J. and Glensor, R.W. (1996) *Community Policing and Problem Solving, Strategies and Practices*, Prentice Hall, Upper Saddle River, New Jersey.

Reiner, R. (2000) *The Politics of the Police* (3rd edn), Oxford University Press, Oxford.

Sadd, S. and Grinc, R. (1994) 'Innovative Neighbourhood Oriented Policing: An Evaluation of Community Policing Programmes in Eight Cities', in Rosenbaum, D.P. (ed.) *The Challenge of Community Policing: Testing the Promises*, Sage, Thousand Oaks, CA, pp. 27–52.

Townsend, P. (1979) *Poverty in the United Kingdom: A Survey of Household Resources and Standards of Living*, Penguin Books, Middlesex.

Trojanowicz, R.C. (1983) 'An Evaluation of Neighbourhood Foot Patrol Programme', *Journal of Police Science and Administration*, 11, 4, 410–19.

—— (1986) 'Evaluating a Neighbourhood Foot Patrol Programme; the Flint Michigan Project', in Rosenbaum, D.P. (ed.) *Community Crime Prevention*, Sage, Thousand Oaks, CA, pp. 258–62.

—— (1990) 'Community Policing is not Police Community Relations', *FBI Law Enforcement Bulletin*, 1, October, 10.

Trojanowicz, R.C. and Bucqueroux, D. (1990) *Community Policing, a Contemporary Perspective*, Cincinnati: Anderson.

Worsely, P. (1987) *New Introductory Sociology* (3rd edn), Penguin, London.

Wright, A. (2002) *Policing – An Introduction to Concepts and Practice*, Willan Publishing, Cullompton, Devon.

Young, M. (1991) *An Inside Job*, Oxford University Press, Oxford.

Useful websites

http://www.homeoffice.gov.uk/crime-victims/reducing-crime/hate-crime/
Hate crime discussed at this Home Office website.
http://police.homeoffice.gov.uk/community-policing/
Community policing website.
http://www.jrf.org.uk/
The Joseph Rowntree Foundation.
http://www.poverty.org.uk/
Website explaining poverty indicators, etc.
http://www.cabinetoffice.gov.uk/social_exclusion.aspx
Social exclusion website.
http://www.statistics.gov.uk/default.asp
The Office for National Statistics.

3 Community and crime reduction

Introduction

Policing in England and Wales has undergone a significant change. Since 1998 and the introduction of the Crime and Disorder Act 1998, one particular new way of working for the police is that of being involved in partnerships working with the community, outside agencies and local authorities, in an effort to reduce crime and disorder and the fear associated with both. The past ten years or so has increasingly seen the development of the partnership approach to policing in general and to crime and disorder prevention and reduction in particular. This is in contrast to the previous reactive style of policing where the police are seen as the only available experts who could tackle crime and control criminals. The situation now arises where practitioners are carrying out functions of crime and disorder reduction work or parts thereof, and may have little or no understanding of why they are doing the work, and on occasions, how to carry out this work effectively, by using the resources of their partnerships.

Perhaps one of the most influential documents to be published has been the report of the Standing Conference on Crime Prevention chaired by James Morgan, which had the responsibility for reviewing the development of crime prevention. This report became known as the Morgan Report (Home Office 1991) and contained many proposals for the structure and coordination of crime prevention strategies, and in particular highlighted the need for the partnership approach, with an increased emphasis on the role of local authorities. These issues, among others, are discussed in greater depth within this chapter.

Historical context of partnerships

If one accepts the argument that the rise of partnerships in crime and disorder control has been dramatic, then an analysis of the component parts of the partnership approach would need clarifying. These usually involve a style of policing that is considered unusual, or different in some way, from the normal reactive style of policing, and the use of crime prevention techniques. Crime prevention techniques appear to contain elements of situational crime prevention and include a consideration of repeat victims of specific crimes. Partnerships also need to include wide consultation with the community they serve, in order to operate economically, effectively and efficiently.

The past 20 years or so have produced a substantial amount of research and advice to the police service urging it to tackle problems with the aid of the community and other agencies. Many of the publications urging this approach stem from the Home Office, and a typical example of the mood for change may be seen in the influential Home Office circular 8/1984. Box 3.1 sums up the approach.

Box 3.1   Important point – the view from the Home Office

Every individual citizen and all those agencies whose policies and practices can influence the extent of crime should make their contribution. Preventing crime is a task for the whole community.

(Home Office 1984: 1)

Kirkholt and other early initiatives

The message in Box 3.1 could not have been clearer for police services. Consequently, throughout the country, partnership initiatives were introduced. Initiatives such as 'The Kirkholt Burglary Prevention Project' (Forrester *et al.* 1988) were promoted as flagships of the partnership approach and the police service was encouraged to engage with other agencies in community crime prevention initiatives. For a number of years the Home Office sponsored and published research into specific areas of tackling criminality that appeared to highlight the successful approach of partnerships involving differing agencies. These initiatives have covered a range of offences, from burglary (Brown 1997), public order and annoyance on housing estates (Morris 1996), to thefts against retail outlets (Tilley 1993). The common theme of all this work was the claimed positive results obtained by several agencies collaborating to tackle highly specific crimes. Indeed, such was the faith in the partnership approach that the Home Office published a document that provided examples of partnership initiatives from various locations within this country that were deemed good practice (Home Office 1997). The intention of this document, it was claimed, was to provide a framework of ideas for those agencies not already engaged in the paradigm of partnership policing.

One of the main reasons behind the introduction of the partnership approach lay in the fact that that there had been a rise in recorded crime and the realisation that the police did not have the resources to tackle this problem alone. In view of what you have read so far, attempt the exercise provided in Box 3.2.

Box 3.2 Exercise 3A Partner agencies

What partner agencies would you consider using in order to reduce instances of domestic burglary in the area where you work or live?

Community safety

The publication of the Morgan Report (Home Office 1991) saw the term 'crime prevention' replaced by the concept of 'community safety' in order to broaden the base of support for such partnerships (Box 3.3).

Box 3.3 Important point – community safety

The term crime prevention is often narrowly interpreted and this reinforces the view that it is solely the responsibility of the police. On the other hand, the term community safety is open to wider interpretation and could encourage greater participation from all sections of the community.

(Home Office 1991: 1)

By using the term community in 'community safety', it was hoped that this approach would be more acceptable to the public at large, since, as Cohen (1985) rightly points out, the word 'community' appeals to the individual perceptions of positive feelings. When the imagery portrayed is positive, the term is associated with concepts of 'natural', 'openness', 'integrative' or simply 'in the community'. Therefore, such concepts as community centres, community prisons and community policing are generally viewed as positive and non-threatening.

Consultation – early ideas

The more complex ideas surrounding consultation are discussed in full in Chapter 5 of this book. However, for partnerships trying to provide a service, the aims of the consultation process may be listed as follows:

1. The drive to reach as broad a cross-section of the population as possible. All parties, it is argued, have an interest in consulting as widely and deeply as possible, as failure to do so could mean that prominent crime and disorder problems are not brought to their attention.
2. The identification of public priorities to influence the annual policing plan, to assist in targeting valuable police resources to particular community concerns.

3. The identification of public priorities for local action, so that local partnerships can be focused on individual community problems, such as the perception of youth annoyance.
4. To provide the public with information on policing and community safety matters feeding back information to the public and improving the quality of consultation.

Responding to community needs

Partnerships are concerned with the management of providing a service to the community and, therefore, organisational attainments are quite high on their list of consultation priorities. For the public, according to Elliot and Nicholls (1996), the main reason for engaging in the consultation process with policing partnerships seems to revolve around two main areas of concern, namely:

1. To obtain rapid police action on public concerns, so that it is likely that the public do not merely wish to be consulted on their views as their priority will be to get the police to address their problems.
2. Obtaining information from the police, such as what the police are doing, how they are performing and the impact the police are having on crime. They may well see consultation as a way to achieve this.

However, the consultation process itself, while a positive idea, is far from infallible. Public meetings, where members of the community are asked to attend to air their views, are not necessarily representative of the community as a whole. Marginalised groups such as gay and lesbian groups, youth elements and those regarded as outsiders owing to minority ethnic background are often not represented at such consultation processes. Consequently, the concerns addressed are those that are normally aired, it may be argued, by locally elected representatives and other community leaders who may not be acting on behalf of the whole community.

One of the biggest influences on the formation of the partnership approach to crime prevention, and touched upon earlier, is the Home Office's Standing Committee on Crime Prevention Report *Safer Communities: The Local Delivery of Crime Prevention through the Partnership Approach* (Home Office 1991). This report, known as the Morgan Report, is so influential in this area that it requires closer scrutiny.

The Morgan Report

By the end of the 1980s the Home Office circular *Tackling Crime* (Home Office 1989) showed the further development of the partnership and community orientation to crime prevention in the Home Office. Particular attention was given in the circular to the problem of coordination – or rather the lack of it – between agencies making up the criminal justice system. This circular led the way for what was considered to be the key inspiration for much of the subsequent local government, multi-agency and seemingly social crime prevention schemes of the 1990s, the Morgan Report (Home Office 1991).

Circular (8/84): *Crime Prevention* (Home Office 1984) may be seen as a watershed in crime prevention policy. Its emphasis lay in the principle that crime prevention must be accepted as a significant and integral goal of public policy, both centrally and locally. In this circular, particular stress was placed on the need for a coordinated approach and joint strategies involving partnerships against crime. Although more often rhetoric than reality around the country the idea of multi-agency 'partnerships' in crime prevention had clearly arrived in Britain.

Effectively, community safety, as a guiding idea, was heralded as a way of moving beyond a situational definition of crime prevention (focusing on the management, design and manipulation of the built physical environment) to a broader social definition (seeking to change criminal motivations which are perceived to lie within people by affecting the social environment).

The Report went on to identify six key elements that needed to be addressed, namely structure, leadership, information, identity, durability and resources, in order to improve the organisation and delivery of multi-agency crime prevention.

This Report supported the notion that local authorities be given the statutory duty (and therefore the resources) to coordinate crime prevention/community safety strategies for their locality. The Report also argued that sufficient resources to make this change must be forthcoming from central government. In passing, it may be noted that the recommendations regarding both local authorities' statutory role and resourcing were not taken up by the government during the 1990s, probably due to its concerns over costs and its ideological hostility to local government per se. With the introduction of the *Crime and Disorder Act 1998* (Home Office 1998), a statutory partnership was introduced rather than Morgan's recommendation of a leadership role for local authorities. The Labour Party's proposals, however, as part of this Act, have stated that no extra resources would be given to local authorities for their new statutory responsibilities for crime prevention. That said, much of the Morgan Report's philosophy of partnerships, multi-agency collaboration and audits is to the fore in current crime prevention policy proposals (Home Office 1997).

Hughes (1998) argues that the Morgan Report appears for the most part to be a report written by local authority and police officers for executive officers. In particular, the discussion of how these multi-agency partnership officer groups relate to issues of democratic accountability, he believes, is never fully addressed. Further, it is argued that citizens are being called upon to play a crucial role in crime prevention through their own actions As in other social policy areas, there is an appeal to the much-vaunted but ill-defined active citizen to play a key role; in this case in both crime surveillance and 'policing'. The Home Office pamphlet *Partners against Crime* (Home Office 1994) confidently asserted that power of partnerships in beating crime was proved and three complementary partnerships were presented as initiatives to be launched or given further encouragement nationally in 1995. These were the already well-established 'Neighbourhood Watch Schemes', 'Street Watch' and 'Neighbourhood Constables'.

Public involvement

Much of the central government proposals for 'community' crime prevention suggested that voluntary community action should replace collective provision, resulting in a voluntary surveillance society, while the extent to which the multi-agency 'call to arms' from both the Home Office Circular 44/1990 (Home Office 1990) and the Morgan Report (Home Office 1991) has affected the thinking, shape and direction of local crime prevention initiatives in the UK is also an important factor. In particular, their research addressed the six elements mentioned previously as crucial to multi-agency partnerships highlighted by the Morgan Report.

Over the past 20 years it has become evident that managing criminal acts has become an increasingly diffuse and diverse problem, with more emphasis on interactive agency work. For Garland (1996), this is a new way of governing crime problems, namely the 'responsibilisation' strategy, with the recurring message that the state alone is not, and cannot, effectively be responsible for preventing or controlling crime. Others must be made aware that they too have a responsibility in this regard, and have to be persuaded to change their practices in order to reduce criminal opportunities and increase formal controls. In the context of crime prevention this strategy is clearly associated with notions of partnership, multi-agency and, of course, self-help. One area that appears to have grown in importance as a result of the partnership approach is that of victimisation. This area has considerable support for the partnership approach as research has shown that some people and places are repeatedly victimised and that patterns of repeat victimisation are often found for different types of offence. Repeat victimisation is usually swift and predictable. It often occurs very soon after the first event, with the risk of becoming a repeat victim diminishing over time.

Further thoughts on partnerships

For partnerships, therefore, there is a need for close cooperation to ensure that more crime is reported, rather than remain hidden and unreported. Further, those repeat offences can be easily identified with this information shared between agencies and that action is taken immediately to prevent re-victimisation. Such strategies it is hoped would place victims' rights firmly on the partnership and therefore political agenda. However, this type of approach has failed to transform practices, and victims' feelings about the criminal justice system remain on the whole negative. While many current partnerships' relationship with victims remains in the domain of purely notification and the supply of information to them, it is suggested that victims could play a greater part in the policy formation which guides many partnerships in crime prevention.

Partnership as buzzword

For some, therefore, the partnership approach has just become the new buzzword of the crime prevention 'industry'. However, it is no bad thing for the responsibility for the 'crime problem' to be owned by an increasingly diffuse variety of individuals and organisations even if the make-up of the partnerships is far from ideal. Alternatively, it is the very diverse make-up of many of the agencies that constitute partnerships which can be problematic. Attention is drawn to the inter-organisational conflict and differential power relationships that can occur. Partnerships, especially within the field of crime control and criminal justice, by their nature, draw together diverse organisations with very different cultures, ideologies and traditions, that pursue distinct aims through divergent structures, strategies and practices. Deep structural conflicts exist between the parties that sit down together in partnerships. Criminal justice agencies have very different priorities and interests, as do other public sector organisations, voluntary bodies, the commercial sector and local community groups.

Not all agencies and groups are equally powerful and certain agencies tend to dominate the policy agenda, such as in the field of crime prevention. This has been pointed out by Sampson *et al.* (1988: 178). Their comments are provided in Box 3.4.

Box 3.4 Important point – domination of agenda by the police

The police are often enthusiastic proponents of the multi-agency approach, but they tend to prefer to set the agenda and dominate forum meetings, and then to ignore the multi-agency framework when it suits their own needs.

(Sampson *et al.* 1988: 178)

While this approach can cause conflict, agencies involved in partnerships use strategies such as conflict avoidance as well as engage in overt conflict. By doing so such measures contribute to the smooth running of partnerships at a formal level.

Partnerships now

The Crime and Disorder Act 1998 as amended by the Police Reform Act 2002 sets out statutory requirements for responsible authorities to work with other local agencies and organisations to develop and implement strategies to tackle crime and disorder and the misuse of drugs in their area. These statutory partnerships are known as Crime and Disorder Reduction Partnerships (CDRPs) or Community Safety Partnerships (CSPs) in Wales. The responsible authorities are:

- the police
- local authorities
- fire authorities
- police authorities
- local health boards in Wales
- primary care trusts in England (which became responsible authorities on 30 April 2004).

Working together, these responsible authorities are required to carry out an audit to identify crime and disorder and misuse of drugs problems in their area, and to develop strategies that deal effectively with them. Partner organisations are required to work in cooperation with local education and probation authorities and invite the cooperation of a range of local private, voluntary and other public and community groups including the community itself.

CDRPs are expected to work closely with drug action teams in two-tier local authority areas and have integrated their work in unitary authority areas since April 2004. Integration/closer working brings many benefits including simplifying local working relationships, giving greater recognition to common interests and providing the right framework to enable the more effective delivery of the crime and disorder reduction and drugs agendas. It is argued that effective partnership working is the key to lasting crime and disorder reduction.

Consequently, there is a need to examine the idea of partnerships dealing with such issues. If dramatic change has taken place, there is a need to understand why this is so and what the consequences are of such a shift in how policing is to be carried out. Police practitioners need to understand why they are engaged in partnership activities as well as understand what powers are available to them, best practice in certain key areas, and importantly what appears to work in crime and disorder reduction. There are several important official documents in being that will help the police practitioner to understand what the government is trying to achieve in this particular area. These include the important document entitled *Building Communities, Beating Crime* (2004), The National Policing Plan (2005–8), Confident Communities in a Secure Britain – The Home Office Strategic Plan (2004–8) and the Home Office publication entitled *Neighbourhood Policing – Your Police, Your Community, Our Commitment*. Each of these documents will be discussed below.

Building communities, beating crime

The previous government's White Paper, *Building Communities, Beating Crime* set out a clear direction of the reform that the police service is undergoing today.

It acknowledges the new challenges that the police and their partners face, and indicates a willingness to support and increase the partnership approach through continued substantial investment that will maintain police numbers and provide for more community support officers. In line with the partnership approach to crime and disorder reduction, the government has stated that the police service will be more accountable to local democratic structures and to their local community. Police authorities will be more closely connected with and visible to their local community so that a clear line of accountability is clear.

A new relationship

The report in particular and most importantly for the theme of this work encourages increasing investment of the public in the quality of the services it receives. While acknowledging the pressure for change to the delivery of police services to the public, there is also an acceptance that the place occupied by the police in communities providing a sense of safety and security is not overlooked. Crime and disorder partnerships are part of this new relationship between the police and the public in which there is active collaboration among police, their partners and citizens in the delivery of police services. Effective policing will only be sustained over the long term if it is citizen focused – responsive to people's and partnerships' needs and performed as a shared undertaking. Tackling crime and disorder and reassuring the public go hand in hand. One cannot deal effectively with one without dealing with the other, so a situation of two-way information exchange between the police and community/partners must lead to improvements in the area of dealing with crime and disorder reduction. Much of what can be achieved will start by introducing neighbourhood policing. There are already some interesting and effective approaches being piloted in this country including the guardian scheme in Leicestershire (Box 3.5).

Box 3.5 Important point – guardians in Leicestershire

In Leicestershire the understanding of the policing approach is based on the idea of 'right people, right numbers, and right place'. The right people starts with a clear understanding of the fundamental policing role as community 'guardians', where the importance is placed upon relationship building, listening and problem solving.

Each police officer is given a unique part of Leicestershire to oversee as 'guardian', the size of which depends upon local issues. It could be a housing estate, village or shopping centre. While the demand-led side of policing means their attendance can be limited, the 'micro area' is a constant which the officer must return to when not engaged on other duties. This encourages ownership, contacts and knowledge of the community, and an easier response to problems.

The Crime and Disorder Act 1998 enhanced

The Crime and Disorder Act 1998 states that local authorities and bodies are required to work together to reduce crime, disorder and fear of crime locally, in order to improve the quality of life and to create a safer living and working environment.

Crime and Disorder Partnerships, consisting of representatives from local authorities, the police and police authority, fire and rescue, probation service and health trusts, were set up across the country when the Act came into force. Partnerships now in operation include statutory and voluntary organisations, and representation from the business sector. Partnership Steering Groups commonly consist of:

- Chief Executive of the Council
- Director of Community Services of the Council
- Police Commander for the area
- The Council's Partnership Officer
- Representatives from Primary Care Trusts.

This list is not exclusive and partnerships may include other agencies, including businesses, charities, etc. to assist in delivering the partnership approach to the reduction of crime and disorder.

Police and Justice Act 2006

Sections 19, 20 and 21 of the Police and Justice Act 2006 set out the requirement for a local authority Crime and Disorder Committee to act as a scrutiny of crime and disorder matters whose duties include:

- The Crime and Disorder Committee is to be an overview and/or scrutiny committee of the authority.
- The Crime and Disorder Committee can review or scrutinise decisions made, or other action taken, in connection with the discharge by the responsible authorities of their crime and disorder functions.

Where a report or recommendation results from the review, a copy must be sent to the responsible authorities and other persons or bodies deemed appropriate. The recipients of the report or recommendations must give consideration, respond to the committee indicating what (if any) action it proposes to take, and have regard to the report or recommendations in exercising its functions.

Crime and Disorder (Overview and Scrutiny) Regulations 2009

The Crime and Disorder (Overview and Scrutiny) Regulations 2009 set out when the sections of the Police and Justice Act 2006 come into force along with some clarification on how the Crime and Disorder Committee will operate, such as:

- The choice of co-opting additional members from those persons and bodies who are responsible authorities under the Crime and Disorder Act 1998 who may have voting rights on crime and disorder matters if the Committee decides this. The Committee may co-opt either employees or non-executive members of a responsible authority.
- Minimum of one meeting per calendar year on crime and disorder.
- Responsible authorities must provide information requested of them by the Crime and Disorder Committee. The Committee may require an officer of a responsible authority or a cooperating body to attend a meeting, on reasonable notice.
- Reponses to any reports or recommendations made must be in writing within one month from the date of the report/recommendation, or, if this is not reasonably feasible, as soon as possible, back to the Crime and Disorder Committee.

The Committee shall review such responses and monitor the action (if any) taken.

The current government's response to dealing with the economic recession will play a part in how these police reforms will continue. At the time of writing (September 2010), several official reports (Audit Commission 2010; HMIC 2010) tend to suggest that austerity policing may mean a reduction in police staff, a restructuring to some extent of police organisations and a greater involvement with community, including charities, cooperatives, volunteer schemes, etc. as part of the government's ideas regarding the ideological change to the 'Big Society'.

Community engagement

Partnerships are now seen at all levels within the criminal justice system and include the amalgamation of agencies that may not otherwise appear to work closely together. The main focus for these is the dissemination of good practice across the country. A good example of this type of partnership is that entitled 'Community Engagement' and may be found on the following website: http://www.communityengagement.police.uk/

A wide definition of community engagement would include consultation, social and marketing research, and community and stakeholder engagement. This project is one of the demonstration projects which form part of the citizen-focus policing and also part of the police reform programme.

On this website one can find out about the National Practitioner Panel for Community Engagement in Policing and access their Guide and database of effective practice examples. The Guide and database have been developed and road tested by practitioners for community engagement practitioners in the polic-ing field. By going into the database, one can also access the Community Engagement forum to post views or questions – and discuss topics with other practitioners.

The project, of which the Panel forms one strand, is a partnership venture between the Home Office and the Association of Police Authorities, and seeks to gather knowledge around – and support improvements in – the effectiveness of police service engagement, consultation and involvement with the public it serves.

Signal crimes

Signal crimes are incidents that act as warning signals to people about threats to their security and that have a disproportionate impact upon the way people think, feel or act. This perspective has informed the development of reassurance policing and neighbourhood policing and examines how crime and disorder are viewed by people in their everyday lives. This helps to shape people's perception and their reaction to them, because signal crimes are communicative in that they send signals to people about the potential risk to their security (Innes 2004). Some signals matter more to people than others and may affect people in different ways and at different times. While 'signal crimes' refer to criminal incidents, 'signal disorders' are physical and social disorders that communicate risk. As a result of identifying signal crimes and disorders, which are known collectively as 'signal events', the responses by police and other agencies are known as 'control signals' which are designed to influence people's perceptions, such as high-visibility patrols. The signal crimes perspective is illustrated in Figure 3.1.

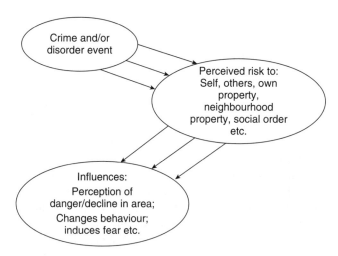

Figure 3.1 The signal crimes perspective.

By clearly identifying the signals that the police may receive from such consultation exercises as PACT (sometimes called Partnerships and Communities Together, or a similar title) meetings, patterns may be identified which means the police and their partners can target resources and provide signal controls.

The approach is not without some criticism, however. It has been argued by Loader (2006), for example, that we need to remember that people's perceptions may not be rational when it comes to risk or harm, and that some people who are actually affected by signal crimes and disorders may not be in a position to be heard, for example, hard-to-reach group members.

Whatever the criticisms attached to this approach, it is a useful way of understanding people's response to crime and disorder within their communities, and was used to inform the ACPO and Home Office-led National Reassurance Policing Programme. The important point to understand is that signal crimes and disorders, if not addressed and dealt with, may undermine another important aspect of reducing crime and disorder within communities, that of cohesive communities.

Cohesive communities

In December 2002, the Local Government Association, Home Office, Office of the Deputy Prime Minister, Commission for Racial Equality and the Inter-Faith Network developed guidance for local authorities on community cohesion. It defined a cohesive community as one where:

- There is a common vision and a sense of belonging for all communities.
- The diversity of people's different backgrounds and circumstances is appreciated and positively valued.
- Those from different backgrounds have similar life opportunities.
- Strong and positive relationships are being developed between people from different backgrounds in the workplace, in schools and within neighbourhoods.

Previous research into cohesive communities and crime suggest that:

- Community cohesion was directly linked to a reduction in mugging, street crime and stranger violence (Sampson and Groves 1989).
- Levels of crime are significantly lower than expected in areas that are disadvantaged but have high levels of social cohesion (Hirschfield and Bowers 1997).
- Higher levels of social control or guardianship apparent in a cohesive community reduce the likelihood of becoming a victim of violent crime such as robbery and assault, regardless of socioeconomic status, lifestyle and neighbourhood characteristics (Lee 2000).

Table 3.1 Decrease in crime by rise in sense of community

Type of crime	Decrease in crime as sense of community increases by one unit
All crime	3%
Domestic burglary	3%
Theft of motor vehicle	4%
Theft from motor vehicle	2%
Violent crime	3%

Source: Wedlock (2006).

More recent research by Wedlock (2006) suggests that local areas with a high sense of community, political trust and sense of belonging show significantly lower levels of 'all' reported crime. As a result of her research, Wedlock provides rates for different types of crime that are predicted to reduce as sense of community increases. Table 3.1 illustrates her work.

Clearly, there appears to be great benefit in the police and their partners promoting the concept of cohesive communities. By encouraging communities and engaging with them, it is believed that they become more resistant to crime and antisocial behaviour.

The use and limitations of crime statistics

Those engaged in crime and disorder reduction activities must be aware of some of these problems if they are to carry out their role effectively. However, there are some apparently basic yet important points that need to be clarified first. What do we understand by the term crime anyway? Where do the statistics we use in everyday life come from and how reliable are they? Do all people who are victims of crime or witness a crime report it? If not, why not? By addressing these questions we can start to understand that the whole idea of crime and statistics is not as straightforward as at first seems. This is especially so if we believe that crime statistics are the bedrock of all that is done in the name of reducing crime and disorder. All countries collect detailed crime statistics for comparison and policy-making purposes. In recent years there has been a realisation that crime is distributed unequally across even small areas and across people inside small areas with similar levels of crime. Combining the crime statistics from a small, quiet area with little crime with a larger, busier area that has a high crime rate to produce a document that purports to represent crime statistics for the combined population really bears little sense.

What is crime?

Before reading on attempt the exercise in Box 3.6.

Box 3.6 Exercise 3B Definition of crime

Write down what you consider to be crime. Once you have compiled the list read the following section and reflect upon your list.

Most people answering the above question would probably include such things as burglary, theft, use of illegal drugs, assault, robbery and so on. These are all crimes as defined by statute or Acts of Parliament. Therefore one definition of what constitutes a crime is a violation of the criminal law. Breaking the criminal law makes someone a criminal and if caught the criminal justice system applies the available legal sanctions against them. Most people have committed criminal acts and few individuals can truly say they have never broken any laws. Under-age drinking, as we have seen, causes antisocial behaviour on many occasions, but in our society, few people actually wait until they are of the legal age to experience their first taste of alcohol. Box 3.7 illustrates what people may or may not consider to be a criminal act.

Box 3.7 Important point – what people may or may not consider as crimes

1. Find money in the street and keep it rather than hand it in.
2. Drive faster than the legal speed limit on a motorway.
3. Take a pen or stationery home from work.
4. Been given too much money in change at a shop and kept it rather than hand it back.

The answer is that all of the above are crimes in the real sense. However, many people would not consider these activities as being identifiably criminal.

By first understanding that there are some problems with the definition of crime itself, we should start to question the validity of what we know about crime. The next step in this critical process is to understand the sources used in producing official criminal statistics upon which much crime reduction policy is based.

Criminal statistics

There are in general three main sources of criminal statistics that are used by the Home Office and those involved in the production of crime and disorder reduction plans and policies. These are:

- Official statistics
- Victimisation studies
- Self-report studies.

Each source has its disadvantages and advantages and these will now be examined.

Official crime statistics

The key publication for crime figures for England and Wales is called *Criminal Statistics*, which is the annual compilation of data produced by the Home Office. This is made up of information from police and court records. In the main, the focus for these crimes revolves around what is known as notifiable offences. This does not mean all criminal offences, as almost all the more minor summary offences are excluded (even though the police may record them for their own investigations). The significance of the term 'notifiable' is that all these offences are notified to the Home Office, and they are collectively known as 'recorded crime'.

The crime recording process is governed by three key stages:

Reporting a crime: someone reports to the police that a crime has been committed or the police observe or discover a crime. In these cases the police should register a crime-related incident, and then decide whether to record it as a crime. From April 2002, the police have complied with the National Crime Recording Standard in making this decision, although generally the police would record these reports of crime if they amount to a 'notifiable' offence and there is no credible evidence to the contrary.

Recording a crime: the police decide to record the report of a crime and now need to determine how many crimes to record and what their offence types are. The Home Office issues rules to police forces on the counting and classification of crime. These Counting Rules for Recorded Crime are mostly straightforward, as most crimes are counted as 'one crime per victim' and the offence committed is obvious (e.g. a domestic burglary). However, it also covers special situations where more than one offence has taken place, maybe on several occasions over a period of time, or there is more than one offender or victim.

Detecting a crime: once a crime is recorded and investigated, and evidence is collected to link the crime to a suspect, it can be detected according to criteria contained in detections guidance within the Home Office counting rules.

In many cases, someone is charged or cautioned or the court has taken the offence into consideration (TIC). The detections guidance covers these detection methods as well as certain others where the police take no further action. The guidance covering these latter methods is stringent, relying on a sufficient amount of evidence that if given in court would be likely to result in a conviction, and in most cases approval by a senior officer.

Victimisation studies

These studies operate at several different levels, including national and, particularly in the case of crime and disorder reduction partnerships, at a local level.

National surveys

The most famous of these types of survey is the British Crime Survey which began in 1982. During this survey respondents are asked to give details of crimes in which they had been a victim in the previous 12 months. The data collected provide a database on crime related topics for policy makers, and include information on drugs abuse, racially motivated crime and the fear of crime. One of the main problems of this type of survey is that they tend to reduce crime and its experience to a level that glosses over some of the significant differences in risk of victimisation.

Local surveys

Local surveys have been carried out for a number of years prior to the introduction of the Crime and Disorder Act 1998 in response to some of the perceived problems of national surveys. By focusing in on particular localities, these surveys attempt to pinpoint the higher levels of crime and associated fear of crime in socially deprived areas, and the disproportionate amount of fear of crime experienced by some vulnerable groups.

All crime and disorder reduction partnerships now engage in this activity in order to conduct their crime audit. This in turn informs their strategic plan for the delivery of their policies.

Self-report studies

Self-report studies were first used in the United States of America during the 1940s, and more recently they have been used to inform international comparisons on criminal activity. These studies involve a researcher asking ordinary members of the public to report their own criminal acts. One of the major drawbacks from the use of these types of studies is that they tend to focus on what might be considered trivial or misdemeanour incidents, not on the more serious crimes committed within a community. However, for the purposes of dealing with antisocial disorder activities this information could be very important indeed.

While all these methods tell us something individually about crime and criminal activity, even when used together they exhibit some problems. Table 3.2 gives a summary of their strengths and weaknesses.

Clearly, use of officially recorded statistics has its limitations and we need to understand that over-reliance on them alone for formulation of crime and disorder reduction policies may be flawed. Perhaps the best that may be said about them is that they are an indicator of what may be happening in an area in terms of crime and disorder, but that they are only a partial representation. Partnerships need to analyse other data sources, including the use of surveys and other qualitative methods of consultation discussed elsewhere in this book, to attempt to obtain a clearer picture.

Table 3.2 Research strengths and weaknesses

Source	Strengths	Weaknesses
Official statistics	1. Easy to obtain from official sources. 2. Quite detailed information about crimes. 3. Can be used to study trends of crime over a period of time.	1. There is the problem of the dark figure of crime. 2. Not all crimes are reported.
Victimisation studies	1. May help us discover more about the dark figure of crime. 2. Can give an insight into crimes rarely reported to the police (e.g. incest). 3. Can help with understanding fear of crime.	1. People may not be supplying accurate information. 2. A very time-consuming and expensive method.
Self-report studies	1. Directly from the person who has committed the offence. 2. May be used to confirm other data from other sources.	1. Some people may exaggerate their crimes, etc. 2. People may not own up to really serious offences.

Why don't people report crime and disorder?

The police become aware of crime through a number of different ways. While their presence on the street is likely to deter criminal acts, the police actually detect relatively few crimes as they are being carried out by the perpetrators. Consequently the police rely on the public to not only report offences to them but also to act as witnesses and provide information which will ultimately lead to detection.

However, many crimes will not be reported to the police. McLaughlin and Muncie (2001) suggest the following to explain why this should be:

- People may not be aware that a crime has occurred (e.g. fraud).
- The victim may be powerless and have no one to report it to (e.g. child abuse).
- There may appear at first glance to be no victim (e.g. prostitution).
- The victim of the crime may distrust the police and may fear the police will not take the incident seriously (e.g. sexual violence against same-gender victim).
- The victim may not believe that the police will protect them against further criminal episodes (e.g. racial victimisation).

Of course the reason why it is important for the police to encourage people to report crime is that it gives a clearer picture of what is happening in their crime reduction partnership area. This means appropriate responses can be formulated in an effort to reduce these occurrences. Therefore it is in the interests of the police and the crime and disorder reduction partnerships to encourage, wherever possible, the reporting of all crimes. It is clear that there is a gap between official figures and the number of crimes actually committed. This gap is called the dark figure of crime.

The hidden figure of crime

This represents those crimes which have not been reported to or recorded by the police and therefore do not appear in the official statistics. Estimates of the amount of hidden crime vary across different offences. Shoplifting and criminal damage, for example, are likely to have a substantial dark figure, and trafficking in illegal drugs and fraud offences probably contain the highest figure. However, it appears that the police come to know about a very high proportion of murders and other homicides. The point to note for the police practitioner engaged in crime and disorder reduction activities is this. Many of the policies designed to solve crime problems are solely based upon what is known about crime and the criminal. However, there is a large amount of knowledge in the same area that does not find its way into official decision-making policies. We should therefore not be surprised if sometimes these policies appear not to work.

Fear of crime

Fear of crime refers to a rational or irrational state of alarm or anxiety engendered by the belief that one is in danger of criminal victimisation (McLaughlin and Muncie 2001). Fear of crime is something that may affect people from all walks of life (which makes it different from actual crime which tends to be concentrated on particular areas and victims and is committed by a small number of offenders) at any stage of their lives. Whether it is a female who feels nervous about walking home, parents who feel anxious about sending their child up the road to buy sweets, or a shopkeeper who tenses up every time a customer enters his shop, if we let it, fear of crime can have a devastating effect on our quality of life. Fear of crime encourages a physical and psychological withdrawal from the community, which weakens the informal social controls necessary for a community to look after itself (Box 3.8).

Box 3.8 Important point – fear of crime and quality of life

Thirty-one per cent of respondents to British Crime Survey interviews conducted in the 2001/2002 financial year said that fear of crime had a moderate impact upon their quality of life; with a further 6 per cent saying that their quality of life was greatly affected by it. Yet the same survey put the statistical probability of becoming a victim of violent crime at just 4 per cent.

Fear of crime can increase for a number of reasons. These include:

- Direct experience.
- Secondary knowledge from friends and family.
- Police officers and politicians who want to increase awareness of criminal activity.
- Private security firms looking for business.
- News media through over-reporting violent and sexual crimes.

However, attempts to tackle the fear of crime may lead to some unexpected results (Box 3.9).

Box 3.9 Important point – lighting and its impact upon fear of crime

People who lived in an area with very poor street lighting were consulted regarding their fear of crime. This was identified as being one of the causes of fear of crime, so the local authority upgraded the street lighting system. Consequently, there was a sharp increase in the number of thefts from vehicles in the area, which again led to an increase in the fear of local residents becoming victims of crime.

Similarly, encouraging people into a town centre at night might create more opportunities for crime, so the police and their partners need to think carefully when considering how to reduce fear of crime. One of the main problems when tackling fear of crime is the lack of good communication between partnerships and the community. Many partnerships have carried out excellent initiatives which have helped reduce crime but have failed to address the perceptions about fear of crime.

Attempt the exercise given in Box 3.10.

Box 3.10 Exercise 3C Fear of crime

Make a list of events that you could do in order to positively affect people's ideas about fear of crime.

You may have thought of some of the following ideas:

- Engage the local newspapers and try to get them on side by reporting good news stories in a prominent position.
- Send out leaflets to affected areas giving examples of the initiatives that the local CDRP has implemented to reduce crime and disorder and improve the local environment.

- Use every opportunity to provide the community with the names, numbers and contact details of those officers (council, police and others) whom members of the community can contact to discuss a particular problem.
- Arrange for a series of face-to-face talks at a variety of social and communal events using not only community police officers but other representatives of the CDRP.
- Find out what different interest, identity and geographical groups are already running in the area and who you can contact to get an invite to address them. Parish councils, schools and voluntary/community groups are always keen for interesting speakers to come along to their meetings.

Fear of crime is one of the most pressing issues for the police at this moment in time. Attempts to engage with and understand communities are vital if attempts to deal effectively with this issue are to occur.

Conclusion

In this chapter, we have considered the rise in importance of partnership policing and the main reasons why this approach has been so prominent. To become effective this approach requires an understanding of such topics as recognising the problems attached to partnership working, how engaging with the community, despite difficulties attached to the processes, is vital, and how concepts such as fear of crime, signal crimes and the official use of crime data influence not only people's perceptions of their own personal safety, but their view of the wider community within which they live.

References and suggested further reading

Audit Commission (2010) *Sustaining Value for Money in the Police Service – a Joint Report with HMIC*, The Audit Commission, London.

Bright, J. (1991) 'Crime Prevention: The British Experience', in Stenson, K. and Cowell, D. (eds) *The Politics of Crime Control*, Sage, London, pp. 62–86.

——(1996) 'Preventing Youth Crime in High Crime Areas: Towards a Strategy', in Bennett, T. (ed.), *Preventing Crime and Disorder: Targeting Strategies and Responsibilities*, Institute of Criminology, Cambridge, pp. 365–83.

—— (1997) *Turning the Tide: Crime, Community and Prevention*, Demos, London.

—— (1999) 'Preventing Youth Crime', in Francis, P. and Fraser, P., (ed.) *Building Safer Communities*, The Centre for Crime and Justice Studies, London, pp. 96–103.

Brown, C. (1997) *Dwelling Burglaries: The Need for Multi-Agency Strategies,* Police Research Group, Home Office, London.

Cohen, S. (1985) *Visions of Social Control*, Polity Press, Cambridge.

Elliot, R. and Nicholls, J. (1996) *Its Good to Talk: Lessons in Public Consultation and Feedback*, Police Research Group Paper 22, Home Office, London.

Forrester, K., Chatterton, M. and Pease, K. (1988) *The Kirkholt Burglary Prevention Project, Rochdale*, Home Office Crime Prevention Unit Paper 13, Home Office, London.

Garland, D. (1996) 'The Limits of the Sovereign State', *British Journal of Criminology*, 36, 4, 445–71.

HMIC (Her Majesty's Inspector of Constabulary) (2010) *Valuing the Police: Policing in an Age of Austerity*, HMSO, London.

Hirschfield, A. and Bowers, K.J. (1997) 'The Effect of Social Cohesion on Levels of Recorded Crime in Disadvantaged Areas', *Urban Studies*, 34: 1275–95.

Home Office (1984) *Crime Prevention Circular 8/1984*, Home Office, London.

—— (1989) *Tackling Crime*, HMSO, London.

—— (1991) *Safer Communities: The Local Delivery of Crime Prevention through the Partnership Approach* (The Morgan Report), HMSO, London.

—— (1990) *Circular 44/90 Crime Prevention. The Success of the Partnership Approach*, HMSO, London.

—— (1994) *Partners against Crime*, HMSO, London.

—— (1997) *Getting to Grips with Crime: A New Framework for Local Action. Examples of Local Authority Partnership Activity*, HMSO, London.

—— (1998) *The Crime and Disorder Act*, HMSO, London.

—— (1999) *Crime and Disorder Act 1998*, HMSO, London.

Hughes, G. (1998) *Understanding Crime Prevention*, Open University Press, Buckingham.

Innes, M. (2004) 'Signal Crimes and Signal Disorders: Notes on Deviance as Communicative Action', *British Journal of Sociology*, 55: 335–55.

Lee, M.R. (2000) 'Community Cohesion and Violent Predatory Victimization: A Theoretical Extension and Cross-national Test of Opportunity Theory', *Social Forces* 79 (2): 683–88.

Loader, I. (2006) 'Policing, Recognition and Belonging', *Annals of the American Academy of Political and Social Science*, 605: 202–21.

McLaughlin, E. and Muncie, J. (2001) *Controlling Crime*, Sage, London.

Morris, S. (1996) *Policing Problem Housing Estates*, Police Research Group Crime Detection and Prevention Series Paper 74, Home Office, London.

Sampson, A., Smith, D., Pearson, G. and Blagg, H. (1988) 'Crime, Localities and the Multi Agency Approach', *British Journal of Criminology*, 28: 478–93.

Sampson, R.J. and Groves. W.B. (1989) 'Community Structure and Crime: Testing Social-Disorganization Theory', *American Journal of Sociology*, 94: 774–802.

Tilley, N. (1993) *The Prevention of Crime against Small Businesses: The Safer Cities Experience*, Police Research Group Prevention Series Paper 45, Home Office, London.

Wedlock, E. (2006) *Crime and Cohesive Communities*, Research, Development and Statistics – Communities Group, Home Office, London.

4 Neighbourhood policing teams and problem solving

Introduction

We have seen in previous chapters how diverse the community can be. Indeed, in Chapter 2 the idea of community was examined in some depth to help explain and understand the complexities that make up communities, and how the police have tried to respond to this in terms of crime reduction partnerships and community policing. This chapter extends the idea of policing communities by examining the introduction of neighbourhood policing and in particular the problem-oriented partnership approach which underpins the community policing idea.

The context of neighbourhood policing teams

In recent years the neighbourhood policing programme has moved through the planning stages to implementation. It was supported by previous government investment in excess of £1 billion, and there are approximately 16,000 police community support officers and 13,000 police constables and sergeants dedicated to neighbourhood policing. In total there are some 3,600 neighbourhood policing teams providing a named police contact in every neighbourhood area across England and Wales (HMIC 2008). In general, the aims of neighbourhood policing teams are as follows:

- To improve satisfaction for the community and increase confidence in the police service.
- To reduce the fear of crime within communities.
- To resolve local problems of crime and antisocial behaviour.

Underlying the way in which these objectives are to be achieved is the citizen-focused approach to policing.

Citizen-focused policing

Before reading on, reflect a while and attempt the exercise given in Box 4.1.

Box 4.1   Exercise 4A Citizen focus

As a member of the community, you expect a certain service from the police organisation. Make a list of what you expect from the police and compare it to the information contained in this section.

Citizen-focused policing is about developing a culture where the needs and priorities of the citizen are understood by staff and always taken into account when designing and delivering policing services. Sir Ronnie Flanagan's *Review of Policing* (Flanagan 2008) emphasised that focusing on the treatment of individuals is one of the key determinants of satisfaction in the police service. Therefore a sustained commitment to quality and customer need is essential to build trust and open up opportunities for active engagement with individuals, thereby creating safer and more secure communities. However, it must be remembered that this approach is a long-term commitment which will yield greater and better results in the fullness of time, and citizen focus is a major factor in the neighbourhood approach.

There is a close relationship between neighbourhood policing and the wider citizen-focused agenda with each being supported by the concept of putting people first. This involves greater engagement with all members of the community, and research has highlighted that those police forces that are strongly embedding neighbourhood policing in their core work have engaged with the public in qualitative value-based commitments such as that highlighted in Box 4.2 entitled the LISTEN principles.

Box 4.2   Case study Surrey police and the LISTEN principles

Surrey police have embedded the LISTEN principles throughout their force and this is now a corporate standard of how staff should deal with everyone with whom they have contact. Each contact conducted by a member of Surrey police is subject to the following:

- Listen to people in the community and take their concerns seriously.
- Inspire confidence and help people feel secure.
- Support with information – give contact details and tell people what is happening locally.
- Take ownership – tell people what you can do to help solve the problem: make realistic promises.
- Explain what the team can and cannot do, and the next steps.
- Notify people of action agreed, progress and the final outcomes.

Unfortunately, despite such initiatives shown above, community engagement is still inconsistent across forces. The methods and effectiveness of engagement vary from one BCU to another within forces, and from force to force.

The elements of neighbourhood policing teams

The Police Reform Act 2002 (Home Office 2002) indicated that substantial change was in store for the police service and it is this Act that enables us, with some accuracy, to predict the future delivery of policing. The introduction of police community support officers, coupled with the use of neighbourhood watch and local warden schemes, was intended to introduce a more flexible method in dealing with community problems.

The scenario given in Box 4.3 illustrates how neighbourhood policing teams may be used.

Box 4.3 Case study neighbourhood policing teams in West Yorkshire

Neighbourhood policing teams should be at the centre of policing communities. They should be able to work together, be contactable and listen to the needs of the community. In Bradford South, West Yorkshire, neighbourhood policing teams now comprise more community support officers than community police officers. The full teams comprise an inspector, two sergeants, 18 police constables and 22 community support officers. CSOs conduct uniform patrols, not in an unstructured manner, but focused on particular problems that have been identified within the previous 24 hours. The whole idea of the local policing team is supported by the use of good local knowledge, and the unit has been very successful in combating vehicle crime and burglaries because of this. CSOs are encouraged by the local commander to visit people, enter their homes and have a cup of tea, thereby gaining their trust and confidence. CSOs have assisted regular officers in arresting an individual for a prolific number of burglaries, pooling their local knowledge to discover his hiding place. The neighbourhood team has built up many contacts in the area, such as schools and the community centre, and this personal involvement means the community believe the teams are working for and with them.

The extended police family, in the form of the neighbourhood policing team, responsible for ensuring the tackling of day-to-day policing of crime and disorder, is worthy of exploration.

Uniformed constable

The role of the uniformed constable is crucial in that he or she will act as the 'manager' of the coordinated service delivery. This enables the constable to perform a more pro-active role in consultation, coordinating delivery through the various officers available, and where necessary being able to use the full powers available to a police constable. The role alters dramatically the idea of constable from one of enforcer of laws to only that of facilitator and leader. This will require a more professional approach and therefore perhaps a more highly qualified individual to perform the role. The constable, it is envisaged, will be directly accountable to his or her line supervisor, the sergeant, who will have responsibility for two or more of the policing teams.

Special constables

The powers exercised by special constables, who are volunteers, are exactly the same as for regular officers. They receive the same amount and level of training as regular officers, wear the same uniforms, and provide invaluable support in many situations. As volunteers, they are able to offer only a certain amount of their time. Despite this fact, they should, if their availability is intelligently managed, provide useful high-visibility patrol, backed up with the lawful authority to use force if necessary, just like regular sworn police officers.

Police community support officer

The police community support officer (PCSO), working with the other members of the delivery team, will be used not only to provide reassurance through visible patrolling at relevant times, but also through use of his or her powers to resolve low-level community problems. They will provide the beat manager with invaluable assistance in dealing with minor instances of public disorder and antisocial problems.

Traffic wardens

With the idea of traffic wardens not only enforcing road traffic offences but also being able to issue fixed penalty notices for certain other offences, this role becomes part of an integrated policing system. Traffic wardens are also employed by private companies but can still be incorporated into the overall idea of policing teams by supplying information for the policing team, as well as supplying criminal and community intelligence through their visible presence on the street. They will be available to deal with local traffic problems as well as being involved in maintaining safety on the roads. This duty is also carried out by Department of Transport traffic officers who operate on motorways.

Parish or neighbourhood warden schemes

While originally conceived as an eyes-and-ears approach for the police, coupled with concierge and reassurance functions, these warden schemes may well be able to issue fixed penalties for various offences such as minor criminal damage (graffiti) to the depositing of litter. The increase in surveillance and reassurance by high-visibility patrolling that these schemes provide will be an invaluable asset to the beat manager.

Private security provision

It is possible that within the neighbourhood teams idea use could be made of private security officers to enhance the policing capability. While the main function of private security industry has in the past been the protection of private property, there has been an increase in their use for such roles as prisoner escort, as well as other custody duties assisting sworn officers. The Private Security Industry Act 2001, which regulates the industry, will have wide repercussions for the use of private security in the public domain of policing. The main areas of current activity include the roles of wheel clamping, guarding premises and as security consultants. Section 40 of the Police Reform Act 2002 introduces the community safety accreditation scheme which is designed to extend limited police powers to persons already engaged in community safety duties. These include local authority wardens as well as security guards within private security industry.

Volunteers

A clear theme of the current government agenda for reform and modernisation of public services is the development of new ways of involving local communities in shaping the priorities and outputs of public service delivery. This involves identifying new and less formalised methods of communication between the public services and service users to make delivery of services more responsive to the needs of local people. Generally speaking, the police service in England and Wales has a modest record in the involvement of volunteers in its activities. The Special Constabulary has been the principal initiative and significant effort has been invested in recruitment, retention and empirical evaluation of the business and community benefits of using these volunteers. However, the term 'volunteer' needs to be expanded to include individuals who are not special constables. The increased use of volunteers and closer engagement with community agencies is a major idea of the current government which refers to the ideological standpoint known as the 'Big Society' (see Halpern 2010).

The Big Society

In essence, the 'Big Society' refers to a tripartite partnership between the citizen, community and local government. This vision requires families, networks and neighbourhoods in a postmodern society to formalise a working partnership that is effective and sustainable in its approach to solving problems, building social cohesion and setting priorities for Britain. In doing so, the government along with the involvement of communities is set on building a 'big society' that is bigger, stronger and accountable to all. How this equates to the practicalities of living in the UK is worthy of examination. The current Prime Minister refers to the ideology of the 'Big Society' as liberalism, empowerment, freedom and responsibly where the top-down approach to government is abandoned and replaced by local innovation and civic action. The government insists that for the 'Big Society' to work, it will require significant involvement, encouragement and support from communities. Fundamentally, there are five key strands to understanding the 'Big Society'.

Empowering communities – the government aims to reform the planning and procedural systems to give local people the ability to determine how their communities will develop and be shaped in the future. Specifically, the 'Big Society' requires local people to have a greater say in the 'construction' of their surroundings. Accompanying these new powers, local people will also have ways of saving local facilities and services that are threatened by closure if they are deemed to be fundamental to the fabric of society. Communities will have the right to take over state-run services and facilities. Bringing about this change, the government will recruit and train 'community organisers' to support the creation of neighbourhood ground all over the UK.

Action-orientated communities – community involvement, philanthropy and a spirit of volunteerism are an integral component of the 'Big Society'. The introduction of a 'Big Society' day and a focus on civic service will aim to increase and stimulate involvement from members of the communities of all socio-economic backgrounds. A 'National Citizen Service' will be established to encourage young people to develop the skills needed in a modern society aimed to break down negative perceptions and stimulate cohesion.

Decentralised power – a drive for decentralisation and 'rolling back the frontiers of the state' are perhaps a synonymous style of governance set by the Conservative Party in previous administrations. Reducing the size and influence of the state by stimulating local initiatives is seen as a key driver in the move to establish a 'Big Society'. Greater autonomy, both financially and procedurally, is likely to be seen as government moves away from micro-management or 'nano-level' management to a more macro-management approach. This cultural change in governance will see local authorities and local officials having greater discretion and influence over the direction of local policy. Decisions on housing and planning are also likely to return to local councils in an effort to make the procedure of allocation and urban design more accountable to local people.

Greater social enterprises – as pluralisation is to be encouraged, it is envisaged that there will be an expansion in social enterprises. Those sectors, companies, industries and organisations that have previously been operating under a monopoly or oligopoly are likely to see an increase in competition as state-run functions may be shared with other social enterprises. Public sector workers will be encouraged to set up employee-owned cooperatives encouraging innovation and quality of service for the end user while being a more economically viable option for the state. Funding the 'Big Society' will come from dormant bank accounts which it is believed will provide the necessary finding for stimulating neighbourhood groups, charities and social enterprise. As previously indicated, it is however unlikely that the 'Big Society' ideology drive will be funded by an unlimited supply of capital, and financial constraints will play a large part in their introduction and use.

Information ability – finally, confidence in official data and statistics has been eroded in recent years with possibly unfounded, incorrect statistics being published resulting in several official apologies being made in Parliament by senior ministers. Underpinning the 'Big Society', the government aims to create a new culture where the public have a 'right to data' that will be published regularly in an attempt to improve accountability.

Implications for the police

Policing in the 'Big Society' will unquestionably have implications for the service and for its partners. It is likely that with community engagement taking precedence, the community policing paradigm that has been adopted by the police over recent years with the roll-out of neighbourhood policing teams will continue, if not be strengthened. The police may need to engage with an ever-empowered community as they work together in setting short-, medium- and long-term objectives for policing within their local community. Becoming more focused at a local level while operating in smaller geographical areas will possibly be of greater importance to the police if they are to facilitate the needs of the community rather than simply prescribe narrative, often enforcement-led solutions. The transfer of power to the local level is likely to be difficult for both the police and community. However, to create value, mobilise wealth in terms of reciprocity and social capital and to operate efficiently, it will be up to both the police and the community to agree and operate under a cooperative productive mutual partnership. As local communities are likely to be part of the setting of objectives, there will be a need for greater involvement from partner agencies, particularly local authorities, charities and local cooperatives in order to address issues which the public needs to tackle. The use of unpaid volunteers is also likely to be increased dramatically as the police attempt to offer a wide range of services in times of austerity. The concept of volunteering within the police service is not a new one. Special constables, who are recruited from members of local communities, are unpaid, fully warranted police officers and are the archetypical volunteer in the police. However, the police service has begun to use volunteers who are unpaid 'civilians' to work within the police organisation. These are members of the public who have expressed an interest in working with the police, undertaking various roles and responsibilities within the organisation; however, they are not special constables, have no police powers and are unwarranted. These 'neighbourhood volunteers' assist when they can, as many volunteers enjoy the flexibility of supporting the service and their local community. Dependent on the role, whether administrative or involving some sort of community engagement, some volunteers work from different police stations, and others work on the street engaging with members of the public directly, engaging in Police and Communities

Together (PACT) meetings, letter dropping and other operations, often working alongside neighbourhood police teams and partner agencies. Although such schemes are used extensively throughout some forces, there will need to be an expansion of this programme if the police are to continue to offer a wide range of services considered necessary by communities. In the mid- to long term, volunteer schemes may have a positive influence on communities in times of austerity. This will be achieved in part because of the extended partnership approach, improving confidence and cooperation. The improved relationship as well as the developed sense of ownership and inclusion may result in targets on community safety being met. As a direct consequence, this may lead to a reduction in overall crime and fear of crime leading to a reduction in the reassurance gap. In terms of structure, the 'Big Society' will result in the devolvement of power to more local levels. The Commission on 2020 Public Services (2010) concludes that directly elected crime commissions will facilitate this change in structure as power and autonomy is transferred away from the police force and basic command unit (BCU) level and back to local communities. It is likely that the previous managerialist, new public management mandate where the primary focus was on centralised targets will change, moving instead to more meaningful local statistics where the locally elected crime commissioner can be held to account. No longer will sanction detection rates or league tables be considered the measurement of all policing. Instead it will be public perceptions that will take precedent. The forces of neoliberalism and pluralisation are likely to increase the number of policing providers in the future. Private contractors and a move to a more European approach to policing where a significant amount of policing tasks are contracted out to private companies and industries may also be a visible change following the implantation of the 'Big Society'. Losing dominance in the market, it is likely that the police service may need to become smaller, more focused and specialised in its approach to policing. As they lose the position of dominance in an ever-dynamic market, there is likely to be an expansion of partner agencies through the creation of more charities, groups and enterprise following the societal shifts. This will increase the importance of better partnership working between the police and other agencies as the need to share knowledge and intelligence becomes even more important.

Extending the role of the volunteer

Members of the community are a valuable source of information for the police. However, their role as volunteers should not be underestimated. Some forces have embraced the idea of using unpaid volunteers not just to help with the increased workload that all police forces have to bear, but also as a means of breaking down barriers that may appear to exist between the police and their communities. A very good example of the use of volunteers may be seen in the case study given in Box 4.4.

This list is not exhaustive and displays the large range of duties that community volunteers can play in assisting neighbourhood policing teams.

Box 4.4 Case study Lancashire Constabulary and their community volunteer scheme

This project has been developed by recruiting volunteers from within the community, and includes an assessment of how volunteer recruitment would bring together the police service and the communities they service.

Launched in 2004 following a pilot scheme, Lancashire Constabulary now has in the region of 644 volunteers from a wide variety of backgrounds. Nearly 60 per cent of the volunteers are female, and the ages of the volunteers range from 18 to 86, with 55 of the volunteers being over the age of 70.

There are four main roles that the volunteers are involved in, namely:

- Assisting in neighbourhood policing.
- Assisting in improving quality of service to the public.
- Volunteers who assist in general administration.
- Public enquiry desk duties.

Three hundred twenty-two of the volunteers are engaged on carrying out neighbourhood policing volunteer duties and work alongside other members of the NPTs. The tasks that they typically carry out include:

- Coordinating PACT (Police and Communities Together) information sheets and inputting information on these on computers.
- Ringing PACT members to confirm or give reminders of dates of meetings.
- Attending PACT meetings and assisting in taking notes.
- Accompanying community beat managers on patrolling their area.
- Attending crime prevention displays.
- Conducting analysis of hotspots.
- Managing the neighbourhood watch database.

While there may be some obvious resistance to the introduction of volunteers by some staff and their staff representatives, who may view volunteers as a 'cheap' option and replacement for full-time positions, where close consultation has taken place the use of volunteers has 'dovetailed' well with existing administrative and police processes. Having discussed the role of volunteers, try the following exercise (Box 4.5).

Supporting neighbourhood policing

In support of the neighbourhood policing team idea, there are several areas that are vital if the approach is to be successful. In particular, two are worthy of closer

---

Box 4.5 Exercise 4B Volunteers

Reflect upon the information discussed above. Make a list of the functions that a volunteer could undertake within the police organisation.

---

scrutiny as they are undoubtedly linked. These are the use of community intelligence and the introduction of IT systems that support effective use of such information, and the problem-oriented partnership approach to solving problems using partnership agencies for long-term problem-solving solutions.

Community intelligence

Defining just what community intelligence actually is has never really been satisfactory. The ACPO *National Intelligence Model Manual of Guidance* defines it thus:

> Community Intelligence is local information, which, when assessed, provides intelligence on issues that affect neighbourhoods and informs both the strategic and operational perspective in the policing of local communities. Information may be direct and indirect and come from a diverse range of sources including the community and partner agencies.
>
> (ACPO 2005)

This attempt to differentiate community intelligence from criminal intelligence is confused further by the same document suggesting that community intelligence may address issues from general quality of life to serious crime and terrorism. Clearly, there appears to be some overlap in just what the intelligence product is or should be, and how it supports community-focused policing. However, the gathering of this type of information is extremely important and relies heavily on the use of information technology systems designed to support those already in use by the police and also designed to support the National Intelligence Model business process system that underpins targeted or intelligence-led policing. However, the introduction of new IT systems that support NPTs and community intelligence work needs to be discussed at greater depth to provide an understanding of the problems that may occur to impede their successful use.

Understanding the problems of introducing community intelligence

The introduction of any new type of technology should be considered as quite challenging, since it directly impacts upon established working practices within an organisation that has a strong occupational culture (see Chan 1997; Reiner 2000). This fact should not be disregarded when considering an evaluation of this kind. As Chan (2003) and Manning (1996) point out, the introduction of new technologies into the police service can often destabilise the power balance between organisational segments by altering communication patterns, roles, relationships, the division of labour, established formats for organisational communication, and 'taken-for-granted' routines. Furthermore, supervisors may be directly affected by the introduction of new technology. Chan's (2003) study came to the conclusion that information technology had led to closer scrutiny of police work by supervisors and made them more aware of the day-to-day activities and workloads of officers under their control which may cause them to change their behaviour towards subordinates. In view of Herzberg *et al.*'s (1959) conclusions that changes in levels of supervision, especially when they are perceived to lead to imbalances, can become a strong hygiene factor and demotivator, it may be reasonable to expect some changes in staff motivation levels. The needs of employees and their behaviour in the workplace modify dramatically following the introduction of information and communication technology (ICT). It is further suggested that cultural change within any organisation is needed to cope with the introduction of new technology and the skills training required to make full use of it.

Mullins (2005) warned that advances in ICT tend to develop quickly irrespective of human and social consequences. He said:

> staff may become resentful, suspicious and defensive. People's cognitive limitations, and their uncertainties and fears, may result in a reluctance to accept change

> (Mullins 2005: 134).

The police as an organisation may also show tendencies to resist change as some groups within the organisation suspect changes to the power and influence of certain groups associated with the organisation such as community safety partnerships. Mullins (2005) stated that where a group of people had established what they perceived to be their 'territorial rights' over a period of time, changes to established working practices may well be resisted.

Reis and Pena (2001) linked motivation levels to resistance to changes in the workplace and, bearing in mind the seminal work of Reuss-Ianni (1999) which identified the problems that exist between 'street cop' and 'management cop' when implementing changes in working practices, one would expect some form of resistance to be evident. However, all the individuals spoken to in the course of this research appeared to be very supportive of the idea in general.

Different models of policing make different assumptions about what police information is for. Traditionally, the police organisation has viewed information in terms of incident-based, operational and administrative purposes. On the other hand, community and problem-oriented approaches see the use of information as being for problem identification, the search for solutions and evaluation of responses.

Resisting change

Hay (2002) warned that as organisations redefine themselves and go through a period of reorientation to ensure effectiveness for the future, the need and demand for change may not be obvious to all levels of the organisation. Kotter and Schlesinger (1979) identified four main areas why employees resist change: parochial self-interest, misunderstandings, different assumptions of the changes proposed and low tolerance to change. Resistance by key police personnel working within the organisation can affect output which reflects the *quality of change management* techniques chosen, rather than the *quality of work* carried out.

Zaltman and Duncan (1977) advocated the need to educate people in the workplace about changes planned, and Coch and French (1944) stated that employees who are involved and participating in the planning for change are more likely to accept and embrace change. It is therefore important for the police to recognise the significance of correct marketing of this and any new initiative with the people who have to use the ideas in the workplace. It is believed that successful management of change tends to occur when managers effectively communicate the reasons for change and embrace change themselves. Situated alongside this is the control of expectations about just what an initiative such as this can or cannot achieve. Vroom (1964) suggested that an employee's motivation to succeed will be influenced by his or her expectancy to achieve. One of the newer ways of obtaining information and community intelligence is through the use of neighbourhood or area profiles.

Neighbourhood or area profiles

An area profile provides a rich picture of the quality of life and public services in your local area. Area profiling is particularly helpful to the police and their partners in local strategic partnerships (LSPs), and to central government and national agencies. Area profiles have been developed in partnership with local services for a number of years and can help agencies to focus on people and places, and identify priorities that cut across service boundaries.

Therefore, area profiles are useful to:

- help local public service providers to identify where improvement is most needed locally;
- make publicly available a summary of data and information on the quality of life and local services;
- aid government and regulators to concentrate strategically on those areas that most need support.

They are created using a variety of tools such as databases, surveys, etc., with each agency helping the user to explore and understand the quality of life and local services with regard to an aspect of the local community. A good area profile involves analysis of the following aspects:

- indicators of local quality of life and context statistics;
- public funding into and spending patterns within a local area;

- local residents' and service users' views on quality of life;
- the LSP partners' views on quality of life and services;

The profiles produced by each of these components are then used in the final process.

The result of this approach is an area profile that may be used in different ways, namely:

1. To provide a summary for the public of all the data and assessments for the local area. For example, key findings could be published online, in a leaflet, or in a local newspaper article. This will help local people to hold public services to account and empower them to take decisions about priorities and services in their local area.
2. LSP partners (council, police, health, voluntary and private sectors) could apply the information to highlight problem areas where improvement is most needed.
4. The government, national agencies and regulators could draw on area profiles to identify strengths, weaknesses and trends in local areas. This will help them to agree on how best to target their support and regulatory activities.

The problem-oriented partnership (POP) approach

Community-based policing, particularly community engagement, involves a shift from reliance upon reactive patrol and investigations towards a problem-solving orientation (Williamson 2008). In essence the approach is not new; police officers have always tried to solve problems in the past, but the difference today is that officers are now able to receive guidance, support and technology for dealing with problems (Peak and Glensor 1996). Herman Goldstein is considered by many to be the principal architect of problem-oriented police work, and his text entitled *Problem-Oriented Policing* (Goldstein 1990) is frequently cited in publications within this area. Goldstein realised that police work tended to revolve around responding to a call rather than concentrating on what was actually carried out once the police arrived at the scene. He therefore advocated a radical change in the way in which the police carried out their duties and that a new framework should be applied, that of a more thoughtful concern with substantive problems.

Defining problems

A 'problem' for the purposes of the POP approach is anything that is of concern or that causes harm to citizens. It must be noted that this is not just something that concerns the police, or just crime or antisocial behaviour. It can mean anything. If this is understood from the beginning, then the use of partner agencies to solve problems becomes apparent.

The basic model of POP

In general, three elements are needed for a problem to occur: an offender, a victim and a location. The problem analysis triangle helps us to visualise this and to understand the relationship between the three elements. The basic idea is that by attempting to influence one or more sides of this triangle, there is a greater chance of negating or reducing the potential for the incident to occur.

Problem analysis triangle

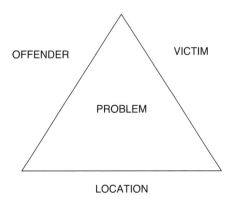

Figure 4.1 The problem analysis triangle.

The role of third parties

As Peak and Glensor (1996) state, there are individuals or groups who can influence or hinder the problem-solving efforts of the police and their partners. These are:

- *Guardians*: people who look out for targets and try to protect them from theft, attack, destruction or harm. Formal guardians are people who are assigned to look out for the targets, such as security guards. Informal guardians are people who look out for targets without such an assignment. Such people may be friends, neighbours, employees and sometimes strangers. Guardians may be human or non-human technology (e.g. CCTV).
- *A handler*: someone who knows the offender well and who is in a position to exert some control over his or her actions.
- *A manager*: a person who has some responsibility for controlling behaviour in a specific location. Their primary interest is in the smooth functioning of the location or place. Managers include store clerks, property managers, lifeguards and librarians. The updated version of the problem analysis triangle is given in Figure 4.2

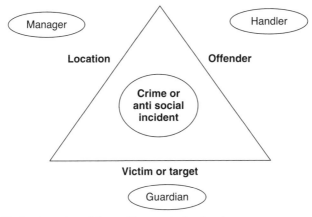

Figure 4.2 Updated version of the problem analysis triangle.

The SARA model

The main problem-solving process is known as SARA, which involves scanning, analysis, response and assessment. Figure 4.3 illustrates the process.

Each part of the process links to another part and should inform it accordingly. Once the assessment phase has been undertaken this should be used to adjust any one or more of the other three parts of the process to ensure effectiveness. Each part of the SARA model is defined in Box 4.6.

In addition to the main component parts of the SARA model, there is a further area that needs to be considered within the application of the problem-solving approach, that of sustainability. Once an initiative has been implemented by police and their partners, the long-term success of this initiative may be judged by the problem having been eradicated or dealt with in such a manner that

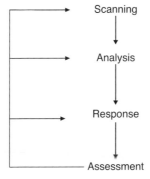

Figure 4.3 The SARA problem-solving process.

Box 4.6 Important point – the SARA components defined

Scanning

Identifying problems through a wide range of data and information such as intelligence logs, crime reports, public information and local police knowledge.

Analysis

Here the details of the problem are examined in more detail. Scanning might tell us that a large amount of criminal damage is taking place, but analysis will tell us the times, dates, methods, types of property witnesses, suspects, etc. Here information from other agencies should be included. This extra information may provide alternative perspectives in trends and patterns.

Response

This is the implementation of suitable action to resolve the problem. It may involve the assistance of other agencies and partnership members where appropriate. Responses may be multi-layered, involving police action against a suspect, victim support for individuals, or changes to geographic features at a location (e.g. lighting, CCTV cameras, etc.).

Assessment

This is the evaluation phase where the effectiveness of the response to the problem is assessed. Here we decide whether all objectives have been met, considering how the response was carried out as well as the effects of the response.

Box 4.7 Important point – sustainability

Sustainability involves the ability for the problem to be solved in such a manner that it does not resurface and therefore does not require ongoing resources to maintain its resolution.

---

resources are not required to deal with it. For the purposes of this report sustainability may be defined according to the elements given in Box 4.7.

Now that the elements of the problem-oriented partnership approach have been discussed, try the exercise given in Box 4.8.

Box 4.8 Exercise 4C Problem-oriented partnerships

Bradey Youth Centre is situated at the edge of a large housing estate. Every Sunday night, groups of youths congregate about 50 yards away from the entrance to the youth centre and the police have received numerous calls from worried elderly people living on the estate. Using PAT and SARA as a guide, explain how you would approach solving this problem.

The benefits of using the POP approach

There are several areas where it is believed that the POP approach benefits the police service. These are:

- All types of crime and disorder problems; existing and potential community problems actually come to the attention of the police and their partners.
- A systematic and analytical approach to the understanding of the sources of these problems is discovered.
- There is the opportunity to implement measures designed to reduce, deflect or eradicate community problems through partnership work.
- Assessing the impact of initiatives introduced under this system can be introduced so that lessons may be learned and good practice disseminated to other agencies.
- Sustainability of problems solved offers the police and their partners the opportunity to target scarce resources elsewhere.

Clearly, the basic idea of using this approach seems sound. A scientific analysis of problems leads to solutions being put forward which are then implemented and assessed for effectiveness. It seems to fit neatly into the world of policing using the partnership approach, namely with crime and disorder reduction partners in England and community safety partnerships in Wales.

Impact upon partnerships

The adoption by the police of the problem-oriented approach has major consequences for those agencies engaged in partnership working. A thorough analysis of a problem often leads to an appreciation of the need for more effective referrals to existing governmental and private services, as well as improved coordination with agencies that exert control over some of the problems or individuals involved in incidents, as well as mobilising the community to help implement a specific response to a specific problem. As Skogan (2008) rightly points out, solutions to the pattern of problems involve other agencies and may be 'non-police' in character. In the traditional reactive response to policing, these problems would be ignored, and this may have contributed to the reduction in support for police from within communities that look to the police for help in solving these types of problems. Problem solving encourages a different approach from police agencies, as the best programmes encourage officers to respond creatively to the problems they encounter or to refer them to other appropriate agencies (Eck 2004). Indeed, problem solving cannot be a police approach alone. For Kelling (2005), every successful problem-solving initiative in which he was involved over a large number of years required some form of inter-organisational relation ship. No one agency, therefore, can claim to 'own' a particular problem. However, the sharing of the problem does not automatically mean it will be solved effectively, as there are problematic areas that require consideration before adopting this approach.

Information technology

Much police data recording revolve around the use of information for management only and are not configured for the deeper type of analysis that is required to successfully implement the problem-solving approach. When relying on police data already in computer systems, community partners often require attention to issues that are not well recorded by the police such as public drinking or excessive noise. This leads to a distinct lack of data for effectively analysing problems. Further there appears to be a major problem with the analysis of problems which is perhaps one of the foundation stones of the problem-oriented partnership approach. Indeed, the analysis section of the approach needs to be a prolonged session, sometimes much more than the time taken to implement tactics to deal with the problem. For example, Kelling (2005) points to the fact that when addressing the problem of 'sqeegeemen' in New York City, the problem was analysed for some four months, while only three weeks were spent in resolving the problem.

External pressures

Another area which greatly impacts upon the ability of partnerships to effectively engage in problem solving lies in the fact that they are subject to external pressures. For example, the drive to satisfy performance indicators for quantitative analysis and dealing with demands for response perhaps leaves little time for problem solving. Police sergeants and inspectors are often caught between the requirements to respond to immediate calls rather than work out solutions to long-term problems. Furthermore, budgetary constraints may influence other agencies in their ability to engage with the police in problem solving, as invariably when involved in this kind of initiative more work is engaged in with little or no increase in resources to tackle the resulting issues.

Organisational and cultural problems

Despite legislation such as the Crime and Disorder Act 1998 (Home Office 1998), local authorities and other agencies sometimes think that the problem-oriented approach is the police's programme, not theirs (Skogan 2008). Many agencies have their own agendas to satisfy when engaging in partnership work and perhaps see little of benefit for them in working in this manner. Furthermore, there are other cultural problems that need to be addressed. As Goldstein (1990) noted, the adoption of the problem-solving approach is a sea change in the way the police and their partners need to think. This does not occur overnight, and involves the retraining of staff, changed promotion systems and an acceptance of a customer focus, among others. It appears to be difficult to involve police officers in problem solving owing to the nature of the occupational subculture, which consistently appears to value 'crime fighting' (see Holdaway 1983; Chan 2003; Reiner 2010). Gardner and Biebel (2005) conducted an in-depth study in San Diego, California, and found that street officers typically defined problems very narrowly, and crafted solutions using heuristic or local knowledge, with two-thirds of their proposed solutions not going further than arresting someone. While great strides have been made in introducing the POP approach, the focus on enforcement as a predominant solution to problem solving tends to be supported in recent work (Rogers 2009) as well as in previous examination of problem-solving databases in England and Wales (Read and Tilley 2000).

Lack of knowledge

Applying the problem-solving approach brings to the table many theories and approaches such as crime prevention theories. In particular, the work of Clarke and Felson (1993) and their ideas about routine activity theory should play a crucial role in problem solving being applied by all employees engaged in crime reduction. However, it is not clear what levels of understanding of these approaches exist within the many partnerships that currently operate in England and Wales despite the number of specialist courses now appearing to help satisfy this demand.

Joint problem solving: the partnership approach

Neighbourhood policing success is underpinned by bringing together three key aspects, namely:

- Coverage of areas by neighbourhood policing teams.
- Effective engagement within that neighbourhood, including the use of community intelligence and area profiles, to enable the identification of priorities.
- Strong joint problem solving addressing those priorities.

Effective partnership working is absolutely key to delivering success.

Crime and disorder reduction partnerships (known as community safety partnerships in Wales) have evolved over the past ten years or so and the HMIC audit (HMIC 2008) has found that there remains some area of improvement in terms of the strategic assessments produced that identify community concerns.

In particular, the community's assessment of how well people think the police and their partners are doing in terms of dealing with local crime and disorder is not as good as expected.

It is believed that by adopting the problem-oriented partnership approach that tackles local priorities this will significantly impact upon this perception.

Tackling local priorities through joint problem solving can be achieved by the following approach:

- Collaborative problem solving involving the community in defining exactly what the problem is and also assisting in the delivery of solutions.
- Using the National Intelligence Model to support this process.
- Using multiple sources of information and rigorous problem definition.

Again, the use of the joint problem-solving approach across England and Wales appears inconsistent. Several areas of the process have been identified as in need of improvement. These include:

- The PACT process which needs reviewing in terms of joint problem solving.
- Training needs for partners and relevant community members.
- Corporate support for the feedback of information to the community.
- Development of a problem-solving database designed to a corporate standard for the sharing of best practice and learning opportunities.
- Ensuring that a common force structure is applied to all of its BCUs.

Box 4.9 describes a case study showing how one leading force approaches joint problem solving.

In support of the strategic approach and the POP policy the application of neighbourhood policing across Lancashire is supported within a framework of NIM (National Intelligence Model) and POP compliance and follows a six-step model:

1. Know your neighbourhood
2. Engage with the public to identify priorities
3. Engage with partners
4. Local neighbourhood action driven by PACT panels
5. Divisional (BCU) action
6. Review progress and communicate results.

Furthermore, there is an extensive network of key individuals within all the divisions, which enables an informal means of regular communication and feedback with communities.

Conclusion

Neighbourhood policing teams promise much in the way of tackling crime and disorder with communities, while also being able to engage with people in order

---

Box 4.9 Case study Lancashire Constabulary joint problem solving

In Lancashire Constabulary joint problem solving is monitored and evaluated throughout the organisation. Effective joint problem solving focuses on local priorities that are determined through the involvement of partners and members of the community. At a strategies level, the chief constable drives a strong engagement with partners and provides leadership for this approach, by showing a close personal commitment to this area of policing.

Shared neighbourhood teams involve a neighbourhood coordinator, a neighbourhood engagement officer, neighbourhood capacity officers, neighbourhood policing sergeants, community beat managers, police community support officers, registered social landlords and accredited antisocial behaviour officers, working to address local priorities and needs.

The forces POP policy applies to all its procedures and all police staff, police officers, special constables and volunteers. The broad aims of this policy are to:

- Establish a structured approach to apply the principles of POP in respect of operational and support functions throughout the constabulary.
- Establish an understanding of the individual responsibilities of all police and support managers, supervisors and staff in the use of POP principles in relation to planning and carrying out their day-to-day functions.
- Establish an understanding among all staff of the importance of working together with partners in problem solving.

---

to increase their belief and faith in the police and their partners. The adoption of the problem-oriented partnership approach, allied to greater use of community intelligence, is one which has many attractions for the police and their partners. It engages with community at a 'grass-roots' level and attempts to provide long-term solutions to those problems that may have been considered low level by the police and other agencies, yet which have a major impact upon the perceptions of community. It allows the police and their partners in particular to regain lost ground in terms of positive engagements with the community, and may positively impact upon perceptions of crime, disorder and the fear of crime. The introduction of such an approach on a wider scale than has hitherto been seen means an extraordinary amount of change in the way policing and partnership work is currently delivered. Kelling (2005) believes that this change will occur naturally and can be developed, since it should grow out of the realisation that to deal with urgent problems, change must take place. However, Kelling perhaps underestimates the strength of the police occupational subculture and its ability to withstand and even manipulate changes and new initiatives (Reuss-Ianni 1999;

Rogers 2002). If this is the case, then, as Tilley (2008) points out, in the absence of a sustained and committed programme, problem orientation is likely to remain an occasional fad, or the preserve of a few exceptional officers, and a golden opportunity to deal effectively with issues that matter to communities in a sustained and economic manner will have been missed.

References and suggested further reading

Association of Chief Police Officers (ACPO) (2005) *Guidance on The National Intelligence Model*, Centrex, NPIA.

Chan, J.B.L. (1997) *Changing Police Culture-Policing in a Multicultural Society*, Cambridge University Press, Cambridge.

—— (2003) 'Police and New Technologies', in Newburn, T. (ed.), *Handbook of Policing*, Willan Publishing, Cullompton, Devon, pp. 655–79.

Clarke, R.V. and Felson, M. (1993) *Routine Activity and Rational Choice*, Transaction Publishers, New Brunswick, New Jersey.

Coch, L. and French, J.R.P. (1944) 'Overcoming Resistance to Change', *Human Relations*, 1, pp. 512–32.

Commission on 2020 Public Services (2010) *From Social Security to Social Production – A Vision for 2020 Public Services*.

Eck, J.E. (2004) 'Why Don't Problems Get Solved?', in Skogan, W.G. (ed.), *Community Policing – Can It Work?*, Wadsworth, Belmont, CA, pp. 185–206.

Eck, J.E. and Spelman, W. (1987) *Problem-Solving: Problem Oriented Policing in Newport News*, U.S. Department of Justice, National Institute of Justice, 1987, Washington DC, p. 43.

Flanagan, R. Sir (2008) *The Review of Policing – Final Report*, available online at http:// police.homeoffice.gov.uk/ (accessed on 7 March 2011).

Gardner, G. and Biebel, E.P. (2005) 'Problem Oriented Policing in Practice', *Criminology and Public Policy*, 4: 155–80.

Goldstein, H. (1990) *Problem-Oriented Policing*, McGraw-Hill, New York.

Halpern, D. (2010) *The Hidden Wealth of Nations*, Polity Press, Cambridge.

Hay, J. (2002) *The Theory and Practice of Change Management*, Palgrave Macmillan, New York.

Herzberg, F., Mausner, B. and Snyderman, B.B. (1959) *The Motivation to Work*, Transaction Publishers, New York.

HMIC (2008) Her Majesty's Inspectorate of Constabulary – Serving Neighbourhoods and Individuals, HMIC, London.

Holdaway, S. (1983) *Inside the British Police – A Force at Work*, Blackwell, Oxford.

Home Office (1998) *The Crime and Disorder Act*, HMSO, London.

—— (2001) *The Private Security Industry Act*, HMSO, London.

—— (2002) *The Police Reform Act*, HMSO, London.

—— (2008), Select Committee on Home Affairs Seventh Report, entitled *Policing in the 21st Century*, Home Office, London.

Kelling, G.L. (2005) 'Community Crime Reduction: Activating Formal and Informal Control', in Tilley, N. (2005) *Handbook of Crime Prevention and Community Safety*, Willan, Cullompton, pp 107–42.

Kotter, J.P. and Schlesinger, L.A. (1979) 'Choosing Strategies for Change', *Harvard Business Review*, March/April.

Manning, P.K. (1996) 'Information Technology in the Police Context: The "Sailor" Phone', *Information Systems Research*, 7(1): 52–62.

Mullins, L.J. (2005) *Management and Organisational Behaviour* (8th edn), Financial Times/Prentice Hall, London.

Peak, K.J. and Glensor, R.W (1996) *Community Policing and Problem Solving – Strategies and Practices*, Prentice Hall, Upper Saddle River, New Jersey.

Read, T. and Tilley, N. (2000) *Not Rocket Science? Problem Solving and Crime Reduction*, Home Office Crime Reduction Series Paper 6, Home Office, London.

Reiner, R. (2000) *The Politics of the Police* (3rd edn), Oxford University Press, Oxford.

—— (2010) *The Politics of the Police*, Oxford University Press, Oxford.

Reis, D. and Pena, L. (2001) 'Reengineering the Motivation to Work', *Management Decision*, 39(8): 666–75.

Reuss-Ianni, E. (1999) *Two Cultures of Policing*, Transaction Publishers, New Brunswick, New Jersey.

Rogers, C. (2002) Community Safety and Zero Tolerance – A Study of Partnership Policing, unpublished Ph.D. thesis, University of Glamorgan.

Rogers, C. (2009) *An Evaluation of a Problem Oriented Partnership Database*, Internal Report Commissioned by South Wales Police.

Sergeant, H. (2008) *The Public and the Police*, Civitas, London.

Skogan, W.G. (2008) 'An Overview of Community Policing: Origins, Concepts and Implementation', in Williamson, T. (ed.), *The Handbook of Knowledge Based Policing – Current Conceptions and Future Directions*, Wiley, Chichester.

Tilley, N. (2008) 'Modern Approaches to Policing: Community, Problem Oriented and Intelligence Led', in Newburn, T. (ed.), *Handbook of Policing* (2nd edn), Willan Publishing, Cullompton, Devon, pp. 373–403.

Vroom, V.H. (1964) *Work and Motivation*, Wiley, New York.

Williamson, T. (ed.) (2008) *The Handbook of Knowledge Based Policing – Current Conceptions and Future Directions*, Wiley, Chichester.

Zaltman, G. and Duncan, R. (1977) *Strategies for Planned Change*, John Wiley, London.

Other useful websites

http://www.neighbourhoodpolicing.co.uk/
NPIA Neighbourhood Policing Website
http://www.popcenter.org/
The POP Centre website POP Centre website

5 Communities

Engagement, communication and accountability

Introduction

This chapter considers methods of communicating within communities and partnerships, as well as how the police are accountable to the public they serve. These are important considerations, and are set against previous government ideas and the current government's framework of the 'Big Society' as discussed in the previous chapter. Recent research by the National Policing Improvement Agency (Myhill and Beak 2008) suggests that positive perceptions of neighbourhood policing and the way the police and their partners treat and interact with local people are major factors most associated with being confident in the police. Providing a satisfactory response to the public may therefore improve their confidence in the police and their partners, while providing an unsatisfactory service and little communication in any contact may reduce public confidence and interaction. It is therefore important to understand the ideas behind engaging with and being accountable to communities if the police are to be successful in maintaining their support and tackling crime and antisocial behaviour.

Community engagement

Community engagement, as a concept, has been in vogue for many years; yet there appears to be little or no common or widely agreed definition. This section summarises what is generally understood by the terms 'community' and 'engagement', while later in the section the idea of community engagement as it applies to policing will be discussed.

There is, as has already been discussed in Chapter 2 of this book, a broad acceptance of the idea that a community is a group of people who all hold something in common. The concept of 'community' has tended to be associated with two aspects:

- People who share a locality or geographical place.
- People who are or share communities of interest.

Communities of interest are groups of people who either share an identity – for example, ethnicity or religion – or share an experience, such as people with a particular disability.

A person will usually be a member of multiple communities at any one time. For example, an individual could be a Muslim musician living in Leicester. Each of us is likely to move in and out of one or more communities over time. However, some people may be unable or unwilling to identify with any community at all.

Defining engagement

Engagement is the involvement of the public, either as individuals or as a community, in policy and service decisions which affect them. In practice this involvement can take a number of different forms. The three main forms of engagement are given in Table 5.1.

A key difference between these three kinds of engagement is the extent of the 'dialogue' that takes place. The word 'dialogue' refers to the exchange of views, ideas and concerns among different groups, such as between a neighbourhood community and a neighbourhood policing team. The information-gathering approach does not involve much dialogue, whereas the participation approach is about continuing dialogue as part of joint working (Box 5.1).

Theories of community engagement

The idea of community engagement has a long history and has been considered in many different and varied ways. The link between the different schools of thought is their view of what makes good governance and a healthy civil society. There is widespread agreement that these factors depend on individuals and communities actively expressing their views, and public services in turn listening and responding. The idea of the 'active citizen' is central to this idea, but it has

Table 5.1 The three main forms of engagement

Information gathering	The collection of information about public attitudes and requirements through surveys, etc. There is no ongoing dialogue between the public and the organisation – for example, force or authority – seeking the information. The public usually participate in this as individuals.
Consultation	Members of the public and the organisation work together for a defined period to discuss a particular policy or service issue. The methods used can range from focus groups to citizens' juries. People are brought together as representatives of the demographic profile of a particular community.
Participation	Members of the public and the organisation work together, on an ongoing basis, on a range of policy or service issues. These tend to focus on the community rather than on individuals. Community forums are an example.

Box 5.1   Exercise 5A Police engagement with communities

Having seen the different forms that engagement can entail, reflect upon how the police engage with their communities. Which is the best approach for neighbourhood policing teams?

---

been interpreted in many different ways. Some models focus on 'empowering' the individual to make decisions. Others emphasise the importance of collective involvement, and prioritise the needs of the community and society above the demands of the individual.

Some of the main philosophies or thoughts and models surrounding community engagement are worthy of examination and are introduced below.

Community development

Community development is action which helps develop sustainable geographic communities or communities of interest. It is also about developing community activity, thereby helping all members of a community to work together to express and achieve their visions for the future.

One of the main organisations for developing and promoting this in Britain is the Community Development Foundation. This is a non-departmental public body and is supported by the Active Communities Directorate of the Home Office.

Active communities, active citizenship, civil renewal

The government in England and Wales is aiming to develop 'strong, active and empowered communities' that can work together to tackle the problems they face. It wants everyone to feel that they belong to, and have a stake in, their society.

Communitarianism

Communitarianism developed as a political philosophy in the 1980s and as a political movement in the 1990s. It was a reaction against perceived problems with liberalism, saying that it placed too much emphasis on the rights of individuals, and too little on social responsibilities and collective moral values. Communitarianism asserts that people are shaped by the values and culture of their community; they are not autonomous individuals. This approach supports a greater focus on community to foster social cohesion.

Social capital

This idea is associated with the work of American academic Robert Putnam (2000). Social capital emphasises the importance of social networks in developing trust, reciprocity and solving shared problems. Much of this approach has been developed of late by Halpern (2007, 2010) who has been influential in assisting the government with its plans for the 'Big Society'.

Localism

Localism focuses on the perceived advantages of devolving power to people at a community level. It makes the case that local people know best what the most important local issues are and it seeks to empower them to make decisions about shared local problems. It places the collective voice above the individual voice.

Deliberative democracy

Deliberation is a process that promotes the informed involvement of citizens in decision making. It encourages citizens to learn about policy issues and to consider different perspectives before making recommendations about how to proceed.

What 'engages' the public?

When looking to engage the public, success is more likely if issues are appropriate and are of the type to which the public tend to respond. These are usually:

- Issues that are close to home and something they can relate directly to in their own life.
- Issues about risk and which raise concerns about safety.

Furthermore, people involved feel that the process used to engage them is appropriate and convenient for them rather than just the organisation they are dealing with, and that their views are likely to be listened to and could lead to change. In addition, if they feel that they will get feedback on their input, including information about what has been done with their information or why their priorities may not necessarily be acted upon, they are more likely to interact.

Choosing a method of engagement

Community engagement methods may be grouped into two main types of approaches: quantitative and qualitative.

Quantitative

These usually take the form of surveys. The aim is to be able to numerically measure people's opinions. They may be used to:

- test hypotheses;

- accurately highlight differences between different groups of people;
- track changes over time.

Qualitative

These approaches may be used to explore and understand people's motivations, desires, behaviour and beliefs. It can help get behind the percentages from quantitative research.

Both quantitative and qualitative approaches are often used in the same project. A qualitative stage before a quantitative stage can help clarify the scope of a research project, and the type of language that should be used in a subsequent survey stage. A qualitative stage after a quantitative one can help explore in more detail some of the findings that have emerged from a survey.

Quantitative methods are mainly used when information gathering, rather than for consultation and participation. Qualitative methods are suitable for all three stages.

Table 5.2 illustrates some of the strengths and weaknesses of both approaches.

Selecting a community engagement approach for a particular project calls for one which is fit for purpose. There is no single method that will work in every situation and it can be tempting to pick a preferred method 'off the shelf' and hope that it will work. However, it is far more effective to clarify the aims of the project first and then select an approach which will deliver these aims. An effective community engagement strategy is likely to employ a wide range of methods.

Table 5.2 Strengths and weaknesses of qualitative and quantitative methods

	Strengths	*Weaknesses*
Qualitative	Enables opinions to be explored in more depth than is possible in a quantitative survey May be used to start and develop a dialogue with the public Is interactive: participants (the organisation and public) can listen and respond to each other	Results cannot be analysed by statistics Is difficult to extrapolate results to the wider population Analysis can be difficult and open to subjectivity and bias
Quantitative	If well designed, can give an accurate picture of people's opinions which can be extrapolated to the wider population May be used to accurately monitor change over time Can involve large numbers of people Allows for objective analysis	Often can only give 'top of mind' rather than 'considered' responses Does not create dialogue between the organisation and interviewees Does not allow for interaction between interviewees Only gives a simple numerical picture of opinion

PACT (partners and communities together or similar) meetings

PACT is the name given to the neighbourhood meetings that help form the structure through which neighbourhood policing is being delivered and is a popular form of community engagement. While there may be some slight variations in the definition of the term PACT throughout the country, in general, PACT stands for partnerships and communities together.

PACT meetings develop into a forum where the partnerships that serve a neighbourhood are tasked with dealing with the priorities identified by that community as requiring partnership attention. The meetings normally take place in every neighbourhood once a month in order to deal with the issues that affect the residents and they should be attended by members from every part of that neighbourhood and the meetings managed by neighbourhood residents. Partner agencies are tasked by and responsible to the PACT meeting for working with the community members and groups in resolving the identified issues. While initially these meetings were to be organised and managed by the police, the idea was that they should be handed over to the community to run and organise. However, it is unclear if this has occurred throughout the country and there is the suspicion that the majority of meetings are police owned and run.

The benefits of the PACT system

In general there are several important areas that PACT meetings support and it is worth noting the main benefits of this approach. These are:

- There is a structure that will deliver the main requirements for neighbourhood policing.
- The approach is about community engagement.
- It involves problem solving of localised policing and partnership issues.
- It is a method of gathering community intelligence.
- It allows community members to meet members of their neighbourhood team in person at least once a month.
- It is an opportunity to inform local people what their neighbourhood team is doing for them.

How PACT meetings should be structured

In order for PACT meetings to be successful, there should be a structure in place that ensures the maximum attendance from all partners. In particular the following should be considered:

- Meetings should be publicised during the last two weeks of every month in key locations.
- Meetings should take place at regular intervals.
- Panels should also take place immediately after the meeting and be open to those who have attended the meeting.

- Panels should comprise members of the public who have attended the meeting and partners who can take action to deal with the priorities.
- Meetings should be developed over time by the neighbourhood team and the public so that the panel comprises only members of the public who task the neighbourhood team on behalf of the meeting.
- Meetings should enable people to task their local partnership in their own neighbourhoods.
- The meetings should identify up to three top partnership priorities at a community level every month.

While PACT meetings open up the possibility for interaction, accountability and engagement with community at a lower level, there is in fact a historical and different form of accountability that should be a communication tool by and for the community using elected representatives: that of the police authority.

Police authorities

Introduction

This section will consider the role of the police authority and its influence upon policing the local community, its use of knowledge management in assisting local policing, its role in terms of performance management including a consideration of the new Assessments of Policing and Community Safety (APACS) and the future of police authorities in terms of governance and accountability.

The Police Act 1964 (Home Office 1964) introduced the so-called 'tri-partite' system which divided responsibility for policing between three main parties, namely the Home Office, chief constables and police authorities. The idea was to balance the national position in terms of accountability with the local perspective so that all levels of policing were 'controlled' and accountable. The chief constable, however, was protected to some extent, in that the chief officer had independence over the operational control of the police force for which he or she was responsible. It was believed that this provided some protection from interference by elected representatives in controlling policy for the police. However, the tri-partite system has not been beyond criticism. Reiner (2010) stated that under the tri-partite system, police authorities 'paid the piper' but never named the tune, indicating that although police authorities provided resources for the police, they had little or no say in how crime and disorder was tackled within the communities which the police authority represented. While there appears to be a prospect for change in the accountability process of the police in England and Wales, the current and possible future changes are discussed here.

The current position

A police authority is an independent body made up of local people. The police authority's job is to make sure that the community has an efficient and effective local police force. There is a police authority for each local police force – 43 in total in England and Wales – plus an additional one for British Transport Police. In Northern Ireland the police authority is called the Policing Board but it has a similar role to police authorities in England and Wales.

All police authorities are members of the Association of Police Authorities.

Most police authorities have 17 members, namely:

- Nine local councillors appointed by the local council.
- Five independent members selected following local advertisements.
- Three magistrates from the local area.

The Metropolitan Police Authority has 23 members owing to the size of London.

The main job of the police authority is to set the strategic direction for the force and hold the chief constable to account on behalf of the local community. Delivering policing services is the job of the chief constable.

In short, the police authority:

- Holds the police budget and decides how much council tax should be raised for policing.
- Appoints (and dismisses) the chief constable and senior police officers.
- Consults widely with local people to find out what they want from their local police.
- Sets local policing priorities based on the concerns of local people as well as targets for achievement.
- Monitors everything the police do and how well they perform against the targets set by the authority.
- Publishes a three-year plan and an annual plan which tells local people what they can expect from their police service and reports back at the end of the year.
- Makes sure local people get the best value from their local police force.
- Oversees complaints against the police and disciplines senior officers.

The function of police authorities

The main function of a police authority therefore is to make sure that the local police are accountable for what they do within the community – that is, the people who live or work in the area – and that they have a say in how they are policed.

It is the police authority that controls the size of the budget and which is ultimately responsible for maintaining an efficient and effective police force. The police authority consists of 17 local councillors, magistrates and independent members, and it is mainly through these members that the police service is accountable to the population at large. The responsibilities of the chief constable and police authority are shown below in Table 5.3.

Table 5.3 Responsibilities of the chief constable and the police authority

Chief constable	Police authority
In overall command of the force and holds ultimate responsibility for operational matters.	Holds ultimate responsibility for the efficiency and effectiveness of the force.
Drafts local plans for basic command units (BCUs).	Sets overall budget and approves any additional expenditure.
Responsible for achieving local force goals.	Drafts local plans and goals for local forces. Drafts three-year force strategy in accordance with National Police Plan.
Has control of expenditure within an agreed budget.	Consults with local population.

Key
City City of London
MPA Metropolitan
Mersey Merseyside
Gtr Man Greater Manchester
W Mids West Midlands

Figure 5.1 The geographic location of the police authorities in England and Wales

Local policing plans

The Police Act 1996 (Home Office 1996), amended by the Police and Justice Act 2006 (Home Office 2006), requires police authorities to produce a local three-year rolling policing plan to be issued annually. Police authorities are required before the beginning of the financial year to determine objectives for the policing of the authority's area and to include them in the local policing plan. The policing plan objectives should be consistent with the strategic priorities determined by the Home Secretary.

This guidance continues to use the terminology 'local policing plan' to refer to the new three-year rolling policing plan which is refreshed and issued annually. The local policing plan contains objectives relating to both the 'national priorities' set by the Home Secretary in the National Community Safety Plan (Home Office 2007), and further 'local priorities' set by the police authority (developed in consultation with the community, policing partners and the local force).

The police authority can set local targets against both national and local priorities. It also assesses the force's performance against the policing plan and makes their findings available to local communities. At a national level, the performance of forces will be assessed using the APACS framework. APACS has been designed around a framework of domains; at present the actual domain structure is subject to consultation and is discussed fully later in this chapter. The domains provide the framework for a set of performance indicators that are agreed nationally: the Statutory Performance Indicators (SPIs).

National

National priorities are set by the Secretary of State and are detailed in the National Community Safety Plan. However, each authority will have its own unique issues (i.e. local priorities). When determining the local priorities for the policing plan, authorities should seek input from:

- *Community consultation.* In keeping with the principles of continuous improvement, authorities should ensure that local communities, including hard-to-reach groups, are consulted and their feedback incorporated into the local policing plan. This may involve surveys, workshops, focus groups or feedback from the website.
- *Partner consultation.* Local police priorities should align with the work of inter-agency working groups and partners seeking to improve community safety and reduce crime. These include crime and disorder reduction partnerships, community safety partnerships, Criminal Justice Boards and local strategic partnerships.
- *Neighbourhood priorities.* Priorities adopted by neighbourhood teams across the force/authority area should be consulted to establish if they can be reflected in and supported by force-wide priorities.
- *Force Control Strategy.* The Force Control Strategy (FCS) is an output of the National Intelligence Model, which forces use to ensure that activities

are intelligence led. The FCS will identify important, intelligence-based priorities.

- *Risk registers.* The force's and authority's risk registers and processes may identify necessary change and therefore be indicative of potential local priorities.
- *Continuous improvement.* Key priorities may also include a focus on internal business processes, systems and enabling functions to ensure that a force is effective, efficient and economic, and delivers the required quality of service. For example, based on the expert view of authority members and staff, efficiency, cost reduction or service improvements may be identified as priorities.

The priorities identified through the consultation and internal process may overlap with the strategic policing priorities identified in the National Community Safety Plan. However, each authority should aim to identify at least one priority that is not a national priority.

The policing plan regulations 2008

The policing plan regulations which came into being in March 2008 (Home Office 2008c) provided further guidance for the production of a policing plan. In particular it stated that in producing a policing plan a police authority should consider:

1. Any performance targets established by the police authority, whether in compliance with a direction under section 38 of the Police Act of 1996.
2. Any matters relating to the efficiency and effectiveness of the police force:
   - arising out of any inspection of the police force by Her Majesty's Inspectors of Constabulary, or
   - raised with the police authority by the Secretary of State.
3. Any direction given to the police authority by the Secretary of State under Section 40 of the 1996 Police Act (power to give directions in relation to a police force) or any information given to the police authority of the grounds on which such a direction might be given.
4. The strategies for the plan period formulated by the relevant responsible authorities under Section 6 (formulation and implementation of crime and disorder reduction strategies) of the 1998 Crime and Disorder Act (Home Office 1998).

The contents of policing plans

In addition to the above the policing plan of a police authority should clearly set out:

- Any strategic priorities determined by the Secretary of State under section 37A (strategic priorities for police authorities) of the 1996 Act that relate to the plan period.

- Any performance targets established by the police authority, whether in compliance with a direction under Section 38 of the 1996 Act or otherwise, that relate to the plan period and how it is proposed to meet those targets.
- A statement of the financial resources the police authority expects to be available for the plan period and the proposed allocation of those resources.
- Any planned increases in efficiency and productivity of the police force during the plan period and how it is proposed that such increases will be achieved.
- Any matters relating to the efficiency and effectiveness of the police force.
- Any direction given by the Secretary of State under Section 40 of the 1996 Act or any information given to the police authority of the grounds on which such a direction might be given and how it intends to address such matters.
- Any planned improvements in the ability of the police force to deliver protective services during the plan period and how it is proposed that such improvements will be achieved.
- Details of any cooperation between the police force and other police forces that is taking place at the time the plan is issued, and is proposed for the plan period.

Publication of policing plans

A police authority should arrange for every policing plan issued by it to be published in an appropriate manner by 30 June of the financial year before the beginning of which it was issued, and shall send a copy of the plan to the Secretary of State.

The Assessments of Policing and Community Safety (APACS)

Mention was made previously of the importance of the use of APACS and local performance indicators which the local police authority uses to establish the performance of its police force. Below is an introduction to this important performance management method.

An important aim of the Assessments of Policing and Community Safety (APACS) is to reflect performance in respect of locally selected priorities set alongside assessments based on Home Office statutory performance indicators. This is a complex business; individual police authorities and forces rightly set different priorities, objectives, indicators and targets so that comparison 'between' forces for these local policing plan priorities has limited value. In addition, it has been necessary to establish a common terminology for discussing and populating APACS with locally selected indicators.

APACS will introduce one national performance framework for policing, crime and drugs. It reflects the performance of the police service working alone or in partnership, and has links to the Communities and Local Government National Indicator Set, the new local performance framework and local area agreements.

Knowledge and performance management

Strong and effective performance management arrangements have been central to the reduction of crime and improvements in the performance of the police and partners on a wide range of crime and community safety issues.

As well as driving higher levels of service delivery nationally, performance management has helped to reduce the gaps between the strongest and weakest performances across England and Wales, through a combined approach of scrutiny and support. A strong performance management culture has now become firmly embedded in the way that the police and its partners plan and deliver services to reduce crime and ensure safer communities. This is not without criticism, since it may appear that the use of statistics and the managerialist approach is thought perhaps to have undermined 'traditional' policing methods in some quarters.

However, the Home Office and its partners are committed to refining the approach to managing the performance of the police, working alone or in partnership with others, on crime and community safety to ensure continued improvements. The Home Office and its partners therefore agreed to develop and introduce a new performance framework which will:

- simplify national and local performance arrangements;
- align the performance management of crime, drugs and policing by combining existing performance assessment arrangements for these areas in the Home Office;
- join up with the wider performance management frameworks of community safety partners;
- broaden the scope of performance management to take account of important community safety work which has not been included in previous performance frameworks.

A public statement of support was released by all the partners in February 2007 which was committed to the introduction of the Assessments of Policing and Community Safety or APACS framework to replace and rationalise the existing assessment systems and harmonise with the principal frameworks of our community safety partners.

APACS has replaced a number of assessment systems that were in use for crime and community safety. Principally, the Policing Performance Assessment Framework (PPAF), which was developed by the Home Office and HM Inspectorate of Constabulary, with support from the Association of Police Authorities and the Association of Chief Police Officers. PPAF was introduced in 2004 and brought together a number of police performance indicators and qualitative judgements that the Home Office and HMIC had previously published separately, with the aim of covering the full range of policing activity and giving the public a rounded view of how their local force was doing across the board. This process brought significant improvements, providing greater transparency to the public, and underpinned work to improve police performance.

The new simplified framework reduces the number of measures by which the police and others are judged in terms of their success on crime and community safety, and reduces the data demands of central government. The framework covers policing and community safety issues in a balanced way which focuses better on the most serious crimes and criminals. It harmonises with other related frameworks and contains indicators and targets which are shared between partners.

APACS was introduced from April 2008 and the first assessments will be published in 2009, reporting on financial year 2008–9 (Table 5.4).

Police authorities, accountability and the future

Reducing crime and disorder is still a high priority for the public, and this has influenced government thinking regarding the subject. Police authorities play a major role in helping to achieve this priority through their part in the accountability and consultation process, producing policing plans that help in the transfer of knowledge to formulating policing objectives. There have been numerous initiatives and much legislation in the past decade or so aimed at addressing the issues of crime and disorder reduction. There has been considerable investment in expanding police powers and increasing police staff numbers, but research has shown that only half of the public believe that their local police are doing a good or excellent job (Kershaw *et al.* 2007).

Furthermore, the majority of the community served by the police feel they have no influence over them and so consequently have little say in police matters. Importantly, those people who have had contact with their local police are less likely to believe they are doing a good job, including individuals who class themselves as victims and witnesses (Kershaw *et al.* 2007). Police accountability has therefore become a topic of great political interest, and has stimulated debate and a number of important papers for discussion, including documents by the Local Government Association (LGA 2008) and the Institute for Public Policy Research (IPPR 2008), and the influential Home Office White Paper concerning the transfer of power to the community (Home Office 2008b).

All of these documents clearly indicate the way in which accountability for the delivery of local services within communities, including the police service, are about to undergo a radical overhaul.

However, the seminal document that illustrates the possible changes in accountability and local policing and that ultimately will affect the present tri-partite arrangement is the government's Green Paper entitled *From the Neighbourhood to the National: Policing Our Communities Together* (Home Office 2008a).

This document covers an extensive amount of policy discussion, including neighbourhood teams, leadership and improving communication between the police and communities. Consequently, strengthening local accountability is a prime feature of this document. In particular the following issues were identified:

- There is at present no direct public participation in the selection of police authority members.

Table 5.4 The new APACS strategic aims and the perceived benefits

Strategic aims	Benefits
Simplify existing frameworks used by the Home Office and align clearly with external frameworks (e.g. for criminal justice, local authorities/Local Area Agreements [LAAs], health and transport)	• Less bureaucracy: fewer frameworks • Better joint delivery via shared priorities, measures and targets • Simpler, clearer and consistent messages about performance
Integrate assessment with policy, delivery and support functions plus associated regimes Related to good practice, inspection and audit	• Improved performance and reduced performance variation among peers • Improved knowledge of 'what works' • Risk-based regulation and support
Promote a balanced regime of accountability, building on the roles – including any collaborative arrangements – of partners locally, regionally and nationally	• Clear roles and responsibilities • Basis of freedoms and flexibilities plus graduated framework of support • Sensitive to different arrangements (e.g. in England and in Wales)
Cover crime, drugs and policing issues comprehensively but in a way that reflects relative seriousness and which minimises data demands on partners	• Less bureaucracy: fewer measures • Balanced and proportionate coverage • Address current imbalances/gaps in performance assessment (e.g. antisocial behaviour and protective services)
Make best use of available data and professional judgements in producing analysis and assessments which: • Reflect relevant Public Service Agreements (PSAs) and other strategic priorities, objectives and targets as well as performance against priorities for improvement selected locally • Use data focused on results (outcomes) but with the capability to use data on inputs, processes or outputs • Monitor implementation of key operational strategies such as neighbourhood policing, alcohol misuse and drug enforcement	• Maximise the value of quantitative and qualitative approaches • Performance data used to inform risk-based audit and inspection. • Clear and consistent expectations • Balance of national requirements and local needs • Scope for innovation in delivery • Option of using other data as proxies where outcome measures are not desirable or feasible • Earlier identification of success / problems thereby facilitating delivery, management and support
Communicate data and assessments in a timely manner and in a way which: • Promotes visibility, accountability and responsiveness of service providers • Supports day-to-day management and which demonstrates service delivery to citizens, communities and opinion-formers • Shows whether services are effective, equitable and provide value for money and whether they are perceived as such	• Practitioner-facing data and analysis with public-facing assessments • Increased local transparency and accountability • Increased data scrutiny to identify and resolve problems • Robust, timely data and comparative analysis plus regular assessments, supported by data and commentary • Balanced understanding of performance across a range of key perspectives

- There appear to be concerns in some police authorities regarding the selection of some councillors to sit on police authorities.
- If a body of citizens are dissatisfied with the service they receive from the police, they have little means to rectify this.

It is anticipated that the government will seek to address these issues through the following means:

- Legislation will be introduced to reform police authorities in an attempt to make them more democratic and more effective in responding to the needs of the local community.

Much of the above discussion will be influenced by the recent White Paper entitled *Policing in the 21st Century: Reconnecting Police and the People* (Home Office 2010). This document sets out the ideas and a structure of the future police organisation as envisioned by the new government. Stating that the previous government had burdened the police with too many targets and thus bureaucracy, which led to a distancing from the communities they serve, several new priorities and changes for the police have been highlighted. These are briefly shown below:

- The new government states that power will be transferred back to communities by introducing directly elected Police and Crime Commissioners who represent their communities. These individuals will hold the local chief constable to account for achieving the crime and disorder priorities.
- These will be supported by greater accountability, accessibility and more transparency for the public, including the ideas of accessible 'street-level' data and information and regular 'beat' meetings.
- There will be a transfer of power away from government to the professionals, i.e. the police, who will no longer have to satisfy centrally driven performance targets.

There are great implications in the introduction of such ideas. The traditional tri-partite agreement of accountability between Home Office, police authority and chief constable will be challenged and there is the fear that the operational independence of the chief constable may be compromised by political considerations. However, it is clear that the present government wishes to transfer accountability to a much more local dimension which will mean a closer engagement by the police with their communities.

Conclusions

The current arrangement for accountability and governance of policing in England and Wales is under review. At present the tri-partite arrangement as introduced with the Police Act 1964, subject to some variations, still stands, but changes are about to be implemented which will alter the make-up and roles of the different members of the tri-partite agreement. Clearly, there is a strong emphasis on more local accountability, with perhaps a stronger 'political' influence, which in turn will mean a greater need for closer contact with the public. This in turn means that there will be more emphasis on local 'hot spotting' and a closing of the gap between what the police believe the community wants and what the community actually needs, which will, it is believed, result in a more efficient and effective delivery of local services to the public. These changes involve the introduction of a different set of management tools such as APACS, and implicit within these changes is the understanding that local success for the police and communities rests on the creation of knowledge, information and intelligence formulated in local policing plans to tackle problems identified by community representatives working in partnership with the police.

References and suggested further reading

Halpern, D. (2007) *Social Capital*, Polity Press, Cambridge.
—— (2010) *The Hidden Wealth of Nations*, Polity Press, Cambridge.
Home Office (1964) *The Police Act*, HMSO, London.
—— (1996) *The Police Act*, HMSO, London.
—— (1998) *The Crime and Disorder Act*, HMSO, London.
—— (2006) *The Police and Justice Act*, HMSO, London.
—— (2007) *Cutting Crime – A New Partnership 2008–2011*, HMSO, London.
—— (2008a) *From the Neighbourhood to the National: Policing our Communities Together*, HMSO, London.
—— (2008b) *Communities in Control – Real People, Real Power*, HMSO, London.
—— (2008c) *Policing Plan Regulations*, Home Office, London.
—— (2010) *Policing in the 21st Century: Reconnecting Police and the People.* Available online at: http://www.homeoffice.gov.uk/publications/consultations/policing-21st-century/policing-21st-full-pdf?view=Binary (accessed 29 November 2010).
Institute for Public Policy Research (2008) A New Beat: Options for More Accountable Policing, IPPR, London.
Kershaw, C., Micholas, S. and Walker, W. (2007) *Crime in England and Wales 2006/2007*, Home Office, London.
Local Government Association (2008) *Answering to You: Policing in the 21st Century*, LGA, London.
Myhill, A. and Beak, K. (2008) *Public Confidence in the Police*, National Policing Improvement Agency, London.
Putnam, R. (2000) *Bowling Alone*, Simon & Schuster, New York.
Reiner, R. (2010) *The Politics of the Police* (4th edn), Oxford University Press, Oxford.

Other useful websites

http://www.apa.police.uk/apa
The Association of Police Authorities
http://www.homeoffice.gov.uk/police/
The Police page on the Home Office website

http://www.ippr.org/
The Institute for Public Policy Research
http://www.lga.gov.uk/lga/core/page.do?pageId =
1 Local government association
http://police.homeoffice.gov.uk/police-reform/policegp/
The government's policing Green Paper
http://www.inspectorates.homeoffice.gov.uk/hmic/
Her Majesty's Inspectorate of Consta-bulary website
www.active-citizen.org.uk
The Active Citizenship Centre
www2.gwu.edu/~ccps/
The home of Communitarianism is the Communitarian Network based at George
　　Washington University in Washington, DC:
www.ksg.harvard.edu/saguaro/
The main site for information and tools relating to social capital is:
www.cpn.org
The Civic Practices Network
www.odpm.gov.uk/stellent/groups/odpm_localgov/documents/page/odpm_locgov_034808.
　　pdf
The Office of the Deputy Prime Minister has published a detailed report presenting case
　　studies of Localism:
www.deliberative-democracy.net
An American website which is dedicated to deliberative democracy.

Part 2

Investigations

One of the main areas of work for the police organisation revolves around investigations. Bayley (2005) states that in England and Wales some 15 per cent of all police personnel are engaged specifically upon this activity. However, criminal investigation is not just carried out by detectives alone. More and more criminal and other types of investigations are being conducted by uniformed police officers and other unsworn police staff such as community support officers and investigators. The recent speech by the Home Secretary appears to highlight the importance placed upon the investigation and prevention of crime when she told the National Policing Conference in June 2010:

'I couldn't be any clearer about your mission: it isn't a thirty point plan: it is to cut crime. No more, and no less' (May 2010).

In general criminal investigation is still reactive; with police responding after the criminal event has occurred. This is despite the greater use of intelligence and IT systems to support a more pro-active and intelligence-led approach to investigating criminal activity. Knowledge of the approaches used, doctrines and the skills required are therefore vital for all police officers and staff.

The chapters in Part 2 consider criminal investigation in historical and organisational context, highlighting the different types of investigations and strategies, legislation and techniques that fit into the wider Criminal Justice System in England and Wales, and as such underpins the professional approach to this important aspect of police work.

References

Bayley, D. (2005) 'Criminal Investigations', in Newburn, T., *Policing: Key Readings*, Willan Publishing, Cullompton, Devon.

May, T. (2010) Speech to the National Policing Conference, 29 June, available online at http://www.homeoffice.gov.uk/media-centre/speeches/theresa-may-sp-NPC (accessed 30 June 2010).

6 Criminal investigations in context

Introduction

Criminal investigation is a complex and sometimes tedious process that requires a certain knowledge base, skills and attention to detail. Each case that is investigated is different, and should be treated individually while adhering to standard policies and procedures. This chapter introduces you to some fundamental topics surrounding criminal investigations, defining the idea and setting it within the context of the adversarial Criminal Justice System in operation in England and Wales. Understanding the historical aspect of criminal investigations is important so as to ensure past mistakes are not repeated, while knowledge of the role of the Crown Prosecution Service and the distinct phases of an investigation are vital in developing an appropriate investigation strategy, whatever the incident under investigation.

The Association of Chief Police Officers (ACPO 2005: 7) state: 'The performance of the police in the area of investigation is continually under scrutiny by the government, criminal justice service and media. There is widespread recognition within the police service that there is a need to improve the professionalism of the investigative response.' The ACPO (2005: 13) continues to explain that 'through increased media coverage and criminal behaviour, and because of the effect that crime can have on individuals and the local community, the process of criminal investigation has attracted considerable attention.'

Newburn (cited in Newburn *et al.* 2007: 5) suggests that the subject of crime investigation has not generally been under academic scrutiny, but agrees that this is changing. 'In contrast to the sub discipline of police studies which is now well established with British Criminology, there has been relatively little systemic research by sociologists, criminologists and social psychologists into how criminal investigations are conducted.'

History of investigations

Maguire (cited in ACPO 2005) discusses the beginning of the 'New Police', which provided street patrols, maintained public order and prevented crime. It was in 1842 that the Metropolitan Police established a small detective branch which adopted an investigative and more disciplined approach to crime, and which was viewed as a radical departure from the more traditional role of a patrolling police constable. Prior to this change the detection of crime had been mainly undertaken by 'thief takers', although their methods were often crude and financially motivated. By 1878 a Criminal Investigation Department (CID) was serving the whole of London; it was quickly established that this was an effective tool in controlling crime and it wasn't long before each force had its own CID.

Morris (cited in Newburn *et al.* 2007) identifies four main periods, showing the changing nature and organisation of criminal investigations:

- 'Heroic' period – this covers the period for the first 50 years after the introduction of the 'New Police'.
- A further period lasting until the interwar years – a process of organisational specialisation began.
- Third half-century-long period – central leadership and oversight of criminal investigation in the Police Service.
- Current era – this started in the early 1980s, a period which saw further centralisation, particularly by the government which moulded crime investigation practices. There have been general changes to policing that have affected investigations more significantly. The gradual centralisation, politicisation and increasing managerial control may be seen in investigation as much as in general policing.

ACPO (2005) discusses two distinct methods of investigation developed within the police service during the twentieth century. Reactive methods of investigation were employed by generalist CID and uniformed officers and the intention was that they would respond to crimes which had been reported. In addition to this method, specialist squads, such as serious crime squads and drug squads, were established to tackle invisible crime or organised crime using pro-active methods of investigation, predominantly intelligence led. Occasionally when a major incident such as homicide or serious sexual assault dictated it, ad hoc major enquiry teams are brought together; these generally adopt reactive methods of investigation, but will use pro-active methods when the circumstances require them. The two methods are similar. These will be looked at closely in the next literature review.

ACPO (2005) states that investigations can vary considerably as crimes can occur under a multitude of circumstances, and the behaviour of offenders and victims who are all key players can never be predicted. Investigators need to develop their skills as the offenders become more sophisticated. The police service today has a wide range of scientific and technical expertise available to assist in the investigation of crime, but it is reliant on investigators to approach all investigations in a methodical and structured manner.

Newburn (cited in Newburn *et al.* 2007) describes how criminal investigation has been the subject of both public and political attention; there have been two

Royal Commissions since 1980 and high levels of media and public interest following a number of miscarriages of justice. There have been a number of more recent, extremely high-profile inquiries, such as Lord Laming's inquiry into the death of Victoria Climbie and Lord Macpherson's inquiry into the death of Stephen Lawrence. Both of these inquiries have identified problems in the way criminal investigations have been carried out and have made recommendations for improvements in the future.

There has been an increased drive throughout the public sector to improve accountability, efficiency and effectiveness according to ACPO (2005). Newburn (cited in Newburn *et al.* 2007) describes how the National Intelligence Model (NIM) brings a process of professionalisation in relation to investigations within police services, developing only recently as it is only in recent times that investigations have been viewed as being separate from other policing skills, despite the CID existing for over a century. There has developed a desire to encourage and stimulate greater professionalism, and this has been supported by the introduction of job descriptions and occupational standards covering all investigative roles. Newburn (cited in Newburn *et al.* 2007: 6) discusses the end product, this being the PIP (Professionalising Investigation Programme) which was established by the Home Office and ACPO. Its key objectives are:

- To achieve professionalism in investigation across the complete spectrum of the investigative process. PIP includes an end-to-end National Learning Development Programme designed to provide a career pathway for investigators and to develop skills in investigation within the police service.
- PIP incorporates training, workplace assessment and ultimately registration for all existing and new-to-role investigators. The programme draws on the practice advice contained within core investigative doctrine and is underpinned by the investigation and interviewing units contained within the National Occupational Standards developed by Skills for Justice.
- National training programmes with investigative elements have been designed to support PIP and to accurately reflect the levels of complexity at which investigators are expected to operate.

Consequently, an accreditation programme has been developed and a continuous development programme has been introduced aimed at officers at all levels and also at police service staff who are involved in criminal investigation.

Newburn (cited in Newburn *et al.* 2007) discusses how the government has recognised the need for a consolidation of knowledge and understanding about criminal investigation, and that the Home Office announced the establishment of the National Police Improvements Agency (NPIA) in 2006 which was then formerly established in 2007. The NPIA is designed to improve the way in which police forces work by providing them with support.

Criminal investigations defined

There are many definitions of a criminal investigation. Before proceeding attempt the exercise given in Box 6.1.

Box 6.1   Exercise 6A Defining a criminal investigation

Write down what you think the definition of a criminal investigation should be. Then compare what you have written with the following section.

Osterberg and Ward (2005) suggest that a criminal investigation is defined as the reconstruction of a past event through which police solve crimes. Here police and other personnel take into account many factors in reconstructing a case in order to determine who committed the crime and under what circumstances the crime was committed. A statutory definition is provided by the Criminal Procedures and Investigations Act 1996 (Home Office 1996) Code of Practice under Part II of the Act which defines a criminal investigation as:

'An investigation conducted by police officers with a view to it being ascertained whether a person should be charged with an offence, or whether a person charged with an offence is guilty of it'. This includes:

- Investigations into crimes that have been committed.
- Investigations whose purpose is to ascertain whether or not a crime has been committed, with a view to the possible institution of criminal proceedings.
- Investigations which begin in the belief that a crime may be committed; for example, when the police keep premises and individuals under observation for a period of time with a view to the possible institution of criminal offences.
- Charging persons with an offence includes prosecution by way of summons.

We can see that while this definition refers specifically to criminal investigations, the ideas set out in this definition apply just as much to other types of investigation such as antisocial behaviour, professional standards, etc. or those enquiries carried out on behalf of Her Majesty's Coroner.

Whichever definition is applied, however, there appear to be four broad objectives of a criminal investigation process. These are:

- To establish whether or not a crime has actually occurred.
- To identify and apprehend any suspect.
- To recover any stolen property.
- To assist in the prosecution process of the person or persons charged with such a crime (Swanson *et al.* 2006).

Reactive and pro-active criminal investigation

There are two methods of criminal investigation, namely reactive and pro-active. The pro-active method is sometimes referred to as 'intelligence-led' or 'covert' type investigations. However, the two approaches should not be considered as entirely separate from each other as they sometimes overlap in a criminal investigation.

The reactive method starts with the discovery of a crime and seeks to bring offenders to justice by uncovering material that identifies suspects and provides sufficient evidence to enable a court to determine their guilt. In the main this process depends upon interviewing victims and witnesses as well as examination of the crime scene and establishing forensic links to suspects.

The pro-active method generally starts with information and intelligence that a particular individual or group of people are engaging in or about to engage in criminal activity. This is often organised crime such as drug dealing or human trafficking. This approach is often used to deal with suspected terrorists. Investigators generally employ a range of covert surveillance techniques which are used to link offenders to the criminal act. These investigations are often complemented by financial and forensic science investigation techniques.

Covert investigations

This type of criminal investigation involves the use of techniques designed to ensure that the operation and sources of information it uses remain concealed. Covert methods of policing may be used in both reactive and pro-active investigations, and the methods include:

o   Static surveillance
o   Mobile surveillance
o   Technical options
o   The use of a covert human intelligence source (an undercover officer or informant)
o   Covert financial applications
o   Undercover test purchases (used when investigating sales of illegal drugs, etc.).

The type of covert technique used during a criminal investigation is normally decided by the intelligence or covert team. However, there are a number of important points that have to be considered before covert methods are used, such as:

o   Investigators need to have a good understanding of the intelligence process and of the National Intelligence Model.
o   Ensure that the amount of covert policing used is proportionate to the overall objectives of the investigation.
o   Have a thorough understanding of the RIPA (Regulation of Investigatory Powers Act 2000) and other relevant legislation.

- Maintain operation security.
- Consult the CPS (Crown Prosecution Service) at the earliest possible opportunity in the investigation.

Preliminary phase of an investigation

In general, the most important phase of a criminal investigation is the *preliminary investigation*, and this is discussed in depth below.

Preliminary investigation phase

Receipt of information – call handling

Very often, the criminal investigation commences when a telephone call is received by the police service from someone reporting that a crime has occurred or is in progress. While different forces have different procedures for dealing and grading such calls they generate a response which could be:

- an immediate one with officers attending straight away;
- a delayed response where police staff attend within a given time;
- a non-attendance response where the receiver of the call applies force guidelines and procedures which allow the matter to be dealt with over the phone.

The initial contact between victims or witnesses with the police service is a key component and should be regarded as the start of the criminal investigation process. Here a wealth of information and knowledge is available from the first contact and it is an opportunity to obtain accurate relevant information, collect evidence and also give reassurance to a victim or witness. Furthermore, good advice can be given to the caller to ensure that vital evidence is retained at the scene, etc.

Research into the use of call handling and screening (Office for Criminal Justice Reform 2006) includes the following:

- Every report of a crime should receive a minimum level of investigation to ensure that an informed and accurate decision is made to determine the initial response.
- Call handling should be considered as key to ensuring the beginning of the investigative process, and call handlers should be trained for this role.
- The expectations of the victim should be an important consideration when determining processes and policies regarding immediate action taken by the police once a crime is reported.

Criticisms of the call handler approach have included:

- Some forces have had no criteria for dealing with callers, and were in direct conflict with the National Intelligence Model.

- Responses to particular crimes were contrary to force policies.
- Ill-trained staff were deployed to deal with initial callers regarding crimes. For example, the IPCC bulletin *Learning the Lessons No. 9* (IPCC 2010) highlights such problems, as seen in the case study outlined in Box 6.2.
- Poor handling of public expectations led to an increase in complaints and a possible decline in public confidence.

Box 6.2   Case study Problems of ill-trained staff

A caller reported a man with a head injury behaving strangely, but the call handler did not understand the local term 'burn' the caller used to describe the location. The call handler sent officers to the wrong place, failing to contact the caller when they could not find anyone. The man was later found drowned.

(IPCC 2010)

Bearing in mind the importance of the first contact with a victim or a witness as outlined above, attempt the exercise outlined in Box 6.3.

Box 6.3   Exercise 6B First contact

You are a call handler at the police station when a person telephones you to report a stolen vehicle. Write down a list of questions that you believe you should ask this person.

You may have considered some of the following questions.

Witnesses – evidence

- Are there any witnesses?
- Is there CCTV at the location where the car was parked?
- Is there physical evidence at the scene (e.g. broken glass)?
- Did the car alarm activate?
- Who was the last person to see the vehicle?

Insurance and registration

- Who is the vehicle insured with?
- What sort of policy is in place?
- Who else has access to the vehicle?
- Is the vehicle registered with the DVLA in the driver's name?

Vehicle's last movements

- When and where was the vehicle last fuelled?
- Where had the vehicle been parked in the days prior to its theft?
- Has the car been to a garage lately for repairs?

Ownership

- How long has the owner owned the vehicle?
- How many keys were given when the car was purchased?
- How many keys are accounted for now?
- Where was the vehicle bought from?
- Is there any finance outstanding on the vehicle?

Maintenance history

- When was the vehicle last serviced?
- When is the test certificate due?
- Where was it last serviced?
- Has this vehicle previously been written off in an accident?

Clearly, there is much information to be gained from correctly interrogating the initial call regarding an incident or crime.

The role of the Crown Prosecution Service

The Crown Prosecution Service was set up in 1986 to prosecute criminal cases investigated by the police in England and Wales. In undertaking this role, the CPS:

- Advises the police on cases for possible prosecution.
- Reviews cases submitted by the police for prosecution.
- Where the decision is to prosecute, it determines the charge in all but minor cases.
- Prepares cases for court.
- Presents those cases at court.

The Code for Crown Prosecutors sets out the basic principles to be followed by Crown Prosecutors when they make case decisions. The decision on whether or not to charge a case against a suspect is based on two tests outlined in the Code. These are the evidential test and the public interest test, and both are discussed below.

1. The evidential test

This is the first stage in the decision to prosecute. Crown Prosecutors must be satisfied that there is enough evidence to provide a 'realistic prospect of conviction' against each defendant on each charge. They must consider whether the evidence can be used and is reliable, and they must also consider what the defence case may be and how that is likely to affect the prosecution case. A 'realistic prospect of conviction' is an objective test. This means that a jury or a bench of magistrates, properly directed in accordance with the law, will be more likely than not to convict the defendant of the charge alleged. (This is a separate test from the one that criminal courts themselves must apply. A jury or magistrates' court should only convict if it is sure of a defendant's guilt.) If the case does not pass the evidential test, it cannot go ahead, no matter how important or serious it may be.

2. The public interest test

If the case does pass the evidential test, Crown Prosecutors must then decide whether a prosecution is required in the public interest. They must balance factors for and against prosecution carefully and fairly. Some factors may increase the need to prosecute but others may suggest that another course of action would be better. A prosecution will usually take place however, unless there are public interest factors tending against prosecution which clearly outweigh those tending in favour. The CPS will only start or continue a prosecution if a case has passed both tests.

The CPS also provides liaison with other agencies and government departments to work together to achieve improvements in the criminal justice system and to meet new domestic, European and global challenges of crime.

The principles that the CPS use are outlined in the following:

- Decisions will be independent of bias or discrimination but will always consider the interests of others. They will act with integrity and objectivity and will exercise sound judgement with confidence.
- In their dealings with each other and the public they will be open and honest. They will show sensitivity and understanding towards victims and witnesses, and treat all defendants fairly.
- They are accountable to Parliament and to the public, and will work together with other criminal justice agencies to maintain public trust and to provide an efficient criminal justice system.

Once satisfied with these two tests a person may be prosecuted and enter the criminal justice procedures. The phases of a criminal trial are shown in Figure 6.1

What is evidence?

Johnston and Hutton (2008: 101) state that 'evidence can be described as information that may be presented to a court so that it may decide on the probability of some facts asserted before it, that is information by which facts in issue tend to be proved or disproved'.

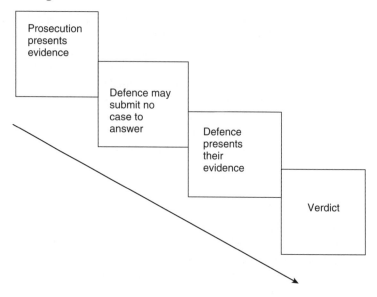

Figure 6.1 Phases of a criminal trial.

According to ACPO (2005: 26), In terms of the law of evidence, all evidence which is sufficiently relevant to the facts in issue is admissible, subject to the exclusionary rules.' Consequently all evidence that is irrelevant should be excluded. The test of relevance is:

> evidence which makes the matter which requires proof more or less probable
> (Lord Simon of Glaisdale in *DPP v. Kilbourne*
> [1973] AC 729, at p. 756).

'Facts in issue' means the facts which the prosecution must be able to prove in order to establish the guilt of the defendant.

Johnston and Hutton (2008) state that two questions need to applied to evidence: its admissibility and its weight. Its admissibility, which is to be decided by the judge in all cases, is to do with whether the evidence is relevant to a fact in issue. All evidence of facts in issue is potentially admissible, and all evidence which is sufficiently relevant to prove (or disprove) facts in issue are potentially admissible also. Johnston and Hutton (2008) continue to discuss how the admissibility of evidence is very important to the outcome of the trial. An investigator should always be mindful when collecting evidence for a case that the evidence is the best available and should always consider whether this evidence will be admissible. Once it has been established that the evidence is admissible then the court will consider how much weight it will attach to the evidence and what effect it could have on proving or disproving the case.

Johnston and Hutton (2008: 113) categorise evidence into two groups: the ways in which evidence can be proved and the main evidential rules.

Evidence can be proved in the following ways:

- Original (primary) evidence
- Real evidence
- Secondary evidence
- Documentary evidence.

The main evidential rules are:

- Hearsay evidence
- Circumstantial evidence
- Presumptions
- Character
- Opinion
- Corroboration
- Judicial notice.

Fisher and Baca (2004) describe how the police deal with evidence on a daily basis and argue that their success as investigators is largely determined by their ability to recognise, collect and use evidence in a criminal investigation.

Evidence may be divided into two broad types, according to Fisher and Baca (2004):

- Testimonial evidence – given in the form of statements, under oath for the majority of people (not children, for example) and usually in response to questioning.
- Real, physical evidence – any evidence with an objective existence, large or small.

What is material?

It is important that investigators understand what material is, how it is generated during a criminal offence, and how it can be located, gathered and subsequently used, as this knowledge is central to the investigation of crime. The CPIA Code of Practice under Part II of the Act defines material as:

> Material is material of any kind, including information and objects, which is obtained in the course of a criminal investigation and which may be relevant to the investigation. Material may be relevant to an investigation if it appears to an investigator, or to the officer in charge of an investigation, or to the disclosure officer, that it has some bearing on any offence under investigation or any person being investigated, or on the surrounding circumstances of the case, unless it is incapable of having any impact on the case.
>
> (OPSI 2009)

It can be difficult, particularly during the early stages of an investigation, to predict what is or is not relevant as to the exact nature of what has occurred, and who was involved in the offence is perhaps still unclear. It is advisable for an investigator to err on the side of caution and, where legally permissible, to gather and retain material; supervisors and Crown Prosecutors are available to be consulted in order to determine whether the material should in fact be retained for investigation (ACPO 2005).

ACPO (2005: 44) provides information about where material can potentially be sourced from:

- Victims
- Witnesses
- Suspects
- Locations, including scenes of crimes and the victim's or suspect's premises
- Passive data generators which are systems that collate or record data automatically and generate material which is not intended solely for the purpose of an investigation (e.g. CCTV recordings, telephone records, banking and credit card records)
- Intelligence databases.

ACPO (2005: 44) goes on to describe the different formats in which material can present itself. The most common formats for material are:

- Statements
- Documents
- Reports
- Physical exhibits such as weapons, clothing, stolen goods and biological or chemical material
- Fingerprints
- Images
- Audio or video recordings.

A skilled investigator will be able to recognise and locate potential sources of material and will also understand how such material should be gathered and stored in a format that is admissible as evidence.

The duty to retain material is covered by Section 5 of the aforementioned Code and includes in particular the duty to retain material falling into the following categories, where it may be relevant to the investigation:

- crime reports (including crime report forms, relevant parts of incident report books or police officers' notebooks);
- custody records;
- records which are derived from tapes of telephone messages (for example, 999 calls) containing descriptions of an alleged offence or offender;

- final versions of witness statements (and draft versions where their content differs from the final version), including any exhibits mentioned (unless these have been returned to their owner on the understanding that they will be produced in court if required);
- interview records (written records, or audio or video tapes, of interviews with actual or potential witnesses or suspects);
- communications between the police and experts such as forensic scientists, reports of work carried out by experts, and schedules of scientific material prepared by the expert for the investigator, for the purposes of criminal proceedings;
- records of the first description of a suspect by each potential witness who purports to identify or describe the suspect, whether or not the description differs from that of subsequent descriptions by that or other witnesses;
- any material casting doubt on the reliability of a witness.

The duty to retain material, where it may be relevant to the investigation, also includes in particular the duty to retain material which may satisfy the test for prosecution disclosure in the Act, such as:

- information provided by an accused person which indicates an explanation for

  - the offence with which he has been charged;
  - any material casting doubt on the reliability of a confession;
  - any material casting doubt on the reliability of a prosecution witness.

Initial actions at the scene of a crime

Stanley and Horswell (cited in Horswell 2004) describe the potential for finding a vast array of material at the scene of a crime that could provide significant forensic evidence.

According to White (2004) there will be three issues that an investigating police officer will need clarification on:

1. Has a crime been committed?
2. If a crime has been committed, who is responsible?
3. If the person responsible has been traced, has enough evidence been gathered to charge the person and successfully prosecute?

Weston (cited in White 2004) describes the actions necessary when a police officer attends the scene of a crime. The first officer to attend a crime scene is called the 'First Officer Attending' (FAO). Weston states that their first role is to reassure the victim; this is essential. The officer is then responsible for checking the crime scene and informs the victim about what will happen next. While doing this, the officer will also begin the process in his investigation. He or she will be looking for information and will aim to identify potential evidence to provide the officer with information as to what has occurred: What evidence has been left behind? Where might the suspect be now? The FAO will inform the control room and ensure that nobody touches anything in the crime scene, to prevent contamination.

Weston continues to describe the role of the crime scene examiner who would attend the scene to make an independent assessment. He will:

- Make a detailed record of the scene, making detailed notes, sketching the scene and taking numerous photographs.
- Carry out a thorough search of the scene, recovering and recording all the physical evidence found.
- Package carefully and securely all physical evidence in appropriate labelled containers.
- Take down a detailed description of each item found and provide an indication of its potential significance.
- Search for and record all traces left behind by an offender.
- Take samples which are called 'control samples' of all materials that it may be possible that the offender has taken from the scene.
- Form a clear impression of how the crime has been committed.

The crime scene examiner will keep in mind 'Locard's exchange principle' as explained by Stanley and Horswell (cited in Horswell 2004: 45): 'every contact leaves a trace'. When an offender is present at a crime scene a transfer of materials may occur, so he not only leaves evidence of his being present at the scene, but may also take evidence away with him that will prove he was there. This is why the control samples are so important; they can provide extremely valuable evidence of a person being at the scene.

The benefits of a good investigation

According to ACPO (2005), investigation should not be considered in isolation from other policing activities even though it does form a large part of the core business function of the police service.

The five police service priorities are outlined by the National Policing Plan (NPP), working in conjunction with their local communities. The National Intelligence Model (NIM) guides this plan with its strategic assessments. The NIM drives policing in the UK according to ACPO (2005) requiring the input of timely and accurate information into intelligence systems, which is vastly generated by investigations. In order for the NPP objectives to be delivered, it is key that investigations are conducted effectively, providing information for the NIM.

Inevitably there will be contact between investigators and members of the public; the effectiveness of the investigator will impact upon the quality of material provided by witnesses and victims.

Each and every investigation will provide each investigator and the police service with an opportunity to understand and recognise the impact of crime and criminality upon the local community. The knowledge gained may be used in a multitude of ways (e.g. to provide reassurance to specific vulnerable persons/ groups or locations within the community, to guide preventive policing patrols, and to promote and disseminate crime prevention advice).

Investigators who connect with suspects are also given the opportunity to gain material relating to crime and criminality in the local community and also in the wider area; this material may be used to improve both the personal and organisational knowledge through the provision of this intelligence. This could go on to assist in the reduction of crime and also the fear of crime within the community, and would encourage positive intervention with the offenders with the aim of reducing recidivism.

The role of the investigator

Who an investigator is and what their role is within an investigation is clearly defined in the CPIA Code of Practice under Part II of the Act:

> An investigator is any police officer involved in the conduct of a criminal investigation. All investigators have a responsibility for carrying out the duties imposed on them under this code, including in particular recording information, and retaining records of information and other material.
>
> (OPSI 2009)

ACPO (2005) points out that if an investigator is to be effective then he or she must be able to make reliable and accountable decisions, often in difficult or pressurised situations.

ACPO (2005) states that investigations may also be carried out by persons, other than police officers, who have investigative duties, such as the Independent Police Complaints Commission (IPCC), Department for Trade and Industry (DTI), Department for Transport (DfT) or the Serious Fraud Office (SFO).

ACPO (2005) states that the investigator is assisted by knowledge in making effective and accountable decisions throughout an investigation, allowing him or her to make use of the maximum amount of material to identify and bring an offender to justice. There are four key areas of investigative knowledge necessary to conduct an effective investigation:

- The legal framework
- Characteristics of crime
- National and force policies
- Investigative skill.

Within the legal framework there is a requirement for all investigators to have an in-depth and current knowledge of criminal law and the legislation that regulates the investigation process. Opportunities to gather material occur frequently, particularly for those investigators working at PIP level one, while those officers are carrying out routine activities such as interviewing victims and witnesses or responding to incidents. Without an in-depth knowledge these investigators will not be able to make full use of these opportunities and will lack good sources of advice to aid on-the-spot decisions as to the most appropriate courses of action. For this reason it is imperative according to ACPO (2005: 18) that all investigators should understand the following:

- Legal definitions of offences likely to be encountered
- Points that have to be proven
- Potential defences available from statute and case law
- Powers that support and regulate the investigation process
- Relevant rules of evidence.

ACPO (2005) argues that without this knowledge it is possible that investigators may take action that is unlawful or may gather material in such a way that makes it unlikely to be accepted as evidence in court. In addition, if an investigator maintains a current knowledge of criminal law this will aid the investigator to deploy his or her full range of investigative techniques and will ensure that the investigator is well equipped to withstand the high level of scrutiny that may be applied by the Criminal Justice System. If an investigator with good knowledge of the law can anticipate possible defences that may be put forward by a suspect then he or she can look to gather more material which will provide the courts with more evidence to test the validity of the defence. During the investigation of a serious or major crime it is quite common for there to be a high volume of material which generates quite complex chains of evidence.

Investigators gain their knowledge through formal training courses and from experience of actually carrying out investigations. Formal training courses include the IPLDP (Initial Police Learning and Development Programme) and the ICIDP (Initial Crime Investigators Development Programme) (ACPO 2005).

Sources of legal knowledge are available to investigators, and should be accessed frequently so that the investigator keeps up to date with current law and any amendments that have been made. ACPO (2005:19) lists places where investigators can gain current information:

- Home Office circulars
- Ministry of Justice circulars
- Textbooks
- Force orders
- The media
- Legal digests
- HMSO website (legislation/statutory instruments)
- Police journals
- Force crime training departments

- Conferences and seminars
- Daily or extended briefings
- Legal databases (PNLD Police National Legal Database and Lawtel).

Ethics in investigations

According to ACPO (2005), with such a wide range of legal powers to enable investigators to effectively conduct investigations, such as depriving individuals of their liberty, the power to enter a person's home or other private premises, the power to use reasonable force, the power to gain private information and to use intrusive surveillance techniques when necessary, there is a huge responsibility placed on them to use these powers and the discretion with which they may be used ethically.

ACPO (2005: 19) states that 'the Police Service Statement of Common Purpose clarifies the basic ethical principles that investigators should use as a guide:

- To uphold the law fairly and firmly;
- To prevent crime;
- To pursue and bring to justice those who break the law;
- To keep the Queen's Peace;
- To protect, help and reassure the community;
- To be seen to do this with integrity, common sense and sound judgement.

It is widely recognised that policing works best when it has the support and cooperation of the community it is serving. At times this support and cooperation can suffer if communities lose confidence in either the way in which the police exercise their powers or the effectiveness of the police. ACPO (2005: 19) suggests that in order 'to encourage a high level of community support and ensure investigations are carried out ethically the following principles should be adhered to:

- When a crime is reported, or it is suspected that one may have been committed, investigators should conduct an effective investigation.
- The exercise of legal powers should not be oppressive and should be proportionate to the crime under investigation.
- As far as operationally practical and having due regard to an individual's right to confidentiality, investigations should be carried out as transparently as possible, in particular, victims, witnesses and suspects should be kept updated with developments in their case.
- Investigators should take all reasonable steps to understand the particular needs of individuals including their culture, religious beliefs, ethnic origin, sexuality, disability or lifestyle.
- Investigators should have particular regard for vulnerable adults and children.

- Investigators should respect the professional ethics of others. This is particularly important when working with those whose role it is to support suspects.

If investigations can be carried out ethically then the confidence of the community and individuals within that community will remain high. The community will be more likely to come forward and report crime, providing investigators with material and to cooperate in the prosecution of offenders if they can see that the police service is performing ethically and effectively and that the processes and techniques in which they do so are fair (ACPO 2005).

It is wise for investigators to keep in mind that offenders are part of the communities and they can influence how members of the community view the police, and that they themselves could at some point become a victim or a witness. If they then feel that they have been treated ethically during an investigation they are less likely to form a negative view of the police and pass that view on to others. They are more likely to be helpful and cooperative with future investigations, whether as a victim, witness or suspect (ACPO 2005).

Conclusion

In conclusion, investigations have been carried out since the first CID in the Metropolitan Police in 1878. It was recognised as an effective tool in policing, and, over the years, as policing has developed and changed so too has the role of the investigator. This chapter has introduced the changes which have contributed to the professionalising of the investigative process and a call from the government to be able to measure outcomes. There has also been a move towards greater pro-active rather than reactive investigations, with the introduction of greater technology and forensic science in support of this. Inquiries such as the Laming Report and the Macpherson Report have certainly brought to the public and media attention the need for change. The role of the investigator is now clearly defined in the Criminal Procedure and Investigations Act 1996 and it has made it clear that in order for an investigator to work effectively on the ground then a sound knowledge of criminal law is necessary, so that good decisions can be made and relevant material recognised and gathered. In turn, good evidence can be presented before the court. The police service recognises that if the public lose confidence in their abilities they are less likely to come forward with information, and therefore the investigators will have a more difficult task looking for material and information. Professional and ethical investigations are vital, since without them material and evidence could go undiscovered, and those individuals who commit criminal and other acts would go unpunished.

References and suggested further reading

Ascoli, D. (1979) *The Queens Peace: The Origins and Development of the Metropolitan Police, 1829–1979*, Hamish Hamilton, London.

Association of Chief Police Officers (ACPO) (2005) *Practice Advice on Core Investigative Doctrine*, National Centre for Policing Excellence, Cambourne, Cambridgeshire.

Fisher, B.A.J. and Baca, D. (2004) *Techniques of a Crime Scene Investigator* (7th edn), CRC Press, London.

Home Office (1996) *The Criminal Procedures Act 1996*, HMSO, London.

—— (2000) *The Regulation of Investigatory Powers Act*, HMSO, London.

Horswell, J. (2004) *The Practice of Crime Scene Investigation*, Taylor & Francis, London.

Independent Police Complaints Commission (IPCC) (2010) Learning the Lessons Bulletin No. 9, available online at http://www.learningthelessons.org.uk/learningthelessons_bulletin9.pdf.

Johnston, D. and Hutton, G. (2008) *Blackstone's Police Manual. Evidence and Procedure*, Oxford University Press, Oxford.

Melville Lee, W.L. (1901) *A History of Police in England*, Methuen & Co, London..

Newburn, T., Williamson, T. and Hutton, H. (2007) *Handbook of Criminal Investigation*, Willan Publishing, Cullompton, Devon.

Office for Criminal Justice Reform (OCJR) (2006) *Redefining Screening*. Available as a download from: http://frontline.cjsonline.gov.uk/_includes/downloads/guidance/general/Redefining_screening_report.pdf (accessed on 7 March 2011).

Office of Public Sector Information (OPSI) (2009) *Criminal Procedure and Investigation Act 1996*, available online at http://www.uk-legislation.hmso.gov.uk/acts/acts1996/ukpga_19960025_en_1 (accessed 9 July 2009).

Osterberg, J.W. and Ward, R.H. (2005) *Criminal Investigation: A Method for Reconstructing the Past* (4th edn), LexisNexis Publishers, Cincinnati, OH.

Swanson, C.R., Chamelin, N.C., Territo, L. and Taylor, R.W. (2006) *Criminal Investigation* (9th edn), McGraw-Hill, Boston, MA.

White, P.C. (2004) *Crime Scene to Court: The Essentials of Forensic Science* (2nd edn), Royal Society of Chemistry, Cambridge.

Useful websites

http://www.cps.gov.uk/index.html
The website of the Crown Prosecution Service
http://www.opsi.gov.uk/acts.htm
A useful website that contains all the details about Acts of Parliament passed in this country
http://www.forensic.gov.uk/index.htm
The website of the Forensic Science Service
http://www.soca.gov.uk/
The Serious Organised Crime Agency website which explains the aims and objectives of this organisation.

7 Legislation and police powers

Introduction

This chapter provides a brief overview of the legal basis of police investigations of alleged crimes (*criminal investigation*) for police officers at the beginning of their service. The chapter seeks to stimulate interest and awareness in the powers and roles of investigators and to give some examples showing how and why criminal law has changed in recent years. Attempt the exercise in Box 7.1 before continuing.

Every member of the public can carry out investigations into crime provided that such investigations do not infringe the law. Most criminal investigations carried out by the police service are made by police officers and police community support officers (PCSOs). However, designated investigating officers (including crime scene investigators) also have powers to enter and search buildings and seize evidence. Other agencies, such as the UK Borders Agency, also employ specialist investigators with the powers to search and arrest.

Definitions of investigation

Section 22 (hereafter abbreviated to s.22) of the Criminal Procedure and Investigations Act 1996 (CPIA) defines a criminal investigation as follows:

> a criminal investigation is an investigation which police officers or other persons have a duty to conduct with a view to it being ascertained:
>
> (a) whether a person should be charged with an offence, or
> (b) Whether a person charged with an offence is guilty of it.

The Act also states that all investigators have a responsibility for carrying out the duties imposed upon them under this Act, including in particular recording information and retaining records of information and other material.

In essence, the CPIA requires that in investigations:

- All reasonable lines of enquiry are pursued.
- Relevant information should be recorded.
- Relevant records and other material should be retained.

Box 7.1 Exercise 7A Who can investigate?

Who has legal powers to carry out criminal investigations? Who carries out such investigations?

Prosecuting staff (such as CPS lawyers) should be informed of the existence of relevant information or material. They will decide whether or not defence lawyers should be given access to the same information or material, a process known as 'disclosure of evidence'.

The Terrorist Act 2000 defines a terrorist investigation as an investigation of:

(a) The commission, preparation or instigation of acts of terrorism.
(b) An act which appears to have been done for the purposes of terrorism.
(c) The resources of a proscribed organization.
(d) The possibility of making an order under section 3(3) (i.e. an order against proscribed organisations).
(e) The commission, preparation or instigation of an offence under this Act.

We are not primarily concerned with the effectiveness of investigations in this chapter, but this is clearly a matter of some importance to both the police, the public and politicians. A study tracking 240 arson investigations (Hopkins 2009) illustrates the difficulty of identifying factors that bring about ('casually impact' upon) detections. This research study suggests that if detection had not been obtained during the initial investigation, then it was less likely that the arson would ultimately be solved. Analysis of the data suggests (perhaps unsurprisingly) that police resource levels and the ways in which arsons were managed may also be important in solving this type of offence.

Legislation, statutory police powers and responsibilities

Legislation specifies the elements that must be proved in order to gain a conviction for an offence to be proved but it also provides protection for those suspected of being guilty. Lawyers sometimes speak of the 'due process (of law)'. This refers to the principle that governments and other agencies (including the police) cannot be selective in deciding which legal rights will be upheld. For example, this principle opposes arbitrary arrest (the illegal arrest of an individual on the whim of officials) as part of an investigation.

Police officers, like other citizens, can engage in non-intrusive investigations and make requests for information without legislative authorisation. The rights of police officers to take actions beyond those of citizens derive from legislation and legal precedent. Laws, such as the Police and Criminal Evidence Act 1984 (PACE), have substituted legislation for the application of common law to police powers, although officers still exercise their powers to deal with breaches of the peace under common law. Police action is also dictated or guided by manuals of guidance and professional doctrine produced by the National Police Improvement Agency and the Association of Chief Police Officers: such guidance is also part of attempts to 'professionalise' the police service by disseminating good practice. In the case of investigations, there is an increasingly consistent approach to the use of technology (such as HOLMES 2), largely brought about by the similar training that investigators receive across England and Wales as a consequence of the Professionalising Investigation Project (PIP).

The discretion exercised by police officers is also constrained by the policies of individual police forces which may state, for example, the conditions under which a fixed penalty is given for minor criminal offences and the action that should be taken in cases of domestic abuse.

Individuals have fundamental rights which derive from international law, including the International Covenant on Civil and Political Rights 1966, the United Nations Convention on the Rights of the Child (1989) and the European Convention on Human Rights (1950) (ECHR). The Human Rights Act 1998 (HRA) is a piece of UK legislation that requires conformity of public bodies (including the courts, the CPS and the police) with ECHR. A legal consequence of HRA is that police action must be legal, necessary and proportional. Torture is explicitly outlawed under Article 3 of the HRA. The HRA, coupled with concerns about the behaviour of the police in some high-profile cases, has stimulated discussions about the ethical basis of police operations and has led to proposals for an ethical framework for police officers. Such considerations have found their way into formal documents of guidance, such as the NPIA *Core Investigative Doctrine* (currently under revision).

UK legislation has expanded police powers connected with evidence gathering, including those allowing arrest which leads to interview, the searching of individuals and premises and surveillance. Examples related to investigation include PACE 1984 (which rationalised many early powers and laws), the Regulation of Investigatory Powers Act 2000 (RIPA), the Criminal Procedure and Investigations Act 1996 (CPIA), the Criminal Justice Act 2003 and the Youth Justice and Criminal Evidence Act 1999. The sheer volume of legislation confirms a wider trend: in common with other organisations in modern society, the activities of the police service are the subject of increasing direction via explicit legislation. For example, there has been a drastic reduction in the use of court warrants to search premises as newer police powers have made such warrants unnecessary. This, together with the formalisation of police authority to detain people, means that suspects are arrested using explicit powers contained in legislation. While detained, a clear definition of their rights, including the right to access legal advice, is stipulated.

The Race Relations (Amendment Act) 2000 outlaws direct or indirect discrimination by public bodies (including the police service) not covered by the Race Relations Act 1976. The discriminatory use of 'stop and search' would be one example of such discrimination.

Although the work of all police officers, and particularly of investigators, is increasingly dependent upon shared information and intelligence, legal cases emphasise that it is individual police officers who are accountable for police actions. For example, the arrest of suspects cannot be a corporate decision and it is illegal for a police officer to arrest a suspect on the basis that the officer suspects that his senior officers have reasonable grounds for suspicion: the arresting officer himself must have such grounds for reasonable suspicion. See *Commissioner of Police of the Metropolis v. Mohamed Raissi* (November 2008).

Evidence and the adversarial system

It is the role of the police service to collect and present evidence, often with the intention of supporting a prosecution at court. The police work with the Crown Prosecution Service (CPS), which has responsibility for the selection of any charges laid against individuals. Legal processes operate within an adversarial legal system in UK courts, but both the police and CPS have an overriding moral and legal responsibility to aid justice (e.g. by disclosing information that strengthens the defence case and by only putting forward evidence that they believe is true) even if the prosecution case is thereby weakened. The defence, on the other hand, do not have to disclose evidence that weakens their case although they must not knowingly deceive the court.

Since the introduction of the Crown Prosecution service it has been said that the role of the police as investigators has become more inquisitorial than adversarial, an approach which is also adopted by forensic scientists.

The 'Code for Crown Prosecutors' is issued under Section 10 of the Prosecution of Offences Act 1985. It gives guidance on the general principles to be used when making decisions about prosecutions, in particular, Crown Prosecutors make charging decisions in accordance with the so-called 'Full Code Test' which has two stages. Crown Prosecutors cannot proceed to the second stage unless the first stage is satisfied. In the first stage, the evidence is considered: there must be enough evidence to provide a 'realistic prospect of conviction' against each defendant on each charge. This is an objective test which will require an evaluation of the quality, reliability and admissibility of evidence gathered by investigators. The second stage involves a decision on whether or not a prosecution is in the public interest. For example, the prosecution of individuals for offences that involve long sentences (which are 'serious') or that are perpetrated by individuals in positions of authority (e.g. a government minister) are more likely to be judged as being in the public interest.

The Crown Prosecution Service also defines a 'threshold test' which it applies to those cases in which it would not be appropriate to release an individual on bail after charge, but where the evidence to apply the Full Code Test has not yet been collected or prepared. The Threshold Test requires the CPS to decide whether or not there is at least a reasonable suspicion that the suspect has committed the offence in question, and if there is, whether it is in the public interest to charge that subject. The Full Code Test must still be applied as soon as reasonably practicable.

(http://www.cps.gov.uk/publications/docs/code2004english.pdf)

Criminal lawyers often debate whether or not a piece of evidence is admissible in court. The modern position is in general that all evidence that is relevant to the facts of the case is admissible. For example, the idea of 'best evidence' was originally important because it was connected to admissibility in court. This has been replaced by the idea that while it is preferable to present best evidence (e.g. original documents) in court, the presentation of other evidence (such as photocopies) will not necessarily mean that evidence is inadmissible.

The distinction between direct and circumstantial evidence remains important. Direct evidence is exemplified by a witness who observes an assault taking place. Circumstantial evidence, however, is evidence of the circumstances of the offence from which a fact may be inferred; an example of circumstantial evidence would be if the suspected assailant was seen to leave the crime scene with blood on his clothes. It will be no surprise to learn that in practice, most evidence presented at court (including forensic evidence) is strictly circumstantial and the key question is whether or not the circumstantial evidence is deemed relevant by the court. The use of 'expert witnesses' is commonplace, but it is the trial judge who decides whether or not a witness is competent to act as an expert (Box 7.2).

[1] PACE was catalysed by serious miscarriages of justice which cumulated in the Philips Royal Commission which reported in 1981.

Box 7.2 Exercise 7B PACE

The latest version of the PACE Codes will be found at http://police.homeoffice.gov.uk/operational-policing/powers-pace-codes/pace-code-intro/.

[1] Find out about the historical events that led to the introduction of the Police and Criminal Evidence Act 1984 (PACE).
[2] To answer the following, refer to the PACE Codes of Practice A–G.
    (a) Give one example of police activity that is covered by PACE which is (1) designed to be *protective* to suspects, and (2) *coercive* in that it forces suspects to do something that they may not wish to do.
    (b) Which part of PACE deals with access to legal advice?
    (c) Can a suspect be interviewed outside the police station?
    (d) What happens if, during a trial, it transpires that an officer fails to conform to PACE?

[2] (a) An example of the protective nature of PACE is where it outlaws the use of oppression in obtaining statements (Code C, 11.5), confirming common law. It is also a source of some of the *coercive* powers of the police, enabling (for example) fingerprints and a mouth swab (for subsequent DNA analysis) to be taken from individuals without consent (see Code D).

(b) Many governments throughout the world provide some level of free legal aid to those who otherwise could not afford it. In the UK, the duty solicitor or Public Defender Service scheme provides free legal aid in a police station. The right to legal advice is specifically guaranteed under s.58 of PACE (see Code of Practice C, s.6.) although there are exceptional circumstances (Annex B) when access is delayed, as where there are reasonable grounds to believe that access to a solicitor would hinder the recovery of stolen property. However, although nearly all detainees have the right of access to legal advice many arrested individuals do not exercise that right (Ashworth and Redmayne 2005: 88).

(c) Code C, s. 11.1 states that interviews should take place in a police station, although questions may be asked if the information is required urgently. The definition of the word 'interview' is crucial here, but at some point questioning becomes an interview, in which case it should be conducted at a police station.

(d) Failure to follow PACE will not automatically destroy a prosecution case: the court will consider each case on its own merits. However, a breach of PACE may result in disciplinary action against the officer.

PACE is one of the most important pieces of legislation involving police powers that have been enacted over the past 50 years. When the legislation that led to PACE 1984 was being considered, some chief police officers maintained that the Act would assist wrongdoers while others were concerned that the Act heralded a new kind of coercive policing. In retrospect, neither set of objections appears to have been realised (Rowe 2008, ch. 3).

Criticisms are often based upon the fact that all detained suspects are, by their circumstances, vulnerable to some extent and that the defendant's lawyers or independent observers are not party to the whole sequence of events whereby an individual is detailed and interviewed. What happens (or could happen) before the suspect is interviewed in the presence of a solicitor? What deals might have been done in return for bail or even a cigarette? What advice might have been given before a suspect is informed of their right to legal advice? Can custody officers, as part of the police organisation, really be expected to be independent decision makers? Furthermore, although custody officers have important and ostensibly independent roles, they are not always in a position to appreciate the full circumstances which would allow them to decide whether or not detention should be authorised.

Some police officers would regard these concerns as exaggerated. Nevertheless, it is valuable to place oneself in the position of an outsider (perhaps a member of

---

Box 7.3 Exercise 7C Checks and balances while an individual is in custody

In principle and often in operation, there are checks and balances against the abuse of power of interviewing investigators. Examples include 'rules' such as:

- Interviews must be taped.
- Detained individuals have the right to legal advice.
- Custody officers (not investigators) must make decisions on whether detention is initially justified.
- Reviews of detention before charge must be made by officers of at least the rank of inspector.

In what way might individuals or organisations outside the criminal justice system regard these safeguards as unreliable, flawed or ineffective? Can you think of a more effective way of monitoring the way in which the rights of suspects are protected?

---

the suspect's family) and appreciate some of their concerns; this may be helpful in ensuring that the standard of care that detainees and interviewees receive is satisfactory and that it *appears* satisfactory to as many people as possible who are involved in the process. It is possible, at least in principle, to imagine an independent professional administrative service that would oversee detention and investigation more effectively but this would be very expensive to implement.

It is important to note that police interviewers are not expected to act passively. Schollum's literature survey (2005: 57) on investigative interviewing quotes Mr Justice Mitchell in the court case *R v. Heron* (1993):

> The police, of course, are not prohibited from putting questions to a suspect merely because he chooses not to answer them. They are not required to accept any answer or answers a suspect chooses to give. Nor are they prohibited from being persistent, searching and robust in their questions. If they do not believe what they are being told they are entitled to say so. Persistence must not, however, develop into bullying; robustness must not develop into insulting or gratuitously demeaning questions, nor must robustness be regarded as an acceptable label for what in truth, is no more than a repetitive verbal pounding . . . Where the line is to be drawn between proper and robust persistence and oppressive interrogation, can only be identified in general terms. Furthermore, questioning, though persistent, searching and robust, must remain fair . . . An assessment of any interview will have regard to the question of how the [overall] interview is best characterised. Was it essentially fair, or was it essentially unfair?

Legislation's role in striking a new balance between the rights of individuals and the effectiveness of the Criminal Justice System

The increasing politicisation of criminal justice of the 1990s catapulted all aspects of policing more or less permanently into the public arena. This led to an unprecedented volume of new legislation and to the qualification (or removal) of some previously 'cherished rights'. For example:

(a) *'Double jeopardy'*, whereby an individual cannot be prosecuted for the same crime twice, was historically part of common law. In England and Wales (but not Scotland) the protection against double jeopardy was removed for serious offences and under certain circumstances by the Criminal Justice Act 2003, leading to the conviction of Billy Dunlop who had been acquitted of the murder of his former girlfriend Julie Hogg, of Billingham, Teesside. It is very unlikely that more than a handful of individuals will be prosecuted in the same way, but presumably the government felt that such legislative changes gave a powerful deterrent message to criminals and a reassuring message to the public.

(b) The long-term detention of individuals without charge was once regarded as a feature of military dictatorships in underdeveloped countries and not of the UK but the extended detention of suspects for terrorism is now part of UK law. In 2008, proposals to increase the maximum detention to 42 days were rejected by Parliament. While it is true that the powers of the police are potentially more intrusive than they were only a decade ago, the counter-argument is that the challenges of terrorism over that period have become very much greater. The argument is over the exact balance between individual rights and the needs of the state. The perceptions of the public on the impact of counter-terrorism legislation are complex and variable (Home Office 2010, Occasional Paper 88).

(c) The Drugs Act 2005 allows courts to presume that a person is guilty of intent to supply drugs if they are found to be in possession of large amounts of controlled drugs. In effect, the 2005 Act (within certain safeguards) places an evidential burden on the defendant to show, to the *civil* threshold of evidence, that he did not have the drug in his possession to supply to others. The prosecution, responding to this defence, has to prove, to the *criminal* threshold of evidence, the defendant's 'intent to supply'.

(d) The 'right to silence' during interview is preserved by the Criminal Justice and Public Order Act 1994 (in accordance with the ECHR), but the Act does allow the jury or court to draw adverse inferences from an interviewee's silence under certain circumstances.

(e) Traditionally the Criminal Justice process follows the sequence: crime report, investigation, report/charge and court. One important deviation from this sequence of dealing with crime arose when the government introduced antisocial behaviour orders (ASBOs) through the Crime and Disorder Act

1998, after becoming concerned with the difficulty of securing court convictions for minor crime or social disorder. The intention is that ASBOs deter or prevent antisocial behaviour without recourse to the criminal courts. Applications for ASBOs are made to court and although breach of the order itself is a criminal offence, the making of such an order is not a criminal process.

(f) Arguments about the retention of private information about individuals who are proved innocent have resurfaced over the collection of DNA samples. In England, Wales and Northern Ireland, body samples that yield a DNA profile are legally acquired after arrest and permanently retained by the police, even where individuals are not charged and even when the prosecution case fails in court. This has led to concerns that young people in particular are being 'criminalised' for petty offences.

Despite the increasing volume of legislation which clarifies and authorises police action, the scrutiny of the courts, of human rights organisations and of the public remains high and the regulations concerning some police practices (including the disclosure of relevant information and the need for accurate records) are detailed. Yet, the support of the public for the police's role in investigation is only likely to continue if the police use their powers proportionately (some members of the public would call this 'sensible usage') and justly ('fairly'). Put simply, 'Just because you have the powers, you don't have to use them'.

(i) Pro-active investigation is based upon intelligence such as information from informers, information about crimes that are being planned or from the detailed analysis of crime patterns. For example, if data show that the number of petty crimes in a shopping centre increases dramatically when a school finishes for the day, additional visible patrols may prevent crimes from occurring in the first place.

(ii) One class of crime that necessarily requires pro-active investigation is so-called *consensual crime* in which it is in the interests of the parties

---

Box 7.4　Exercise 7D Reactive and pro-active criminal investigation

Traditionally the investigation of crime has been reactive – in response to a complaint or an incident – but, where possible, the police service also attempts to investigate pro-actively so as to deter or prevent crime.

(i) Give an example of a pro-actively based investigation, stating what type of information is acquired.
(ii) What types of crimes necessarily require pro-active investigation?
(iii) Do you think that pro-active investigation is more cost-effective than responsive investigation?

involved that the crime is kept private. Examples include supplying and taking drugs and smuggling. Serious crime of all classes (including terrorist offences) is always best investigated pro-actively, but legislation is as important in restraining the actions of investigators *before* the commital of a crime as it is when a suspect is held in custody. For example, the police service has no universal right to intercept private correspondence or to use covert surveillance in private dwellings and such practices must remain within the law.

(iii) This is something of a hypothetical question, but it raises a number of interesting albeit complex issues. Whether or not pro-active investigation is more cost-effective than reactive investigation depends upon the nature of the crime and how the costing is done. It could be argued that the investigation of serious crime after the event involves the sifting of a large volume of evidence which is extraordinarily expensive and where a successful outcome is uncertain and that, therefore, pro-activity saves money. Of course, there is more at stake than cost. Pro-active investigation may prevent injury or large-scale criminal damage and it is difficult to attribute a cost to these benefits.

Surveillance and covert policing

Attempt the exercise in Box 7.5.
   Possible answers (see Clark 2008) include:

- The move away from reactive to pro-active policing.
- The availability of high-quality ('near-confession quality') evidence from surveillance.
- The reluctance of members of the public to provide evidence to the police.
- Improvements in surveillance technology with lower risks of detection by the suspect.

One of the latest developments in this field is the automatic number plate recognition system. The technology captures images to identify vehicle number plates. It uses optical character recognition to read the registration mark from passing vehicles. These systems can use images from dedicated cameras, which are primarily in police vehicles, fixed sites, or from existing video cameras which have been modified, such as town centre closed circuit television (CCTV) cameras, as in the 'ring of steel' around the City of London. The ability to centrally search across the UK and analyse ANPR data from all cameras in the

---

Box 7.5 Exercise 7E Police operations

State four reasons why investigators have sought to increase their reliance on the use of covert police surveillance and police operations.

infrastructure have provided excellent intelligence in numerous high-profile investigations including the terrorist attack in June 2007 at Glasgow airport and the links to the failed car bombs in London's West End the same weekend.

The Regulation of Investigatory Powers Act 2000 (RIPA) regulates investigative and other so-called intrusive powers. Such powers may be authorised for a range of purposes, including the investigation of crime (prevention or detection), the protection of public health or to maintain national security. Surveillance, as defined in s.48(2), includes 'monitoring, observing or listening to persons, their movements, their conversation or their other activities or communications'. The recording of anything monitored, observed or listened to (with or without the use of a surveillance device) is also defined as part of 'surveillance'. A distinction is made between surveillance carried out outside of residential properties or vehicles (*directed surveillance*) and surveillance carried out inside properties or vehicles (*intrusive surveillance*).

Codes of practice are issued under s.71 of RIPA and the Police Act 1997 makes interferences lawful if properly authorised. Oversight of RIPA is the responsibility of the Chief Surveillance Commissioner and the Interception of Communications Commissioner. RIPA provides statutory controls on the use of informants or undercover police officers, who are now given the rather grand title of 'covert human intelligence sources' (CHISs). Section 17 of RIPA specifically excludes the use of intercepted communications as evidence in court. This is widely interpreted as a concession to the security and secret intelligence community who are naturally anxious to prevent details of their operations from being revealed in court. However, the consequence of this restriction is that intercepted communications are generally of investigative value only (Box 7.6).

(a) The chief concern is that many informants are criminals themselves and accordingly, that the evidence or information they provide may be dubious or unreliable. The motives of informants must also be subjected to scrutiny. If it is in their interest to provide false information, the defence may legitimately question why such information was provided in the first place. On the other hand, information from informants which is found to link a suspect to a crime and so lead to more evidence being uncovered that is both admissible and credible is a highly valuable part of the investigator's armoury.

Box 7.6 Exercise 7F Informant information and entrapment

(a) What might be the concerns of the courts in relying upon information from informants?

(b) 'Entrapment' is a form of pro-active policing which involves the creation of circumstances that may lead to crime followed by prosecution of that crime. What might be the objections to the use of this tactic by the police?

(b) Entrapment may be thought of as 'state-created crime'. Since the state is also effectively the prosecuting authority, cases of entrapment are sometimes viewed as abuses of state power, and prosecution cases based on such events may be dismissed by the courts. Large-scale entrapment operations are relatively rare because of their contentious nature and because of the associated operational costs.

Stop and search

Most 'stop and searches' are authorised under PACE 1984 and the purposes of 'stop and search' powers are defined in s.1.4 of Code A:

> The primary purposes of stop and search powers are to enable officers to allay or confirm suspicions about individuals without exercising their power of arrest. Officers may be required to justify the use or authorisation of such powers, in relation both to individual searches and the overall pattern of their activity in this regard, to their supervisory officers or in court.

Two things are apparent from this definition. The first is that stop and search may be regarded as a pro-active form of investigation. Second, the use of stop and search has to be justified. It is a power that cannot be used lightly and police officers who use this power may be held accountable for their actions.

PACE dictates that even when a person is prepared to submit to a search voluntarily, that person must not be searched unless the legal power exists. The only exception applies to searches of persons entering sports grounds or other premises carried out with their consent given as a condition of entry. Where the power to stop and search requires 'reasonable suspicion', the statement (in s.2.2) that there must be an *objective basis* for 'reasonable suspicion' effectively outlaws stop and searches based on stereotypical images, gender or race. Furthermore, the responses of individuals being stopped and searched cannot be used retrospectively by a police officer as the basis for reasonable suspicion.

The Criminal Justice Act 2003, linked to governmental initiatives to help combat antisocial behaviour, extended the powers of police officers to look for articles concerning the commission of the offence of criminal damage as defined in s.1 of the Criminal Damage Act 1971. It also widened the definition of prohibited articles (PACE 1984, s.1) to include objects connected with criminal damage, including spray cans, and allows for non-police officers (e.g. IT experts) to take an active part in the search provided that they remain accompanied by a police officer.

The powers of 'stop and search' under the Terrorism Act 2000 are discussed in Box 7.7.

Health and safety

The Health and Safety At Work Act 1974 and Police (Health and Safety) Act 1997 also apply to investigations. Risk assessments must be carried out under the

Box 7.7 Case study 1 Report of the MPA scrutiny on MPS stop-and-search practice

http://www.ligali.org/resource/mpa_scrutiny_on_mps_stop_and_search_practice.pdf

The Metropolitan Police Authority's (MPA's) Report of the MPA scrutiny on MPS stop-and-search practice provided a snapshot of practice between June 2003 and January 2004 together with detailed discussions of what is a complex phenomenon. The statistics showed that the proportion of people from black and minority ethnic groups stopped has been increasing. Most stops and searches were justified by the police as part of investigations into illegal drug activity. The fact that members of the black and minority ethnic population are disproportionately stopped and searched may lead to further alienation of these groups from the police service. On the other hand, it may be argued that the legitimate use of stop-and-search powers contributes to crime reduction and crime prevention.

Case study 2 The Terrorism Act 2000

http://www.opsi.gov.uk/acts/acts2000/ukpga_20000011_en_1

Stop and search in relation to terrorism offences is the subject of separate legislation. Under s.43(1) of the Terrorism Act 2000, a constable may stop and search a person whom the officer reasonably suspects to be a terrorist to discover whether the person is in possession of anything which may constitute evidence that the person is a terrorist. The arrest power under the same Act (s.41 (1)) is that a constable may arrest without a warrant a person whom he or she reasonably suspects to be a terrorist.

However, the police have the authority to designate areas as 'cordoned areas' and within these further powers apply (s.44): constables have the right to stop and search vehicles, drivers and pedestrians. There is no requirement that the constable should have reasonable suspicion.

The use of s.44 to stop and search individuals who are 'simple protestors' and who have been exercising their right to protest peacefully was declared a breach of the European Convention on Human Rights by the European Court of Human Rights in December 2009, and the UK government's appeal against the ruling was refused in June 2010. Examples of the concerns of such legislation will be found on the Liberty website at http://www.liberty-human-rights.org.uk/ and the ECHR declaration is reported at http://www.guardian.co.uk/uk/2010/jan/12/terrorism-stop-and-search-illegal.

In March 2010, The Equality and Human Rights Commission (EHRC) published its 'Stop and Think Review'. The report, including its recommendations, is available at: http://www.equalityhumanrights.com/uploaded_files/raceinbritain/ehrc_stop_and_search_report.pdf.

In line with previous reports, the review expresses concern over the disproportional numbers of black and Asian searches. It also contains some interesting statistics and conclusions:

- It is estimated that searches only reduced the number of 'disruptive' crimes' by 0.2 per cent.
- Neighbouring police areas often have markedly different search statistics.
- In 2008/2009, there were one million searches conducted under PACE and 256,000 under s.44 of the Terrorism Act.
- Of the searches conducted under s.44, only 0.6 per cent led to a subsequent arrest.

In July 2010, and following a change of government, the new Home Secretary Theresa May reported to Parliament that in accordance with a judgment of the ECHR the use of s.44 to stop and search individuals would be suspended. Therefore police must now use other powers where appropriate, including those based on reasonable suspicion under s.43.

Management of Health and Safety at Work Regulations 1999. Attempt the exercise given in Box 7.8.

In (1), there are risks that the officer could be identified and attacked or caught up in a public order situation; therefore it may be more appropriate to send a pair of uniformed officers wearing body armour who remain in contact with the control room. In (2), the potential dangers of a booby-trap device or of dealing with explosive materials may require that explosives specialists accompany police officers. In (3), the potential for an ambush, the disruption of radio signals

---

Box 7.8 Exercise 7G Risks and control measures

Briefly consider the risks and 'control measures' that might apply to the following parts of a long-standing investigation:

1. A detective constable is sent to retrieve a car registration document from a lock-up located in an area with a high level of crime and social unrest.
2. A team is dispatched to check out the flat of a potential suicide bomber.
3. A surveillance operator follows a suspect into an old abandoned multi-storey warehouse.

and the presence of dangerously dilapidated buildings would probably result in an instruction to the operative to delay entry until support arrives.

The senior investigating officer (SIO)

In most police forces the investigation of serious crime is led on an all-force basis, through specialised units (e.g. Major Crime Unit, Drug Squad, Child Protection Unit, Special Branch, Fraud Squad). The police officer in charge of an investigation or review into serious crime, and the individual primarily responsible for fulfilling the operational requirements of CPIA for that investigation, is known as the *senior investigating officer* (SIO). He or she must be both experienced and well trained, with a history of successful and properly conducted investigations. Their training will have been equivalent to Level 3 under the Professionalising Investigation Programme. Figure 7.1 illustrates some of the responsibilities of an SIO and it is clear that many of them relate to the legislation discussed in this chapter. Although training and an analytical and reflective mind are required to produce a good investigator, experience is also essential. If you have the opportunity, watch how senior investigators approach their work; how they bring out the best in others and use the expertise of others; and how they create time and space away from the fine operational detail of the investigation in order to identify the next stage in its progress.

Interviewing young and vulnerable people

PACE offers certain protection for those in custody which applies to all detainees, but legislation also exists which applies to particularly vulnerable persons. It is important to understand that vulnerability (e.g. to questioning) depends on the individual as well as the circumstances. Generalising, if two suspects are posed the same questions at interview and endure the same conditions of detention, it is unlikely that they will react in similar ways and there will be 'a spectrum of

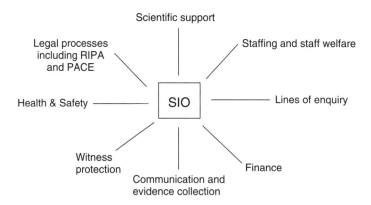

Figure 7.1 Responsibilities of an SIO.

vulnerability' from (at one extreme) a person who will confess to anything to please the interviewer and (at the other extreme) someone who will sit in stony silence. Ultimately, it will be the court that will decide whether or not the evidence which the police have obtained from such suspects is reliable.

PACE 1984 (s.1) effectively specifies vulnerable persons as including those under 17 years of age, the blind, deaf and the mentally vulnerable. Taking a mentally disordered person as an example, he or she should only be interviewed in the presence of a relative or a person experienced in dealing with mental disorders.

Usually police officers compile a written statement of the information that a witness provides but in some situations a video interview is carried out. The police take into consideration the witness's age, physical and mental state and vulnerability. If the witness is under the age of 17 in a case which is likely to go to court, they will almost always video record the interview.

In such cases the police officer will explain the procedure to the witness but will not discuss the evidence before the interview is recorded. This is to ensure that the most accurate description of what the witness saw or knows is contained in the video, so providing the best evidence possible.

Vulnerability may obviously extend from the police station to the court, and concerns that some witnesses in court are likely to suffer fear or distress if they give evidence in the traditional way are reflected in the Youth Justice and Criminal Evidence Act 1999. For example, a young witness may be allowed to give evidence by live audio link or (if giving evidence in person) from behind a screen. Such special measures do not apply to the accused.

The subject of vulnerable adult witnesses is considered in further detail by Stone (2009). Such witnesses with learning disabilities, mental disorders or those who are easily intimidated, are not always identified by the police or CPS. Government guidance (Achieving Best Evidence in Criminal Proceedings: Guidance on Interviewing Victims and Witnesses and Special Measures 2007) provides a series of prompts to help officers identify vulnerable witnesses (e.g. witnesses who appear to have difficulty understanding questions, have limited speech, have a short attention span, are unable to read or write, are unable to remember personal information, or those who repeat what officers say) (Box 7.9).

Intrusions into traditional freedoms as a consequence of police action

A recurring theme of this chapter will now be examined further: the conflict that may occur between the need for more intrusion into people's lives and traditional freedoms in order to facilitate the prevention or investigation of serious offences.

Some observers are particularly concerned that legislation principally designed for one purpose is now being used for another previously unforeseen purpose and that there appears to have been very little political debate about the application of such legislation. A frequently cited example is the Protection from Harassment Act 1997, an act widely believed to have been designed to protect individuals

---

Box 7.9 Case study Research

What makes a good investigative interviewer of children?

Rebecca Wright and Martine Powell (2007) attempted to establish the factors that make a good interviewer of children in child abuse cases by the in-depth interviewing of 23 police officers from three states in Australia. The aim of any investigative interview is to extract an accurate and detailed account of any relevant information. Information that is obtained from several sources may then be used to corroborate the account of the victim. This is particularly important with child abuse, since physical and medical evidence is sometimes lacking. Young witnesses require skilful interviewing since they have a less developed sense of time than adults.

The study showed that the limitations in the competency of police officers in child interviewing are not simply a reflection of their ability to ask open-ended questions. The personal skills of the police officer are also important in developing a rapport with the child, with some officers believing that certain officers are naturally better at interviewing than others. This does not prove that interviewing skills cannot be improved, but it does emphasise that practitioners themselves recognise the importance of personal qualities (such as patience and empathy) in such skilled and demanding work.

---

from stalkers. As early as 2000, a Home Office Report (Harris 2000) showed that the Act was rarely used for 'classic' stalking cases and that it may have been inappropriately used in some cases, particularly where a civil remedy was available. One likely reason that the 1997 Act is favoured by police officers is that like ASBOs, it is preventive in nature: so that, for example, action (such as a restraining order) can be taken without having to await for an assault to take place.

The use of covert surveillance by Poole Borough Council to monitor whether a family lived in the school catchment area made the headlines in August 2010 when the Investigatory Powers Tribunal ruled that this was a disproportionate use of RIPA and was therefore illegal. The coalition government, elected in 2010, have stated that RIPA powers should only be used to investigate serious crime.

One could argue that the practice of storing personal data is over 100 years old, as illustrated by the creation of a vehicle register after the Motor Car Act 1903. The vehicle register was created so that vehicles and their owners could be traced in the event that a vehicle was involved in a crime or accident, and the modern Police National Computer (PNC) system may be viewed as an elaborate extension of this early database. In modern times a more controversial issue has been the extent to which it is appropriate for the police service to investigate, store and pass on personal information in the interests of public protection (i.e. to prevent criminal offences occurring in the future). This is sometimes called 'preventive intelligence gathering'. The exchange of such data has always been regarded as acceptable when vetting individuals who work under the Official Secrets Act but its extension to 'ordinary serious crimes' is much more recent. The Bichard inquiry into the murders of Jessica Chapman and Holly Wells revealed failures in information sharing about the murderer Ian Huntley's past. Although Huntley had no previous convictions before his arrival in Cambridgeshire, many allegations had been made that he had committed sexual offences in Humberside, and had these been known to the local authority in Cambridgeshire it would have almost certainly prevented his appointment as a school caretaker.

The implications of the Huntley case are more than simply improving the technology and implementation of data sharing: what has to be decided is *what kind* of behavioural information about an individual should be shared, *with whom* and *when*. In the Huntley case, it could be argued that the allegations, although unproven, were of sufficient weight to justify transmission and disclosure to a potential employer. What of other cases? Just how far should the police go in recording and collating individual behavioural traits and who decides when such traits, although they did not lead to successful prosecution of the individual, are sufficiently worrying to justify wider dissemination? One of the UK Labour government's responses to the Huntley case to these and similar questions has been the creation of the Independent Safeguarding Authority (ISA; see Chapter 14); although the UK Conservative Liberal Democrat Government (elected 2010) has indicated that it may give the ISA a narrower focus.

The traditional and overriding objective of criminal investigators of securing a conviction in the courts (in other words, of establishing the guilt of the suspect) is not always regarded as the best way of preventing a crime. This is most obvious in some terrorist investigations, where attempting to collect and present evidence of criminal activity for court cases poses two disadvantages. First, revealing police methods and information sources in open court may be damaging to subsequent or ongoing operations. Second, such investigations are complicated, time consuming, and insofar as criminal convictions in court are concerned, uncertain in their outcome when the stakes for society (particularly in terrorist cases) are very high. A controversial response to these perceived disadvantages has included UK Labour government plans to introduce a 42-day pre-charge detention for certain terrorist suspects, proposals which were later rejected by Parliament. Equally controversial is the introduction of 'control orders' under the Prevention of Terrorism Act 2005. Such control orders represent a shift away from making the production of evidence the highest priority in terrorism matters: control orders are controversial because they can be applied to individuals even if they have not been proven to have been involved in crime. The use of such control orders, often portrayed as a 'last resort', has been supported by Lord Carlisle, the UK government's independent reviewer on counter-terrorism legislation (Box 7.10).

If legislation such as control orders can be justified, it is because the impact of terrorist crime is so much greater than acquisitive crime, for example (such as burglary.) William Blackstone once said that 'it is better that ten guilty escape than one innocent suffers'. It may not be too far-fetched to suggest that in the interests of preventing very rare events that lead to mass panic or large-scale

---

Box 7.10 Exercise 7H Control orders

How might 'Control Orders' be justified?

---

damage or injury, modern anti-terrorist laws legitimise an alternative philosophy: that of protecting the rights of the many against those of the few. However, even if such a view is correct, it does not abrogate the police service from attempting to communicate the principles of its actions to the public.

In his paper 'Slippery Slopes and Civil Libertarian Pessimism', Waddington (2005) attempts to counterbalance some of the pessimism about the erosion of human rights. He places civil libertarian pessimism at the erosion of freedoms in its historical context and gives examples of where civil liberties have been enhanced and extended.

Police and the media

It is well known that the press obtain much of their information about investigations from official police sources and that the police service uses televised broadcasts to seek further information from members of the public. However, the relationship between the police service and the media is in fact more complicated and controversial than such a simple description suggests, and in 2008 the Home Office Affairs Committee (a select committee of MPs) announced its intention to probe this relationship more deeply. Its report, published in 2009, is available on the internet.

The committee was particularly concerned with the damage caused by off-the-record briefings by police officers and also with allegations that some police forces were attempting to 'spin' crime figures by not releasing crime information to the media. The committee also investigated the way in which a Channel 4 programme, *Undercover Mosque*, was dealt with by the West Midlands Police (Box 7.11).

Box 7.11 Case study *Undercover Mosque*

On 15 January 2007, Channel 4 broadcast a programme entitled *Undercover Mosque*, which included footage of extracts from the speeches of several speakers in mosques and other organisations which contained extreme and offensive views by three speakers about non-Muslims, women and gay people. The speeches had been recorded covertly and sold to Channel 4.

West Midlands Police (WMP) and the Crown Prosecution Service examined the footage. It was decided that there was insufficient evidence to convict the speakers recorded on tape on charges such as stirring up

---

racial hatred and soliciting murder. However, WMP and the CPS believed at the time that Channel 4 had distorted the meaning of the speakers by editing the tapes. WMP asked CPS to consider whether any prosecution could be brought against Channel 4 for broadcasting material likely to stir up racial hatred. WMP also referred this matter to Ofcom, the media regulator, believing that the broadcasting had undermined community cohesion and feelings of public reassurance, as well as the safety of those communities in the West Midlands.

Ofcom investigated the film and concluded that Channel 4 had broadcast the film accurately and that *Undercover Mosque* was a legitimate investigation, uncovering matters of high public interest. Channel 4 took legal action against WMP and the CPS, and won their case. WMP and CPS publicly recognised that the film had not been misleading.

Both the WPS and CPS were widely criticised for referring this matter to Ofcom because such an action might be interpreted as an attempt to restrict the freedom of expression by the public and other organisations. To refer the film to Ofcom in the knowledge that the film *was* accurate might imply that the goals of improved public confidence and social cohesion took precedence over the truth and the right of organisations to bring to the public's attention matters which are both important and interesting, but it appears that WPS/CPS acted solely because they believed the film was inaccurately portrayed.

References and suggested further reading

Ashworth, A. and Redmayne, M. (2005) *The Criminal Process*, Oxford University Press, Oxford.

Clark, D. (2004) *The Investigation of Crime*, Lexis Nexis Butterworths, London.

—— (2008) 'Covert surveillance and Informer Handling', in Newburn, T., Williamson, T. and Wright, A. (ed.) *Handbook of Criminal Investigation*, Willan, Cullompton (this chapter also contains a short section on 'Preventative Intelligence Gathering'). pp. 426–450.

Cook, T. and Tattersall, A. (2008) *Blackstone's Senior Investigating Officer's Handbook,* Oxford University Press, Oxford.

Harfield, C. and Harfield, K. (2008) *Covert Investigation: A Practical Guide for Investigators* (Blackstone's Practical Policing), Oxford University Press, Oxford.

Harris (2000) Reference is http://rds.homeoffice.gov.uk/rds/pdfs/r130.pdf (accessed 7 March 2011).

Home Office (2002) *Vulnerable Witnesses: A Police Service Guide*, Home Office, London

—— (2010) 'What perceptions do the UK public have concerning the impact of counter-terrorism legislation implemented since 2000?' *Occasional paper 88*, HMSO, London.

Hopkins, M. (2009) 'Why are Arson Detection Rates so Low? A Study of the Factors that Promote and Inhibit the Detection of Arson', *Policing*, 3, 1: 78–88.

Neyroud, P.W. and Beckley, A. (2001) *Policing, Ethics and Human Rights,* Willan, Publishing, Cullompton, Devon.

Ozin, P., Norton, H. and Spivey, P. (2006) *PACE: A Practical Guide to the Police and Criminal Evidence Act 1984* (Blackstone's Practical Policing), Oxford University Press, Oxford.

Roberts, P. (2008) 'Law and Criminal Investigation', in Newburn, T., Williamson, T. and Wright, A. (eds) *Handbook of Criminal Investigation*, Willan Publishing, Cullompton, Devon.

Rowe, M. (2008) *Introduction to Policing*, Sage, London.

Sanders, A. and Young, R. (2008) 'Police Powers', in Newburn, T. (ed.), *Handbook of Policing* (2nd edn), Willan, Cullompton.

Schollum, M. (2005) *Investigative Interviewing – The Literature*, Office of the Commissioner of Police, Wellington, New Zealand.

Stone, K. (2009) 'Criminal Justice and Vulnerable Adults: Who Does What?', in Pritchard, J., *Good Practice in the Law and Safeguarding Adults*, Jessica Kingsley, London.

Waddington, P.A.J. (2005) 'Slippery Slopes and Civil Libertarian Pessimism', *Policing and Society*, 15, 3: 353–75.

Wright, R. and Martine B Powell, M.B. (2007) 'What Makes a Good Investigative Interviewer of Children?', *Policing: An International Journal of Police Strategies and Management*, 30, 1: 21–31.

Useful websites

http://www.opsi.gov.uk/acts/acts1996/ukpga_19960025_en_1
The Criminal Procedure and Investigations Act 1996
http://www.opsi.gov.uk/acts/acts2000/ukpga_20000034_en_1
The Race Relations (Amendment) Act 2000
http://www.lawgazette.co.uk/in-practice/law-reports/criminal-law-4
Commissioner of Police of the Metropolis v. Mohamed Raissi (November 2008)
http://www.cps.gov.uk/victims_witnesses/code.html
The 'Code for Crown Prosecutors'
http://www.police.govt.nz/resources/2005/investigative-interviewing/
The Schollum review of the literature on investigative interviewing (2005)
http://security.homeoffice.gov.uk/ripa/about-ripa/
The Regulation of Investigatory Powers Act (RIPA) 2000
http://www.police-foundation.org.uk/files/POLICE0001/Briefing%20-%20Stop%20%20Search%20Final.pdf
A section on 'stop and search' published in November 2008 in *The Briefing* by the Police Foundation
http://www.npia.police.uk/pip
The Professionalising Investigation Programme
http://www.opsi.gov.uk/acts/acts1999/ukpga_19990023_en_1
Youth Justice and Criminal Evidence Act 1999
http://www.cps.gov.uk/publications/docs/achieving_best_evidence_final.pdf
Achieving Best Evidence in Criminal Proceedings: Guidance on Interviewing Victims and Witnesses and Special Measures (2007 revision)
http://www.harassment-law.co.uk/pdf/rds.pdf
The Protection from Harassment Act 1997 – an evaluation of its use and effectiveness. Jessica Harris – Home Office Research, Development and Statistics Directorate 2000

http://www.homeoffice.gov.uk/rds/pdfs/r130.pdf

The Bichard Inquiry (2004) initiated as a response to the Solam Murders

http://www.homeoffice.gov.uk/publications/counter-terrorism/independent-reviews/ind-rev-terrorism-annual-rep-09?view = Binary

A report by Lord Carlisle (2010), the independent reviewer of terrorism legislation

http://www.official-documents.gov.uk/document/other/9781849871518/9781849871518.pdf

Fifth Report of the independent reviewer pursuant to section 14(3) of the prevention of Terrorism Act 2005 by Lord Carlisle, February 2010

http://www.telegraph.co.uk/news/uknews/law-and-order/7879164/Anti-terrorism-stop-and-search-powers-dropped.html

Suspension of the use of s.44 Terrorism Act 2000

http://rds.homeoffice.gov.uk/rds/pdfs10/occ88.pdf

What perceptions do the UK public have concerning the impact of counter-terrorism legislation since 2000? Occasional Paper 88, Home Office, March 2010

http://www.telegraph.co.uk/news/uknews/law-and-order/7922427/Councils-warned-over-unlawful-spying-using-anti-terror-legislation.html

Councils warned over unlawful spying using anti-terror (RIPA 2000) legislation

http://www.publications.parliament.uk/pa/cm200809/cmselect/cmhaff/75/7503.htm

Home Affairs Committee, Police and the Media, Second Report of Session 2008–9

8   Methods of investigation

Introduction

This chapter will explore the subject of methods of investigation. It will be divided into different yet connected areas, such as the use of hypothesis in investigations and methods of investigations. It will consider a model for the investigative process, heuristic knowledge, the investigative mindset, the importance of the golden hour in investigations and what happens during the early stages of a missing person case. Further, it will consider what positive actions can be taken when dealing with domestic violence incidents, and the importance of forensic evidence and its role in investigation. It also includes a brief introduction to the National Intelligence Model (NIM) and the management of critical investigations.

The use of hypothesis in investigation

The definition of a hypothesis is 'as a suggested explanation for a group of facts either accepted as a basis for further verification or accepted as likely to be true' (Collins English Dictionary 2009). ACPO (2005a: 70) describes a hypothesis as 'building a scenario that best explains the available material'. Hypotheses can aid an investigator to progress investigations according to ACPO (2005a: 70), explaining that an investigator must consider the following before using hypotheses:

- Has all the available material been gathered?
- Does the investigator understand all the material?
- Are there lines of enquiry which have not yet been pursued and which could generate more material?
- What benefit will the use of a hypothesis bring to the investigation?

It will depend on the amount of material an investigator has gathered whether he or she will decide to use hypotheses. ACPO (2005a) states that it is generally the case that investigations progress because the material gathered generates actions, which in turn generates more material. This continues until enough material has been obtained to identify a suspect and support a successful prosecution. It is often the case that the link between the material and the subsequent action is straightforward enough and does not require an investigator to form a hypothesis.

However, ACPO (2005a) acknowledges that there are times when the amount of material available to an investigator does not identify the actions necessary to further the investigation of the case. In these cases hypotheses may enable the investigator to regain the momentum of the investigation.

An investigator will apply the investigative mindset when locating, gathering and using material; once done, all the material should be evaluated using the investigative and evidential evaluation process which will be discussed later in this review. This ensures that all the material is explored fully and all the potential of the material is identified. It will also indicate what further actions are necessary (ACPO 2005a).

Hypotheses are also useful when an investigator is testing the interpretation that has been put on material gathered, and will decide if this interpretation is reasonable. If alternative hypotheses can be formed from the same material it may direct enquiries and the investigation to help confirm which interpretation is likely to be correct. This is helpful with the investigator's decision making as well as being useful during the investigation, and is also a very useful way of looking at the possible interpretations of material in court.

It is important to remember that hypotheses which are formed from uncertain or limited information can only lead to an assumption of what occurred and this can possibly be influenced by stereotyping or personal bias, so investigators should avoid trying to fill gaps in material during the early stages of investigation with hypotheses about what happened; they really need to have sufficient knowledge before developing hypotheses. It is advisable that investigators seek advice from colleagues or supervisors, and ACPO (2005a) suggests that in serious or more complex cases the assistance of a behavioural investigative adviser (BIA) from the Specialist Operations Centre which is part of the NPIA is sought.

It is likely, therefore, that there will be a series of hypotheses, each of them offering an alternative explanation (ACPO 2005a).

Hypotheses are developed to facilitate investigators in seeking further material or to test interpretations put on material that has already been gathered. The collection of further material may prove one particular hypothesis to be correct (ACPO 2005a).

ACPO (2005a: 73) outlines some considerations that have to be met when building hypotheses:

- Ensuring a thorough understanding of the relevance and reliability of all material gathered.
- Ensuring that the investigative and evidential test has been applied to all material gathered in the investigation.
- Ensuring there is sufficient knowledge of the subject matter to interpret the material correctly.

- Defining a clear objective for the hypothesis.
- Developing hypotheses that 'best fit' with the known material.
- Consulting with colleagues and experts to formulate hypotheses.
- Ensuring sufficient resources are available to develop or test the hypotheses.
- Ensuring that hypothesis building is proportionate to the seriousness of the offence (Box 8.1).

Box 8.1   Exercise 8A Building a hypothesis

- Consider a criminal offence that you have dealt with or are aware of through the media. Using the information provided in this chapter, build a hypothesis or a series of hypotheses about the case.

Methods of a criminal investigation

ACPO (2005a) describes two methods of criminal investigation – pro-active and reactive. The pro-active method is sometimes referred to as intelligence-led or covert investigation. ACPO (2005a) further explains that the main difference between reactive and pro-active methods are that the reactive method starts with the discovery of a crime that has been committed and seeks to bring offenders to justice by gathering material that identifies suspects and provides sufficient evidence for a court to decide upon their guilt. The techniques of reactive investigation focus on the interviewing of victims, witnesses and suspects, the examination of the scene and the development of forensic links between the offence and the suspect. ACPO (2005a: 47) states that 'The proactive method usually starts with an intelligence analysis that a particular individual or group is involved in criminal enterprise'. This is commonly organised crime such as people trafficking, fraud or drug dealing. Since individual instances of such crimes are often not reported to the police it is usually the case that reactive methods of investigation cannot be used. This results in the necessity for investigators to adopt a range of covert surveillance techniques which can link offenders to the criminal enterprise. These surveillance techniques are often used alongside forensic science techniques and financial investigations. Both of these methods of investigation have been discussed fully in Chapter 6.

A model for investigative process

According to ACPO (2005a) the type of material gathered by an investigator and the type of activity that an investigator engages in is dependent upon whether the investigator used the reactive or pro-active method of investigation. Both types of investigation undergo a similar process. This process is shown in Figure 8.1

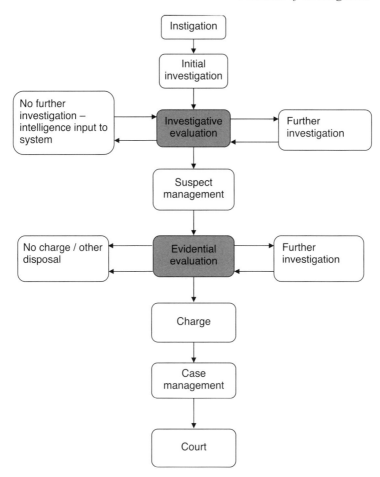

Figure 8.1 The processes of investigation.

The basic elements of this process are discussed more fully below.

Instigation

Criminal investigations may be instigated in a number of ways according to ACPO (2005a: 49):

- Report from the general public such as attendance at police stations, phone calls, online and to patrol officers.
- Referral by other agencies.
- Intelligence links to other crimes (linked series).
- Re-investigation as a result of new information, cold case or other type of review.
- Discovered as a consequence of other police actions.

Force policy will guide the patrol officers, public counter staff or call takers as to the information that needs to be gathered and the action that is to be taken in any given case. All staff should be mindful that they are commencing an investigation and the material they receive is relevant to the investigator, and should be recorded and retained and communicated to the investigating officer. If the investigators are aware of and familiar with the investigative strategies they will be able to exploit early opportunities and to gather material by means of questioning (ACPO 2005a).

ACPO (2005a) describes sources of instigation in pro-active investigations; these are often called intelligence packages by investigators and they have been developed by national, force or local intelligence systems. These systems can identify individuals or groups who are involved in ongoing criminal activity:

- Crime pattern analysis
- Market profiles
- Network analysis
- Target profile analysis
- Operational intelligence assessment
- Tactical assessment
- Problem profile
- Tactical profile.

Initial investigations

It is not necessary for every report of a crime to require an initial investigation. For example, referrals from other agencies and intelligence packages would usually be allocated for further investigation without any need for initial investigation. That said, the majority of reports of crime are dealt with by deploying police officers to a scene. Some forces deal with the initial investigation entirely over the telephone prior to making a decision as to whether any further investigation is necessary (ACPO 2005a). Whether over the telephone or in person, the initial investigation is a vital stage in gathering material that can lead to the detection of crime. Those involved in the initial investigation must take positive action to ensure material is not lost. For example, scenes that are not secured will deteriorate quickly, CCTV images may be recorded over days later if they are not recovered immediately, and witnesses who are not interviewed straight away may be contaminated by talking about the events with others. It is recognised by ACPO (2005a: 50) that officers who are deployed to incidents are likely to have a variety of competing demands placed upon them as they arrive; 'before they can begin an investigation they may have to:

- deal with a violent situation;
- provide first aid and call for medical assistance;
- reassure victims and witnesses;
- prevent public disorder.'

Once these demands are dealt with an officer can then plan how best to conduct the investigation. It may well be that the officer who attends the scene is the only investigator throughout the enquiry as the majority of crimes reported to the police are not major incidents (ACPO 2005a). During complicated investigations the distinction between the initial and further investigation may not be clear. ACPO (2005a: 51) discusses when the initial investigation phase is complete:

- The investigator has obtained an account from the victim and any witnesses who are immediately available (individual force policy will determine whether these accounts are obtained in the form of a witness statement (MG11), notebook entry or verbally).
- The immediate needs of victims and witnesses have been met.
- The crime scene investigation has been instigated.
- All fast-track actions indicated by the material to hand have been taken.
- All records required by the CPIA and individual force policy have been made.
- All intelligence gathered during the initial investigation has been submitted.

ACPO (2005a) discusses why it is important for comprehensive records during the initial investigation to be completed. These will aid the investigator during his or her investigative evaluation; they will add to the intelligence picture of crime in the area; the quality of the investigation may be assessed by supervisors; and they will facilitate a comprehensive hand-over of the investigation if it is allocated to another investigator.

Investigative evaluation

For a case to progress, decisions need to made about the value and meaning of material, and the investigator should continually evaluate material. In some forces a formal evaluation is carried out at the conclusion of the initial investigation by a crime evaluator, who is an investigator with experience, who will be looking at the material gathered and will make a decision as to whether further investigation is required. Investigators should still carry out their own evaluations as new material becomes available (ACPO 2005a).

Further investigation

When intelligence packages or a crime are allocated for further investigation, a clear plan should be decided upon by the investigator about how he or she intends to bring this investigation to a conclusion. Some cases will identify a suspect during the initial investigation, perhaps where victims and witnesses have been able to name them, these cases are likely to move directly to the suspect management phase. When a suspect has not been identified any further investigation will concentrate on gathering material that will lead to the identification of the suspect (ACPO 2005a).

ACPO (2005a: 52) discusses the importance of the investigative plan being based on rigorous evaluation of material and this evaluation should include:

- The specific objectives of the investigation; these will depend on the unique circumstances of the crime and the material that has already been gathered.
- The investigative strategies that are to be used to achieve those objectives.
- The resource requirement of the investigation. In many cases this will be limited to the investigator, crime scene examination and forensic analysis of the material recovered from the scene or the suspect. In more complex cases resource allocation will be greater. It is part of an investigator's responsibility to articulate his or her resource requirements to managers.

Suspect management

A suspect is defined as 'someone who the police would have to caution if they wanted to interview them' (ACPO 2005a). It is required that there are some reasonable, objective grounds for the suspicion, which is based on known facts or information which is relevant to the likelihood that the offence has been committed and that the person they want to question has committed it (ACPO 2005a).

Evidential evaluation

This process takes place when the investigator believes that there is sufficient material to justify charging the suspect. Crown Prosecutors will work closely with the investigators to ensure that the most suitable charges are used for the material that is available to them (ACPO 2005a).

Case management

There is a variety of matters that the investigator needs to manage once a suspect has been charged before the case goes to court. The Crown Prosecution Service (CPS) has responsibility for the prosecution of the case once a suspect has been charged. If it is necessary for any further investigative action the CPS will liaise with the investigator. It is possible that new material arises following the charge, and the impact on the case should be minimal if the investigator has been thorough. All new material needs to be evaluated and any further reasonable lines for enquiry that are identified must be pursued (ACPO 2005a).

The investigative mindset

According to ACPO (2005a) if an investigator applies his or her investigative mindset it will bring some order to the way in which the investigator examines material and therefore makes effective decisions. The mindset is one which can be developed over time with experience and continued use; there is no process guidance that will assist the investigator to develop the mindset. According to ACPO (2005a: 60), 'it is a state of mind or attitude which the investigator adopts'.

ACPO (2005a) describes how an investigator will be enabled to develop a disciplined approach by applying a set of principles; this ensures that appropriate decisions are made and that the decisions are reasonable and can be explained to others.

ACPO (2005a: 60) states the five principles involved in the investigative mindset:

- 'understanding the source of material
- planning and preparation
- examination
- recording and collation
- evaluation.'

These will be discussed further below.

Understanding the source of material

It is argued by ACPO (2005a) that in order to conduct an effective examination of any material it is important to understand the provenance or origin of the material and indeed the characteristics of its source. An understanding of the source of material will assist the investigator in determining whether special measures are available to assist victims/witnesses, for instance.

Planning and preparation

ACPO (2005a) states that the first opportunity an investigator has to examine material is usually the only opportunity. It is true that the process of a crime scene investigation will inevitably alter the scene, and for this reason it is vital to get it right first time. It is important to obtain victims'/witnesses' accounts of events as soon as possible, as their recollection can fade after time and may be contaminated by details they hear from others' accounts. This principle applies for many other sources of material. It is for these reasons that ACPO suggests that an investigator plan carefully in order to ensure that any examination reveals all the available material possible from any particular source. ACPO recommends that investigators work through 'Checklist 4' and should produce a detailed written plan before the examination begins during complex cases to ensure that important material is not missed. Checklist 4 sets out clear objectives for the retrieval of material from sources, identifying the most appropriate method of examination, the need for specialist equipment or expertise and the most appropriate location for the examination.

Examination

This process may be divided into three areas. The source and characteristics will determine the extent to which any of these is relevant:

- **Account** – During interview situations victims, witnesses and suspects provide an account of their knowledge of, or indeed involvement in an incident. The account will be interpreted by the investigator, and the investigator should be able to explain his or her interpretation and findings to others. An investigator should always consider other possible alternative explanations.
- **Clarification** – Once an account has been obtained from a source the investigator should look for and clarify any inconsistencies; these may be tested against other material which has been gathered.
- **Challenge** – It is the case that sources of material which in the first instance can appear to be of unquestionable reliability may indeed be wrong or material that can indicate one thing may eventually turn out to suggest an entirely different scenario. It is therefore advisable for an investigator to continually challenge both the reliability and the meaning of any material gathered. Investigators should always consider that material may be wrong and that all sources may potentially be misleading. Investigators should apply the ABC approach: Assume nothing, Believe nothing, Challenge everything (ACPO 2005a).

Recording and collation

Before an examination can be closed an investigator should always consider the records that need to be made of the examination, how the source should be stored, the security of the source and, if the source is going to be under third-party control, any access arrangements that need to be made (ACPO 2005a).

Evaluation

Any immediate actions that need to be taken will be identified during an evaluation. This may include any fast-track actions that are needed to secure other material or any actions necessary to test the reliability of the source or material (ACPO 2005a).

While applying the investigative mindset investigators should consider the limitations in decision making. They should be careful not to be influenced by first impressions. It is necessary for an investigator to keep an open mind and to remain receptive to alternative explanations and views, and he or she should never rush into making judgements (ACPO 2005a).

The golden hour in investigations

According to the Metropolitan Police (cited in ACPO 2005a: 47), 'Golden hour is the term for the period immediately following the commission of an offence when material is abundant and readily available to the police'. During the period immediately following the report of a crime, positive actions can prevent or minimise the erosion of material and can improve the chances of securing material that will be admissible in court. The Metropolitan Police continue to discuss some considerations for the investigation during the golden hour:

- Victims – It is important to identify victims, provide support and sensitively preserve evidence.
- Scenes – It is vital to identify the scene of a crime, to preserve the scene, and to assess and commence a log of material identified.
- Suspects – It is important to identify possible suspects, arrest them and preserve evidence.
- Witnesses – It is important to identify witnesses, provide support and prioritise them (key and significant). It is also important to take a record of the witness's first account and possible description of any suspect(s).
- Log – It is vital to prepare a log of any decisions made and the rationale of the investigator, the circumstances, resources and conditions.
- Family/community – It is important that the investigator identifies the needs and concerns and expectations of the family or even the community, and ensures these are dealt with sensitively.
- Physical evidence – This needs to be preserved, i.e. – CCTV, escape routes, etc.
- Intelligence – During the golden hour it is important to identify, prioritise, maximise, exploit and consider any intelligence.
- Prevent contamination – Of victims, scenes, witnesses and suspects.
- Lines of responsibility – These need to be identified, people need to be informed, briefings need to take place, and resources need to be coordinated, and all this needs to be reviewed.

Early investigation in missing persons cases

According to ACPO (2005b: 8) a missing person is 'anyone whose whereabouts is unknown whatever the circumstances of disappearance. They will be considered missing until located and their well-being or otherwise established.' Before reading further, attempt the exercise given in Box 8.2).

ACPO (2005b: 18) outlines the responsibilities of the first officers attending a report of a missing person:

- Establish the facts and keep accurate records of what was said and by whom.
- Make an assessment of the circumstances of the disappearance in order to form a judgement regarding the risks to which that person or the community are likely to be exposed. The decision, the evidence supporting it and where the information came from should be recorded on the appropriate form.

Box 8.2   Exercise 8B Missing persons case

Imagine you are on duty and have been called to a report of a missing 15-year-old female from her home. Write down a list of ideas/topics you will need to consider when first attending the home address. When you have done this, compare your list to the ideas below.

- Gather sufficient information about the missing person to enable an effective and thorough investigation to be conducted. The depth of that information will vary according to the assessment of risk. Very detailed information and a lifestyle profile will be needed in high-risk cases.
- Notify a supervisor immediately in high-risk cases. In the case of medium risk do this without undue delay and in all other cases by the end of tour of duty.
- Conduct a search of the premises and its environs in accordance with Section 3.10 Search and Evidence Gathering – 3.17 Sightings.
- Make all immediate relevant enquiries in order to locate the missing person.
- Circulate details of the person reported missing on PNC.
- Circulate details of the person on local information systems.
- Consider obtaining any physical evidence of identity such as recent photographs, fingerprints, DNA samples.
- Identify the person who is the point of contact for the police and assess levels of support required for the family.

Following this initial risk assessment it should be clear with whom the ownership and supervision of the investigation lies. The case should not be left for long periods without any active investigation taking place.

ACPO (2005b) discusses the initial reporting of a missing person and the importance of recording detailed and accurate information about the circumstances of the disappearance at the time of reporting. During the taking of the initial report of a missing person, the person taking the report must ensure that all steps are taken to assess the level of risk and to determine the appropriate course of action. ACPO (2005b: 14) acknowledges that 'missing person reports will need to be resourced in light of priority and competing demands'. This will be decided once all the facts are ascertained and a detailed and accurate record has been taken.

According to ACPO (2005b: 18) the Human Rights Act 1998 'places a positive obligation on police officers to take reasonable action within their powers, to safeguard the rights of individuals who may be at risk'. It is acknowledged that where a person is considered to be at medium or high risk it is necessary to take this positive action at every stage of the missing person investigation.

The judgements made by the initial officer on scene will affect the progress of the investigation significantly. It is vital that the officer understands that he or she is not merely taking details of a report but is conducting an investigation. Officers must consider at all times that this may be the first report of a serious crime. The involvement of a supervisor should be a priority. It is the case that most missing person reports do not lead to major crime investigations but it is the case that where they do, early identification is vital to the investigation (ACPO 2005b).

Positive action when investigating domestic violence incidents

According to Rawstorne (cited in Summers and Hoffman 2002: 32), the police have come under criticism for their responses to domestic violence in the past. During the 1970s it was a topic that feminists concentrated on, calling for the police to take action in what they referred to as 'domestics'. It was rare for a man to be arrested for assaulting his wife or partner back then and the victim was rarely offered assistance. A Home Office Circular 60/1990 stated that 'domestic violence is a crime as serious as assaults by strangers, and … the primary duty of police is to protect the victim and take action against the assailant'. By the 1990s the majority of forces had a domestic violence policy document and most of them had a dedicated domestic violence unit which aimed to provide advice, help, support and information to victims.

Rawstorne (cited in Summers and Hoffman 2002) continues to discuss the fact that domestic violence is a crime and that the police involved in the case must first protect the victim, and anyone else who may be at risk. The second task for the officer is to investigate the offender, securing evidence and eventually bringing the offender to justice. Information should be given to the victim at all stages, and assistance should be provided regarding available resources and the protection of children in the household. There is strong recognition that a multi-agency/interagency approach and coordination has great potential.

The role and importance of forensic evidence

Caddy and Cobb (cited in White 2004: 1) provide a definition of forensic science as 'a science used for the purpose of the law'. They explain that the services of a forensic service provider is required when a police officer investigating an incident will need clarification of three issues:

1. Has a crime been committed?
2. If so, who is responsible?
3. If the person responsible has been traced is there enough evidence to charge the person and support a prosecution?

Forensic science can contribute in the clarification of these issues; when considering whether a crime has been committed, there is, in most cases no doubt. There are sometimes occasions when it is possible that only a scientific examination of items can confirm to the investigator that this is indeed the case (Caddy and Cobb, cited in White 2004).

When considering the issue of who is responsible for the crime, if a latent fingerprint is recovered from the scene and that person's fingerprint is on the database, it is likely that the person has been identified. It is also possible that a suspect can be identified if he or she has bled at the scene, or if other bodily fluids have been recovered, possibly in a sexual assault. Specific identification of an offender may not be discovered following scientific examination; the examination could provide useful leads which could then allow the investigator to narrow the field of enquiry (Caddy and Cobb, cited in White 2004).

With regard to the question 'Is the suspect responsible?' it is often the case that a diligent police investigator will be able to provide a suspect, and the investigator will need the forensic scientist to examine the evidence and provide corroborative evidence to enable a charge to be made and subsequently help the court to decide guilt. The forensic service provider will usually be directed to two aspects, as explained by Caddy and Cobb (cited in White 2004: 8):

1. 'Examination of material left on the victim or at the scene which is characteristic of the suspect.
2. Examination of the clothing and property of the suspect for the presence of material of the victim or the scene.'

The ultimate role of the forensic scientist is to present an expert testimony to the court that is trying the issue and, when fulfilling this role, he or she is solely responsible and accountable for the experimental results presented and for the opinions expressed. His or her duties will include:

- Examining material that has been collected and submitted by an investigator with an aim to providing information that was previously unknown or to corroborate information that is already available.
- Provide the investigator with a written report containing all the results from any examination; this will enable the investigator to identify an offender or possibly corroborate other evidence which will facilitate the preparation of a case.
- To present written and/or verbal evidence to the court which will aid it to reach an appropriate decision as to the guilt or innocence of the defendant.

According to ACPO (2005a), forensic science will allow the investigator to maximise the potential of any material found during the crime scene investigation phase. Forensics may also prove useful to the investigator in providing information that may be used during interview.

A brief introduction to the National Intelligence Model

The National Intelligence Model (NIM) is discussed in greater depth elsewhere in this book. However, it is vital to understand NIM in the context of investigation procedures. Maguire (cited in Newburn 2008: 456) describes how in the United Kingdom interest in, and the use of, problem-solving approaches has grown steadily over recent years, and has been given 'significant new momentum by the linking up of two major policy initiatives which had previously been pursued largely in isolation from each other: the implementation of the National Intelligence Model (NIM) and the development of Crime and Disorder Reduction Partnerships (CDRPs).' Maguire continues to explain that the NIM is based on the notion that the core business of policing is to:

> collect relevant information to allow clear and accurate identification and analysis of current and likely future 'problem'; to prioritise the most important of these problems and plan responses to them; to implement plans; and, finally, to evaluate what has been done to feed back the experience and knowledge.

ACPO (2007) states that the NIM is a business model that is used by the police service, which is being increasingly used by other partners, and which ensures that policing is delivered in a targeted manner through the development of intelligence and information. It is helpful, as it can prioritise issues and allocate resources to deal with these issues. ACPO (2007: 6) lists the aspects of operational and investigational policing practices that the NIM applies to:

- Direct patrols
- Target prolific and priority offenders, and resolve crime and disorder problems
- Work effectively with partner agencies
- Drive problem solving
- Improve road safety
- Manage priority locations and high-risk issues
- Guide neighbourhood policing activity
- Increase the understanding of criminality and antisocial behaviour issues.

ACPO (2007) continues to explain that NIM is based on pro-active policing methods which identify, understand and address underlying problems and trends. Looking at the bigger picture NIM allows for prioritisation of police activity which in turn makes it easier for the police to respond to the increasing demands placed upon them. It is possible, however, for elements of NIM to be used in reactive investigations, for example, when establishing a fuller picture of an issue under investigation and directing resources.

Managing critical investigations

ACPO (2005b: 30) states that a critical incident is: 'any incident where the effectiveness of the police response is likely to have a significant impact on the confidence of the victim and/or the victim's family and/or the community'.

ACPO (2005b) continues to explain that the police can find guidance within the *Murder Investigation Manual*; this guidance may be applied to the management of critical incidents which can be classed as critical. The decision of whether or not an incident is critical normally lies with command or the control room, and this decision will initiate the local Critical Incident Plan; this usually sees the appointment of a senior investigating officer, along with the adoption of a major incident room to manage the enquiry. When a decision is made that an incident is critical there are immediate consequences, so it is better to make the decision early rather than delay. One of the benefits of calling it critical is that it makes the deployment of other national assets available.

Conclusion

It is clear that material is an important element in an investigation and the use of hypotheses can aid an investigator when looking for more material and when testing theories. It is also argued that material and information discovered during an investigation can aid pro-active (intelligence-led) policing methods as well as reactive methods, and that it is sometimes the case that both methods may be used side by side.

This chapter has also discussed the importance of the model of investigative process, and how it can guide an investigator through decision making during an investigation. The investigator's mindset has also been looked at, and the importance of applying the five principles: understanding the source of material; planning and preparation; examination; recording and collation; and evaluation throughout an investigation. Investigators can also use heuristic knowledge, which comes from experience, and from immersing themselves within a topic.

The importance of the golden hour can never be overemphasised. An abundance of material is available at this time and, through the correct actions from an officer, an incident such as a missing person can be prevented from becoming a critical incident which may harm the reputation of the police force.

Forensic evidence and the importance of forensic science during an investigation is also vital for investigators to understand, as an investigator can gain further material and evidence with their assistance and this can prove vital to the case.

References and suggested further reading

Association of Chief Police Officers (ACPO) (2005a) *Practice Advice on Core Investigative Doctrine*. National Centre of Policing Excellence, Cambourne, Cambridgeshire.

—— (2005b) *Guidance on the Management Recording and Investigation of Missing Persons*. National Centre of Policing Excellence, Hook, Hampshire.

—— (2007) *Practice Advice Introduction to Intelligence-led Policing*. National Centre of Policing Excellence, Wyboston, Bedfordshire.

Collins English Dictionary (2009) *Collins Language.com.* Available online at http://www. collinslanguage.com/results.aspx (accessed on 25 July 2009).

Hawk, B. (2007) *A Counter-history of Composition toward Methodologies of complexity.* Available online at http://books.google.co.uk/books?id = dnHFgu43x1oC&printsec = frontcover&dq = a+counter-history+of+composition (accessed on 28 July 2009).

Newburn, T., Williamson, T. and Hutton, H. (2007) *Handbook of Criminal Investigation.* Willan Publishing, Cullompton, Devon.

Newburn, T. (2010) *Handbook of Policing.* Willan Publishing, Cullompton, Devon.

Oxford Dictionary (2009) *Ask Oxford.com.* Available online at http://www.askoxford. com/concise_oed/heuristic?view = uk (accessed on 29 July 2009).

Summers, R.W. and Hoffman, A.M. (2002) *Domestic Violence: A Global View.* Greenwood Press, Santa Barbara, USA.

White, P.C. (2004) *Crime Scene to Court: The Essentials of Forensic Science* (2nd edn). The Royal Society of Chemistry, Cambridge.

9 Investigation strategies

Introduction

This chapter will explore the subject of investigation strategies. In particular the chapter will consider a number of important areas, including the role of a victim in an investigation, and the role of a witness and how important they are. It will also consider the TIE (trace/interview/eliminate) strategy and the suspect strategy. Further, the impact of the professionalising investigation process (PIP) will be discussed and reviewed to discover what impact this has had on investigations. Finally, the use of intelligence and other sources during an investigation will be examined.

The role of the victim in investigations

Black's *Law Dictionary* (cited in ACPO 2005: 84) describes a victim as 'a person harmed by a crime, tort or other wrong'. Before reading this section, complete the exercise in Box 9.1.

Victims are extremely important to the Criminal Justice process. Carrabine *et al.* (2004) discuss the experiences of victims and describe how an incident that may only have lasted for a few moments can propel a victim into a process that may take months or even years to go through and that often victims who come to court expecting to find justice discover instead that their integrity and honesty is on trial. Carrabine *et al.* (2004) go on to explain how the role of a victim in the process is largely restricted to the reporting of a crime and providing evidence. The vast majority of crimes actually come to the attention of the police when a victim reports it rather than the police discovering the crime through their patrolling activities. This compounds the significance and importance of a victims' role. Davies *et al.* (2005) suggest some victims believe that the police may not take them seriously so they do not report the crime, which is problematic, since the police are very reliant on this information. Reiner (cited in Carrabine *et al.* 2004) agrees with that statement and says that the majority of crimes are solved through information provided by victims opposed to independent 'leads' discovered by the police. Newburn and Merry (1990) also state that it is broadly recognised that the detection of crime and subsequent conviction of criminals is

---

Box 9.1   Exercise 9A Victims

Using a score of between 1 and 10, list in order of importance the value of a victim's evidence in the following incidents:

1. Auto crime
2. Antisocial behaviours
3. Rape
4. Murder
5. Domestic violence
6. Criminal damage.

Once you have complited this list, keep it safe and read the rest of the section.

---

highly dependent upon the provision of information to the police by victims and witnesses, but criminal justice agencies and the police often fail to reciprocate this by keeping the victim informed about the progress of their case. Davies *et al.* (2005) argue that the police and victims have different priorities. The victim will be seeking reassurance, protection, advice and information, while the police are primarily concerned with the detection and prosecution of the offender.

The prosecution of criminals is difficult and in many cases impossible without willing victims who are prepared to go to court. As the defendant is presumed innocent, the victim is required to play an active role in explaining what happened and identifying the culprit, and needs to be able to demonstrate this beyond reasonable doubt (Davies *et al.* 2005). This is surely at the very heart of why victims should be supported; their evidence is vital if offenders are going to be brought to justice. The Home Office (1999) in their crime reduction strategy discuss how supporting and helping victims will not only encourage a criminal justice system that recognises the needs of victims and witnesses but it will also contribute to an increase of confidence in the criminal justice system and will encourage communities to be more confident; they will in turn be more willing to stand up against criminals and tackle local crime effectively. The Home Office (1999) pledged to increase the funding for Victim Support (Box 9.2).

So important is the role of victims to investigations that the need to protect and provide a service for them has been reinforced by the introduction of the Victims' Charter.

The Victims' Charter

First published in 1990, the Victims' Charter sets out the standards of service victims can expect from criminal justice agencies such as the police and the courts, and what they can do in cases where they do not feel they have received the treatment to which they are entitled.

Box 9.2   Excurise 9B Victims

In Exercise 9A you were asked to rate the importance of victims' evidence in different incidents. Having read this section and seen the importance of victims as witnesses, etc. reflect on why you have placed them in this order. Then try to explain why you differentiated between them in the light of what you read about the importance *of all* victims.

Important point

Victims and other witnesses are a fundamental component of the criminal justice system. They provide information, intelligence and ultimately the evidence to assist in bringing offenders to justice.

The current government recently reviewed the Victims' Charter as part of the drive to place victims at the heart of the criminal justice system. As a result, the old Victims' Charter has been replaced with the Victims' Code of Practice – a document that gives victims of crime statutory rights for the first time. The Code of Practice for Victims of Crime was published on 18 October 2005, and became law in April 2006.

The Code of Practice for Victims of Crime sets out the services victims may expect to receive from the criminal justice system, including:

- A right to information about their crime within specified time scales, including the right to be notified of any arrests and court cases.
- A dedicated family liaison police officer to be assigned to bereaved relatives.
- Clear information from the Criminal Injuries Compensation Authority (CICA) on eligibility for compensation under the scheme.
- All victims to be told about Victim Support and either referred on to them or offered their service.
- An enhanced service in the cases of vulnerable or intimidated victims.
- Flexibility with regard to opting in or out of receiving services to ensure that victims receive the level of service they want.

Criminal justice bodies, including the Prison Service, the Criminal Injuries Compensation Authority and all police forces in England and Wales, need to ensure that victims of crime and their families receive information, protection and support. The government's current programme of work for victims also includes the establishment of Witness Care Units, a consultation on Victims' Advocates, the forthcoming Prosecutor's Pledge and the commitment to the appointment of a Victims Commissioner. The current government also aims to ensure that every victim, including relatives of people who have died as the result of a crime, has access to information on support services in their local area.

Witnesses and their importance in investigations

Some witnesses present themselves to the police, or are self-evident, while other witnesses may be much harder to locate (ACPO 2005). Before reading on, attempt the exercise in Box 9.3.

Box 9.3   Exercise 9C Potential witnesses to an assault

Imagine you are investigating a serious violent assault that took place in a busy high street on a Saturday afternoon. How would you go about trying to identify potential witnesses?

Investigators may use a variety of ways to try to identify potential witnesses:

- Viewing CCTV
- Media appeals
- House-to-house enquiries
- Interviews with victims and other witnesses
- Suspect interviews
- Anniversary appeals.

Witnesses also need a degree of support during the process of an investigation, especially as witness interviews are 'a means by which an investigator can both obtain and impart information' (ACPO 2005: 89). It is essential that the investigator gains the trust of the interviewee, as witnesses can be afraid of providing the police with information. If they can trust that the officer is competent enough to deal with the information they provide, then they are more likely to provide the investigator with a full and accurate account. ACPO (2005: 89) states that 'Witnesses have a right to expect that they will be listened to and will receive fair treatment' (attempt the exercise in Box 9.4).

Box 9.4   Exercise 9D Consideration for witnesses

Before you interview a witness of an incident or offence, what welfare issues would you need to consider? Write down a list of things you may need to consider.

You may have thought of some of the following points:

- Age and mental capacity of the witness – legal requirements dictate how material may be obtained from individuals.
- The emotional health and welfare of the witness.

- The language skills of the witness; interpreters should be used in accordance with ACPO policy and local guidelines.
- How to prevent further offences from occurring, such as intimidation.

It may also be beneficial for the witness to receive some third-party support, providing they are not connected with the investigation.

The TIE strategy (trace/interview/eliminate)

The term trace/interview/eliminate (TIE) strategy is taken from the investigation of major incidents; it first appeared in 1985. It allows the investigator to identify groups of people who are likely to include the offender. It is possible, once the group has been identified, for an investigator to make enquiries and eliminate those people within the group who could not be the offenders, and implicate those in the group who could. The investigator is then able to focus his or her attention on those who are implicated with the intention of identifying the suspect. The use of a TIE strategy can be very resource intensive, and without effective management it can have the potential to incorrectly eliminate an offender.

A TIE category is a group of individuals who share a common characteristic; this group is likely to include the offender. This common characteristic will depend on the circumstances surrounding the crime. ACPO (2005: 95) states that TIE categories are typically based on:

- Those with access to the scene at the time of the offence.
- Those living in, or associated with, a certain geographical area.
- Those associated with the victim.
- Those with previous convictions for similar offences (usually known as MO suspects).
- Those with physical characteristics that are similar to the offender.
- Those with access to certain types of vehicles.

This list will become more accurate once more information is known regarding the circumstances of the crime.

Once an investigator has worked out which groups are likely to include the offender, he or she must identify as many of the members of the group as possible. This is something that on occasions the investigator can be certain about; for example, a check of a company's records will provide a list of all the employees. ACPO (2005: 96) discusses useful ways of populating TIE categories:

- Official records, such as memberships lists, payrolls, electoral registers.
- Police intelligence databases.
- Media appeals.
- 'Snowballing' – this technique involves interviewing known members of a TIE category to identify other members of the group. Like a snowball rolling down hill, this technique can start from a single point, gathering additional material as it goes.

On occasions, the number of people in a TIE category is very large and it is not possible to carry out enquiries on each individual. In these cases the investigator should begin with the members of the category who are most likely to be the offender. It is possible for the investigator to apply a number of filters to the category. ACPO (2005: 96) suggests that these filters may include:

- Proximity to the scene.
- Date of last conviction of MO suspects.
- Age (where the age of the suspect is not known, investigators may wish to prioritise those who fall within the most likely age range of offenders for that category of crime).
- Sex (where the sex of the offender is not known, investigators may wish to prioritise those who are of the sex which is most likely to have committed the crime).

There are certain characteristics of an offender that may be used to implicate or eliminate those individuals within a TIE category; these are called suspect parameters. ACPO (2005: 96) says that these parameters are:

- Sex
- Age
- Physical characteristics
- Fingerprints
- Forensic characteristics such as DNA, fibres, footprints
- Ownership of a particular make or colour of vehicle
- Ownership of particular clothing.

These characteristics can vary in value. While a fingerprint will eliminate everyone but the offender, knowing the sex of the offender offers limited assistance, although it may still narrow it down to half of the population. It is advisable for investigators to set these parameters wider than is suggested by the material in order to allow for errors in descriptions that are given by victims or witnesses.

The time frame within which a crime has been committed is useful when eliminating people from the TIE category, as some individuals will be able to provide proof that they were somewhere else when the crime was committed. It is important that an investigator is as accurate as possible when setting the time parameters based on the material available. If an exact time of a crime is not known then the time parameter should start at the earliest time that a crime could have been committed and should end at the latest time (attempt the exercise in Box 9.5).

You may have thought of some of the following which are commonly found on the HOLMES database to assist investigators to eliminate members of a TIE category from a crime:

1. forensic elimination (e.g., DNA, footwear, fingerprint);
2. description (suspect parameters);

Box 9.5 Exercise 9E Using the TIE approach

What would you consider using to eliminate an individual from a crime?
Write down your answers before reading on.

---

3. independent witness (alibi);
4. associate or relative (alibi);
5. spouse or common law relationship (alibi);
6. not eliminated.

Depending on the material available, the nature of the offence and the characteristics of the TIE category, an investigator will decide on the level of elimination
he or she will apply. For example, there may be no description of an offender
available or there may be no forensic evidence.

An important principle of TIE strategies which investigators consider is that
implication and elimination are 'always provisional and should be rigorously
tested against the material to hand and any new material that later becomes available' (ACPO 2005: 97). Best practice may be to regard any person eliminated or
implicated as being eliminated or implicated from the category, not as being
eliminated or implicated as the offender. For example, a person who is eliminated
because of an alibi provided by a spouse (criterion 5) can be re-examined at a
later stage if new material comes to light which then allows for forensic elimination criteria to be set.

Investigators should be aware that subjects of a TIE category may well also be
witnesses. Each should be interviewed using the PEACE model of investigative
interviewing, in order to gather information relating to the characteristics that the
investigator is interested in.

The suspect strategy

According to ACPO (2005), an investigator decides whether a suspect, once they
have been identified, can or should be arrested. Once a suspect has been identified
there are a number of investigative strategies that will either eliminate them or
implicate them (attempt the exercise in Box 9.6).

Box 9.6 Exercise 9F Arresting an individual

As an investigator, what would you need to consider when deciding to
arrest an individual?

You may have thought of some of the following important points:

- *Power of arrest* – Some investigative strategies, such as interviews under caution, can only be undertaken with the suspect's consent. Where there are grounds for arrest then the investigator must consider how and when the arrest should take place.
- *Timing an arrest* – When considering how and when an arrest should be made the way in which the suspect was identified will have some bearing on this decision. The choice is usually between making an early arrest and making a planned arrest. There are a number of factors that should be considered when thinking about the timing; these factors are reviewed continuously. Factors that could alter the circumstances and make an immediate arrest necessary are:

  - The suspect poses a serious risk to the safety of the victim, witnesses or the general public.
  - It is likely that the suspect will commit further or more serious crimes.
  - The suspect is likely to destroy, conceal or falsify evidence, and this will obstruct the investigation.
  - Further surveillance or other covert surveillance is necessary.

Other issues that will dictate the timing of an arrest is any background information about the suspect. When a suspect has been identified, research can be conducted into the suspect's lifestyle and background. These checks can assist and strengthen the case. Things that should be taken into consideration are:

- Is the suspect violent?
- Is the suspect known to be in possession of a firearm and/or is there any history of firearms use?
- Does the suspect use any other premises?
- Are there any previous criminal convictions/arrests?
- What is the suspect's modus operandi?
- Are there any known associates?
- Is there any habitual behaviour? Are they a known drug addict or gambler?
- Is there any intelligence regarding previous behaviour during interviews?
- *Searches* – The timing of an arrest provides the investigator with the opportunity to plan searches of the suspect's home address or other premises and their vehicle(s). It may also be crucial and provide opportunities for the recovery of incriminating or corroborating material before the suspect has a chance to alter it, dispose of it or destroy it. Searching the suspect's property may also uncover property from other offences or intelligence that can aid the identification of other offenders or their associates. All searches of a suspect's premises should be done in accordance with Code B of PACE Codes of Practice.
- *Community impact* – The impact upon the community as a whole or parts of the community as a result of the planned action. How the community will

react following high-profile arrests needs to be considered, as does the use of media to negate such problems.

Wherever possible, an arrest should be planned. While this plan is formulated consideration should be given to logistics and resources. For example, where there are several suspects it may well be that investigators feel the arrests need to be coordinated. Other considerations are search warrants, search methods and interpreters, and likely defences should be identified and considered before interview. If an investigator prepares an initial interview plan at this stage it makes better use of the detention time once a suspect has been arrested.

Briefings before arrest and search

Arrest-and-search teams need to be briefed prior to the arrest-and-search stage to ensure everyone is aware of their role and the reason for the arrest. Attempt the exercise in Box 9.7.

Box 9.7   Exercise 9G Briefings

Imagine you are about to brief teams involved in the arrest of a suspect and the search of the suspect's house. What topics do you think you will need to cover in the briefing?

Points that should be considered during a briefing are:

- Circumstances of the offence
- Authority for search
- Nominated officer in charge of the arrest team
- Nominated officer in charge of the search team
- Communications
- Method of entry
- Items to be searched for – clothing, footwear, trophies, weapons
- Recording significant statements for silences
- Methods of recovery and cross-contamination
- Exhibits officer
- Health and safety
- Transport of suspects – the location of the custody office
- Interview teams
- Debrief – time and location.

Once a suspect is in custody, their detention is controlled by the Police and Criminal Evidence Act 1984 (PACE). Anything they say at the time of arrest and during their transportation to the police station must be fully recorded.

However, it must be made clear to arrest teams that they should not question or interview the suspect further unless there is imminent threat to life or property. All questioning should be carried out in accordance with PACE, and the investigator may challenge any significant statements during the formal interview, after contradictory evidence has been presented to the suspect.

Suspect identification

With regard to the identification of a suspect, according to ACPO (2005), in some cases the suspect has been identified from the outset of the investigation; they may have been caught red-handed or been arrested during the initial investigative response. In other cases the suspect may have been identified from material gathered during the investigation through DNA or fingerprint evidence. Consideration may be given in these cases to the formal identification of the suspect. PACE Codes of Practice Code (D) provides an investigator with guidance on appropriate identification procedures.

A description of the suspect needs to be accurately recorded as soon as it becomes available and if an investigator fails to use that description during the identification process it can seriously undermine any chance of a successful prosecution. An identification officer will assist the investigator when deciding on the appropriate identification procedure he or she should adopt. Consideration should be given to the witnesses, and the most appropriate procedure for them.

ADVOKATE

Investigators are urged to apply the ADVOKATE mnemonic when obtaining a description, using the guidelines contained in *R v. Turnbull* (1977) in order to secure best evidence. ADVOKATE stands for the following:

- A – amount or length of time the witness had the suspect under observation;
- D – distance between the witness and the suspect during observation;
- V – visibility conditions during the observation;
- O – obstructions to the observations, whether they temporarily or partially inhibited the observation;
- K – whether the suspect is known to the witness in any way;
- A – any particular reason the witness has for remembering the suspect or event;
- T – time the witness had the suspect under observation and the amount of time elapsed since the event;
- E – errors in the description provided by the witness compared with the actual appearance.

It is believed that any description that is obtained as soon as possible while it is fresh in the witness's mind is vital, especially if the suspect is believed to be still in the locality and may not have altered their appearance or had the opportunity to conceal or dispose of any incriminating evidence.

Identification procedures

ACPO (2005: 108) suggests the identification procedures that should be used when a suspect is not known. These are:

- Street identification – when a witness may be taken to a particular location to see whether identification of a suspect can be made.
- Showing photographs to the witness.
- Showing video footage or photographs of an incident to a witness.
- Using facial imaging techniques which may include artist impression, composites and E-fits (electronic facial imaging technique).

Where there is sufficient information known to the police to justify the arrest of a particular person as a suspect, and a witness is available to take part in an identification parade, the identification procedures should follow this sequence:

- Formal identification parade or video identification parade electronic recording (VIPER) or other approved video identification techniques.
- Group identification.
- A video film.
- A confrontation.

The advantage of using VIPER is that the suspect does not have to be present, thus reducing the time required to arrange a formal identification procedure and allowing the witness an early opportunity to view the parade. Another advantage is that the witness will feel less intimidated picking the image from a screen as opposed to attending a formal identification at a police station; a disadvantage, however, is that the witness is not able to see the suspect walk or move, or use a particular phrase or word, known as 'voice identification', where a person is able to identify the voice of a person whom they know, or recognise the voice of a suspect and pick it out as being distinct from other voices (ACPO 2005).

Planning interviews

A suspect interview needs to be very carefully planned. The investigator should demonstrate a comprehensive knowledge of all the material gathered during the investigation and should have a clear plan how this should be used during interview. Competent and capable staff should be used during the interview. In volume crime cases it is possible for inexperienced investigators to seek advice and assistance in planning and conducting their interviews from more experienced colleagues and supervisors. In more serious cases, additional support is available, and the experience from officers with advanced interviewing skills, specialist interview advisers or behavioural analysts can all be helpful when preparing interview plans (Box 9.8).

Box 9.8 Important point Preparing interview plans

According to ACPO (2005: 110) an investigator 'must develop a clear strategy for pre-interview briefing'. This briefing needs to provide sufficient information for a legal representative to properly advise his or her client while avoiding giving too much information which could have an adverse impact upon the subsequent interview. In suspect interviews it is advisable for an investigator to build a rapport with the suspect and his or her legal representative, and to avoid confrontation.

The professionalising investigation process and its impact upon investigations

More professional investigation will lead to shorter investigations, better quality of evidence, more convictions, fewer not-guilty pleas by defendants, fewer cracked trials and better targeting of offenders (Home Office 2003).

Commissioned by the Home Office, the Association of Chief Police Officers (ACPO) leads the project of 'professionalising investigations'. ACPO works in partnership with the National Policing Improvement Agency (NPIA) and the Skills for Justice Organisation (PSSO) in order to examine, develop and make recommendations concerning the professionalising of investigation.

It was recognised in the Police Reform Act 2002 that the police service in England and Wales needed to professionalise the business of investigation. The police service has, in recent years, developed various initiatives across the forces to support this idea, including the following:

- The National Centre for Policing Excellence (NCPE).
- The Senior Investigating Officers Development Programme.
- The identified need to develop training and accreditation of civilian investigators linked to specialist roles and rapid progression through the different levels of investigation and accreditation.
- Police knowledge maps and manuals.
- Implementation of the National Intelligence Model (NIM).
- The development of National Occupational Standards.

One of the aims of the project is to develop a process to professionalise the investigation process with recommendations for implementation. This is being delivered in two phases:

1. **Development** – The accreditation process that is being developed is intrinsically linked to the National Occupational Standards and the National

Competency Framework. The accreditation of investigators will be bench-
marked against these standards and the process will have to withstand both
internal and external scrutiny.

2. **Implementation** – The development work completed by the project team
will be handed over to the National Policing Improvement Agency (NPIA)
for implementation.

According to Skills for Justice (2009), the aim of professionalising investigation
is to enhance the skills and abilities of police officers who are better qualified and
better skilled in investigations and there will be more focused training provided
for investigation, with national qualifications and consistent training
programmes.

Use of intelligence and other sources in investigations

Intelligence, information and the National Intelligence Model are situated at the
heart of most policing activities, so these concepts are discussed throughout this
book, in various chapters, to illustrate how they are used in support of different
strategies and approaches. The collection of information and its use within the
NIM process for investigative purposes cannot be underestimated. This
is supported by ACPO (2007) which states: 'The concept of intelligence-led
policing underpins all aspects of policing, from neighbourhood policing and
partnership working to the investigation of serious and organised crime and
terrorism' (ACPO 2007: 3).

Therefore it is quite clear that intelligence and information is a vital part of
any investigation. The police gather information that they require for
policing purposes. These purposes include one, or possibly a combination, of the
following:

• protecting life and property;
• preserving order;
• preventing the commission of offences;
• bringing offenders to justice;
• Any duty or responsibility arising from common or statute law (ACPO
2007).

These five policing purposes provide the legal basis for collecting, recording,
evaluating, sharing and retaining police information. They will include information relating to the key policing functions, including crime investigation, antisocial behaviour, road policing, public order, counter-terrorism, racial and
community tension, or the protection of children and other vulnerable people.
Before reading on, attempt the exercise in Box 9.9.

ACPO (2007) discusses the types of sources the police can use during
the search for information; the police should consider the type of information
that may be available and whether there is any likelihood of the information

---

Box 9.9   Exercise 9H Sources of information

As a senior officer leading an investigation into a serious sexual assault, make a list of sources you would consider for information. Now read on and compare your list with what is written below.

---

having any value as intelligence. The types of sources available to the police are:

- Victims and witnesses
- Communities and members of the public
- Crimestoppers
- Prisoners
- Covert human intelligence sources (CHI)
- Covert operations (e.g. surveillance)
- CCTV and automatic number plate recognition (ANPR)
- Crime and disorder reduction partnerships
- Commercial agencies (e.g. banks and credit card agencies)
- Fixed penalty tickets database
- Forensic Science Service (FSS)
- Internet – open sources (e.g. http://www.homeoffice.gov.uk)
- Media
- Neighbourhood Watch scheme
- Police IT systems (e.g. Police National Computer [PNC])
- Other law-enforcement agencies (e.g. Serious Organised Crime Agency (SOCA)
- Primary care trusts (PCTs)
- Local education authorities (LEAs).

ACPO (2007) believes that the police have a duty to gather information about issues that affect the force by openly engaging with the community. The public will gain confidence in providing information to the police from this effective community engagement. The police have a duty of care and must ensure the confidentiality of any individual who provides information. Some people may be at more risk due to their personal or professional circumstances. In such cases when an increased risk of harm is apparent, specific action needs to be taken. ACPO (2007) outlines such situations:

- The nature of the information, the way it was obtained, or the circumstances of the person providing the information indicates that the information should be treated in confidence or in a sensitive manner.
- The frequency of contact between an individual and the police indicates that the information should be treated in confidence or in a sensitive manner,

or that the individual may be maintaining a relationship in order to obtain that information.

- A member of the public has been tasked to provide information by a member of staff. This does not include the requirement to provide statements or the completion of diaries to record witness or victim experiences of a particular problem.

Some information of significant intelligence value may be handled with a high level of confidentiality and sensitivity. The reasons why this should be include:

- The vulnerable environment in which the individual lives (e.g. a person living in an area with a history of witness intimidation).
- The individual's close proximity to the subject of the information (e.g. a family member, neighbour or employee).
- During the deployment of technical or other surveillance activity, and for any resulting material.

Conclusion

This chapter has reinforced the view that the victims and witnesses of crimes are crucial to any investigation. Without their information, investigators would have a difficult time bringing offenders to justice. It is therefore important that victims feel confident in the ability and competence of the investigator and ultimately the police. Consequently the professionalisation of investigations will encourage individuals such as victims and witnesses to provide information and be more forthcoming. Due to the use of guidelines, strategies and other training programmes, investigators are now better equipped for the task of carrying out thorough investigations in a professional manner.

References and suggested further reading

Association of Chief Police Officers (ACPO) (2005) *Practice Advice on Core Investigative Doctrine*. National Centre for Policing Excellence, Cambourne, Cambridgeshire.
—— (2007) *Practice Advice Introduction to Intelligence-led Policing*. National Centre for Policing Excellence, Wyboston, Bedfordshire.
Carrabine, E., Lee, M., Iganskis, P., Plummer, K. and South, N. (2004) *Criminology. A Sociological Introduction*. Routledge, London, England. Available online at: http://books.google.com/books?id = eNUUG6USXd8C (accessed on 25 May 2009).
Davies, M., Croall, H. and Tyrer, J. (2005) *Criminal Justice: An Introduction to the Criminal Justice System in England and Wales* (3rd edn). Pearson Education, Harlow, Essex.
Home Office (1999) *Governments Crime Reduction Strategy. Helping Victims and Witnesses*. Available online at http://www.crimereduction.homeoffice.gov.uk/crsdoc9.htm (accessed on 9 June 2009).

—— (2003) *Professionalising Investigation*. Available online at http://police.homeoffice. gov.uk/publications/operational-policing/pip_flyerv3.pdf?view = Binary (accessed on 8 August 2009).

Newburn, T. and Merry, X. (1990) *Keeping in Touch: Police–Victim Communication in Two Areas*. Home Office Research Study No. 116. Available online at http://www. homeoffice.gov.uk/rds/hors1990.html (accessed on 29 May 2009).

Skills for Justice (2009) *Professionalising Investigation*. Available online at http://www. skillsforjustice.com/websitefiles/POLICE_PDR_CeinwenThompson_presentation.pdf (accessed on 8 August 2009).

Victims Charter. Available online at http://www.homeoffice.gov.uk/documents/victims-charter?view=Binary (accessed on 31 September 2009).

Part 3

Intelligence

Intelligence has, since the 1990s, become increasingly prominent in policing and police policy in the UK. The National Intelligence Model is the current zenith of such developments, representing the first nationally introduced business process under which all UK forces are obliged to operate.

There are a number of identifiable reasons for the growth in the perceived importance and therefore development of intelligence. Certainly, as discussed in more detail throughout Part 3, technological advances have allowed information to be collected, stored, collated and analysed more readily than before. However, technology alone does not explain the shift in emphasis. After all, intelligence systems operated effectively for centuries with no supporting technology.

Perhaps the clearest reason has been the proposition that intelligence-based decision making allows resources to be allocated and used most effectively. Such a rationale ties in with the information required to make accurate risk assessments. In the police service particular criticism had arisen of the 'fire-brigade' method of operating – responding to random incidents as they were reported and the resource management issues that this raised.

The potential afforded by intelligence to target resources more effectively and allow the police to become more pro-active has certainly been an important developmental factor. These developments have recently gained prominence through the national adoption of the National Intelligence Model. This section of the book explores these themes and developments, commencing with a discussion of what is meant by 'intelligence'.

10 What is intelligence?

Introduction: what is intelligence?

This chapter is concerned with intelligence. More specifically it examines the issues around the acquisition and management of intelligence by the police. The background to this chapter is provided by the Bichard Inquiry, established following the Soham murders and reporting in 2004, which was highly critical of the way the police forces concerned managed and shared intelligence. The chapter discusses how the inquiry's findings have shaped the subsequent police management of intelligence, principally through the Impact Programme and introduction of the statutory code of practice for the management of police information (MoPI). The chapter then considers issues around ethics and integrity in intelligence management, particularly some of the issues that arise in relation to covert intelligence and covert human intelligence sources (CHIS). It concludes by looking at methods of assessing the quality and veracity of intelligence, particularly the use of the 5x5x5 form by the police, and compliance with its requirements.

Initially it is important to establish what we mean by intelligence, not least because intelligence in policing has a number of different connotations and usages. Indeed, there is little consensus about what 'intelligence' is in policing terms, with an apparent degree of overlap between the key concepts of intelligence, information and evidence, and differences in the understanding of what constitutes intelligence on the part of practitioners, academics and in official sources (ACPO and HMIC) (Harfield and Harfield 2008). Indeed in a recent article McKay states that:

> it is interesting that there is no real definition of what intelligence is. This is extraordinary in any view. None of the legislation defines it … and while there are countless references to intelligence in the cases, none grapple with the elusive concept of what it may actually be.
>
> (ACPO Centrex 2007)

Before we commence therefore, attempt the exercise in Box 10.1.

> **Box 10.1 Exercise 10A Defining intelligence**
>
> Write down in your own words what you think the definition of intelligence is and compare it with the information in this chapter.

'Intelligence' is often, and traditionally, used to identify a piece of information gained from a covert source, from an informant, for example. This chapter, however, is principally concerned with intelligence in its more current usage: intelligence as processed, actionable information derived from any number of sources. The chapter therefore begins with a discussion of the distinction between information and intelligence as a means of establishing the focus for intelligence in this and subsequent chapters.

Distinctions between intelligence and information

Some pieces of information may be immediately actionable by the police. Being told, for example, that somebody has been seen entering a house through a broken window would most probably suggest a burglary was taking place. The relevance of another piece of information, however, might only become clear once the context within which it sits becomes apparent. An example might be a van parked on double yellow lines near a bank. A fairly innocuous piece of information in its own right but, when linked with similar sightings near the times of bank robberies, it might potentially become an important piece of intelligence. In other words, intelligence is created from pieces of information. It is a process that converts raw data that might have little apparent value in its own right into information that becomes actionable – into intelligence. Established definitions emphasise this point. For example, a significant report commissioned by the Association of Chief Police Officers to review intelligence within the police, the Baumber Report, defined criminal intelligence in the following way:

> Criminal intelligence can be said to be the end product of a process, sometimes physical, always intellectual, derived from information which has been collated, analysed and evaluated in order to prevent crime or secure the apprehension of offenders.
>
> (ACPO 1975, par.32)

For Whitaker (1999), intelligence is 'the systematic and purposeful acquisition, sorting, retrieval, analysis interpretation and protection of information' (1999: 5). The definition favoured by John Grieve summarises the position – intelligence as 'information designed for action' (2004: 25).

The three definitions clearly establish, therefore, that intelligence is a *process* that does something to *information* in order to make it *actionable* and useful to perform policing functions. This chapter, and those that follow, examine what that something is and what some of the outcomes can be. It begins by examining some key sources of information, before looking at the process of conversion into intelligence.

Information

Pieces of information are the building blocks of intelligence; they are the raw material of the intelligence process. The police have a tremendous range of information sources available to them – overt and covert, and from open and closed sources. Some of this information will be generic and non-specific, often created initially for another purpose. An example could be a simple map of a residential area. Some information, however, will be collected very specifically in the context of a particular investigation or in order to increase understanding of a particular crime issue. Identifying where burglaries have taken place on a residential map, for example, would represent a stage in the translation of various pieces of information into a potentially actionable piece of intelligence.

Information may be gathered in a multitude of different ways, and from myriad sources. A distinction is frequently made between sources that are 'open' or 'closed' to a particular organisation. For example, the Police National Computer is open to the police service. It is generally closed to other organisations although the police may supply the information to them.

Grabiner (2000) recognises that a great deal of information on individuals is held by a variety of governmental departments, agencies and local authorities. He also discusses obstacles (institutional, legal and technical) that prevent or hinder the information being shared – that make potentially 'open' sources 'closed' to the police. He develops this overview by suggesting that:

> a critical aspect of the data sharing debate is the potential for using information held by the private sector. Currently, huge amounts of information are held, and some made available commercially, yet this valuable source cannot generally be tapped by Government under current legislation … For example, if someone claiming a means-tested benefit admits to having a bank account, staff are entitled to call for bank statements in order to check for any savings or signs of regular payments from a job. But if the claimant does not reveal the account, there is no way for the Benefits Agency to know that it exists without access to information which currently resides only in the private sector.
>
> (Grabiner 2000: 22)

There are therefore some obstacles to the police gaining access to certain sources of information available to other state agencies, and vice versa. Increasingly, data-sharing protocols are developed between police and, in particular, other state agencies, in order to allow sharing of, at least, anonymised data that may be used to provide information and therefore ultimately intelligence from a range of agencies (John *et al.* 2006).

Translating information into intelligence

Intelligence may be viewed as the collation and analysis of pieces of related information in order to build up a more accurate picture. Each police officer will, on a daily basis, be the recipient of a range of information from a variety of different sources. These will range from the daily briefing to a conversation with a member of the public, through to direct observation of an event or sighting of a suspect or suspicious activity. Across the policing personnel in a basic command unit or police force, therefore, there is tremendous potential for the organisation to learn more about its business on a daily basis. In order to do so, however, it is necessary to take this information, and that derived from other sources, and determine how useful it is likely to be (Box 10.2).

Box 10.2   Exercise 10B Influences upon information

Write down a list of factors that you think might influence the perceived value of a particular type of information to the police service.

There are a number of factors that influence the value of information to the police and you may have thought of some of these. Ultimately, it is very difficult to say, with certainty, what will or will not be important now or in the future. A seemingly innocuous sighting of a suspect might, for example, serve to undermine a subsequent alibi if it is recorded. It is recognised, however, that some factors are generally significant in determining value. You may well, for example, have considered factors such as: the source of the information, whether that information is already known to the police, the age and currency of the information, and whether it is likely to add value to a particular priority within a policing area at that particular time.

Relatively early formal considerations of information and intelligence within policing recognised that a process was required to establish such considerations. The Baumber definition of intelligence above, for example, included a recognition that information needs to be 'evaluated' as part of the process of converting it into intelligence or, as Harfield and Harfield put it, assess 'to what extent can we believe each different piece of information before us' (2008: 65). This evaluation traditionally involved an assessment of the source of the information and of the quality of the information itself and was known as the 4x4 system. More recently, the police and other agencies who deal with intelligence have adopted the 5x5x5 system of evaluating intelligence. This adds an additional dimension which has been described as 'essentially a risk assessment for dissemination' (Sheptycki 2004: 12) – it denotes the extent to which the information should be circulated within and beyond the police service.

Validation of intelligence

Harfield and Harfield (2008) suggest that there are a number of dimensions to the validation of intelligence:

- What is the provenance of the information? Where does it originate?
- How does the source providing the information come to be in possession of it (i.e. directly or indirectly)?
- Has the source provided reliable information in the past?
- If the source is only able to provide information in relation to part of the issue, why does he or she not know the remaining pieces?
- Can any of the information be corroborated by a second source?
- If this is the case, is the second source providing independent, direct knowledge of the information, or merely confirming that the first source had indirect access?
- Is there a chance that the information, even if it can be corroborated, is being provided to confuse and mislead? And, subsequently,
- If anticipated events did not occur, can information be obtained to ascertain why this was not the case? (Harfield and Harfield 2008: 66–67).

The police and other agencies record, evaluate and disseminate information via the national information/intelligence report (the 5x5x5 form). As well as the above, the aim of the form is to ensure consistency among forces, enabling them to share intelligence more easily and provide an audit trail. In addition, the 5x5x5 is used to assess the risk of exposure to the source of the information or to the use of the material and, therefore, protect the individual or police operation to which the information relates (ACPO 2007).

According to the guidance provided by ACPO, the 5x5x5 form should be used to record 'any information for a policing purpose that is generally not recorded on other systems. The 5x5x5 can be used during routine, volunteered and tasked information collection' (ACPO 2007: 26).

This includes:

- Information given to the police, in confidence, by members of the public.
- Information from anonymous sources (i.e. Crimestoppers, Anti-Terrorism Hotline).
- Information of a personal or confidential nature received from someone who has access to it because of their occupation (i.e. hotel or airline staff).
- Sanitised information derived from a CHIS.
- Sanitised information obtained by covert means (i.e. surveillance activity).
- Information from other law-enforcement agencies that is supplied in confidence, or is from a sensitive source (i.e. information that, had it originated in the police service, would have been recorded on a 5x5x5).
- Information from liaison with other partner agencies (i.e. CDRPs, Youth Offending Teams).

- Information obtained by police officers (patrol officers, front desk staff, PCSOs and interviewing officers) in the course of their duties (ACPO 2007).

As a rule of thumb, the guidance states that the 5x5x5 form should not be used when information is recorded through other systems, whether this is via crime or incident reports, custody records or neighbourhood problem-solving files. However, a number of exceptions to this broad guidance are mentioned, and it is suggested that the 5x5x5 *should* be used to record the following information:

- Reasons for the revocation of a firearms licence.
- Details about a person who may be a risk to children or vulnerable adults.
- Details about a known or suspected domestic violence perpetrator.
- Allegations of threats to life or of serious harm.
- Details of potentially dangerous people who pose a threat to the public.
- Where it is necessary to restrict or control the subsequent dissemination of the information.
- Information contained in other formats that may not be readily searchable or identifiable as having relevant intelligence value (ACPO 2007).

The 5x5x5 report contains basic details identifying the person completing and submitting the report, their organisation, as well as the time and date of submission and, if a paper copy is used, the signature of the person submitting the report (electronic submission of a 5x5x5 usually contains automatic identifiers and does not require a signature). These details are important for auditing purposes and as part of a potential evidential chain (ACPO 2007).

On the 5x5x5 form there are three dimensions that are considered: the reliability of the source for the intelligence, the reliability of the intelligence itself, and how the intelligence should be handled.

Source evaluation

The 5x5x5 report provides an assessment of the reliability of the person, agency or technical equipment which has provided the relevant information or intelligence. While the assessment of reliability will initially be made by the person recording the information, this is not a static process and may be subject to review subsequently (particularly in relation to decisions about the sharing and retention of the information and the need to retain it). The ACPO guidance stresses that the 'assessment of the source must be accurate as it will affect both the evaluation of the information recorded, and the potential action of that information as intelligence' ACPO 2007). The five gradings for source evaluation are:

A – Always reliable – 'where there is no doubt about the authenticity, trustworthiness and competence of the source. Information has been supplied in the past and has proved to be reliable in all instances' (ACPO 2007: 28). According to the guidance this grading 'should only apply to cases where reliability can be assured.

It will *not* be used frequently.' Examples cited are information received from technical products – DNA, interceptions, fingerprints. However, it does not include information received from officers or staff, 'as they are subject to human error' (ACPO 2007: 28).

B – Mostly reliable – used to describe information received from a source which in the past has proved to be reliable in the majority of instances, i.e. police officers, (some) covert human intelligence sources and prosecuting agencies (e.g. United Kingdom Immigration Service (UKIS)).

C – Sometimes reliable – used to describe information where some of the information received from this source has proved to be both reliable and unreliable. The ACPO guidance suggests that any information with this grading should generally not be acted upon without corroboration (e.g. a CHIS or information received from the media or product of a technical deployment where the quality of the product is poor). Where a response is required in the light of the information, 'the intelligence manager will need to obtain as much corroboration as possible before commissioning action' (ACPO 2007: 28).

D – Unreliable – used for individuals who have provided information in the past which has routinely proved unreliable or where there may be some doubt regarding the authenticity, trustworthiness, competency or motive of the source. Consequently any information given this grading should not be acted upon without corroboration. Examples would include information received from members of the public who have a potentially malicious motive (neighbourhood disputes), or information received from an individual with a history of making false allegations.

E – Untested source – used for information received from a source that has not previously provided information to the person recording. The information may not necessarily be unreliable but it should be treated with caution, and again, corroboration of the information should be sought (this grading would usually apply to members of the public, and the majority of information received from Crimestoppers).

Information/intelligence evaluation

As well as an assessment of the reliability of the source, it is essential that any information received or recorded should be evaluated for reliability – an assessment based on the person recording it and their knowledge of the circumstances at the time (the ACPO guidance stresses that 'the evaluation will involve using an objective professional judgement, and the value of the information must not be exaggerated to encourage action to be taken' ACPO 2007: 29). Five information/intelligence evaluation grades are provided by the 5x5x5:

1 – Known to be true without reservation – used where the information has been generated from a technical deployment or an event which was witnessed by a law-enforcement officer or prosecuting agency – in other words, the information has been generated first-hand, i.e. live evidence or where an officer witnesses an incident. The ACPO guidance stresses that 'information received from technical deployments must be treated with caution as the information may have been recorded accurately but the content may be misinterpreted' (ACPO 2007: 29).

2 – *Information is known personally by the source but not to the person reporting* – used where the information is believed to be true by the source although it is not personally known by the person recording the information (the information is provided second-hand – in the case of a CHIS giving information which they know of first-hand, to the person recording the information).

3 – *Information is not known personally to the source but can be corroborated by other information* – where the information given has been received by a source from a third party, but its reliability has been corroborated by other information (CCTV, other force systems).

4 – *The information cannot be judged* – used where the reliability of the information cannot be judged or corroborated (i.e. anonymous information received from members of the public that a crime has occurred but where it is not possible to corroborate the claim). The guidance suggests that information with this grading must be treated with caution.

5 – *Suspected to be false* – an example would be where a CHIS who is engaged in criminal activity provides exaggerated information against others in order to deflect attention from themselves, or to prepare a defence of working for the police should they be arrested. Information with this grading should be treated with extreme caution, and information should be corroborated by a reliable source before any action is taken. In addition, any person applying this grade must justify within the body of the report why it is appropriate to use this grading (Box 10.3).

For the circumstances above the following codes would be appropriate:

- Example i 2 (the information is known personally by the source, but not by the person reporting)
- Example ii 1 (known to be true without reservation)
- Example iii 4 (the information cannot be judged)
- Example iv 3 (the information is not known personally to the source but can be corroborated by other information)
- Example v 5 (suspected to be false).

Handling codes

The intelligence-handling codes are designed to provide an initial risk assessment prior to recording material on the intelligence system. The codes used are as follows:

1. Dissemination allowed within the UK police service and to other law enforcement agencies as specified.
2. Dissemination allowed to UK non-prosecuting parties.
3. Dissemination to (non-EU) foreign law-enforcement agencies.

Box 10.3   Exercise 10C Grading for reliability

Consider the intelligence in the examples below. In each scenario, how would you grade it for reliability?

i.   A CHIS provides intelligence about an incident, which they witnessed first-hand, to the police officer recording the information.
ii.   The incident to which the intelligence relates, has been witnessed by a police officer.
iii. Information has been received from an anonymous member of the public that a burglary has been committed, but details about the offence cannot be verified.
iv.   A CHIS has been told that an individual has been seen driving a particular car. A PNC check has confirmed that the individual is the registered keeper of the car.
v.   A CHIS, suspected to be dealing in drugs, provides intelligence about the activities of another individual he alleges is engaged selling class A drugs.

The grades available are

1 – Known to be true without reservation
2 – The information is known personally by the source, but not by the person reporting
3 – The information is not known personally to the source but can be corroborated by other information
4 – The information cannot be judged
5 – Information is suspected to be false.

---

4.   Dissemination permitted within originating force/agency only (reasons and internal recipients should be specified and a review period set).
5.   Dissemination permitted but receiving agency to observe specified conditions.

The handling codes 'allow recording staff and others involved in the dissemination of intelligence material to clearly record their decisions on the suitability, or otherwise, of sharing the intelligence with other parties' (ACPO 2007: 30). The ACPO guidance suggests that 'staff completing the 5x5x5 will not generally complete the handling code unless they are involved in the intelligence discipline as, for example, trained intelligence officers or specialists' (ACPO 2007: 30 – wording to this effect is also contained in the attached sample 5x5x5 form; see Figure 10.1). However, the authors' own experience suggests

NOT PROTECTIVELY MARKED UNTIL COMPLETED

GPMS:	RESTRICTED ☐	CONFIDENTIAL ☐	SECRET ☐

5x5x5 Information Intelligence Report Form A

ORGANISATION AND OFFICER		DATE/TIME OF REPORT	
INFORMATION/INTELLIGENCE SOURCE/INTELLIGENCE SOURCE REF NO. (ISR)		REPORT URN	

SOURCE AND INFORMATION/INTELLIGENCE EVALUATION TO BE COMPLETED BY SUBMITTING OFFICER

SOURCE EVALUATION	**A** Always Reliable	**B** Mostly Reliable	**C** Sometimes Reliable	**D** Unreliable	**E** Untested Source
INFORMATION/ INTELLIGENCE EVALUATION	**1** Known to be true without reservation	**2** Known personally to the source but not to the person reporting	**3** Not known personally to the source, but corroborated	**4** Cannot be judged	**5** Suspected to be false

REPORT

PERSON RECORD:	DoB:	NIB CRO:

OPERATION NAME/NUMBER:		S	I	H

INTELLIGENCE UNIT ONLY

HANDLING CODE	**1**	**2**	**3**	**4**	**5**
To be completed by the evaluator on receipt and prior to entry onto the intelligence system. **To be reviewed on dissemination.**	**Default:** Permits dissemination within the UK police service AND to other law enforcement agencies as specified [see guidance] ☐	Permits dissemination to UK non prosecuting parties [conditions apply see guidance] ☐	Permits dissemination to (non EU) foreign law enforcement agencies [conditions apply see guidance] ☐	Permits dissemination within originating force/agency only: specify reasons and internal recipient(s) Review period must be set [see guidance] ☐	Permits dissemination but receiving agency to observe conditions as specified [see guidance on risk assessment] ☐

5x5x5 REVIEWED BY: RE-EVALUATED: Yes ☐ No ☐	CROSS-REF URN:	TIME/DATE OF REVIEW:
DISSEMINATED TO:	PERSON DISSEMINATING TIME/DATE:	
DETAILED HANDLING INSTRUCTIONS:	PUBLIC INTEREST IMMUNITY:	
INPUT ON TO AN INTELLIGENCE SYSTEM Yes ☐ No ☐		
SIGNATURE (PAPER COPY):		

GPMS:	RESTRICTED ☐	CONFIDENTIAL ☐	SECRET ☐

Figure 10.1 Information intelligence report form A.

that this is not always the case, and in one force at least, response officers are encouraged to complete the handling code at the point that they submit the intelligence form.

Interestingly there is also evidence of officers in this force being encouraged to use different handling codes as a default by divisional LIOs when submitting intelligence forms. Thus officers in one division were encouraged to routinely code material as a '1' (as the ACPO guidance suggests), allowing the information to be disseminated within the police service and other agencies. Conversely, intelligence staff in a neighbouring division suggested that officers use '4' as the default handling code, restricting the dissemination of the intelligence to the police force concerned. While it is clearly the case that the ultimate determination of the appropriate handling code will be made by Intelligence Unit staff, the example serves as an interesting insight into the different presumptions operating within the intelligence community about how widely (and routinely) submitted intelligence should be circulated, particularly outside the police.

Sanitisation

According to the 2007 guidance, sanitisation occurs when

> material is removed which explicitly or implicitly identifies a source. It also occurs when identifying details of a data subject are removed. This process will be undertaken by the intelligence unit prior to the dissemination or inputting onto an intelligence system. Staff can help this process, however, by ensuring that only 'relevant information' is included in the 5x5x5.
>
> (ACPO 2007: 30)

Again, in the authors' experience there is a wide variety of practice in terms of the expectations of intelligence staff about the level of detail that will be provided on intelligence logs – while response officers were encouraged to sanitise information prior to the submission of the intelligence log by an LIO from one division (indeed, this was described in terms of reflecting their professionalism as police officers), LIOs in another division suggested that officers should provide intelligence in a more unstructured, verbatim account, as the LIOs would subsequently sanitise the intelligence. The upshot of this was to leave the response officers concerned confused and uncertain about what they should include on the intelligence log. On a divisional basis, the LIU had attempted to overcome this by providing a pro forma that indicated to staff how logs should be completed.

The primary considerations are, therefore, the reliability of the source and of the quality of the information received. There are some management issues associated with the use of this system. Primarily, if intelligence is to be shared with colleagues or managers (which it should, as discussed below), there is a temptation for those who have received the information to give it as 'high' a rating as possible to make themselves look effective. Hence objectivity can potentially be lost (and hence the requirement for an 'objective' assessment by an LIO usually responsible for the intelligence process as a whole). However, there is some suggestion that these officers may be over-cautious in their evaluations of intelligence and its dissemination (particularly following the passing of the Human Rights Act 1998). Again, this was a key finding in the

Bichard Report (2004). In considering the codes above you will note that a seemingly poor evaluation of, for example, E4 (derived from an untested source and that cannot be corroborated), does not inherently mean that it is not useful – in retrospect it may prove to be of significant value.

Conclusion

In this chapter we have discussed the means by which information is translated into intelligence and how its veracity is evaluated. We will now turn to a consideration of the means by which intelligence becomes integrated into policing practice. First, we will examine the underlying principles of a basic intelligence process. We will then turn to a discussion of the increased status of intelligence achieved through pro-active policing developments, and the implementation of intelligence-led policing strategies.

References and suggested further reading

Association of Chief Police Officers (ACPO) (1975) *Report of the Subcommittee on Criminal Intelligence* (the Baumber Report). Association of Chief Police Officers, London.

ACPO Centrex (2007) *Practice Advice: Introduction to Intelligence-led Policing*. Association of Chief Police Officers, London.

Bichard, M. (2004) *The Bichard Inquiry Report*. House of Commons, London.

Byford, L. (Sir) (1981) *Report By Sir Lawrence Byford into the Police Handling of the Yorkshire Ripper Case*. Home Office, London.

Fortune, J. and Peters, G. (2005) *Information Systems: Achieving Success by Avoiding Failure*. Wiley, London.

Grabiner, Lord. (2000) *The Informal Economy*. HMSO, London.

Grieve, J. (2004) 'Developments in UK criminal intelligence', in J. Ratcliffe (ed.) *Strategic Thinking in Criminal Intelligence*. Federation Press, Annandale.

Harfield, C. and Harfield, K. (2008) *Intelligence; Investigation, Community and Partnership*. Blackstone, Oxford.

John, T., Morgan, C. and Rogers, C. (2006) *The Greater Manchester Against Crime Partnership Business Model: An Independent Evaluation*. Centre for Criminology, University of Glamorgan, internal document.

McKay, S. (2009) 'Defining intelligence', *Police Professional*, 10 September, p. 37.

Sheptycki, J. (2004) *Review of the Influence of Strategic Intelligence on Organised Crime Policy and Practice*. Home Office, London.

Whitaker, R. (1999) *The End of Privacy; How Total Surveillance is Becoming a Reality*. New Press, New York.

11 Developing and employing intelligence

Introduction

The previous chapter demonstrates the need to establish the quality of information that, ultimately, forms the building blocks of any subsequent intelligence system. Assessing the veracity of information is, though, only the first stage in developing it into intelligence. Put simply, even if every piece of information received was absolutely verifiable, it would still need sifting to determine what is likely to be useful and what is not. Without such a process any intelligence system would be swamped with non-actionable information. The Pearce Report considered this issue by pointing to the overarching purpose of maintaining intelligence records:

> For working purposes we therefore define criminal intelligence records as containing *inferential and speculative* matters about criminals and crime that *do not form part of the criminal record.* It does not preclude the inclusion of some criminal record information such as summaries of convictions where it would be helpful, but we would expect this to be minimal and duplication to be avoided as far as practicable.
>
> (ACPO 1978, para.7; emphasis added)

The distinction is important. A fundamental purpose of an intelligence database is that it should be used for pro-active analysis and action. Too much reliance on factual, verifiable information such as that contained in criminal records can detract from this purpose in concentrating on the past, rather than on current or future criminal actions of the suspect. Studies into the use of intelligence databases have suggested that they are frequently used as an electronic library of information – i.e. as a reactive tool – rather than for the production of actionable intelligence (e.g. Maguire and John 1995).

Innes *et al.* (2005), in a discussion around defining intelligence, helpfully provide an overview of the various forms of intelligence and the value to policing that they bring. These are shown in Box 11.1.

Box 11.1   Important point–values of different forms of intelligence

1. *Criminal* intelligence: detailing the activities of a 'known' suspect or suspects.
2. *Crime* intelligence: enhancing the police's understanding about a specific crime or series of crimes.
3. *Community* intelligence: based on data provided to the police by 'ordinary' members of the public.
4. *Contextual* intelligence: relating to wider social, economic and cultural factors that may impact upon levels of crime and patterns of offending.

(Innes *et al.* 2005: 44)

Increased awareness of the differing focuses of these various forms of intelligence is a useful way of recognising that different forms of intelligence serve different purposes. Using the table in Box 11.1 attempt the exercise given in Box 11.2.

Box 11.2   Exercise 11A Examining the intelligence category

Consider the extent to which the categories in Box 11.1 above might be mutually exclusive or the extent to which they might overlap. Which type of category may be of value to which particular department of the police service and/or other agencies that play a role in policing?

Often, the popular, and to some extent policing imagination is captured by the first of Innes *et al.*'s categories: criminal intelligence, with its association with information gained by detectives from informants and criminal networks. As Ratcliffe observes, '[intelligence] has also been misunderstood to mean the type of information gathered from informants or surveillance' (2008: 87). In contemporary policing in the UK, though, the breadth of intelligence in its various forms, derivations and uses is embodied within the National Intelligence Model and its ambitions to be the mechanism by which all policing priorities are recognised and resourced. While we return to the National Intelligence Model later, it is important for now to bear in mind that it is the broad approach to intelligence with which we are concerned. However, the broad approach is a relatively recent innovation so the discussion below charts its development through criminal intelligence into the mainstream. Turning the verified information (pieces of intelligence) that we discussed above into actionable intelligence is done through a particular cyclical process.

The intelligence process

Good, effective intelligence gathering is infrequently a one-off event (such as a reliable informant giving precise information on the identity of an offender, and the time and place at which an offence will be committed). Rather, it is part of a more long-term process of incrementally increasing knowledge. The intelligence may initially be gathered about a specific individual suspected of committing a crime, or about a type of crime about which little is currently known. This latter is frequently a starting point in the investigation of fraud (Levi 1981).

A process is therefore necessary to ensure that intelligence is collected and analysed in a logical and structured manner. A commonly adopted starting point for this is that the intelligence resource at a particular level of an organisation is sited at one location and operated or managed by specialists – an intelligence unit.

Effective analysis of intelligence will ideally result in the formation of an intelligence package that will form the basis of subsequent actions. 'A package contains all known relevant information about a target offender – description, accomplices, vehicles, favoured *modus operandi*, – plus a tactical approach to securing arrest' (Audit Commission 1993: 36). The intelligence process that results in a package should, however, be viewed as an ongoing cycle rather than as having a beginning and end. A typical example of an intelligence cycle is outlined by Barton and Evans (1999), and is presented diagrammatically in Figure 11.1. Information and intelligence is *collected* and its veracity and importance *evaluated*, before it is *analysed* in further depth. A package is *developed* and the intelligence *disseminated* before the *direction* it takes is decided upon. It may be passed on to a surveillance team for the offenders to be followed and 'caught in the act'. Or it may be put back into the cycle for more information to be gathered – hence the cycle continues.

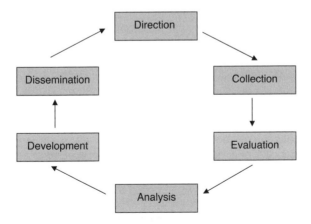

Figure 11.1 The intelligence cycle.

Source: Adapted from Barton and Evans (1999: 10). For slightly different versions of the intelligence cycle see e.g. Blades (1997) and Friedman *et al* (1997).

The strength of good intelligence is self-evident. The weaknesses therefore lie in the gaining of the knowledge. Effectively these are weaknesses within the intelligence cycle. Two major difficulties with the intelligence flow within the cycle have been identified in the literature (e.g. Maguire and John 1995; Barton and Evans 1999). The first lies at the inception of the process: ensuring that sufficient information enters the system for patterns to be identified. There are a number of reasons for this hiatus. Perhaps the most significant is cultural resistance to the sharing of information – individuals preferring to keep back good information so that they get the credit for resulting successes. This has been recognised within the police service – a policing culture that traditionally rewards individual initiative in 'getting a good result' – in being identified as a 'good thief-taker' (see Maguire and Norris 1992 for a discussion of detective culture, and Reiner 2000 for police culture generally). It can consequently be difficult to encourage investigators to share information – to enter it into a process in which they may have no involvement, or recognition for, the eventual result.

A related weakness has been identified in the private sector. Friedman *et al.* argue that: 'Intelligence systems cannot be created without creating a culture of intelligence' (1997: 8). Without the importance of intelligence being emphasised to *all* staff, even those without direct involvement in intelligence or investigation; insufficient information will be fed into the system to make it effective. Recognising this, attempt the exercise in Box 11.3.

Box 11.3   Exercise 11B Encouraging participation

Write down a list of methods by which police and other staff might be encouraged to pass on information into the intelligence system.

The second major difficulty lies in ensuring that the information and intelligence is analysed, problems identified, and intelligence actioned. Recent investment in specialist roles of intelligence analysts (Cope 2003; John and Maguire 2004) has improved this area significantly.

Although progress in developing an intelligence culture had been made with the introduction of the National Intelligence Model, variations in local interpretations of it detracted from uniformity, and therefore the ability for intelligence to be shared. Possession of knowledge is of little value if it is not disseminated.

The intelligence cycle does, therefore, have weaknesses. Nevertheless, it represents an established process for converting raw information into intelligence – information prepared for action. To some extent, the weaknesses identified within this process have been associated with intelligence traditionally being the preserve of specialist units within the police service. It was often only those officers (or civilians) with direct investigative experience of intelligence that were fully committed to developing the process. To those outside of this clique, the potential or relevance of intelligence to their daily function had been ambiguous. The past two decades have seen a determined move towards elevating the use of intelligence within the police.

Bichard and the management of police intelligence (MoPI)

In terms of the dissemination of intelligence, the 5x5x5 system outlined in the previous chapter provides some guidance concerning the routes for sharing. The dissemination of intelligence, and the way in which the police and other agencies manage intelligence, has to be viewed in the light of the Bichard Inquiry set up in the aftermath of the murders of Jessica Chapman and Holly Wells by Ian Huntley in 2002. The lessons emerging from Bichard and the development of the IMPACT programme following Bichard have had a fundamental impact on the way in which intelligence is managed and shared by criminal justice agencies.

The Bichard Inquiry

On 17 December 2003 Ian Huntley was convicted of the murders of Jessica Chapman and Holly Wells. At the time there was a great deal of disquiet about the fact that Huntley had been known to the authorities over a period of years, having come to the attention of Humberside Police in relation to allegations of eight separate sexual offences between 1995 and 1999 (and been investigated in another). This information had not emerged during the vetting check, carried out by Cambridgeshire Constabulary at the time of Huntley's appointment to Soham Village College late in 2001.

As a result an inquiry was set up by the Home Secretary, chaired by Sir Michael Bichard. The terms of the inquiry were to

> urgently enquire into child protection procedures in Humberside Police and Cambridgeshire Constabulary in the light of the recent trial and conviction of Ian Huntley for the murder of Jessica Chapman and Holly Wells. In particular to assess the effectiveness of the relevant intelligence-based record keeping, the vetting practices in those forces since 1995 and information sharing with other agencies, and to report to the Home Secretary on matters of local and national relevance and make recommendations as appropriate.
>
> (Bichard 2004:1)

A report outlining the findings from the inquiry was produced in 2004.

While the report identified a number of serious errors made by Cambridgeshire Constabulary (largely related to the operation of the force's Criminal Records Bureau) it concluded that these were not systematic or corporate. However, this was the term the report used to describe the failures in the way Humberside Police managed their intelligence systems – 'failures…all the more surprising given the emphasis all the witnesses placed on the importance of intelligence and the need to identify patterns of criminal behaviour as early as possible' (ibid.: 2).

Specifically, the process of creating records on Humberside's main local intelligence system was 'fundamentally flawed' during the relevant period and police officers at various levels 'were alarmingly ignorant of how records were created and how the system worked. The guidance and training available were inadequate and this fed the confusion which surrounded the review and deletion of records once they had been created' (ibid.: 2).

In addition, the report concluded that there was no common understanding of what was meant by 'weeding', 'reviewing' and 'deletion' in the force, and that while it was impossible to say how many records had been lost, 'the only sensible inference' was that it was a 'significant number' in what the report called a 'haemorrhaging' of intelligence (ibid.: 2). The failings in the intelligence system were compounded by the fact that other systems (the crime system and the child protection database) were also not being operated properly.

Initial responses by Humberside Police, for example, in a press release on 17 December 2003, suggested that data protection legislation was a principal reason for information about their dealings with Huntley not being available to them in 2001. This suggestion was rejected by Bichard, and was subsequently withdrawn by the Chief Constable of Humberside. However, the inquiry found that police officers were nervous about breaching data protection legislation, in part because too little had been done to educate and reassure them about its impact. Overall the inquiry concluded that, while there was no need to revise the Data Protection Act in the light of the events in Soham, there was a need for 'better guidance...on the collection, retention, deletion, use and sharing of information, so that police officers, social workers and other professionals can feel more confident in using information properly' (ibid.: 4).[1]

The Impact Programme and MoPI

Bichard identified the need to improve the management and sharing of information and intelligence by the Police Service at national and local levels, and for IT systems to support this. As a result the government established the Impact Programme (now overseen by the National Policing Improvement Agency (NPIA) to put Bichard's recommendations into practice. The overall aims of Impact were 'to improve the ability of the police service to manage and share information to prevent and detect crime and provide safer communities' (NPIA website), and to help achieve this, a statutory code of practice on the management of police information (MoPI) was introduced in 2005.

The code itself is a concise document – some six pages, including the title page. It states that 'police forces have a duty to obtain and use a wide variety of information (including personal information), in order to discharge their responsibilities effectively...the purpose of this code and associated guidance is to assist the police to carry out that duty' (ACPO Centrex 2006: 68). Recognising that 'the effective use of information for police purposes required consistent procedures to be in place throughout the police service' the code aims 'to ensure that there is broad consistency between forces in the way information is managed within the law, to ensure effective use of available information within and between individual police forces and other agencies, and to provide fair treatment to members of the public' (ACPO Centrex 2006: 68). To this end the code sets out procedures:

- to be applied in obtaining and recording that information;
- to ensure the accuracy of information managed by the police;
- for reviewing the need to retain information and, where it is no longer needed, to destroy it;
- governing [the] authorised sharing of information within the police service and with other agencies; and
- to maintain consistent procedures for the management of information within all police forces so as to facilitate information sharing and the development of service-wide technological support for information management' (ACPO Centrex 2006: 68).

Under 'key principles', the code identifies the police duty to obtain and manage the information needed for police purposes. These purposes are defined as:

(a) protecting life and property;
(b) preserving order;
(c) preventing the commission of offences;
(d) bringing offenders to justice; and
(e) any duty or responsibility of the police arising from common or statute law (ACPO Centrex 2006: 70).

In addition, the obtaining and management of police information[2] has to be done in a manner that complies with the code (section 4.1.2) and with the National Intelligence Model (NIM section 4.2.1). Subsequent sections of the code deal with issues around the ownership of police data (section 4.4), the review of police information (4.5), the retention and deletion of police information (4.6), and the sharing of police information within (4.7), and outside (4.8) UK police forces. Section 4.3.2 of the code specifically states that 'the source of the information, the nature of the source, any assessment of the reliability of the source, and any necessary restrictions on the use to be made of the information should be recorded to permit later review, reassessment and audit' where appropriate (ACPO Centrex 2006: 71). Interestingly the guidance on MoPI, published by ACPO and Centrex in 2006, runs to some 60 pages, followed by a further 40 pages of appendices (although, in fairness, the latter do include the code itself). A central component of the guidance, clearly critical in the aftermath of Bichard, is the identification of who has responsibility for the various requirements under the code.

Pro-active policing: intelligence, surveillance and informants

Legislation governing the management and acquisition of information

Explicit in MoPi is the recognition 'that there is an existing legal framework for the management of information in legislation relating to data protection, human rights and freedom of information' (ACPO Centrex 2006: 6). Police activities are clearly guided and constrained by a number of pieces of legislation. In circumstances where, as Maguire found, surveillance techniques have increasingly been targeted at lower level crimes and police contact with the public is often restricted and reduced, legislation is needed to do what increasingly the public cannot (Maguire 2000). Laws relevant to intelligence are broadly divided into two groups:

1. Mechanisms and methods for acquiring intelligence.
2. The management of intelligence (definition of rights, obligations, exemptions and powers relating to data held by public authorities) (Harfield and Harfield 2008).

Principles of intelligence acquisition

According to Harfield and Harfield, to prevent 'fishing trips' and avoid the collection of data for data's sake, the acquisition of intelligence has to conform to four principles, represented by the mnemonic PLAN:

- Proportionality (is it proportionate to obtain the intended intelligence in the manner proposed?). As Ratcliffe observes, 'proportionality applies not only to target selection but also to the methods of targeting...tactics that the public may deem acceptable for organized crime families may therefore not be viewed as appropriate when used to target the boy living in the next street', particularly in the light of findings which suggest that the police sometimes increase the status of offenders beyond their actual abilities (Ratcliffe 2008: 218).
- Lawfulness/legitimacy (the proposed action must be lawful). In RIPA the legitimacy tests are: the prevention of disorder or crime; the interests of national security; the interests of public safety; the interests of the economic well-being of the country; the protection of health or morals; or the protection of the rights or freedoms of others).
- Authority to undertake proposed action (what is the lawful foundation/authority for the proposed action, and from whom must authorisation be sought?).
- Necessity of proposed action (why is the proposed action necessary?) (Harfield and Harfield 2008: 119).

The critical pieces of legislation that determine the acquisition of intelligence are outlined below.

1. Police and Evidence Act 1984 (as amended), and subsequent Codes of Practice. The acquisition of personal identification data (DNA profiles, fingerprints, etc.) is critical in the identification of suspects. The power to acquire such personal data derives from the powers provided to the police by PACE.

2. Police Act 1997 (part 111) gave specific public authorities the ability to trespass upon and interfere with private property in order to facilitate restricted forms of covert surveillance.

3. Regulation of Investigatory Powers Act (RIPA) 2000 – while the 1997 Police Act enabled certain covert surveillance tactics, RIPA provides the statutory authority to undertake covert surveillance. RIPA outlines the various surveillance powers that are available to specific agencies in specific circumstances, which are stipulated in various statutory instruments. An authorisation for intrusive surveillance (available to law-enforcement agencies, including SOCA, and intelligence services) may be authorised under RIPA if it is supporting an investigation that is necessary:

   (a) in the interests of national security
   (b) to prevent or detect serious crime
   (c) in the interests of the economic well-being of the United Kingdom.

   Directed surveillance (including the deployment of CHIS, and which is available to a wider range of public authorities, including local councils) may be authorised under RIPA if the intelligence operation is supporting an investigation required:

   (a) in the interests of national security
   (b) to prevent or detect crime or prevent disorder
   (c) in the interests of the economic well-being of the United Kingdom
   (d) in the interests of public safety
   (e) for the purpose of protecting public health
   (f) for the purpose of assessing or collecting any tax or duty
   (g) for any purpose additional to the above specified by an order made by the Secretary of State (Harfield and Harfield 2008: 122–123).

4. The Proceeds of Crime Act – part 7 imposes obligations to report suspicious financial transactions to combat money laundering.

The management of intelligence

Intelligence comprises information and data. Consequently, when it is held by public authorities it is subject to the various laws that exist on data protection and information disclosure, with certain restrictions, considered under the following two headings:

1. Statutory duty to disclose information.
2. Statutory duty to protect data (adapted from Harfield and Harfield 2008).

1. Statutory duty to disclose information

- Section 1 of the Freedom of Information Act 2000 states that 'any person making a request for information to a public authority is entitled (a) to be informed in writing by the public authority whether it holds information of the description specified in the request, and (b) if that is the case, to have that information communicated to him'. However, sections 30 (1) and (2) and 31 (1) of the Act provide exemptions to the general premise above, which mean 'essentially, intelligence in relation to criminal activities, investigations and proceedings is exempt from the general principle of disclosure enshrined in the FIA' (Harfield and Harfield 2008: 128).[3]

- The Criminal Proceedings and Investigations Act 1996 (CPIA) – which arose out of a number of miscarriages of justice in the 1980s and 1990s where prosecutions had taken place despite the existence of evidence indicating the innocence of the accused. The CPIA imposed the obligation on investigators to reveal to the prosecution unused material that did not form part of the prosecution file, and for the prosecution to disclose to the defence unused material that tended to support the defence case.[4]

- The Police Act 1997 – under sections 112–127 of the Act, authority was provided to disclose information held by the Criminal Records Bureau under certain conditions.

- The Crime and Disorder Act 1998 – created a statutory power for the exchange of information between agencies for the purposes of crime reduction. This was subsequently amended by the Police and Justice Act 2006 to give the Secretary of State the ability to *specify* information that had to be shared by relevant CDRP authorities (discussed in greater detail in Chapter 13).

2. Statutory duty to protect data

- Covered by the Data Protection Act 1998 – under which there are eight principles of data protection.

Covert human intelligence sources (CHIS)

Informants, whether paid or unpaid, or staff working undercover or on test-purchase operations, are all covert human intelligence sources (CHIS), and their use and deployment require authorisation (Harfield and Harfield 2005). According to guidance issued by ACPO in 2007, 'a CHIS represents a potentially useful source of information and a valuable tool for law enforcement. All staff must have a basic understanding of how, and under what circumstances, someone becomes a CHIS' (ACPO 2007: 22). Notwithstanding this straightforward exhortation, it is still the case that a degree of confusion remains about when somebody should be registered as a CHIS.

The legal definition of a CHIS is provided by RIPA. Section 26(8) of RIPA classifies a person as a CHIS if:

(a) he establishes or maintains a personal or other relationship with a person for the covert purpose of facilitating the doing of anything falling within paragraph (b) or (c);
(b) he covertly uses such a relationship to obtain information or to provide access to any information to another person; or
(c) he covertly discloses information obtained by the use of such a relationship or as a consequence of the existence of such a relationship (ACPO 2007: 22).[5]

Professionalism and ethics in intelligence gathering

Innes and Roberts, writing about the police use of community intelligence, refer to the pejorative associations of intelligence in a policing context: 'intelligence as a concept routinely connotes notions of covert, secretive and politicized social control' and is seen as 'part of the dirty work of democratic policing', although they suggest that the increased emphasis on 'community' rather than 'criminal intelligence' has led to a movement away from covert towards open sources (Innes and Roberts n.d.: 2). Ratcliffe, writing in 2008, states that there is a 'misconception among both police and the public that the meaning of intelligence retains a suggestion of subterfuge, a clandestine and covert activity conducted by officers of a shady disposition and involving a degree of moral ambiguity' (Ratcliffe 2008: 213).

However, the extent to which Ratcliffe is correct in describing this view as a 'misconception' is open to debate. In work published in 2005, Innes *et al.* described how they had conducted fieldwork in four intelligence units in two UK police forces. They suggested that while crime analysts made use of both 'open' and 'closed' sources in the course of their work, police intelligence workers tended to rely on 'closed' sources, namely police databases and informants, particularly where the latter were established and had supplied pertinent and reliable information in the past. They concluded that, in part, this reflected cultural beliefs within the police, earlier identified by Manning, that the most trustworthy individuals were least likely to be in possession of reliable information about ongoing criminality (Innes *et al.* 2005).

This notion of the benefits of covert intelligence is echoed by Harfield and Harfield, who suggest that the 'significant advantage' of covert investigation is that it produces evidence which is often 'considered to be incontrovertible', where investigation subjects incriminate themselves without realising it (2005: 4). However, in contrast to the regulation of overt investigation, the secrecy of covert investigation limits the ways in which investigators can be managed and held to account.

Risks in the use of covert investigation

The risk of the inappropriate use of confidential human sources and attempts to control their usage is nothing new (see, for example, Grieve's account of the development of intelligence use in the Metropolitan Police, and attempts by the head of CID in the 1970s and 1980s to reform the payment and handling of informants, described in Ratcliffe 2008). Similarly, academic studies in the 1990s suggested that the legislative response to increased use of covert sources had been ad-hoc, piecemeal and insufficient (Maguire and John, cited in Ratcliffe 2008) (Box 11.4).

Box 11.4   Exercise 11C The use of covert intelligence

The use of covert intelligence may have negative as well as positive repercussions for the police. Before proceeding, take time to consider what some of these negative consequences might be.

The use of covert intelligence can have negative as well as positive consequences – crime is facilitated as well as repressed, criminals are allowed to commit crimes by officers rather than being apprehended, rule-bending may be condoned rather than condemned within the police, and relations among colleagues within the police may suffer where there is distrust and secrecy, rather than openness. In turn, this may have a consequent impact upon police morale (Norris and Dunningham, cited in Ratcliffe 2008). What the greater use of covert sources obviously points to is the need to check and verify the information that is obtained.

'Helping with Enquiries: Tackling Crime Effectively'

A key watershed in moving intelligence into the mainstream of policing was the publication of the Audit Commission Report 'Helping with Enquiries: Tackling Crime Effectively' in 1993. The report argued that:

> The police are caught in a vicious circle of reactive policing in which crime threatens to overwhelm them.
>
> (Audit Commission 1993: .40)

The vicious circle, represented in Figure 11.2, presented a summary of the Audit Commission's view of inefficiencies resulting from a reactive, 'fire-brigading' model of policing with resources focused around responding to incidents on an ad hoc basis. Despite long-term increases in investment into the police force, the volume of crime was rising inexorably. The pressures associated with responding to the incidents as they occurred provided the police with little resources or

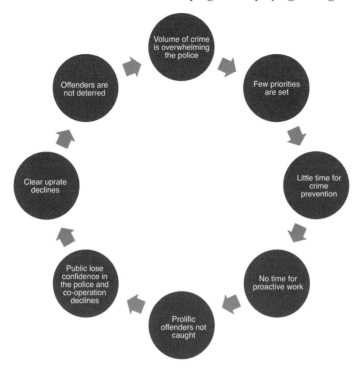

Figure 11.2 The vicious cycle of reactive investigations.
Source: Adapted from Audit Commission (1993).

space to adopt a strategic, prioritised approach. For example, in responding to individual incidents, opportunities to concentrate on the arrest and successful prosecution of prolific offenders who were responsible for a disproportionate number of crimes were minimal. When such offenders were arrested and charged it would tend to be for a single offence, with the potential for attaching them to other offences committed through intelligence gathered missed. As a result deterrence would be minimal, both in terms of the chances of being caught, and of the extent of the sentence given being restricted to a small proportion of the individual's offences. And so, the Audit Commission argued, the cycle would continue with little opportunity for it to be broken. This cycle is illustrated in Figure 11.2.

The Audit Commission presented a strong case for an alternative approach to policing to be adopted, an approach that would draw on the pro-active policing techniques of intelligence, surveillance, informants and crime prevention. Using the mantra of 'target the criminal, not the crime', the Audit Commission argued that the vicious circle could be broken by the police focusing on the activities of serious and prolific offenders. Using intelligence, surveillance and informants to target this relatively small group of people would allow for a more efficient use of resources. A proactive concentration on the offenders rather than reactive investigation of the crimes they had already committed would produce more significant results – more arrests and ultimately longer sentences – as a clearer picture would be established of the range of offences for which an arrestee was responsible. At the same time, the resultant reduction in crime-related demands on the police would free up resources which would then be focused on addressing priorities set by the police themselves – removing the reliance on ad hoc, inefficient response. The Audit Commission argued that this approach would produce a 'virtuous' circle through pro-active policing, represented in Figure 11.3.

The Audit Commission's report received widespread attention within the police, and many forces introduced or developed existing systems and processes around the pro-active policing techniques. In an early review for the Police Research Group (Maguire and John 1995), the authors identified a range of approaches across the forces in which they conducted their research. For example, a particular focus of the Audit Commission was the use of informants as an effective and efficient use of resources. They saw informants as the 'lifeblood of

Figure 11.3 The virtuous cycle of pro-active investigations.

Source: Adapted from Audit Commission (1993).

the CID', and in one review of a force's results from informants over a six-month period it was noted that the police paid out:

> £60 ... per person arrested and £57 per crime detected. For every £1 paid to informants, stolen property to the value of £12 was recovered. Some 219 crimes were cleared up at a cost for the period equivalent to one detective constable.

Although the presentation of these figures has subsequently been criticised for ignoring the costs in police time in the recruitment and management of informants (Dunninghan and Norris 1999), they were persuasive at the time. Maguire and John (1995) reviewed in some detail progress made within forces in developing their informant networks and support structures. Particular obstacles around the sharing of informants and their resultant information were identified and considerable progress in this area has subsequently been made. In the context of this chapter, a salient point to note was the identification of the need for resources to be available to act on 'live' information as it came in. This partly applied to intelligence in general terms also. For forces that developed intelligence and informants in isolation from the creation of dedicated surveillance or response teams, there was often a gap in being able to provide a response. Quality intelligence/information from an informant was being gained but there were not the available resources to act on it while it was still live.

Conversely, for forces which concentrated their resources on the creation of a sophisticated mobile surveillance squad, problems existed if it was not supported by accurate, timely and actionable intelligence and information from informants. Mobile surveillance squads are an expensive resource (£400,000 per annum in 1995). In order to be deployed effectively they need to be targeted to activities that will produce results. In the absence of reliable intelligence and informants this resource could be wasted by itself being used in an ad hoc, loosely managed way.

Intelligence-led policing

In recognising the weaknesses in these piecemeal moves that some forces had made to implementing the central findings of the Audit Commission Report, Maguire and John (1995) identified the activities of several forces which had taken an integrated approach to developing the various strands of pro-active policing. Kent police, in particular, had introduced a pilot in several of its BCUs that attempted to reorient a range of policing functions – not only those associated with CID – around intelligence, supported by information from informants and the use of surveillance (see also Amey *et al.* 1996). This Crime Management Model sought to ensure that intelligence informed the activities of all branches of the police. For example, uniform patrol officers might be asked to determine which vehicle a particular target was currently using. It also involved the introduction of a call centre to screen calls to determine which would need a police response and which could be dealt with by other means. In so doing it sought to free up police time away from the demands of reactive policing and towards a more pro-active approach. Of the approaches reviewed by Maguire and John, the holistic approach developed by Kent and some other forces seemed to provide the most appropriate mechanism for supporting the Audit Commission's ambitions with respect to the benefits of adopting a pro-active rather than reactive approach to policing:

> [W]hile many forces are convinced of the need for a shift to pro-activity in criminal investigations, it is only in those forces which have taken the calculated risk of investing in major organisational reforms to support this kind of work that it is beginning to make a substantial contribution to the overall picture of crime control. Neither 'good intentions' nor 'exhortations', nor isolated reforms to enhance the use of individual forms of proactive work, are likely to be sufficient. Without holistic, structured systems in which officers are given clearly defined and protected roles, initiatives are frustrated by constant abstractions to cope with reactive demand, and by blockages and hiatuses in what should be a steady flow of information and actions.
>
> (Maguire and John 1995: 54)

This holistic approach and the organisational reforms they reflected began, through the 1990s, to be referred to as 'intelligence-led policing' (ILP) (John and Maguire 2004). This distinguished the more structured and holistic approach from the pro-active policing deployment of the individual (or combined) tactics. Intelligence-led policing models typically sought to place intelligence at the heart of police decision making, although they still retained a bias towards police activities focused on crime and criminality. Maguire has described this approach as reflective of a general move towards:

> a strategic, future-oriented and targeted approach to crime control, focussing upon the identification, analysis and 'management' of persisting and devel- oping 'problems' or 'risks' (which may be particular people, activities or areas), rather than on the reactive investigation and detection of individual crimes.
>
> (Maguire 2000: 315)

The ILP approach typically involved some substantial reorganisation of the police structure, placing a greater emphasis on Intelligence Units informing the activities of a range of police departments outside of the CID. In order to free up resources from reactive response, mechanisms for screening calls were intro- duced to determine whether a physical police response was necessary (Maguire and John 1995). The reactive, investigative side of detective work was frequently 'hollowed out' to create roles that could pro-actively pursue the management of 'problems' and 'risks'.

Intelligence-led policing (ILP)

> conveys the relatively obvious notion that policing activity (be it focused on community safety, the investigation of crime, the regulation of trading standards, the collection of customs and excise, or organizational (*sic*) priorities expressed in terms of intelligence requirement, prevention, enforcement, and reassurance) should be informed and directed rather than undertaken randomly.
>
> (Harfield and Harfield 2008: 5)

The aim of ILP is to provide 'information designed for action' (Grieve 2004: 25), to identify 'criminal capability, [assess] criminal intention, then [manage] interventions against these two factors in timely fashion' (Harfield and Harfield 2008: 6).

It should be stressed that ILP is not a modern concept – the Harfields, in their discussion of the concept, refer to Vincent's 1881 'Police Code and General Manual of Criminal Law', and Grieve provides a short summary of the Met's intelligence function from the late nineteenth century onward (Grieve 2004). However, the specific term 'intelligence-led policing' originated in Kent Police in England during the 1990s and was closely associated with the then Chief Constable David Phillips and the subsequent development of the National Intelligence Model (NIM).

While the emergence of ILP has been linked with the ethos of new managerialism, with a focus on performance indicators and targets, value for money, and achieving more from resources, the architect of the approach (Phillips) stressed its importance in supporting criminal detection and CID at a time when they were under increasing pressure from community policing during the 1980s and 1990s (Harfield and Harfield 2008).

Nevertheless, ILP is perhaps best seen as part of what Innes *et al.* describe as a 'move away from an ad-hoc intuitive and largely unstructured mode of analytic work, to a more ordered rationalized approach, based upon specific methodologies, on the basis that this provides a more 'objective perspective on patterns of crime and offending' (Innes *et al.* 2005). Clearly, in this respect, intelligence-led policing sits comfortably within well-established principles in the community safety and crime prevention field of partnership and multi-agency working (beginning with the HO circular 8/84, then continuing with the Morgan Report 1991, the Crime and Disorder Act 1998, the National Policing Plan, Police and Justice Act 2006, and continuing into the present with the Green Paper on policing and the current emphasis on neighbourhood policing).

CompStat (computerised statistics)

A related development that has arisen from a focus on intelligence and its availability has been the introduction of CompStat and equivalent programmes. CompStat was introduced in New York City by Police Commissioner William

Branton in the 1990s. CompStat combines elements of crime mapping with four core principles: timely and accurate information and intelligence; effective tactics; rapid deployment; and relentless follow-up and assessment (Home Office 2005). Identification and interpretation of crime hotspots forms the basis of the CompStat system, and the role of live intelligence and information is key to this. There is a strong element of review of operational tactics' success or failure. The American model introduced a publicly visible, high-profile and somewhat adversarial system of accountability of senior officers for success or failure in addressing the hotspots and reducing the problems associated with them. While CompStat principles have been adopted in other countries (the Thames Valley is a notable example in the UK), its long-term contribution to tackling the problems it identifies has not been convincingly evaluated. In New York, for example, its introduction coincided with a range of other initiatives including a substantial expansion in police numbers and the deployment of zero-tolerance policing strategies. Managerially within police forces, however, the contribution that CompStat can make to raising the profile and active use of intelligence and retaining a focus on particular issues and hotspots until issues are resolved are frequently welcomed. There is also potential for links between CompStat and other approaches to managing policing, such as community policing, to be more explicitly made (Willis *et al.* 2010).

Concluding comments

This chapter has described the development of intelligence from its embodiment in the police as a specific tactic that is used alongside surveillance and informants as part of a move towards more holistic pro-active policing approaches that then develop into intelligence-led policing. This theme is developed in subsequent chapters. It should be emphasised here, though, that the developments discussed above still locate intelligence within the crime-fighting sphere of the role of the police. The broader forms of intelligence identified by Innes *et al.* are marginalised within this particular approach. More recent developments, in particular the National Intelligence Model in the UK, have sought to place intelligence at the heart of the management of all police (and, increasingly, the relevant functions of multi-agency partners) resources and functions. It is to these developments that we turn in Chapter 12.

References and suggested further reading

ACPO (1978) *Third Report of the Working Party on A Structure of Criminal Intelligence Offices above Force Level* (the Pearce Report). Association of Chief Police Officers, London.

ACPO Centrex (2006) *Guidance on the Management of Police Information.* ACPO, Wyboston, Bedfordshire.

—— (2007) *Practice Advice: Introduction to Intelligence-Led Policing.* ACPO Wyboston, Bedfordshire.

Amey, P., Hale, C., and Uglow, S. (1996) *Development and Evaluation of a Crime Management Model*. Police Research Series Paper 18. Home Office, London.

Audit Commission (1993) *Helping with Enquiries: Tackling Crime Effectively*. Audit Commission, London.

Barton, A. and Evans, R. (1999) *Proactive Policing on Merseyside*. Police Research Series, Paper No.105, Home Office, London.

Bichard, M. (2004) *The Bichard Inquiry Report*. House of Commons, London.

Blades, A.J. (1997) *The Development and Application of a Security Intelligence System to Support the Security Manager as a Decision Maker*. Unpublished M.Sc. thesis, University of Leicester.

Cope, N. (2003) 'Crime analysis: principles and practice', in Newburn, T. (ed.), *Handbook of Policing*. Willan Publishing, Cullompton, Devon.

Dunningham, C. and Norris, C. (1999) 'The detective, the snout, and the audit commission: the real costs of using informants', *Howard Journal of Criminal Justice*, 38(1): 67–86.

Friedman, G., Friedman, M., Chapman, C. and Baker, J.S. (1997) *The Intelligence Edge*. Random House, London.

Grieve, J. (2004) 'Developments in UK criminal intelligence', in Ratcliffe, J. (ed.) *Strategic Thinking in Criminal Intelligence*. Federation Press, Annandale.

Harfield, C. and Harfield, K. (2005) *Covert Investigation*. Oxford University Press, Oxford.

—— (2008) *Intelligence; Investigation, Community and Partnership*. Oxford University Press, Oxford.

Home Office (2005) *Crime Mapping: Improving Performance – A Good Practice Guide for Frontline Officers*. Home Office, Communications Directorate, London.

Innes, M. and Roberts, C. (n.d.) 'Community intelligence in the policing of community safety'. UPSI website.

Innes, M., Fielding, N. and Cope, N. (2005) ' "The appliance of science?" The theory and practice of crime intelligence analysis', *British Journal of Criminology*, 45: 39–57.

John, T. and Maguire, M. (2004) *The National Intelligence Model: Key Lessons from Early Research*. Home Office Online Report 30/04.

Levi, M. (1981) *The Phantom Capitalists: The Organisation and Control of Long-term Fraud*. Heinemann, London.

Maguire, M. (2000) 'Policing by risks and targets: some dimensions and implications of intelligence-led crime control', *Policing and Society*, 9: 315–336.

—— (2003) 'Crime investigation and crime control', in Newburn, T. (ed.), *Handbook of Policing*. Willan Publishing, Cullompton, Devon.

Maguire, M. and John, T. (1995) *Intelligence, Surveillance, and Informants: Integrated Approaches*. Police Research Group Crime and Prevention Series, Paper No. 64. Home Office, London.

Maguire, M. and Norris, C. (1992) *The Conduct and Supervision of Criminal Investigations*. Research Study No.5, Royal Commission on Criminal Justice. HMSO, London.

Ratcliffe, J. (2008) *Intelligence-Led Policing*. Willan Publishing, Cullompton, Devon.

Reiner, R. (2000) *The Politics of the Police 3rd Edition*. Oxford University Press, Oxford.

Wills, J.J., Mastrofski, S.D. and Kochel, T.R. (2010) 'Recommendations for Integrating Compstat and Community Policing', *Policing Journal*. Oxford University Press, Oxford, Vol 4(2), pp. 182–193.

12 Intelligence-led policing and the National Intelligence Model

Introduction

This chapter develops the previous discussions on intelligence-led policing that began in Chapter 10. The chapter recognises that, while being *a* development that arose from ILP, the National Intelligence Model is not *only* about ILP, and can equally embrace other policing tactics. Its development and prominence is also explained by its contextualisation of knowledge management principles within policing, and through its specific recognition and articulation of strategic intelligence. The chapter therefore begins with an overview of these two areas.

Knowledge management principles

Since the early 1990s the notion and application of knowledge management principles has extended considerably, from the private to the public sectors. Knowledge management recognises that the individuals within an organisation are the principal owners of knowledge. In essence, knowledge management seeks to ensure that organisational structures are enhanced to ensure such knowledge is available to the organisation as a whole, and barriers to this goal are minimised. As Ratcliffe (2008) discusses, using the Bichard Inquiry Report as an example, failures within policing for knowledge to be disseminated can have tragic consequences. Intelligence management weaknesses in one force area prevented background information from being passed on to another force which in turn would have prevented Ian Huntley from gaining employment as a school caretaker.

In specific areas, the police have for some time recognised the importance of shifting the focus of knowledge ownership away from individuals and towards the organisation. A clear example is that of informants, or Covert Human Intelligence Sources. CHIS can be a valuable resource but in the past have tended to be 'owned' by a sole detective. Co-handling and management of informants introduces a degree of continuity should the primary handler retire or move to another force area (Maguire and John 1995).

The discussion of the National Intelligence Model (NIM) that follows precludes a detailed analysis of knowledge management principles. Nevertheless, the NIM represents a significant contribution to reorienting the police service within a consistent knowledge-based framework of decision making and prioritisation. A useful overview of knowledge management and knowledge organisations within the policing context is provided by Gottschalk and colleagues (2009). A significant arm of the development of knowledge-based decision making has been an increased focus on the creation of strategic intelligence.

Strategic intelligence

In part, this reorientation has involved a recognition that intelligence in the police has traditionally been focused on tactical and operational issues rather than on longer term challenges and goals. As Flood has identified, 'Intelligence activity in most police forces had exclusively short-term operational objectives' (2004: 40). This served to reinforce the problems associated with reactive policing models as discussed in Chapter 10 of this book. The past two decades have seen a deliberate move, in the UK and elsewhere, towards a strategic approach to addressing challenges and managing policing resources. While tactical intelligence remains significant, a strategic view provides an overarching knowledge-based assessment of crime, criminality and other policing issues – as well as responses to them.

Despite the logic of the arguments for evidence-based and long-term, strategic approaches however, their integration into mainstream policing has proved to be a 'hard-sell'. Sheptycki and Ratcliffe (2004) identify a number of factors that contribute to this position across policy and practice arenas within the police. For example, a strategic approach does not necessarily produce a measurable outcome in the same way that operational intelligence might – this is of significance in a policing environment driven by performance measurement. This is an obstacle to both the setters of the performance indicators and those operational personnel who seek to meet them. In addition, within the police, it is argued that 'Tactical or operational analysts, detectives and investigators view strategic intelligence work as lacking day-to-day relevance' (2004: 195). In essence, it appears, strategic intelligence has been viewed as abstract from day-to-day policing and policing deliverables.

Despite such challenges, the relatively new focus on strategic intelligence has developed and become increasingly invested in and supported. Offering potential for resource allocation, and tying into developments in risk management, it satisfies a demand for decision making to be taken on the basis of a firm foundation of knowledge. In the UK, the requirement for strategy to be considered explicitly has been formalised within the National Intelligence Model.

The National Intelligence Model

The National Intelligence Model (NIM) was launched in 2000. The Police Reform Act 2002 made it a requirement that each police force adopt the Model by April 2004. As such, the NIM represents a significant development in advancing standardised police procedures and means of operating police business. As discussed in Chapter 10, the NIM is a development in a continuum of policing that marks an evolution from the adoption of individual pro-active policing techniques, to the more holistic approach denoted by 'intelligence-led policing'.

It should be noted, however, that the NIM has a much broader purpose than its genesis suggests. Its ambition is to act as an overarching business process that informs the decision making and prioritisation decisions within policing at various levels – from the local BCU through to major organised crime with national and international ramifications. The Model encompasses all police business and not only that associated with crime and criminality. This is emphasised in the Code of Practice, in a subheading entitled 'A National Model for Policing':

> The National Intelligence Model is a business process. The intention behind it is to provide focus to operational policing and to achieve a disproportionately greater impact from the resources applied to any problem. It is dependent on a clear framework of analysis of information and intelligence allowing a problem solving approach to law enforcement and crime prevention techniques. The expected outcomes are improved community safety, reduced crime and the control of criminality and disorder leading to greater public reassurance and confidence.
>
> (National Intelligence Model Code of Practice: 6)

Note, in the context of the discussion in Chapter 10 in this book, that it explicitly relies on a 'framework of analysis of *information and intelligence*' – a further indicator that the remit of the Model is broader than reliance on criminal intelligence. Neither is the NIM solely a mechanism for the management of intelligence-led policing. As a 'business process' that adopts a 'problem solving approach' its tactics are dictated by the nature of the problem. The knowledge, or intelligence, on a particular issue dictates the appropriate response from the resources at the police's (or their partners') disposal. Hence a neighbourhood policing presence might be as acceptable a resolution under the NIM as the use of a surveillance team.

In order to achieve this intention, the National Intelligence Model establishes a range of structures and procedures to support its business. A brief account will be presented here. Fuller details are contained in the 'Guidance on the National Intelligence Model' produced by ACPO Centrex in 2005.

NIM components

1. Levels

The NIM establishes clear levels of operation, local, force/cross-border, and national/international. The NIM processes and structures are essentially replicated at each level, and the particular level reflects the focus of the business conducted. The Guidelines for the NIM provide an overview.

As Flood (1999: 9), the principal author of the Model puts it:

> The model is, therefore, very ambitious, for in describing the links between the levels it offers for the first time the realisable goal of integrated intelligence in which all forces might play a part in a system bigger than themselves. How can we have a sound crime strategy if we cannot paint the picture of crime and criminality from top to bottom?

In specifying the levels in this way, a clear intention of the NIM is to allow a detailed national picture to be developed. Each BCU will produce a detailed picture of policing challenges in its area, principally through its strategic assessments (see below). In drawing together this information from across all of its BCUs a force will be able to develop a resultant force-wide picture. In turn, a national picture can be developed by pulling together the information and intelligence from each police force. This upward transmission of information and intelligence should potentially allow centrally set priorities (e.g. performance indicators) to be taken from common issues derived from the more local pictures.

Operationally, the levels are capable of being used to allow a coordinated approach to particular policing problems. John and Maguire (2004) provided an example in relation to drugs with Level Two focusing on operations around class A drugs distribution affecting the region, and open drugs markets in the particular force area. At the same time, BCUs were coordinating local activities through Community Against Drugs-funded activity at Level One. In the case study that they provided, there were clear links between the NIM levels in the coordination of these activities. It would be consistent with the model for Level Three to also have an input, focusing, for example, on international drug networks and importation issues. Hence the levels allow a coordinated response to a particular issue with each level owning responsibility for the resolutions at its particular focus of impact.

The NIM introduces a similar set of structures and processes that operate at each level. The following provides an account of these.

2. Assets

The Guidance on the National Intelligence Model identifies crucial assets upon which the model is based. These are established as shown in Box 12.1.

Knowledge assets are those that establish the framework within which policing operates, and includes:

- Current legislation and case law
- Codes of practice
- Manuals of standards and ACPO guidance
- Force policies
- Briefing products.

Box 12.1   Information point – The model's crucial assets

Knowledge assets – Knowing the business of policing and understanding law, policy and guidance.
System assets – Having appropriate systems and structures in place, including secure environments and practices.
Source assets – Ensuring information is effectively gathered and managed from as many sources as possible.
People assets – Establishing a professional personnel structure with trained and suitably skilled staff to carry out the required functions within the model.

(ACPO Centrex 2005: 13)

The level of knowledge about a particular area will be dictated by the role of an individual within their police force.

System assets are designed to ensure that appropriate technical and computer equipment is available to the model for its effective operation and to minimise inefficient practices such as the use of incompatible IT systems that act as a barrier to the sharing of information. They are also used to ensure that access is secured across the different levels, and to other agencies, and to international law-enforcement bodies. System assets also identify key security issues relating to the handling and dissemination of information and intelligence.

> System assets create the infrastructure which supports NIM. These assets must provide or supply access arrangements to systems and facilities for the secure capture, recording, reception, storage, linkage, analysis and use of information. They provide:
>
> - Information storage, retrieval and comparison during the research process.
> - A capability and process for the acquisition of new information and intelligence.
> - Security systems.
>
> (ACPO Centrex 2005: 23)

A particular focus of the system assets is the effectiveness of briefing and debriefing arrangements within the police service to ensure the appropriate dissemination and collection of information and intelligence from operational officers.

> Source Assets refers to the range of information sources available to the police specifically, focussing upon those which are capable of being managed by the police. Whilst specifically recognising the potential benefits of using

informants (Covert Human Intelligence Sources, or CHIS), the source assets are recognised as being much broader, including:

- Victims and witnesses
- Communities and members of the public
- Crimestoppers
- Prisoners
- Forensic information
- Undercover operatives
- Surveillance products
- CHIS.

(ACPO Centrex 2005: 33)

People assets are effectively a consideration of the human resources require-ments to ensure that the NIM is run effectively. The People assets establish a range of key roles that drive and support the NIM, ensuring that issues such as appropriate staff development and succession planning are managed appropriately.

Taken together, the assets form the basis by which the NIM is informed. They collectively feed into the rest of the system. The guidelines are specific in being clear that in order for the Model to operate effectively the assets need to be in place, and drawn upon and developed appropriately.

3. Tasking and coordinating groups

Sitting above the assets is the system and process which manages policing business. The driver of business at each level is the tasking and coordinating group (T&CG), comprising managers who can agree and allocate appropriate resources, usually advised by heads of intelligence units. At Basic Command Unit level, for example, the Chair will typically be the superintendent, with a membership of inspectors and other resource owners (not necessarily limited to police personnel, drawing, for example, on local partners such as local authorities), as well as the detective inspector running the local Intelligence Unit. The T&CG is the owner of policing 'business' at its particular level, and is responsible for achieving the relevant outcomes. The decision making of the group is informed by data and intelligence products provided by analysts. Each level runs both strategic and tactical tasking and coordinating groups (ST&CGs and TT&CGs), which often overlap considerably in personnel but have different purposes: ST&CGs set the broad 'control strategy' for the area while TT&CGs focus more closely on planned operational responses to specific problems or threats – they have ownership of the 'tactical resolution' as illustrated In Box 12.1.

This separation of function between the two T&CGs is one of the critical distinguishing factors of the NIM against other policing models. It specifically provides an opportunity for decision making to be taken strategically and is removed from the pressures of daily demands. As discussed in Chapter 10, this satisfies one of the Audit Commission's (1993) prerequisites for the police to be able to break out of a vicious circle in which they are constantly responding to reactive demands, and to develop a more pro-active, evidence-based focus. To summarise the discussion above, the ST&CG determines strategy and priorities. The TT&CG determines how to make progress against the strategy set and address the priorities.

4. Intelligence products

The primary resources upon which the T&CGs base their decision making are the intelligence products, of which there are four (see Box 12.2).

Box 12.2   Information point – Intelligence products

- **Strategic assessments** – drive the business of the ST&CG. The assessment gives an accurate overview of the current and long-term issues affecting the police force, BCU or region. The T&CG use the assessment to set the control strategy and intelligence requirement.
- **Tactical assessments** – drive the business of the TT&CG. The assessment identifies the shorter term issues in a police force, BCU or region in accordance with the control strategy. The T&CG use the assessment to amend the intelligence requirement where necessary.
- **Target profiles** – the T&CG commission target profiles to secure a greater understanding of either a person (suspect or victim) or group of people, in line with the control strategy priorities or high-risk issues.
- **Problem profiles** – the T&CG commission problem profiles to secure a greater understanding of established and emerging crime or incident series, priority locations and other identified high-risk issues. It also recommends opportunities for tactical resolution in line with the control strategy priorities or high-risk issues.

(ACPO Centrex 2005: 64)

These four documents are crucial to the work of the T&CGs and therefore to the level of operation at which they are focused. The strategic assessment provides a detailed picture against which prioritisation and resourcing decisions can be based. It is supplemented by the detailed pictures and plans provided in the tactical assessments, target profiles and problem profiles which move into actionable priorities.

A range of analytical techniques and products are used to provide the analysis that forms the basis for the intelligence products. These are briefly considered below.

5. *Analytical techniques and products*

Analytical techniques and products represent the key approaches for analysis of information and intelligence from a variety of sources (within and outside the police). They vary in form and content according to the techniques employed and the sources of data from which they are drawn. The techniques and products, in isolation and/or in combination, provide the analytical basis upon which subsequent parts of the process will rely. Critically they inform the intelligence products discussed above. A clear intention is that these techniques and products should be standardised and recognisable. The NIM specifies nine key analytical techniques and subsequent products, as detailed in Box 12.3.

Taken together, the analytical techniques and products provide a comprehensive set of tools upon which the rest of the NIM processes are ultimately based. Application of these techniques and the quality of the resultant products – analytical and intelligence – is reliant upon the development of specialised analytical skills, provided by intelligence analysts. This, typically civilian, role has been developing since the 1990s and has become mainstream within policing since the introduction of the NIM. All levels of operation will employ analysts to support the processes.

The National Intelligence Model in practice

The above discussion identifies the overarching purpose of the NIM and its central mechanisms, processes, and sources of information and intelligence. To summarise, the NIM is a business process replicated across three policing levels: local; force/regional; and national/international. The core drivers of policing business at each level are the tasking and coordinating groups. The strategic T&CG provides the potential for the police to break out of a reactive cycle by identifying key priorities to be addressed over the medium to long term. It is principally supported in this function by the production of the strategic assessment which provides an evidence-based overview of threats and opportunities, and the resources available to address and embrace them. In turn, the tactical T&CGs operationalise appropriate responses to the strategic priorities, while maintaining reactive responses to short-term policing challenges. The work of the T&CGs is supported by a range of intelligence products and analytical techniques. The National Intelligence Model is consistent with knowledge management principles.

The National Intelligence Model is unique in being rolled out nationally. Previous policing models, notably Problem-Oriented Policing (POP), while receiving widespread recognition and adoption, did not have the requirements to be adopted that forces have had for the NIM. Nevertheless, with POP and subsequently with intelligence-led policing, implementation gaps develop which to some extent separate the abstract intention from its implemented version (for a discussion on POP in this context see Leigh *et al.* 1996, 1998, and for intelligence-led policing, Maguire and John 1995).

Box 12.3   Information point – Nine key analytical techniques

- **Crime pattern analysis** – a generic term for a number of related disciplines such as crime or incident series identification, crime trend analysis, hotspot analysis and general profile analysis.
- **Demographic/social trends analysis** – centred on demographic changes and their impact upon criminality. It also analyses social factors such as unemployment and homelessness, and considers the significance of population shifts, attitudes and activities.
- **Network analysis** – not only describes the links between people who form criminal networks, but the significance of these links, the roles played by individuals, and the strengths and weaknesses of a criminal organisation.
- **Market profiles** – continually reviewed and updated assessments that survey the criminal market around a particular commodity, such as drugs or stolen vehicles, or of a service, such as prostitution, in an area.
- **Criminal business profiles** – contain detailed analyses of how criminal operations or techniques work, in the same way that a legitimate business might be explained.
- **Risk analysis** – assesses the scale of risks posed by individual offenders or organisations to individual potential victims, the general public and also to law-enforcement agencies.
- **Target profile analysis** – embraces a range of analytical techniques to describe the criminal, their criminal activity, lifestyle, associations, the risk they pose, and their strengths and weaknesses, in order to give focus to the investigation targeting them. Profiles may also focus on victims and vulnerable persons.
- **Operational intelligence assessment** – involves evaluating incoming intelligence to maintain the focus of an operation on previously agreed objectives, particularly in the case of a sizeable intelligence collection plan or other large-scale operation.
- **Results analysis** – evaluates the effectiveness of law-enforcement activities, for example, the effectiveness of patrol strategies, crime reduction initiatives or a particular method of investigation.

(ACPO Centrex 2005: 61)

This section of the chapter reviews the roll-out of the National Intelligence Model and provides an overview of the key challenges that arose in doing so. It is based on previous work conducted by the author with Mike Maguire, specifically on the review conducted for the Home Office on the roll-out itself (John and Maguire 2003, 2004). As noted above, a Code of Practice and considerably extended set of guidelines for the NIM were introduced in 2005.

Subsequent guidelines and practice notes on a range of related issues have also been introduced. The impact of these is, in the absence of a detailed research study, difficult to assess. They clearly hold the potential, however, to mitigate some of the concerns arising from the evaluation of the initial roll-out. The clear minimum standards, for example, provide detailed benchmarking and improve the environment for standardisation to develop. To some extent, then, the originally identified issues discussed here may be viewed as legacy issues. However, legacies continue to have an impact so the extent to which they have been resolved is open to interpretation. The following discussion provides an overview of key areas identified in the evaluation of the roll-out of the NIM.

Perceptions of the NIM

An issue for the National Intelligence Model is perception about what it is, particularly its compatibility with other, apparently conflicting policing approaches. As noted above, this is largely attributed to its association with intelligence-led, or pro-active policing. In its original roll-out of the NIM, Lancashire Constabulary, which had previously invested heavily in promoting and implementing problem-oriented policing (POP) throughout the force, specifically linked the NIM to the scanning, analysis, response and assessment (SARA) stages of POP by, for example, equating the T&CG process to that of 'analysis and response'. By adopting this approach it secured better understanding and 'buy-in' from its officers than had been experienced in some other forces which presented it as an entirely new innovation. Furthermore, and as a linked point, it allowed the NIM to be promoted without reliance upon the various facets being spelled out in detail – making it more approachable and understandable as a concept to those who were not directly engaged in its mechanics (John and Maguire 2004). Nevertheless, the Model's association with ILP remained strong, arguably distancing it from those forces and/or individuals who had pursued alternative strategies such as neighbourhood policing and reassurance policing. Indeed, as noted by Maguire and John (1995), these developing initiatives appeared, at first glance, to be competing approaches to the NIM. As noted above, however, the NIM is primarily a business process that supports the full range of policing tactics. Indeed, the 2005 Code of Practice introduces the NIM as a 'National Model for Policing' and goes on to emphasise that:

> The National Intelligence Model is not confined to or restricted for specialist usage. It is relevant to all areas of law enforcement: crime and its investigation, disorder and community safety. Overall, it is a model for operational policing.
>
> (Code of Practice 2005: 6)

Had this message been made more strongly in the original launch of the NIM it is likely that some of the subsequent implementation difficulties observed by John and Maguire (2004) could have been significantly reduced.

Development of strategy under the NIM

One of the major potential contributions that the NIM provides is a structured opportunity for key strategic decisions to be taken on the basis of a considered evidence base. Specifically this is achieved through the ST&CG on the basis of, primarily, the analysis provided in the strategic assessment. Produced annually, it is therefore critical that the strategic assessment is comprehensive, and identifies the full range of considerations that the group need to be aware of for prioritisation decisions to be made appropriately.

Certainly in the early roll-out of the NIM, widespread variations in practice were noted. While in some areas the assessments were sufficiently robust, in others they were scant, drawn mainly from established crime statistics and performance indicator data with little additional application of the analytical techniques (John and Maguire 2004). A key determinant of quality of the strategic assessments (and subsequently other aspects involving analysis within the Model) was related to the role of the analyst. Intelligence analysis of this form, and strategic analysis in particular, requires extensive analytical skills and capacity that, at least at that time, represented a significant step-up from the management analysis typically undertaken previously (Cope 2004). In turn, the professionalisation of the analyst role demands a clearer understanding of the potential of analysis from relevant managers. Education and awareness in both groups was embryonic. A combination of experience in developing and using the strategic documents, and of more extensive training seemed to quite rapidly raise the game. However, the distinction between strategic intelligence and tactical intelligence should be protected and reinforced. In the action-focused arena of policing there is a danger of mission drift away from strategic priorities and back towards reactive responses to problems as they present themselves. The strategic approach, if robust, supports this separation through the priorities set. For a fuller consideration of strategic thinking with the police more generally, see Ratcliffe (2009).

The role of the analyst

The analyst's role has been evolutionary in nature. Consequently, analysts have broad and divergent career backgrounds with differing levels of experience and qualifications. John and Maguire (2004) found a fairly even divide between those who had reached their position by moving through a number of administrative roles (mainly with the police service), and those (typically younger and more recently appointed) who held degrees, often with social science research training, but relatively little practical experience. The different routes have their own advantages and disadvantages and none is necessarily 'the best', but the diversity in itself creates significant challenges for police forces in terms of developing and exploiting their analysts' skills.

The retention of existing analysts was a major issue for many of the police managers interviewed by John and Maguire (2004), due partly to the absence of national agreed pay structures and a clear (hierarchical) career path for analysts.

This produced two significant problems. First, the lower paying forces quite frequently lose analysts to more generous neighbours or to other, non-police employers. For example, one of the development sites experienced a 48 per cent turnover of analytical staff in the two-year period ending October 2001; in contrast, their higher paying neighbouring force retained all its analysts over the same period. Given the expense of training analysts (estimated by one principal analyst at £5,500 for basic skills and £10–15,000 for comprehensive training), and the time taken for them to become accustomed to the way a BCU operates, this is a clear financial as well as human resources issue. Second, for those analysts who do remain within one force, there is little career incentive for them to seek to excel. Senior and principal analyst posts are very low in number. One principal analyst summed up the position thus:

> Staff retention depends upon job satisfaction, which includes professional development, career progression, salary and training. There is no professional structure within the analytical function to ensure analysts' development and to guarantee quality assured work. There is no career structure for analysts to enhance their development and to ensure their accountability for performance.

Some inroads have been made in rectifying these difficulties, such as the introduction of recognised accredited training programmes and the development of a career structure and pay spine. However, the early weaknesses in this regard hampered the development of the potential of the NIM in key aspects of its analytical capacity.

Standardisation

In the discussion above, we noted the ambition of the NIM to be able to piece together local pictures in order to provide a national overview. The model at launch sought to standardise the procedures and processes within the NIM. It did not, however, provide detailed guidance on, for example, the structure, format and content of key documents such as the strategic assessment. Consequently a force would receive a number of sometimes dramatically different documents from its respective BCUs. This provided an obstacle to the information being brought together to provide the force-wide picture. A similar situation existed at the national level. The original evaluation of the roll-out of the NIM saw this as an opportunity lost. The subsequent Code of Practice and related Guidelines are likely to have made substantial progress on standardisation, notably with the introduction of minimum standards and relevant templates.

Partnership engagement

Aspects of the NIM would clearly benefit from partnership engagement. For example, if the strategic assessment is to meet its goals of providing a comprehensive overview, data gained from partner agencies could be a crucial element in providing as full a picture as possible. Similarly, the resolutions for particular issues might fall outside of the enforcement remit and require a combined approach among several agencies to produce an effective long-term result. While the Model encourages cooperation with partner agencies, in practice it has tended to be a police-focused enterprise. Direct partner involvement within the NIM has tended to be ad hoc, and barriers to data sharing – both to the police and back out from them – have been identified (John and Maguire 2004). Links with partner agencies therefore tend to be maintained and developed through a parallel path of community safety partnerships with few instances of formal links with the NIM business process. In only very few instances are partners represented on the T&CGs.

In response to this position, Greater Manchester Police made a positive move towards incorporating their partners within a NIM-based framework at local and county levels. The Greater Manchester Against Crime Partnership Business Model (GMAC) is explicitly owned and managed by the partnership. Its analysts are employed directly by them, rather than by the police, emphasising GMAC resources as a partnership, rather than solely police resource. The equivalents of the T&CGs comprise resource owners from across the partnership. A common data hub is maintained by a third party, supported by clear data-sharing protocols across the partnership. An early independent evaluation of the GMAC approach (John *et al.* 2006) recognised particular resultant strengths in: the breadth of data and strategic use of it, coordination of partnership resources and clear evidence of joint working, and a resulting clarity of focus on community issues and priorities. Aspects of the ACPO Guidance on the National Intelligence Model (ACPO Centrex 2005) encourage similar developments but do not specify that the GMAC approach be followed. Further integration of police and partnership-shared business might, it is argued, be a specific ongoing focus in the coming period.

Conclusion

This chapter has provided an overview of knowledge management principles and of strategic intelligence. It has discussed in some detail the purpose and mechanics of the National Intelligence Model, and some of the issues that have arisen during its implementation. In doing so it has pointed to areas of likely improvement.

John and Maguire (2003: 38) described the NIM as:

> a means of organising knowledge and information in such a way that the best possible decisions can be made about the use of resources. It ensures that actions are coordinated between the various levels of delivery, and that lessons are continually learnt and fed back into the system.

As with the implementation of any major change to business processes in large organisations, there will be a gap between the stated objectives of a model and its implemented version. If the fundamental concepts underlying the developments are sound, it will be anticipated that as learning curves are achieved, understanding improves and cultural resistance declines, this gap will begin to close. It is likely that the additional support and guidance provided by the Code of Practice for the NIM and its related guidelines will accelerate this process, more visibly allowing the potential identified above to be realised. That the NIM is a framework rather than a policing tactic ensures that it can encompass the full range of operational responses available to the police (and their partners). As such it is anticipated that it will be subject to continual evolution rather than whole-scale replacement.

References and suggested further reading

Audit Commission (1993) *Helping with Enquiries: Tackling Crime Effectively*. HMSO, London.

ACPO Centrex (2005) *Guidance on the National Intelligence Model*. NCPE, Wyboston Bedfordshire.

Code of Practice (2005) *The National Intelligence Model*. Centrex, Wyboston, Bedfordshire.

Cope, N. (2004) 'Intelligence-led Policing or Policing-led Intelligence? Integrating Volume Crime Analysis into Policing', *British Journal of Criminology* 44(2): 188–203.

Flood, B. (1999) 'Know your business: NCIS has brought together best practice in intelligence-led policing', *Nexus 7* (winter): 8–9.

—— (2004) 'Strategic aspects of the UK National Intelligence Model', in Ratcliffe, J.H. (ed.), *Strategic Thinking in Criminal Intelligence* (1st ed., pp. 37–52). Federation Press, Sydney.

Gottschalk, P., Holgersson, S. and Karlsen, J. (2009) 'How knowledge organizations work: the case of detectives', *The Learning Organization* 16(2): 88–102.

John, T. and Maguire, M. (2003) 'Rolling out the National Intelligence Model: key challenges', in Bullock, K. and Tilley, N. *Crime Reduction and Problem-oriented Policing*. Willan Publishing, Cullompton, Devon.

—— (2004) *The National Intelligence Model: Early Implementation Experience in Three Police Force Areas*. Cardiff School of Social Sciences, Cardiff. Available online at http://www.cardiff.ac.uk/socsi/research/publications/workingpapers/paper-50.html (accessed 11 December 2009).

John, T., Morgan, C. and Rogers, C. (2006) *The Greater Manchester Against Crime Partnership Business Model: An Independent Evaluation*. Centre for Criminology, University of Glamorgan, internal document.

Leigh, A., Read, T. and Tilley, N. (1996) *Problem Oriented Policing: Brit Pop*. Crime Detection and Prevention Series, Paper 75, Home Office, London.

—— (1998) *Brit Pop II: Problem Oriented Policing in Practice*. Policing and Reducing Crime Unit, Police Research Series, Paper 93, Home Office, London.

Maguire, M. and John, T. (1995) *Intelligence, Surveillance, and Informants: Integrated Approaches*. Police Research Group Crime and Prevention Series, Paper No 64 Home Office, London.

Ratcliffe, J. (ed.) (2004) *Strategic Thinking in Criminal Intelligence*. Federation Press, Leichhardt.

—— (2008) *Intelligence-led Policing*. Willan Publishing, Cullompton, Devon.
—— (ed.) (2009) *Strategic Thinking in Criminal Intelligence* (2nd edn). Federation Press, Leichhardt.
Sheptycki, J. and Ratcliffe, J.H (2004) 'Setting the strategic agenda', in Ratcliffe, J.H. (ed.), *Strategic Thinking in Criminal Intelligence*. Federation Press, Leichhardt.
Willis, J., Mastrofski, S. and Kochel, T. (2010) 'Recommendations for integrating Compstat and community policing', *Policing Advance Access*. Available online athttp://policing.oxfordjournals.org/content/early/2010/04/08/police.paq005.full.pdf+html (accessed on 7 March 2011).

13 Multi-agency approaches and intelligence

Introduction

The concept of partnership working, and the need for various agencies to work together to combat crime and disorder, has been a consistent theme in the community safety field in the UK for the past decade. Beginning with the Crime and Disorder Act 1998, this chapter examines how policy has evolved – with the movement away from the three-year cycle of crime audits and strategies towards the introduction of the annual rolling strategic assessment and emphasis on the National Intelligence Model (NIM) in supporting an 'intelligence-led' approach. The importance of data sharing between agencies in ensuring effective partnership working is also examined, with consideration of the increasingly coercive policy being used to ensure the exchange of data between responsible authorities. The chapter also examines the constraints on data sharing, as well as providing examples of how the use of health data can provide a more comprehensive understanding of certain crime problems.

Bearing in mind the lack of precision about precisely what is meant by 'intelligence' in a policing context, it is perhaps a little ironic that one of the most detailed definitions is to be found for the form of intelligence which police systems most struggle to handle: community intelligence. In 2005 HMIC and ACPO described community intelligence as:

> local information which, when assessed, provides intelligence on issues that affect neighbourhoods and informs both the strategic and operational perspectives in the policing of local communities. Information may be direct and indirect and come from a diverse range of sources including the community and partner agencies.
>
> (ACPO/HMIC 2005)

This definition remains extremely inclusive and general. In this respect it reflects the problematic notion of both community and community safety that has been previously identified by commentators. Discussing the concept of community intelligence, Innes and Roberts (n.d.) suggest that there is a risk that community intelligence is defined in terms of what it is not, rather than of what it is; it becomes a 'generic term to account for a range of intelligence data that does not fit the traditional types of intelligence the police have accessed'.

Crime and Disorder review

A review of the partnership provisions of the Crime and Disorder Act (CDA) 1998 was carried out by the Home Office, the Local Government Association (LGA), the Association of Chief Police Officers (ACPO) and the Association of Police Authorities (APA) between November 2004 and January 2005, and published in January 2006.

The review suggested that in order to be responsive, CDRPs/CSPs needed to be

> well informed about the crime, anti-social behaviour and substance misuse risks and problems in their area through the use of real time intelligence and data. It is the use of this real time intelligence that should direct partnership activity both at a strategic level and at the level where strategic priorities are translated into action, at neighbourhood level.
>
> (HO 2006: 13)

Moreover, 'intelligence led decision making lies at the heart of effective delivery. We want every CDRP/CSP to undertake an intelligence led, problem-solving and outcome orientated approach to community safety' (HO 2006: 3).

The CDA review and the National Intelligence Model (NIM)

More specifically, the review suggested that the existing police National Intelligence Model provided a good framework for the analysis of data and intelligence, and could be used 'to inform strategic direction, accurately direct resources and manage risk. We will be adapting many of the principles and practices behind NIM to a partnership setting' (HO 2006: 3). The review described NIM as a system

> for using intelligence and information to direct police activity enabling police forces to trace the continuum between anti-social behaviour and the most serious crime, and to identify those local issues most in need of attention. It ensures that information is fully researched, developed and analysed to provide intelligence that senior managers can use to inform strategic direction, make tactical resourcing decisions about operational policing, and manage risk.
>
> (HO 2006: 13–14)

While it recognised that the business processes of NIM were not directly transferable to the multi-agency environment, it concluded that its principles and practices were, not least because of the 'huge range' of intelligence gathered, produced and retained by the many bodies operating within a locality.

Brought together, it was suggested, this intelligence had the power to produce a much more focused assault on the drivers of crime, antisocial behaviour and substance misuse (HO 2006: 14).

Assessment rather than audit and strategy

The review concluded that:

> at the strategic level, intelligence led partnership working will mean more effective and co-ordinated strategic planning across partner agencies and with other local partnerships. Chief Officers of partner agencies will need to consider strategic intelligence assessments on a six-monthly basis, in order to set – and then review – the strategic priorities for the area' (HO 2006: 13). It was anticipated that the assessments would include crime, victim and offender data, 'along with other relevant local profiling for the purposes of risk assessment and resource allocation and draw on softer intelligence generated through community consultation and engagement carried out at district and neighbourhood level' (HO: 13).

The review also identified that while the existing requirement on CDRPs to carry out triennial audits of crime and disorder and drugs misuse and to implement strategies for tackling the problems identified was useful, it was also 'resource intensive and often now seen as a distraction from delivery, tying up key partnership staff for up to a year in their production'. The reality was that many partnerships were now 'becoming increasingly performance focussed and intelligence-led; informed by real-time information and community intelligence' (HO 2006: 15). As a result it recommended that the three-yearly audits should be replaced by regular strategic assessments, preferably at least on a six-monthly basis (subsequently amended to annual), which would need to be tied into the progress reports for Local Area Agreements.

The changes arising from the review were contained in the Police and Justice Bill published in January 2006. As a result, a new set of national minimum standards came into force in England in August 2007 and in Wales in November 2007 (HO 2007a: 1). As identified in the CDA review, the Police and Justice Act also repealed two major existing partnership duties: to produce three-yearly audits and strategies; and to report annually to the Secretary of State on their work and progress.

In addition, in response to the review the Home Office developed 'six hallmarks of effective partnership', described in the 2007 document 'Delivering Safer Communities; A guide to effective partnership working' (HO 2007b: 4).[6] The government's justification for the introduction of the hallmarks was that they would:

- ensure that all partnerships are functioning to an acceptable level of performance;

- embed an intelligence-led way of doing partnership business;
- enable communities to see the difference that effective partnerships can have in their area;
- ensure that local communities are involved in shaping local priorities;
- support the development of skills and knowledge across all partnerships;
- increase partnership accountability in addressing crime and disorder matters (HO 2007b: 11).

Strategic assessment

According to the Home Office guidance, a strategic assessment 'presents and interprets the summary findings of an intelligence analysis' (HO 2007a: 6). The assessment is an internal document designed to inform the partnership plan, and does not need to be published. It should contain the following elements:

- analysis of the levels and patterns of crime, disorder and substance misuse;
- changes in the levels and patterns of crime, disorder and substance misuse since the last strategic assessment;
- analysis of why these changes have occurred;
- assessment of the extent to which the previous year's plan has been implemented (HO 2007a: 6).

The purpose of the strategic assessment is to 'provide knowledge and understanding of community safety problems that will inform and enable the partners to:

- understand the patterns, trends and shifts relating to crime and disorder and substance misuse;
- set clear and robust priorities for their partnership;
- develop activity that is driven by reliable intelligence and meets the needs of the local community;
- deploy resources effectively and present value for money;
- undertake annual reviews and plan activity based on a clear understanding of the issues and priorities' (HO 2007a: 6–7).

It is important not to exaggerate the magnitude of the change from audit/strategy to strategic assessment. The content of the strategic assessment and the audit and strategy remain broadly similar – something recognised in Home Office guidance to CDRPs which stated that 'the strategic assessment will be similar in some respects to the previous crime and disorder audit, insofar as it will include an analysis of information from partners and from the community and will identify the trends and patterns of crime, disorder and the misuse of drugs'. However, the guidance goes on to say that the information provided via the strategic assessment will be 'more up to date' and cover a shorter time period, which should make it more relevant to effective delivery, and the assessment itself shorter and quicker to produce (although it is interesting to note that the original suggestion that the assessment be undertaken on a six-monthly basis was subsequently amended to annual 'in response to views expressed by practitioners'. The movement away from audit and strategy is best seen, perhaps, as recognition that under the old system the process had become rather static, and provided a 'snapshot' of crime and disorder rather than serving to support the ongoing analytical process envisaged by the 1998 Act. In addition, the production of an annual strategic assessment fits much better with the annual cycle of the Local Area Agreements into which it is expected to feed (HO n.d.).

However, there are issues around the extent to which agencies other than the police are in a position to undertake a NIM-based strategic assessment. This is a model that has been developed within the policing context – and which the police have comparatively well-resourced units to support (force and local intelligence units, intelligence officers, analysts and researchers – although even here there has been research questioning the extent to which these units/individuals, and the work that they produce, is fully integrated within the wider police organisation).[7] However, the extent to which other agencies have similar intelligence resources is questionable. The result is the risk that the strategic assessment, rather than being a true 'partnership exercise' becomes, by necessity, a 'rebadging' of police work and police priorities.

Similarly, under the old model, the fact that the consultation conducted as part of the audit and strategy process was undertaken only once every three years tended to ensure that partnerships could devote substantial levels of resource to the exercise (e.g. undertaking bespoke victimisation surveys). Indeed, as mentioned above, this became part of the problem; the production of the audit and strategy risked becoming an end in itself rather than a means to an end. However, the movement to an annual cycle begs the question as to whether CDRPs will have the time or resources to consult as comprehensively as they did in the past. There is a risk that the quality of consultation undertaken by CDRPs with members of the public will suffer, and that undue reliance will be placed upon information emerging from sources that are readily available; for example, Policing and Communities Together (PACT) meetings, and the data provided by the British Crime Survey and the Place Survey (which provides data at a CDRP level on the quality of service of local agencies, including community safety – although it is not available in Wales) (Box 13.1).

Information sharing

Sharing of information between agencies is clearly an integral part of partnership working. In 2007 the Home Office paper *Delivering Safer Communities* stated that:

> information sharing is the cornerstone of delivering shared understanding of issues and arriving at shared solutions. Effective delivery relies on good decision making and those decisions should be based on good information.

Box 13.1   Exercise 13A Quality of service of local agencies

Before continuing, consider the differences and similarities between the previous requirement on CDRPs to produce crime audits and strategies, and the current requirement to produce strategic assessments, under the following headings.

1. Purpose
2. Contents
3. Membership
4. Frequency.

The right information enables partners to carry out evidence-based, targeted community safety interventions and to evaluate their impact. The improved outcomes of an intelligence-led, problem solving approach to community safety can only be achieved when partners have access to relevant, robust and up-to-date information from a broad range of sources.

(Home Office 2007a: 36)

Section 115 of the 1998 Crime and Disorder Act

Section 115 of the 1998 Crime and Disorder Act had provided the legal basis for data sharing with relevant authorities where it was necessary in order to fulfil the duties contained in the Act, although partnerships' processes in deciding both when to share information and how those who receive the information should retain it had to comply with the 1998 Data Protection Act which aimed to make sure that when personal information was shared, it happened in a fair and transparent manner (Home Office 2007a: 2). Nevertheless, the operation of section 115, notwithstanding the importance that had been attached to information sharing, had often been sporadic and problematic (Box 13.2).

Box 13.2   Exercise 13B Potential barriers to information sharing

Before reading on, spend some time thinking about what some of the potential barriers to information sharing between different agencies might be.

The Home Office crime reduction website identifies the following barriers to effective information sharing:

- Misconceived ideas about legislation governing information sharing, particularly data protection legislation.
- A lack of guidance and plain language explanations.

- An absence of formal protocols between crime and disorder reduction partnerships.
- A tendency to take an overly cautious approach.
- A lack of awareness of the benefits.
  (http://www.crimereduction.homeoffice.gov.uk/infosharing00.htm)

Information sharing and the Crime and Disorder Act review

Problems with effective information sharing were explicitly addressed by the Crime and Disorder Act review. The report from the review concluded, under the heading 'Improving information sharing', that:

> we know that many stakeholders are frustrated by partners who do not always co-operate fully when approached with a request for information. Uncertainty over what is legally permissible is, in many cases, inhibiting data sharing. The issue is not just that legislation around data sharing can be misunderstood or misapplied. There is also a sense that the law can be used as an excuse; sometimes held up to 'justify' an inherent reluctance to share information outside a particular agency, or for purposes that might not be that agency's primary objective.
>
> (Home Office 2006: 15).

Similar findings had emerged from Michael Bichard's inquiry into the Soham murders in 2004 (Bichard 2004). The CDA review recognised that there were issues surrounding the exchange of data that might identify specific individuals, and that there was a need to 'carefully control' these circumstances. However, these restrictions did not apply to data that had been 'cleansed' (i.e. where personal identifiers had been removed), but which was still not being shared between agencies in all cases. Those undertaking the review concluded that there was a need to strengthen section 115 of the 1998 Act.

The review also concluded that it was 'vital for every CDRP/CSP to have an information sharing protocol in place which formally sets out the principles of the partnership's data sharing arrangements, detailing what will be exchanged, by whom, with whom, for what purposes and with which safeguards in place' (Home Office 2006: 16). In addition, it was essential that, at the strategic decision-making level, someone in each of the responsible authorities was given formal responsibility for facilitating data and information sharing across all partnership agencies. The requirements to introduce an information-sharing protocol and to nominate a designated liaison officer were given statutory footing by the Crime and Disorder (Formulation and Implementation of Strategy) Regulations (2007).

Police and Justice Act 2006; statutory duty to disclose information

In addition, the Police and Justice Act 2006 introduced a statutory duty upon some agencies to disclose certain sets of depersonalised information at least quarterly in electronic form to other relevant section 115 authorities.[8] Details of the relevant datasets are contained in Table 13.1. The introduction of this new duty was designed 'to increase the effectiveness of partnerships by ensuring that they have the necessary multi-agency data for identifying priorities, mapping trends and patterns in crime and disorder, and managing their performance' (Home Office 2007a: 52), although the 2006 Act excluded any personal data from the duty to disclose; thus, for example, where, in the case of a domestic incident, the sharing of precise location details would enable the identification of the individual, the duty did not apply.

Guidance from the Information Commissioner's Office

Further guidance on the sharing of information between agencies was provided in late 2007 by the Information Commissioner's Office in its *Framework Code of Practice for Sharing Personal Information*. This aimed to assist organisations in drawing up their own codes of practice for sharing information (either within or outside the organisation) and to 'help organisations to make sure that they address all the main data protection compliance issues' (ICO 2007: 4). The document suggested what such codes of practice should do, outlined legal requirements, and listed 'points to remember' in relation to the following headings:

1. Deciding to share personal information – legally, 'information sharing must be necessary. Any information shared must be relevant and not excessive' (ICO 2007: 7).
2. Fairness and transparency.
3. Information standards – information must be 'adequate, relevant, not excessive, accurate and up to date' (ICO 2007: 11).
4. Retention of shared information – 'personal information shall not be kept for longer than is necessary' (ICO 2007: 13).
5. Security of shared information – personal information should be 'protected by appropriate technical and organisational resources' (ICO 2007: 15).
6. Access to personal information.
7. Freedom of information.

It also stressed the need to review the continued relevance/adequacy of the code, while providing an example of a 'simple' information-sharing procedure (Boxes 13.3 and 13.4).

Information sharing prior to 2006

Clearly it is possible to overstate the difficulties that existed in the exchange of information between partnership agencies before 2006, and there had been a number of CDRPs which had established successful data-sharing arrangements soon after the introduction of the 1998 Act.

Table 13.1 Details of information sets that must be shared on at least a quarterly basis

Agency	Dataset (for area)
Police	1. Records of antisocial behaviour, transport and public safety/ welfare incidents recorded according to the National Incident Category List.* 2. Crime records recorded according to the Notifiable Offences list.*
Fire and rescue authorities	3. Records of deliberate fires, whether it was a deliberate primary fire (not in a vehicle), a deliberate secondary fire (not in a vehicle) or a deliberate fire in a vehicle. In addition, records of incidents of violence against employees and records of fires attended in dwellings where no smoke alarm was fitted.* 4. Records of malicious false alarms.*
Local authorities	5. Records of road traffic collisions. Whatever information is recorded about the time, date, location and the number of adults and children killed, seriously injured and slightly injured in each road traffic collision must be shared. 6. Records of fixed term and permanent school exclusions. Whatever information is held about the age and gender of the pupil, the name and address of the school from which they were excluded and the reasons for their exclusion must be shared. 7. Records of racial incidents.* 8. Records of antisocial behaviour incidents identified by the authority or reported by the public.*
Primary Care Trusts (lying entirely or partly in the area)	9. Records of various categories of hospital admissions. The relevant admissions are those relating to the following blocks within the International Classification of Diseases: a) assault (X85-Y09) b) mental and behavioural disorders due to psychoactive substance use (F10-F19) c) toxic effect of alcohol (T51) d) other entries where there is evidence of alcohol involvement determined by blood alcohol level (Y90) or evidence of alcohol involvement determined by level of intoxication (Y91). For each record, whatever information is held about the date of the admission, the subcategory of the admission and the outward part of the postcode of the patient's address must be shared. 10. Records of admissions to hospital in respect of domestic abuse. Whatever information is held about the date of the admission and the outward part of the postcode of the patient's address must be shared. 11. Numbers of mental illness outpatient first attendances and persons receiving drug treatment. 12. Records of ambulance call-outs to crime and disorder incidents.*

Key * = For each category of data, whatever information is recorded about the time, date, location and category of each crime/incident/alarm call/ambulance call-out must be disclosed.
Source: HO (2007a: 132–3).

Box 13.3   Exercise 13C Information-sharing procedure

What sort of factors do you think would be included in such a procedure? Before continuing, take some time to outline the headings you think such a procedure would contain. Then compare your answer to the model provided by the ICO below.

Box 13.4   Example of a simple information-sharing procedure (taken from ICO 2007: 21)

An example of an information-sharing procedure between the police, reporter to the children's panel and social work departments.

1. Contact details
Named individuals in council social work departments and area children's reporters.

2. Types of information

- Child Protection Initial Report Form NM/59/2 to be sent to appropriate social worker.
- Department and children's reporter. These will be marked *Confidential*.
- Memoranda as required. These will always be marked *Confidential*.
- Crime reports may also be disclosed.
- Verbal information will be shared at case conferences. This information will be either *Restricted* or *Confidential*. Minutes should be classified according to the value of information in them.

3. How to handle the information

Transmission
Restricted information can be transmitted over the telephone or sent by fax. Confidential information must be sent in a double envelope with the protective marking shown on the inner one.

Storage
All information must be kept under lock and key when not in the custody of an authorised person. The 'need-to-know' principle will be strictly enforced. Confidential information needs to be protected by two barriers, for example, a locked container in a locked room.

Release to third parties
No information provided by partners to these procedures will be released to any third party without the permission of the owning partner.

In Northamptonshire the ComPaSS (Community Profiling and Shared Solutions) unit was established in 2001 to provide technical support (analysis, problem solving and community profiling) to safer partnerships in the county, aiming to 'routinely profile crime and disorder on behalf of the seven Crime and Disorder Reduction Partnerships (CDRPs) within Northamptonshire'. This task involved the 'regular collection and analysis of relevant data, on behalf of all Local CDRP's, highlighting hotspot areas and more prominent issues, as well as identifying evaluated solutions' (ComPaSS).

To assist the work of the ComPaSS unit a 'community profiling protocol' was drawn up in 2002 between the unit and its statutory partner agencies (the police, police authority, probation, the youth offending team and relevant borough, district and county councils). As well as stressing the commitment of the various agencies to the work of the unit the protocol identified the purposes to which the data would be put, and the types of data that would be required (discussed in greater detail below). The protocol also identified the obligation of the various partners to undertake the following: collect information on a postcode basis, identify the data that needed to be analysed (and any changes in the future), collect the data for which they were responsible, ensure compliance with the Data Protection Act, and regularly review the information produced by ComPaSS to ensure it remained relevant.

Under the heading 'Principles of the Compass Unit' the protocol stated that the unit intended 'to obtain and analyse data relevant to crime and disorder reduction that is lawful, fair and relevant to the principles of this agreement and to do so for the purpose of aiding the reduction of crime and disorder. Data provided by the various agencies would only be used for the following purposes:

- To provide an overview of crime, disorder, victims and offenders that is specific to each District/Borough CDRP within Northamptonshire.
- To identify the context of crime and disorder problems and underlying risk factors.
- To identify patterns and trends both over time and geographically.
- To assist in the identification of priorities, enabling agencies to allocate resources accordingly.
- To assist in the identification of gaps in the provision of data, subsequently aiding the development of joint initiatives to overcome these.
- To assist in the evaluation and monitoring of "what works" within Northamptonshire by way of crime prevention and reduction programmes (ComPaSS).

In turn, the data covered by the protocol would be that needed to allow the unit 'to reach its maximum potential', namely to provide data/analysis relevant to the following areas:

- *Area profile:* information concerning the demographics, employment numbers and structure; education, health and leisure facilities: and any other information/data that depict or describe the area concerned.

- *Risk profile:* data/information on social and economic factors that are seen, when clustered, to have a probable influence upon an individual's involvement within criminal or antisocial behaviour.
- *Crime profile:* primarily police crime and incidence data, but from other agencies where necessary.
- *Offender profile:* information on numbers of offenders and offences, most predominant type and place of offence, and other information relevant to routine profiling of predominant or prolific offenders.
- *Victim profile:* individuals and locations most susceptible to becoming victims of crime, numbers of repeat victims and most victimised groups by age, gender and ethnicity.
- *Disorder profile:* data about the extent of antisocial behaviour, the number of evictions, number of homeless individuals and any other data that might highlight disorder.
- *Impacts:* explanatory/statistical information that offers a review of initiatives existing countywide, where the intention is to assist in the reduction of crime and disorder.

Subsequently, however, in addition to the community profiling protocol, the unit also established a Data Exchange Agreement (DEA) with East Midlands Ambulance Service (EMS) to receive Ambulance Service CAD data on a regular basis, so that this data could be analysed alongside the datasets above. Interestingly, ComPaSS had been involved in initial discussions with the local Drug Alcohol Action Team (DAAT) and Primary Care Trust, who were also interested in obtaining the ambulance data, but who eventually signed a separate DEA with EMAS to obtain the specific information they needed (www. compassunit.com). Nevertheless, the account of the establishment of the DEA with EMS refers to difficulties the unit had in overcoming initial reluctance on the part of the ambulance service to transfer information between the NHS's secure system and the police system (PNN) which ComPaSS uses (*MiRAN* 2009).

Data sharing: use of accident and emergency data

A further example of a CDRP/CSP seeking to supplement its understanding of local crime patterns by uising data obtained from health sources is provided by the use of A&E data in Cardiff, South Wales to provide the community safety partnership there with a more comprehensive picture of the nature and trends in violent crime in the city. According to a briefing paper produced in 2007 for the then Health Secretary:

Emergency Departments (EDs) can contribute distinctively and effectively to violence prevention by working with Crime and Disorder Reduction Partnerships (CDRPs) and by sharing, electronically wherever possible, simple anonymised data about precise location of violence, weapon use, assailants and day/time of violence. These data, and the contributions of consultants in CDRP meetings, enhance effectiveness of targeted policing significantly, reduce licensed premises and street violence, and reduce overall A&E violence related attendances – in Cardiff, by 40% since 2002.

(Cardiff University 2007: 3)

Similarly, in Oxford the Nightsafe project has involved the sharing of data from Thames Valley Police, ambulance data from the South Central Ambulance Service NHS Trust, and the Oxfordshire Primary Care Trust. From this a monthly report is produced which indicates problematic licensed premises in the city centre (with counts and details of incidents), hotspot maps of incidents of violence and incidents involving glasses, bottles or weapons, the location of ambulance pick-ups in the previous month and details of the streets where most fixed-penalty notices have been issued (Box 13.5).

Box 13.5   Exercise 13E Benefits of A&E in tackling crime

Research suggests that there are a number of benefits which may arise from involving accident and emergency departments in efforts to tackle violent crime. Take some time to consider what these benefits might be under the following headings:

- Understanding of the nature of violent crime
- Impact on the reporting of crime
- Benefits to partnership working
- Impact on the level of demand on the police and A&E.

Benefits of using health data for community safety

The briefing document produced by the Cardiff project identified a number of reasons why health, and in particular emergency medicine, should be involved in community violence prevention (aside from the fact that it was a statutory requirement). They included claims related to the accuracy of the picture of violent crime in the city:

- A&E data provided information about location and time of assaults, which could be easily collected in EDs and help police and local authorities target their resources more effectively.
- ED staff could facilitate the increased reporting of violence to the police by injured people who were not otherwise in a position to report.
- The approach could identify trends in weapon use (the Cardiff report claimed that the use of glasses and bottles as weapons was first recognised not by the police but by ED services).

- That even very serious violence (e.g. knife and gun crime) might not otherwise be reported to the police, especially if gang-related. Thus it served as a supplement to the partial police recorded crime data.
- Data sharing provided a new 'objective' measure of community violence which helps the public, the police, local government and the Home Office to understand the true size of the problem.

Claims were also made about the benefits that might arise in relation to improved partnership working:

- ED professionals, particularly senior doctors, could be 'powerful and effective advocates for community safety' particularly when they worked in local crime prevention partnerships.
- ED health professionals tended to act from a patient/victim perspective: most crime prevention activity tended to be oriented towards offenders/offending perspectives.
- Involvement could help other agencies to realise the seriousness of violence from a health standpoint, particularly the numbers and seriousness of injury sustained (Cardiff University 2007: 3).

Other claims made for the initiative were perhaps more tenuous, or open to challenge, as they depended upon the successful resolution of identified problems, but included the following:

- Burdens on EDs could be reduced, particularly late at night and at the weekends when services were stretched and alcohol-related disorder was commonplace, including in the ED itself.
- Involvement could lead to improvements in local transport services, pedestrian safety and alcohol licensing, all of which were important in violence prevention.

The Cardiff project identified the following as 'essential ingredients' for the successful operation of the scheme:

- Data-collection system (preferably electronic) in the Emergency Department.
- Capacity on the part of the Hospital Trust to anonymise and share Emergency Department data.
- Crime analyst in Crime and Disorder Reduction Partnership (CDRP) with the skills to integrate and summarise information about violence from Emergency Department and police sources.
- 'At least one NHS ED consultant who is committed to injury prevention, and prepared to lead ED implementation and attend CDRP task group meetings.'

- Prioritisation of violence as a public health issue by the local public health service.
- CDRP task group dedicated to continuous scientific violence prevention which includes senior police, local authority and ED practitioners (Cardiff University 2007: 7).

The Cardiff model suggested the following 'data delivery chain':

1. Twenty-four-hour electronic data collection by Emergency Department clerical staff when patients first attend.
2. Monthly anonymisation and sharing of data by Hospital Trust IT staff with CDRP analyst.
3. Monthly combination of police and ED data by CDRP analyst.
4. Summary of violence times, locations and weapons by CDRP analyst.
5. 'Continuous implementation and updating of prevention action plan by CDRP violence task group.
6. Continuous tracking of violence trends – overall trends and trends in violence hotspots' (Cardiff University 2007: 7).

Conclusion

The assertion that crime reduction and community safety is not merely a matter for the police, but requires concerted, and coordinated, action on the part of a number of agencies has become something of a cliché in the years since the introduction of the 1998 Crime and Disorder Act. What this chapter has identified is that the context for this partnership approach has evolved over the past decade. Agencies are now encouraged to work together towards different outputs (strategic assessments rather than audits and strategies), within a different, but unifying, framework (the national intelligence model). While the impact of these changes should not be overplayed, they illustrate attempts by the government to overcome some of the practical problems that have arisen in trying to implement partnership working in the UK, as does the introduction of statutory requirements for data sharing between agencies, replacing previous exhortations about the benefits of good practice in this regard.

References and suggested further reading

ACPO/HMIC (2005) *Practice advice on Professionalising the Business of Neighbourhood Policing*. ACPO, London.
Bichard Inquiry Report (2004) HC 653. HMSO, London.
Cardiff University (2007) 'Effective NHS contributions to violence prevention; the Cardiff model'. Cardiff University, Cardiff.
Compass (n.d.) 'Compass Community Profiling Protocol'. Available online at http://www.compassunit.com/docs/CompassUnitDataSharingAgreement-PROTOCOL.pdf (accessed on 7 March 2011).

Cope, N. (2004) 'Intelligence-led policing or policing led intelligence?', *British Journal of Criminology*; 1 March: 188–203.

Grieve, J. (2004) 'Developments in UK criminal intelligence', in Ratcliffe, J.H. (ed.), *Strategic Thinking in Criminal Intelligence*. Federation Press, Sydney, Australia.

Harfield, C. and Harfield, K. (2008) *Intelligence, Investigation, Community and Partnership.* Oxford University Press, Oxford.

Home Office (HO) (2006) *Review of the Partnership Provisions of the Crime and Disorder Act 1998 – Report of Findings.*

—— (2007a) *Developing a Strategic Assessment. An effective practice toolkit for Crime and Disorder Reduction Partnerships and Community Safety Partnerships.*

—— (2007b) *Delivering Safer Communities; A Guide to Effective Partnership Working.*

—— (n.d.) Available online at http://www.crimereduction.homeoffice.gov.uk/regions/CD RP%20Reform%20Implementation%20Annex%20B.pdf.

Information Commissioner's Office (ICO) (2007) *Framework Code of Practice for Sharing Personal Information.* ICO, Cheshire.

Innes, M. and Roberts, C. (n.d.) 'Community intelligence in the policing of community safety'. UPSI website.

Innes, M., Fielding, N. and Cope, N. (2005) 'The appliance of science?', *British Journal of Criminology*; January.

Midlands Researcher and Analyst Network Newsletter (MiRAN) (2009) April.

Tilley, N. (2008) 'Intelligence-led policing', in Newburn, T. and Neyroud, P. (eds), *Dictionary of Policing*. Willan Publishing, Cullompton, Devon.

Tilley, N. (n.d.) 'Problem-oriented Policing, Intelligence-led Policing and the National Intelligence Model'. Available online at http://www.jdi.ucl.ac.uk/downloads/ publications/crime_science_short_reports/problem_oriented_policing.pdf (accessed on 7 March 2011).

Part 4

Investigative practices

Part 4 synthesises many of the previous chapters discussions, philosophies and approaches, and includes them in several important investigative areas of police work.

In particular it considers the nature and investigation of prominent criminal offence such as sexual offences, including paedophilia and rape, and considers the problems associated with investigating and dealing with these issues.

Chapter 15, 'Organised and transnational crime', considers the impact of globalisation upon crime and criminality, and discusses such issues as terrorism, money laundering and white-collar crime.

Forensic examination has become a major part of all investigative practices, and Chapter 16 examines in detail some of the major techniques and issues surrounding the use of technology by the police. The police have always played a part in controlling public disorder, and Chapter 17 introduces the student to some more complex ideas and approaches that the police could adopt as society progresses into the twenty-first century.

Part 4 highlights many professional practices surrounding the above topics and invites the student to reflect upon how investigative practices could be improved.

14 The nature and investigation of sexual offences

The content of this chapter is centred on five main themes:

- The nature and evolution of sexual offences.
- Police investigation of allegations of sexual offences.
- Multi-disciplinary responsibilities for the risk assessments of likely victims (vulnerable people) or likely sex offenders.
- The treatment and monitoring of sex offenders.
- The responsibilities of named agencies and organisations in protecting vulnerable people.

Although the word *investigation* appears in only one of these headings, investigation is also a crucial element in both risk assessment and in the pro-active monitoring of offenders.

Sexual violence and abuse

The UK report *Cross Government Action Plan on Sexual Violence and Abuse* (2007) outlines both the scale and nature of sexual offences:

- 62,081 sexual offences were recorded by the police during 2005 to 2006 (representing about 1 per cent of all recorded crime and about 5 per cent of all recorded violent crime). There were 14,449 offences of rape, of which 92 per cent were rape of a female. Many sexual assaults remain unreported: it is estimated that only 15 per cent of rapes come to the attention of the police. Childhood sexual abuse is more prevalent in the 5 to 14 age group and is believed to be massively under-reported. One study published by the National Society for the Prevention of Cruelty to Children in 2000 found that three-quarters of sexually abused children do not tell anyone about it.
- Most sexual offences committed against young people or children are committed by individuals known to the victim – including members of their family. Offences by strangers are rare. The British Crime Survey

Interpersonal Violence Module 2005 to 2006 found that 51 per cent of serious sexual assaults were committed by former or current partners of the victim: only 11 per cent were committed by strangers.

- Adult sexual violence is most likely in the 16 to 19 age group. Statistically, single, divorced or separated people, those who are ill or disabled, those in prison, those who are victims of domestic abuse, those involved in street prostitution and those who have been drinking are more likely to be sexually assaulted.

- Sexual assault during childhood is a risk factor in adult life, making such adults more likely to be assaulted. However, sexual offenders are more likely to have been assaulted in childhood than other members of the population. Boys who demonstrate sexually abusive behaviour appear to be more likely to commit any form of crime in adulthood. However, it appears that most sex offenders are not genetically disposed to their crimes. The graduation of offenders from minor sexual offences to more serious ones is sometimes called the 'spiral of sexual abuse'.

- Some sexual offences, including those involving 'grooming' and child pornography, have become more commonplace since the widespread availability of the internet and this poses new challenges. The Child Exploitation and Online Protection Centre (CEOP) is a UK national agency which seeks to eradicate the sexual abuse of children particularly through the internet. The CEOP tracks offenders, working with the police, child protection agencies and the IT industry.

- Sex offenders are not homogeneous in their nature and habits, and sexual assaults are committed by people with a range of motivations and social backgrounds (Hudson 2005). An interesting classification of offenders is based on their own view of their criminality by dividing them into 'total deniers', 'justifiers' and 'acceptors'. This is relevant to the ability of offenders to self-manage their own risk of offending (Box 14.1).

Box 14.1 Exercise 14A Alcohol consumption and crime

Take a few minutes to answer the following question:

Suggest four reasons why alcohol consumption is often associated with sexual violence and abuse.

Drinking is associated with decisions involving greater risks (e.g. staying out later and walking home on their own) and drinkers may also appear more vulnerable to potential offenders. Alcohol consumption of potential offenders may increase their physical aggression. Culturally, it may be wrongly assumed that people who come to bars or pubs to drink are more receptive to extreme behaviour including sexual advances. Some offenders may regard a drunken victim as less capable of contesting that consent for sex has not been given.

A snapshot of the public's view of sexually assaulted victims was reported by Amnesty International in 2005: many people believed that the victim is partly to blame (e.g. by being drunk or by wearing revealing clothing). It is important that this view is challenged at every opportunity. While being drunk increases the risk of sexual attack it neither justifies such attacks nor mitigates the guilt of the perpetrator. Neither is the sexual history of the victim likely to be relevant to any defence case: section 41 of the Youth Justice and Criminal Evidence Act 1999 prohibits questions in cross-examination relating to the sexual behaviour of the complainant unless judged relevant by the court.

Tackling sexual abuse and violence in its most general sense requires multi-agency action and cooperation (Table 14.1).

The nature and evolution of sexual offences

Although we are used to most criminal offences being fully defined by legislation, the history of sexual offences (Thomas 2005) shows that statute law,

Table 14.1 Main organisations involved in tackling sexual abuse and violence

Organisation	*Responsibilities*
Police Service	Often the agency which is the first to respond to an allegation of assault but also responsible for elements of victim care, for criminal investigation and, through partnerships, for dealing with sex offenders.
Crown Prosecution Service	Prosecution of offenders. Increasingly, the CPS takes responsibility for the creation of an appropriate environment in court for vulnerable witnesses or victims.
Law Courts	The Courts have a responsibility to adjudicate over legal cases and to provide appropriate facilities for witnesses who are easily intimidated.
NHS Trusts	Victim care and (where patients are victims) for the initial identification of possible violence or abuse.
Prison and Probation Services as part of the National Offender Management Service	Responsible for the management and treatment of offenders in prisons or in the community.
Social Service departments in local authorities	Responsible for the management of individuals identified as being 'at risk', for alerting the police to possible abuse cases and for assisting the police in investigations.
Voluntary organisations	These provide a range of services to victims, including specialist legal advice and counselling. Examples include the National Rape Crisis Network and the Survivors Trust.
Sexual Assault Referral Centres (SARCs)	These are regionally based centres funded by central government, the local Police Service and the NHS. They provide care for victims following an assault, and have specialist facilities to provide medical and forensic examinations.

common law and ecclesiastical law have all prohibited certain different types of sexual offences over the centuries.

What constitutes a sexual offence has changed over time. For example, male homosexual activity was unconditionally a criminal offence until 1967 and rape in marriage remained largely unrecognised as a crime until the 1980s. Despite some debates as to whether or not offences relating to prostitution are sexual offences, as opposed to offences involving public nuisance or public disorder, there are specific offences relating to prostitution under both the 2003 and 1956 Sexual Offences Acts. For example, under the Sexual Offences Act 2003, it is an offence to cause or incite prostitution, or control it for personal gain.

The distinction between 'private' and 'public' space is sometimes relevant in the definition of sexual offences. For example:

- The Sexual Offences Act 2003, s.66, defines the offence of 'the intentional exposure of genitals'. This is not restricted to a public place. A related offence, that of 'outraging public decency' under common law, requires that a lewd, obscene or disgusting act be committed where it might be seen by more than one member of the public.
- The Sexual Offences Act 2003, s.71, creates an offence in a highly specific location: the offence of 'sexual activity in a public lavatory'. The legislation does not define sexual but states: 'an activity is sexual if a reasonable person would, in all the circumstances but regardless of any person's purpose, consider it to be sexual'.
- Under the Sexual Offences Act 1967, homosexual activities were defined as legal only if the activity took place in 'private'. The Sexual Offences Act 2003 superseded the 1967 Act and removed the requirement to distinguish between homosexual and heterosexual sexual acts by introducing neutral offences (redefining rape in which the victim might be male or female) and in which the location of the offence – private or public – is irrelevant.
- S.46 of the Criminal Justice and Police Act 2001 created the offence of 'placing an advertisement relating to prostitution' on or in the vicinity of a public telephone. There is no definition of advertisement: the act states that 'any advertisement which a reasonable person would consider to be an advertisement relating to prostitution shall be presumed to be such an advertisement unless it is shown not to be' (Box 14.2).

  (a) The Sexual Offences Act 2003 abandons the idea of 'indecency' (a feature of earlier legislation) and replaces it with the term 'sexual' as considered by a 'reasonable person' who will take into account the nature of the act, the intentions of the alleged offender and other circumstances (see e.g. the reference to sexuality in s.71, above).
  (b) Although the Sexual Offences Act 2003 is central to the prosecution of many sexual offences, and the Act clarified and extended existing legislation and common law, older legislation is still used. Examples are Criminal Justice and Police Act 2001 (see above) and the use of the

---

Box 14.2 Exercise 14B Revision: the Sexual Offences Act (SOA) 2003

Revise your knowledge of the Act by studying the appropriate section in the latest edition of *Blackstone's Police Manual* (Vol. 1, Crime) or by studying the Act on the web at http://www.opsi.gov.uk/acts/acts2003/en/ukpgaen_20030042_en_1.

(a)   Does the SOA 2003 define the term 'sexual'?
(b)   Does the SOA 2003 encompass all sexual offences?
(c)   How does the SOA 2003 define 'consent'?
(d)   Many of the offences contained within the SOA 2003 may be classified as:

   (i)   Non-consensual offences (i.e. where it must be proved that the consent of the victim was not given).
   (ii)   Sexual activity which remains unlawful despite the ostensible (i.e. apparent) consent of both parties.
   (iii) Preparatory offences.
   (iv)   Exploitation offences.

Give one example of each class of offence.

Offences Against the Person Act 1861 to prosecute the intentional or reckless sexual transmission of infection (such as HIV).
  (c) Consent is defined in s.74: 'a person consents if he agrees by choice, and has the freedom and capacity to make that choice'. To find a defendant guilty under s.1–4 of the Act, it must be proved that the offender did not reasonably believe that the victim consented to the sexual act in question. Evidential presumptions about consent are given in s.75 and s.76 of the Act. For example, if it can be shown that a person impersonated a victim's partner in order that the victim would allow a sexual act, it is presumed that consent was not given.

   (i) Sexual offences that are only committed (i.e. established) where there is no consent are referred to as 'non-consensual offences'. They include rape, assault by penetration, sexual assault and causing or inciting sexual activity.
   (ii) Sexual activity involving ostensible consent but which remains unlawful includes any sexual activity involving a person below the age of consent (e.g. sexual activity with a child under 16) and where one party holds a position of power over the other (e.g. under s.30, where the victim suffers a mental disorder and is susceptible to exploitation or coercion.)

(iii) Preparatory offences include 'sexual grooming' (s.15) and administering a substance with the intent to stupefy or overpower a person for sexual activity (s.61).

(iv) Exploitation offences include offences relating to the taking of indecent photographs of children (s.45) and trafficking for sexual offences (s.57) (Box 14.3).

Box 14.3   Exercise 14C Sentencing guidelines for offences under the Sexual Offences Act 2003

The Criminal Justice Act 2003 dictates that the seriousness of an offence depends upon the *culpability* (roughly speaking, blameworthiness) of the offender and the *harm* caused or risked by the offence, including the impact on the victim of the offence.

Study the following factors and label them either as indicating 'more than usually serious degree of harm' or as indicating 'higher culpability'.

Factor

(1) Repeated assault on the same victim
(2) Taking photographs of the victim during a sexual assault
(3) Offender is mentally ill
(4) Offence committed on bail
(5) Young children witnessing the sexual attack
(6) Abuse of position of trust
(7) Offence motivated by the victim's disability
(8) Offender played only a minor role in a sexual attack.

The answers are:

'More harm': (1), (2), (5), (8)
'Higher culpability': (3), (4), (6), (7).

Current sentencing guidelines relating to the Sexual Offences Act 2003 may be found under 'Sentencing guidelines' followed by 'Guidelines to download' at http://www.sentencingcouncil.org.uk/docs/web_SexualOffencesAct_2003.pdf.

Public protection and risk

The response of public bodies, including the police, to the risks posed by potential sex offenders involves the minimisation of harm. Hebenton and Seddon (2009) discuss two approaches to public protection with particular emphasis upon sexual crime and violence. The first, known as 'Community Protection', is an attempt to prevent crime by incapacitating individuals believed to be dangerous. The second, 'the Public Health Approach', attempts to prevent crime through the elimination of risky conditions and by concentrating on the environments that make crime more likely (Box 14.4).

Box 14.4   Exercise 14D Examples

Give an example of both the 'community protection' and 'public health' approaches.

Community protection strategies include:

- The screening of employees (see the role of the ISA below) for 'potential risk' to vulnerable people.
- The control of sex offenders using a range of instruments, including the 'Sex Offence Register'. In 2008, the UK government stated its intention to make legal amendments under the Sexual Offences Act 2003 to permit the police the use of the following civil prohibitive orders: Sex Offences Prevention Orders (SOPOs), Foreign Travel Orders (FTOs) and Risk of Sexual Harm Orders (RHSOs).

Public health approaches include:

- Providing advice on avoiding 'spiked drinks' or concerning personal security late at night.
- 'No-blame' health initiatives, concerned not with sexual offences but with attempts to reduce the harm to society through sexually transmitted diseases by warning advertisements and free advice clinics for sex workers.

Other initiatives may not fall neatly into either category; for example:

- Clear institutional policies where sexual assaults are suspected or reported (for example, clear guidelines stating how to communicate concerns about the suspicious behaviour of a care worker or hospital patient in an NHS Trust).
- The formal coordination of relevant agencies to pool knowledge and more accurately assess the level of risk posed by an offender. For example, the managed release of higher risk sex offenders into the wider community using Multi-Agency Public Protection Panels (MAPPPs). Such panels comprise the three 'Responsible Authorities' (police, prison and probation services) with relevant information being stored on a confidential and secure database known as the Dangerous Persons Database ('ViSOR').

The Sex Offender Register

The basic premise of the Register is that the best way to protect the community is through increasing the monitoring of potential offenders and restrictions on those potential offenders depending on the risk that is determined.

- The Sex Offender Act 1997 implemented a registration process where certain sex offenders who were convicted or cautioned of an offence as listed under Schedule 1 of the Act (or other criteria[9]) were to register their personal details with the police within a specified time[10] and to notify them of any changes to these details for a specific length of time (Cobley 2000).
- While no Register actually exists, the length of time an offender will be subject to the notification requirements (the basis of the Register) is dependent upon the sentence imposed:

    o *An indefinite period* on the Register is imposed upon those sentenced to a term of imprisonment of 30 months or more and those admitted to hospital subject to a Restriction Order.
    o Sentences of more than six months' but less than 30 months' imprisonment attract a *period of 10 years* on the Register.
    o Sentences of six months' imprisonment or less and admissions to hospital without a Restriction Order attract a *period of seven years* on the Register.
    o A person in whose case an order for conditional discharge is made in respect of the offence is subjected to being on the Register for the period of the conditional discharge.
    o A person who is cautioned (within section 80(1)(d) of the Sex Offences Act 2003) is subjected to a *period of two years* on the Register.
    o Any other offenders are subject to the requirements for a *period of five years* on the Register.

- Young sex offenders (under 18 years of age) on the Register have their notification requirements halved in comparison with adult offenders (Thomas 2008).
- A relevant offender must register their personal details (e.g. name, address, date of birth) within three days at a police station where their photograph, fingerprints and DNA may also be recorded.
- The offender must also notify the police of any changes to their movements (e.g. new home address, being away for more than seven days) and they must liaise with the police every year to confirm their registered details are correct even if there have been no changes in movements within the year (Sex Offences Act 2003 s.83–s.85)
- The Offender Assessment System (OASys) (used by the National Probation Service [NPS] and the Prison Service) and the Risk Matrix 2000 (used by the police in England and Wales) are assessment tools used to identify the risk posed of violent and sexual offenders reoffending (Home Office 2003).

- The Risk Matrix 2000 may only be used on male sex offenders. A risk assessment specifically designed for female sex offenders does not currently exist.
- As it is the responsibility of the police to complete the Risk Matrix 2000, it is important that resources are put in place for adequate training of officers on how to complete the matrix successfully; otherwise offenders could be placed in an incorrect risk category for monitoring purposes.

Both assessment tools place offenders into levels of risk:

  o low;
  o medium;
  o high;
  o very high risk.

- The police carry out visits to offenders' homes based on the offenders' level of risk (Criminal Justice Act 2003). The high- and very high-risk offenders would expect a minimum monthly visit from assigned public protection officers, while low-risk offenders would expect an annual visit from community officers. If an offender refuses an officer entry into his home, police can apply to a magistrate for a warrant to enter in order to assess the risk which that offender might pose by way of reoffending (Violent Crime Reduction Act 2006).
- When an offender's period of registration expires, their history of offending and length of registration remains on the Police National Computer (PNC).
- Research suggests that about 20 per cent of offenders subject to the notification requirements will remain subject to them for an indefinite period (Cobley 2000).

In 2006, the number of offenders on the Register stood at just under 30,000 (Thomas 2008) (Box 14.5).

You may have identified high-profile cases and the role of the media as significant, but anxieties are part of a more complicated picture.

The influence of negative reports and the growing rate of crime through the 1960s saw government policy shift from a rehabilitative model towards a more punitive one. Crime surveys, the role of the media in bringing visual news both local and global into one's home, the many social changes taking place and the feminist movement in the 1970s, which 'pushed for broader definitions of sexual crime [and] more vigorous enforcement of sex crime laws' (Janus 2000: 84) created a sense of anxiety that crime was a problem and something needed to be done. As crimes such as robbery and burglary were perceived to be committed by a stranger, the fear of such strangers committing crimes of violence to the person escalated. This fear was transferred from women who it was believed had some power to protect themselves from strangers, to children who were regarded as being the most vulnerable. Anxieties and the threat of danger tended to be posed

Box 14.5   Case study A Multi-Agency Public Protection Panel (MAPPP)

An MAPPP meeting was called regarding the recent behaviour of a 27-year-old predatory high-risk sex offender 'J'. 'J' has been registered 'very high risk' from the age of 20 following his previous history of breaching probation orders and abducting a young boy. Having completed a prison sentence he was now living in the community and his old patterns of behaviour were re-emerging. These patterns included:

- Befriending boys aged 10 to 12 years in local snooker halls or local parks playing football and offering them either money or supplying them with alcohol.
- Carrying inoffensive photos of young females.
- Taking photos of boys near school property.
- His main form of transport is a popular commuting train line while taking his bicycle with him and disembarking at various towns and villages en route (covering approximately a 25-mile radius).

As this offender was 'very high risk' and regarded as one of the 'critical few' when determining an MAPPP meeting, members of the police, probation and housing were brought together to determine what could be done to prevent a possible offence from being committed.

The outcome of the MAPPP was to place a Sex Offender Prevention Order (SOPO) on him. Once a file containing evidence from probation, British Transport Police and the local police force was collated, it was requested that the requirements of the SOPO would consist of:

- Not approaching children under the age of 18 years.
- Not entering schools, parks or cinemas.
- Not to be in possession of inappropriate photos.
- Not to be in possession of photographic equipment.
- Not to use any train as a form of transport.

While the intention of this particular SOPO was to prevent 'J' from potentially committing an offence, it was important that the SOPO was harsh but proportionate at the same time. In this scenario 'J' was allowed to keep and use his bicycle. By clearly informing 'J' of what the SOPO stated, 'J' knew exactly what the unacceptable behaviour was and that any breach of his SOPO would lead to a custodial sentence for him.

Exercise 14E Risk of assault

What factors have made more people anxious about the risk of assault by strangers ('stranger danger')?

by a recognisable group. Cohen's 'Mods and Rockers', for example, were 'visible' – they had a particular dress code and possessed particular modes of transport. With the Mods and Rockers, this visibility meant that one could avoid or be wary of those who matched their description in the community (Cohen 2002). The problem with the concept of danger today is that the sexual offender who poses a threat is anonymous and technically invisible. They don't have a dress code or identifiable accessories. They could live in one's community, in one's street, but one doesn't know. The pre-war integrated communities, where neighbours knew each other and discussed local news and events, have almost disappeared, and so the reliance on the media to inform has contributed to the levels of insecurity and anxiety.

The responsibility of employers in identifying, investigating and protecting vulnerable individuals: the role of the ISA

Police officers will frequently be asked to visit both public and private employers in response to allegations of sexual assault. Many larger employers, particularly those providing services to vulnerable individuals, have policies which define the procedures by which concerns or allegations about misconduct (including sexual offences) are dealt with: police officers should ask for these policies as part of any investigation. For example:

- The Council for Healthcare Regulatory Excellence (CHRE) has published guidance on sexual boundaries between healthcare professionals and patients.
- The Central and North West London NHS Foundation Trust (2008) has published a Sexual Assault Policy, with particular emphasis upon the protection of vulnerable people (such as mentally disordered patients) from offences listed under sections 30–44 of the Sexual Offences Act 2003.

The proposal to create the Independent Safeguarding Authority (ISA) is a major development in protecting vulnerable people. The ISA arose from the Bichard Report following the Soham murders. The role of the ISA is to prevent unsuitable people from working with children and adults ('vulnerable people') by acting as a vetting and barring body. This is achieved by checking the worker against the Criminal Records Bureau (CRB) and Police National Computer databases and also using police and other forms of intelligence. Originally, the proposal involved placing every person (including teachers, social workers, hospital porters and nurses) who currently works, or intends to work, with vulnerable people (even as a volunteer) on the ISA register. Criminal convictions and other intelligence would then be added to the file of the registered individual as a matter of course, and many organisations (including employers) would have to inform the ISA of all information deemed relevant to registration. Members of existing workforces were to be phased into the scheme from January 2011 and individuals who were deemed as posing a risk to work with vulnerable people would be refused registration. However, in June 2010, Home Secretary Theresa May announced that registration would be put on hold and that there will be a review of the ISA vetting and barring scheme, and at the time of writing the future and scope of the ISA remain unclear.

Responsibilities of Social Services departments

The responsibilities of Social Services departments, including partnerships such as local safeguarding children boards, are particularly onerous since they are responsible for children living at home or away from home, children in public care and unborn children. S.47 of the Children Act 1989 states that the local authority has a duty to investigate when 'they have a reasonable cause to suspect a child who lives, or is found, in their area is suffering, or is likely to suffer significant harm'. The resulting enquiries are often referred to as 's.47 enquiries'. Guidance as to how to respond to a child or young person who reports abuse or neglect is often applicable to both local authority and police investigations. For example, the child's information should be listened to impartially and the child should be reassured that they are not to blame for any abuse or negligence they have suffered (see e.g. the referral and investigation policy produced by the Durham Local Safeguarding Children Board 2009, which also provides a useful checklist of possible indicators of physical abuse, sexual abuse or neglect). Where there is a risk to the life of a child or the possibility of serious immediate injury or harm, the police may be asked to provide immediate protection.

The following should always be referred to and investigated by the police: physical abuse (amounting to 'ABH and above' in severity), serious cruelty and all sexual assaults.

Police investigation of sexual offences

Investigating sexual offences poses numerous challenges:

- Sexual offences are not typical crimes. In many of the crimes with which the police deal, the occurrence of the crime is not itself in question. Whether or not a sexual offence has occurred is often contested by the victim and defendant, particularly where there are no witnesses or substantive forensic or medical evidence.
- Many victims refuse to pursue their allegations. While it is not essential that a victim complains or otherwise provides other evidence about a sexual assault in order for action to be taken, the Criminal Prosecution Service may instigate prosecution anyway. However, there is often very little evidence without the victim's testimony.
- Most sexual offences committed against adults involve the question of consent: the exception is a sexual offence committed by a stranger, where it would be expected that lack of consent would be easier to prove.

- Sexual offences may also be part of a longer term pattern involving other long-standing offences such as domestic abuse or assault and often involving repeat victimisation.
- Victims are often very traumatised by the assault, and investigating officers must be particularly patient and sensitive to the victim's needs. This is particularly true of rape, which is 'not just a physical assault but also a violation of personal, intimate and psychological boundaries. Most commonly the offender is known, which also involves a betrayal of trust' (Kelly and co-workers, Home Office Research Study 293, 2005). Since 2003, victims of rape and other sexual offences have been able to give their evidence as a video-recorded interview.
- The investigation of sexual offences which go back many years is both difficult and complex. Such investigations may generate further allegations as part of the rolling investigation and enquiries have an institutional dimension with many possible witnesses. This is the case, for example, where sex offences have taken place within a care home, school or church.
- Paedophilia cases involving the internet are resource-intensive, technically challenging and may involve liaison with law-enforcement agencies in other countries. For example, Operation Ore was intended to prosecute those accessing child pornography images on the web. The operation involved the investigation of over 7,000 suspects and resulted in over 3,000 arrests. Some suspects have since been proved innocent because their credit card details had been fraudulently used by others without their permission.
- Working with the victims of sexual offences, particularly when children are involved, can be harrowing for investigators. Police managers must be aware of this, and make appropriate counselling available.

Reports of sexual offences to the police often come from third parties or partner organisations (e.g. neighbours, Social Services or hospitals). Victims are often reluctant to report an offence directly to the police because they fear embarrassment, that they will not be believed, that the police will be unsympathetic, or that 'there is no point' in coming forward because they believe that the offence will be too difficult to prove in what they view as an aggressive adversarial legal system, or because a court appearance would prove too upsetting.

Historically, there has been general dissatisfaction and frustration of the media, victims and politicians with the outcomes of police investigations of sexual offences (particularly investigations of rape). The victim's experience of rape is reported in Sarah Payne's review (Home Office 2009). The Cross-government Action Plan on Sexual Violence and Abuse (2007) noted:

> Notwithstanding the inherent difficulties in proving that an offence took place where the case hinges on whether or not one party consented, the current rate of serious sexual offences convicted is unacceptable.

There are two implications of this statement that are worth teasing out. First, that the current rate of rape convictions is very low. This was examined in the Stern Review and is discussed further below. Second, that a significant number of individuals who have committed serious sexual assaults are escaping conviction.

The response of criminal justice agencies (and of the police in particular) to continued criticism falls into four main categories:

- Modified behavioural and procedural responses. A greater sensitivity is now shown by police officers and other officials towards victims. Police officers are now trained to be more respectful and supportive of victims and to create 'a culture of belief' that the victim's allegations are true. Good practice includes keeping victims updated on the progress of the investigation, and formal 'cold case reviews' by experienced detectives are encouraged.
- Improved facilities, such as Sexual Assault Referral Centres (SARCs), which provide a calming environment. It is also general practice to use Sexual Offences Investigator Trained (SOIT) officers (or equivalent) in investigations. The CPS uses specialist lawyers in court. Taken together, such initiatives maximise the likelihood that important evidence is not lost early in the investigation and that where possible officers pool experience and best practice across all services. The role of forensic evidence is particularly important: prosecutions involving forensic evidence are more likely to be successful in securing convictions.
- Closer working between police officers and the CPS to 'build cases' more effectively from the beginning of an investigation.

The government is also keen to use preventive strategies to minimise risk with a renewed emphasis upon pre-emptive action against likely offenders. For example, if the use of Sex Offences Prevention Orders (SOPOs) becomes widespread, it is likely that some sexual offences will have been prevented from occurring in the first place.

These responses are resource-intensive and it might be argued that similar levels of resources have not been allocated to many other types of serious assault (e.g. to the investigation of serious [not sexual] assaults caused by drunkenness). The fact that such resources have been provided is a reflection of the priority accorded to the detection and conviction of serious sexual offenders by society and by government.

Rape

At first sight, the 'presumption of truth' appears to go against the idea of the 'sceptical investigator' – the idea that police officers must keep an open mind in their investigations and leave decisions of guilt or innocence to others. It might be argued that assuming that the victim's statement is true is part of the fair treatment that victims should receive, although this is somewhat controversial

---

Box 14.6   Exercise 14F Rape allegations

The City of London Rape and Serious Sexual Offence Investigation Policy contains the statement that 'It is the policy of the City of London Police to accept allegations made by any victim in the first instance as being truthful. An allegation will only be considered as falling short of a substantiated allegation after a full and through investigation.' Do you think that assuming that the victim is 'telling the truth' is justified in police investigations of serious sexual offences, such as rape?

(http://www.cityoflondon.gov.uk/NR/rdonlyres/8AC30EAB-3127-47A4-B791-948B8D026779/0/rapeSSOI.pdf)

---

since this approach is not universally applied to the investigation of other serious criminal offences. However, the presumption of truth is also a strategy designed to maximise the criminally valuable information extracted from a traumatised victim: the safeguard against false allegations is that the CPS still has to decide whether or not there is sufficient evidence to proceed with the prosecution.

Kelly and co-workers (Home Office Research Study 293, 2005) provides a detailed evaluation of two Sexual Assault Referral Centres. They identify four stages of attrition in rape cases: the decision to report; the investigative stage; discontinuance by prosecutors; and the trial, with the greatest withdrawals occurring in the first two stages. The authors report that there appears to have been an improvement in the care of the victim by police compared to previous studies; nevertheless, many of the victims appear frustrated or dissatisfied with the 'culture of scepticism' of some police investigators. However, such concerns have to be balanced with the duty of investigating officers to reach, partly through detailed questioning, the burden of proof required to convict under the current adversarial legal system.

The investigation and detection of rape offences was studied by Feist and co-workers (2007). The familial nature of many rape offences was highlighted by the fact that over two-thirds of rape offences took place in the victim's home: the suspect rapist was named in two-thirds of cases. The study found an association between police force area and conviction rates, suggesting that force procedures or investigations were influential in securing convictions. In turn, this suggests that there is still much to be done at the operational level.

An example of force procedures for dealing with the investigation of sexual offences is provided by West Mercia (2005). The document lists the responsibilities of first responder, of specialist officers trained in sexual offence investigation, the SIO and the family liaison officer.

It is expected that updated guidance for police officers on investigating serious sexual offences will be periodically published by the NPIA.

The Stern review

In March 2010, Baroness Stern reported on how rape complaints are handled by public authorities in England and Wales. The review was very wide-ranging, and the report (in particular Chapter 2 – the role of the police) should be read by all police officers. She notes that: 'The obligations the state has to those who have suffered a violent crime, and a crime that strikes at the whole concept of human dignity and bodily integrity, are much wider than working for the conviction of a perpetrator'. Stern made numerous recommendations, including that forensic medical services should be transferred from the police to the NHS. She also concluded that while the policies underpinning the way in which rape complaints are dealt with are correct, implementation by public authorities is patchy. Further, the obligations to victims should be recognised more widely, for example, by ensuring that every victim who so wishes should be supported by an independent sexual violence adviser. Such initiatives allow public authorities to take a broader approach to measuring success in rape cases, in which support for the victim is given a higher priority.

The Stern Review also considered the frequently quoted conviction rate of 6 per cent. This figure arises because the way in which conviction rates have been calculated for rape cases is different from that of most other offences. About 6 per cent of all rape cases recorded by the police end up with convictions for rape but 58 per cent of all rape cases that are brought to court end with the defendant being convicted. Stern reports that 58 per cent represents a higher percentage than for some other serious and violent crimes.

Paedophilia and child exploitation

While sex offending may appear to be a phenomenon of the late twentieth century, especially in relation to children, it has always existed, and 'molesters of children have spanned the entire age and social spectrum' (Prins 1995: 206). Historical research shows that sex offending has existed for a long time. In 1875, the age for consent was raised from 12 to 13 years (Thomas 2005): marriage at 13 years of age was permitted until 1929. Smart (2000) describes how venereal infections found in children in the early 1900s were as a direct result of rape. Such accounts 'acknowledged that children were being sexually abused as a result of the belief that sexual intercourse with a virgin produced a cure for venereal disease' (2000: 59).

Over 100 years later, sex offending has shifted into a new medium. The introduction of television in the 1950s 'visually' brought the news into people's homes. The perceptions of risk became more intensified and the increasing use of 'expert opinion' in media discussions confirmed that the dangers were real. With 24-hour news coverage being available in recent years, the needs and pressure for the media to fill the hours with 'exclusive' and up-to-date information has led to constant repetitive analysis of available information.

This level of news through television and newspapers could be regarded as a factor in making the general public aware of the concept of 'risk' – the fear that something may happen in the future. This fear that one may be at risk of being sexually assaulted, burgled, attacked or robbed in the future by a dangerous person (a stranger) has increased the level of paranoia within society about 'stranger danger', not only to themselves but especially to children.

The fear of personal danger has increased as technology has rapidly developed in recent years. The internet and mobile phone technology allow one to communicate with people all over the world instantly. With young people being more computer literate and aware than most of their parents, they become naturally vulnerable to 'stranger danger' coming into their homes through the medium of a computer or mobile phone (Box 14.7).

Box 14.7   Case study Paedophile: what's in a name?

The idea of the sinister stranger who molests children may have originated from suspicious vagrants who were blamed for much of the crime in towns and villages in earlier centuries. In 1931, Peter Lorre (later famous for his role in horror and detective films and conspicuous for his bulging eyes and cherubic features) took the part of a psychotic child murderer in a film based on child murders in Dusseldorf in Germany. The film was simply named *M*. In many ways, Lorre became the caricature of a paedophile.

Reality can be distorted by the media and by increasing public hysteria. For example, the word 'paedophile' is unhelpful in that it suggests that the offender is intrinsically different from other people. This is distracting, because the reality is very different: many convicted paedophiles have good jobs, have stable family relationships, are married and have children (for more information, see Thomas 2005: ch. 2).

Film clip from Fritz Lang's *M*, a film about a paedophile released in 1931:

http://www.youtube.com/watch?v=jUDUbxsNjV0.

The Child Exploitation and Online Protection (CEOP) Centre

The Child Exploitation and Online Protection Centre (CEOP, www.ceop.gov.uk) is part of the UK police dedicated to protecting children from sexual abuse. They rely on intelligence – how offenders operate and think, how children and young people behave and how technological advances are developing. The CEOP also works alongside government, charities, industries and other policing communities in order to explore all the options. CEOP consists of many specialised areas of investigation:

- *Intelligence Faculty* – manages the flow of information across the organisation and to external agencies such as local UK forces or international authorities. Any intelligence is researched and developed, and specialist units work with local and international forces to manage the risks posed by sex offenders.

- *Harm Reduction Faculty* – works to deliver market intelligence, to liaise with the technology industry and fine-tune guidelines to minimise the possibility of present and future technology increasing the risk of sexual abuse to children.

    o It also assists in training, education and public awareness. Specialists work together to raise the knowledge, skills and understanding of parents, children, young people, and a wide and diverse community including dedicated skills training for those working with sex offenders.

    o The international team takes the overall approach onto a much wider stage, working with overseas authorities and specialist agencies to share good practice, enhance tracking capabilities and minimise the risk caused by the global internet.

- *Operations Faculty* – works with forces to minimise volume, risk and impact, and to provide a law-enforcement response that connects the online and offline environments.

    o Specialist policing focus is placed on issues such as organised crime prof-iteering from the publication or distribution of images, support for local forces in areas such as computer forensics and covert investigations as well as working with international authorities to maximise policing powers.

    o The Operations Faculty also incorporates the UK's only national victim identification programme which works solely to focus on identifying child victims of online abuse backed up by a sophisticated database and cutting-edge software to support investigators in sharing any intel-ligence that can be gathered from seized images.

Box 14.8   Case study Victim identification

In 2001, a man was accused of abuse within familial circles. However, on release from a prison sentence, he is regarded as 'low risk' of re-offending on the Matrix 2000. The police are suspicious of whether he ever actually committed the offence(s) of which he was accused. Being in the 'low-risk' category would indicate the offender being supervised on an annual basis. It is decided at an MAPPP meeting to deliberately move him into the 'high-risk' category which would require at least one visit per month to his home by public protection officers. The reason for the MAPPP decision was because the police were more suspicious of his wife than of him. As they felt she was the actual offender and not her husband, they wanted to keep surveillance on her instead. She had access to children daily and regularly cared for children in the neighbourhood. She was described by the police as 'wearing the trousers' in the relationship while the husband was regarded as a 'harmless character' who did everything his wife told him to do.

Concluding remarks

We began this chapter by showing how the nature of sexual crimes has changed over the years, and we now look at a recent example which illustrates this development. Prostitution 'behind closed doors' is now a burgeoning industry in the UK, particularly in London. On 1 April 2010, s.14 of the Policing and Crime Act 2009 came into force, making it illegal to pay for a person ('the client') to have sex with a prostitute who has been induced or encouraged by a third person to provide sexual services by force, threats or any other form of coercion or deception: and where the client is, or ought to be, aware of the exploitive conduct of the third person. One reason for this Act is the concern that demand for prostitution is fuelling sex trafficking. It is difficult to unpick the moral dimension in such proposals, although such motivations have been rehearsed elsewhere, notably in Australia (Weitzer 2009).

Also in 2010, the UK coalition Conservative–Liberal Democratic government announced its intention to grant rape defendants anonymity, with such anonymity being removed if they are convicted. This proposal has divided politicians according to gender. Opponents against the proposals argue that it will deter victims from coming forward. Supporters of the proposal argue that such anonymity will limit the damage of malicious allegations on the innocent.

References and suggested further reading

Cobley, C. (2000) *Sex Offenders – Law, Policy and Practice*. Jordans Publishing Ltd, Bristol.

Cohen, S. (2002) *Folk Devils and Moral Panics* (3rd edn). Routledge, London.

Feist, A., Ashe, J., Lawrence, J., McPhee, D., Wilson, R. (2007) *Investigating and Detecting Recorded Offences of Rape*, HMSO, London.

Hebenton, B. and Seddon, T. (2009) 'From dangerousness to precaution', *British Journal of Criminology*, 49: 343–362.

Home Office Circular (HOC 20/2001) *Criminal Justice and Courts Services Act 2000: 'Amendments to the Sex Offenders Act 1997'*. Home Office, London.

Home Office (2003) *MAPPA Guidance – 'Multi-agency Public Protection Arrangements'*. National Probation Directorate, London.

—— (2009) *Rape: The Victim Experience Review*, Available: http://webarchive. nationalarchives.gov.uk/+/http://www.homeoffice.gov.uk/documents/vawg-rape-review/rape-victim-experience2835.pdf?view=Binary, (accessed on 7 March 2011).

Hudson, K. (2005) *Sex Offenders' Perspectives on their Treatment and Management*. Willan Publishing, Cullompton, Devon.

Janus, E. (2000) 'Civil commitment as social control', in Brown, M. and Pratt, J. (eds) *Dangerous Offenders – Punishment and Social Order*. Routledge, London.

Kelly, L., Lovett, J. and Regan, L. (2005) *A Gap of a Chasm?* Attrition in Reported Rape Cases. HMSO, London

Letherby, G., Williams, K., Birch, P. and Cain, M. (eds) (2008) *Sex as Crime?* Willan Publishing, Cullompton, Devon.

Prins, H. (1995) *Offenders, Deviants or Patients?* (2nd edn). Routledge, London.

Smart, C. (2000) 'Reconsidering the recent history of child sexual abuse, 1910–60', *Journal of Social Policy*, 29(1): 55–71.

Thomas, T. (2005) *Sex Crime, Sex Offending and Society*. Willan Publishing, Cullompton, Devon.

—— (2008) 'The Sex Offender "Register": a case study in function creep', *The Howard Journal*, 47(3). Blackwell Publishing,

UK report (2007) *Cross Government Action Plan on Sexual Violence and Abuse*. Available online at http://webarchive.nationalarchives.gov.uk/+/http://www. homeoffice.gov.uk/documents/sexual-violence-action-plan2835.pdf?view=Binary (accessed on 7 March 2011).

Weitzer, R. (2009) 'Legalizing prostitution', *British Journal of Criminology*, 49: 88–105.

West Merica (2005) *Force Policy: Managing Sexual Offenders, Violent Offenders and Other Potentially Dangerous Persons. Available*: http://www.westmercia.police.uk/ assets/files/documents/sep09/wmp1252412491 Managing Sex Offenders & Viole.pdf (accessed 7 March 2011).

Useful websites

http://news.bbc.co.uk/1/hi/uk/4453820.stm
BBC Report of the Amnesty International Survey on attitudes to rape victims (2005).

http://www.nspcc.org.uk/Inform/Research/Findings/childmaltreatmentintheunitedkingdom_ wda48252.html
Child maltreatment in the United Kingdom: a study of the prevalence of child childhood sexual abuse and neglect. London NSPC (2000).

http://www.nice.org.uk/CG89
'When to suspect child maltreatment' and related documents. Detailed clinical guidelines by the National Collaborating Centre for Women's and Children's Health.

http://www.cps.gov.uk/legal/h_to_k/intentional_or_reckless_sexual_transmission_of_ infection_guidance/
CPS Legal Guidance on Intentional Or Reckless Sexual Transmission Of Infection.

http://www.homeoffice.gov.uk/rds/pdfs07/rdsolr1807.pdf
Feist, A., Ashe, J., Lawrence, J., McPhee, D. and Wilson, R. 'Investigating and detecting recorded offences of rape' (2007).

http://www.guardian.co.uk/technology/2007/apr/19/hitechcrime.money/print
Guardian Report on Operation Ore (2007).

http://www.homeoffice.gov.uk/rds/pdfs05/hors293.pdf
Kelly, L., Lovett, J. and Regan, L. 'A gap or a chasm? Attrition in reported rape cases', Home Office Research Study 293 (2005).

http://www.justice.gov.uk/inspectorates/hmi-probation/docs/inspectionfindings-rps.pdf;
Managing Sex Offenders in the Community (2005) – Summary of a joint section by HMIC and HMiP.

http://www.homeoffice.gov.uk/documents/sex-offence-protect-learning-dis?view=Binary
Protecting you from sex abuse': a booklet about sexual abuse and the law for people with a learning disability.

http://www.durham-lscb.gov.uk/Procedures/procedures.shtml
Referral and Investigation Policy Section of Durham Local Safeguarding Children Board (2009).

http://www.cnwl.nhs.uk/uploads/Sexual_Assault.pdf

The Central and North West London NHS Foundation Trust's (2008) policy on Sexual Assault.

http://www.ceop.gov.uk/about/

The Child Exploitation and Online Protection Centre.

http://www.npia.police.uk/en/10510.htm

The Dangerous Persons Database (ViSOR) on the NPIA site.

http://www.isa-gov.org.uk/

The Independent Safeguarding Authority.

http://www.nhsemployers.org/SiteCollectionDocuments/CHRE_Clear_Sexual_Boundaries_doc_fb210509.pdf

The Council for Healthcare Regulatory Excellence (CHRE) guidance on sexual boundaries between healthcare professionals and patients.

http://www.thewnc.org.uk/publications/doc_download/421-rape-the-victim-experience-review.html

Rape: The Victim Experience Review, S. Payne, Home Office 2009.

http://www.westmercia.police.uk/assets/_files/documents/mar_10/wmp – 1268741168_Investigation_of_Serious_Sexua.pdf

West Mercia Force Procedure: The Investigation of Serious Sexual Offences (2005). Reviewed 2010.

http://www.equalities.gov.uk/stern_review.aspx

The Stern Review (March 2010) published by the Governmental Equalities Office.

15 Organised and transnational crime

> [W]herever there is money to be made, the tentacles of criminality will spread if not resisted.
>
> HMIC Thematic Audit, 'Getting Organised' (2009)

Introduction

This chapter is concerned with the nature of organised crime and how governments and police services have sought to respond to its threats. Depending upon the precise definition of organised crime the subject is potentially vast, covering illegal human trafficking across countries, cybercrime against commerce, youth gang crime and gang violence within cities, international and national terrorism, and the activities of the 'Mafia', and so this account must necessarily be selective. Police officers do not usually join specialised units to combat organised crime until they have gained sufficient experience, but the stance taken here is that acquiring a knowledge, through selected examples, of the ways in which the police service organises itself against the threats of organised crime is an important and valuable precursor to future specialist squad attachments.

For our purposes, we will define *transnational crime* as crime being perpetuated by a criminal organisation that displays substantial organisational structure in several countries. Organised crime may be translational. The illicit drug industry, for example, is truly transnational, with huge production markets in South America and Afghanistan, and sophisticated and lucrative supply chains through major European countries to domestic markets. UK-based drug busts will not, by themselves, influence networks on this scale and the long-term solutions are both political and economic, and involve many countries.

What is organised crime?

Organised crime is not defined by statute (as, say, theft is). Organised crime is associated with high-profile groups, such as the infamous Krays of the 1960s, the

Mafia, youth knife gangs in towns and cities as well as with white-collar fraud consortia (Box 15.1).

Box 15.1   Exercise 15A Definition of organized crime

Write down three characteristics that would feature in your own definition of 'organised crime'.

Many attempts have been made to define organised crime and organised criminal groups. Historically, different definitions have evolved as different types of criminal organisations (the permanent structures that *deliver* organised crime) became amenable to study. The definition of organised crime used by the European Union (see Lewis 2007) is not particularly helpful or informative. The United Nations Convention Against Transnational Organized Crime (2000) states that:

> Organized criminal groups shall mean a structured group of three or more persons, existing for a period of time and acting in concert with the aim of committing one or more serious crimes or offences established in accordance with this Convention, in order to obtain, directly or indirectly, a financial or material benefit organised crime.

While some criminal organisations are hierarchical, as in the so-called *Cosa Nostra* model (Wright 2006), some do not even show the characteristics of a formal organisation, much less the characteristics of an industrial organisation. Not all criminal organisations limit membership to family. Some do not display a high degree of rational thought in goal setting. Not all organised crime is associated with a gang structure: white-collar fraud crime being an example. Much (but not all) organised crime is related to the trafficking or sale of drugs: criminal organisations are often very adaptable and adjust their criminal portfolio according to external demand and the degree of scrutiny by government or the police. While all organised crime is focused on financial gain (as is much crime generally), some organised crime activities are also concerned with acquiring power over individuals, groups, governments or other organisations. Fraud, theft and robbery are just as much a part of organised crime as the provision of illegal drugs (von Lampe 2008).

Although the preoccupation with definitions may appear to be less important to the practising law-enforcement officer, definitions are important when it comes to the demarcation of roles and in identifying the aims of organisations whose resources are very limited and in practice, the use of the term *organised crime* is usually qualified by scale and by the seriousness of the crime. For example, SOCA gives one of its aims as being concerned with 'Level 3' serious organised crime, leaving more localised organised crime to local police forces.

The social impact of organised crime is considerable. For the government and for society at large, this includes economic instability and the loss of business confidence, fear and anxiety, gang warfare, loss of educational and recreational opportunities, drug dependency, loss of tax revenue and even loss of life.

What is the scale of organised crime in England and Wales? The Association of Chief Police Officers organised crime national coordinator's office produces maps showing organised crime groups (OCGs). The HMIC's Thematic Audit 'Getting organised' (HMIC 2009) summarised recent data on identified OCGs as follows:

1   About 2,800 OCGs operate in England and Wales, covering all force areas.
2   Two-thirds of all OCGs are involved in multiple criminal enterprises. This increases the impact of OCGs upon the community while increasing the opportunities for law enforcement to detect and act against the OCGs.
3   60 per cent of OCGs are involved in drug trafficking.
4   10 per cent of OCGs have an international dimension.

Attempt the exercise in Box 15.2 before reading further.

Box 15.2   Exercise 15B Policing of organized crime

Give three reasons why the policing of organised crime may be particularly challenging.

Here are five reasons:

- Some criminal organisations are relatively secure in that information is retained by individuals with a common interest in preventing the police from discovering how and when a crime is committed. The activities of such organisations are often nearly 'invisible'. Such organisations are adept at intimidating witnesses or obtaining advance knowledge of police action through corrupt officials.
- Much organised crime operates over regional, national or international boundaries, and the greater the geographical spread, the greater the challenge to law enforcement, since it is easier for criminal organisations to use increasingly accessible communication and transport systems than it is for individual countries to control or limit the use of such facilities. The effect of globalisation upon international organised crime has been particularly dramatic in the drug supply chains that fuel much domestic crime.
- Organised crime may be transnational, and the capacity and alignment of judicial and legislative processes varies from country to country. There is no international court (operating under a universally accepted legal system) that can try perpetrators of organised crime. This means that while

international borders do not give organised crime complete protection, substantial resources are required to communicate and work with criminal justice agencies internationally to achieve convictions or to disrupt criminal operations. The expenditure of such resources can only be justified for serious crime.

- Organised crime is often well planned because it represents a profitable criminal business: it is motivated by profit and power. For example, by the time cocaine has reached the streets of the UK from Columbia, its value may have increased by 200 per cent. If one organised crime structure is disbanded or destroyed, the financial advantages of participation in the business are strong incentives for others to fill the vacuum: fighting certain types of organised crime is a continuous struggle in which the battle (but rarely the war) can be won.

- Organised criminality is often complex because different activities support each other. For example, the trafficking of women, terrorism, illegal immigration and the illegal drug industry are often linked to the importation and trade of illegal firearms and also to money laundering.

The 'Ethnic Succession Thesis'

In the 1970s, Ianni studied the rise (and systematic control) of criminal activity in some American cities by black and Puerto Rican criminals. Ianni proposed that organised crime is not necessarily bound to ethnicity but that crime is one of the few ways in which distinctive ethnic groups can escape from their underclass status in society. These ideas are often referred to as the 'Ethnic Succession Thesis'. They are discussed further in Wright (2006) (Box 15.3).

Box 15.3 Exercise 15C The Ethnic Succession Thesis

How relevant do you think the Ethnic Succession Thesis is to organised crime in Britain today?

The Ethnic Succession Thesis forms a useful starting point when discussing organised crime and ethnic minorities in contemporary Britain, from the Caribbean 'Yardies' of the 1980s to the involvement of Albanian and Romanian gangs in sex trafficking in the 2000s. The cigarette black market in Germany is controlled by ethnic minority criminals (see case study in Box 15.4), but much organised crime in the UK is controlled by white UK nationals. The key point, though, is that it is commonplace for members of *any* ethnic group who are criminals (perhaps in their home country) to continue to act as criminals in the UK; and that some members of *any* ethnic group who are economically disadvantaged will become criminals. Environmental and economical factors rather than ethnicity are likely to be important in catalysing crime (including organised crime). If ethnic minorities have high profiles in organised crime, this may be because they are from the economic underclass that is always more likely to generate more crime.

There are two connected issues that are worth unpicking. First, that a corollary of the importance of the economy and social exclusion in giving rise to organised crime groups is that tackling the conditions which generate organised crime (and indeed, any crime) is as much the responsibility of government officials, local authorities and economists as it is of the police or SOCA. Second, the lack of a simple causation between ethnicity and crime should not prevent the investigator from probing and gaining intelligence from any parts of the community which generate crime. This may, of course, often raise tensions between the police and the communities they serve.

Box 15.4   Case study The cigarette black market in Germany and the United Kingdom

Von Lampe (2006) reviewed the cigarette black market, dividing the market into procurement (getting the cigarettes without paying tax) and distribution (distributing the cigarettes 'under the counter'). Procurement occurs by bootlegging (buying cigarettes in low tax countries for sale in the UK or Germany), the smuggling of cigarettes destined for non-EU countries with taxes suspended (so that the cigarettes are illegally diverted back to the UK or Germany) and counterfeiting (producing fake brand cigarettes). In 2004, about 2 per cent of all packets of cigarettes were estimated to be counterfeit.

In Germany, small-scale smuggling is evident along the German Poland and German Czech borders where strict tax allowances for cigarettes apply to all travellers. In the UK, cross-channel smuggling is believed to be particularly significant but the legal regime is different: travellers can bring any amount of cigarettes into the UK as long as these cigarettes are for the traveller's own use. The importation of excessive amounts of cigarettes for sale within the UK is often referred to as the 'white van trade'. Although the illegal cigarette market in the UK does not appear to be associated with one ethnic group, the participation of polish and Vietnamese groups is often emphasised in reports on the black market in Germany. The black market for cigarettes appears to show a strong regional variation, being particularly active in Northern England.

Exercise 15D Scale of the cigarette black market

Speculate as to how HM Customs and Excise estimate the scale of the cigarette black market.

For obvious reasons the estimates are obtained indirectly! HM Customs and Excise rely on consumer survey data, statistics on legal cigarette sales and small-scale evidence from detected smuggling which is then extrapolated to the wider population. In the UK, illegal cigarettes are thought to have contributed about 15 per cent of the total market in 2003 to 2004, with large-scale (organised) smuggling being responsible for most of the illegal sales.

Tackling organised crime

Attempt the exercise in Box 15.5 before continuing.

Box 15.5   Exercise 15E Organised crime: approaches

List four general approaches used by the police in tackling organised crime.

These might include the following:

- Formulating specific National Strategies. An example is the National Fraud Strategy, 'A new approach to combating fraud' (Attorney General's Office 2009). Fraud is estimated to cost the UK £14 billion per year (more than double the value of the illicit drug market) and is expected to become even more significant during an economic recession. The proposals include the creation of a lead police force for fraud (the City of London force) and include plans for a national reporting mechanism. Organised crime is part of wider strategies which emphasise inter-agency cooperation, including the National Policing Plan 2005 to 2008 and the National Community Safety Plan 2008 to 2011.
- Improving the collection and flow of intelligence by and between the police, the regions and SOCA.
- Forming Specialist Squads, such as those concerned with the investigation of armed robberies, endangered animals or antiquaries. Specialist Squads are often given high levels of personnel and technological resources, and have expertise in surveillance. Specialist squads are often attached to named operations, such as Operation Trident (with the remit of investigating gun crime in London's black community).
- Empowering civilian investigators. The Serious Fraud Office (SFO) is often the prosecuting authority for serious or complex fraud: under s.2 of the Criminal Justice Act 1987, the director of the SFO may authorise non-police investigative staff (including accountants) to demand the immediate production of documents and the attendance of individuals at interview. Such powers are known as 'compulsory questioning' and there is no right of silence, although admissions by the accused are not deemed to be admissible

by the courts. A comprehensive list of UK and public sector groups involved in fraud advice, regulation or prosecution is given by (Levi 2008a) in the second edition of the *Handbook of Policing* (2008).

- Cooperation between police forces and enabling existing agencies to assist the police. For example, the four Welsh police forces have formed a joint group ('Tarian Plus' – Tarian is Welsh for shield) investigating crime relating to Class A drugs within Wales. The Intelligence Services Act 1996 formally extended the role of MI5, MI6 and GCHQ to provide assistance to the police and other agencies in investigating serious and organised crime.

- Legislation. This includes laws relating to money laundering, improved extradition laws and committing states to improved levels of international cooperation. Police cooperation in Europe is described by Brady (2008).

- 'Follow the money' (Levi 2010). This is easier said than done, but the movement of large sums of illegal money is generally indicative of organised crime. SOCA defines money laundering as 'any action taken to conceal, arrange, use or possess the proceeds of any criminal conduct'. Money laundering is now a highly professional business, involving bankers, accountants and lawyers. The Money Laundering Regulations (2007) require some businesses to institute controls against laundering and to report suspicious activity.

- Work with other professionals and organisations outside the criminal justice and intelligence fraternity. For example, closer cooperation between customs and the tobacco industry is alleged to have reduced the volume of illegal cigarette sales in the UK (von Lampe 2006).

- Levi (2008b) discusses non-traditional approaches to organised crime prevention, including:

  - Community approaches, such as encouraging the community to provide information to the police and supplying 'hotlines'.
  - Disruption and non-justice approaches, including suspicious financial activity reporting by banks.
  - Other private sector involvement, such as the use of anti-fraud and money laundering software.

Box 15.6 Case study Targeting the markets for stolen goods

The idea of disrupting parts of the chain involved in the disposal of the products of organised crime rather than target the criminals themselves is another example of 'intelligence-led policing'. The basic premise of this approach is that a reduction in the market for stolen goods influences decisions to steal in the first place.

In 2004, a Home Office Development and Practice Report examined two initiatives in detail and concluded that:

- Interventions must be devised to suite local circumstances – one type or size of intervention will not suit all.
- Those involved in projects must attempt to balance resource expenditure against benefits, including how and whether a marketing campaign can contribute to the objectives of the project.
- Second-hand shops can provide useful information on stolen property.
- Undercover filtration can be effective, but it is expensive and carries with it certain risks.
- For many reasons, it has proved impossible to demonstrate that these projects reduced crime.

(http://rds.homeoffice.gov.uk/rds/pdfs04/dpr17.pdf)

Are police services structured appropriately to respond to organised crime?

One question that has been raised in various arenas is whether or not the current policing organisations in England and Wales can cope with the demands of organised crime which is not dealt with by SOCA. The O'Connor report entitled *Closing the Gap* (HMIC 2005), noted the 'growing appreciation of the threat posed by local and regional organised crime groups'. The preferred response of government and HMIC to this gap was the creation of larger police forces which could mobilise greater resources against organised crime and terrorism, with individual ministers adamant that the failure to act could be very serious, but the political will to rapidly implement such a strategy evaporated as a scandal involving 1,000 foreign prisoners who had avoided deportation engulfed the Home Office (Savage 2007). Whatever the advantages of force mergers may be, they will have to wait.

While the *Closing the Gap* report was written before the creation of SOCA, it is likely that many concerns remain. For example, the report records that fewer than 6 per cent of over 1,500 organised crime groups active at regional or force level were targeted by police on an annual basis in 2003, and it is unlikely that this figure has risen substantially in recent years. This raises a second question: how are resources to be prioritised or, put another way, which organised crime groups and which geographic areas should receive the 'light touch'? Of course, the demands upon police services fluctuate, so available resources do vary from year to year. Nevertheless, as the economic recession bites (and perhaps as the numbers of police personnel fall), there are likely to be heightened challenges if low-level crime, organised crime and neighbourhood disorder all rise. This will force chief constables to continually review 'who gets what' and for how long. This is a daunting and complicated task.

Gilmour (2008) brings his practical experience to look at organised crime from 'the bottom up'. He reiterates the view that organised crime is mainly a local phenomenon and that it should be tackled more by prosecuting members of organised crimes for minor offences rather than using expensive techniques such as surveillance. For example, the operatives and leaders of serious organised crime do not suddenly appear, and they will often pass through early stages of apprenticeship with similar organisations, perhaps starting with street gangs. In this sense, street youth gangs are the nurseries of serious organised crime. To the extent that succession to leadership can be prevented, the future prospects of criminal organisations may be damaged but 'denting', such succession represents an enormous challenge not only for the police service but for government and wider society.

Gilmour also anticipates greater pressures on police resources. He advocates consideration of the three factors harm, threat and risk before police intervention and operations should be considered. The extent to which such factors can be objectively measured is uncertain, but the success of such an approach will be gauged by the better use of resources and when the benefits of police action regarding organised crime become clearer to the communities they serve.

The effectiveness of SOCA, the major UK-wide anti-crime organisation dedicated to investigating the most serious NIM Level 3 crimes, and the way in which it interacts with and supports local police forces, cannot be properly assessed after only a few years of existence. One intriguing question is whether or not there is a difference in emphasis between SOCA (unashamedly driven by Home Office objectives) and local police forces which also have to respond to local need. The HMIC Thematic Audit 'Getting organised' (HMIC 2009) placed great importance on 'national governance', stating:

> National governance is not clear – a number of groups and bodies are competing to set directions and priorities for the service, reporting to different Home Office directorates...Clarity is needed urgently in order to define the threat, agree on priorities and assess progress. Interestingly, the counter-terrorism model provides such clarity and, with an appropriate degree of tailoring, useful lessons can be imported from this work.

The report also emphasises the importance of better performance management of serious and organised crime, raises the question of whether or not resources should be targeted to forces with greater levels of organised crime (e.g. London, North West England and the West Midlands), and suggests that there is an urgent need to produce 'professional doctrine' on policing organised crime, along the lines of guidance that is already available for homicide.

In July 2010, the Home Secretary of the coalition government announced plans to replace SOCA with a new National Crime Agency and we await further announcements.

Box 15.7   Case study Does law enforcement reduce the availability of illegal drugs?

The UK illicit drugs market is currently valued at over £5.3 billion. A 2008 UK Drug Policy Commission's report produced by King's College London found that drug markets are highly resilient and that enforcement has had very little success in reducing the availability of drugs in the UK. Furthermore, some police interventions have had unintended outcomes outside of the immediate police operations (e.g. by increasing the incidence of violence through displacing dealers to areas which already have dealers in place).

The authors review the literature that is available on the supply of drugs and law-enforcement measures and conclude that there has been no 'comprehensive published UK evidence of the *relative* effectiveness of different law enforcement approaches'. Perhaps unsurprisingly owing to the lack of understanding of the drug markets and trafficking networks, no 'value-for-money' analyses appear to have been attempted. Since the sums spent on the law enforcement of organised crime around illegal drugs is vast, the absence of such research may mean that large sums of money are being misdirected.

(McSweeney, T., Turnbull, P.J. and Hough, M. 'Tackling drug markets and distribution networks in the UK: a review of the recent literature' [UK Drug Policy Commission], http://www. ukdpc.org.uk/resources/Drug_Markets_Full_Report.pdf)

Terrorism as organised crime

It is self-evident that most terrorism also qualifies as organised crime: terrorism requires organisation, involves considerable planning and terrorist activities often constitute serious criminal offences. Much terrorism is also transnational. The following points set the scene:

1   The threat of terrorism has forced governments to provide vast resources which dwarf those available to other law-enforcement agencies, even those charged with tackling drug crime.
2   No part of policing is so contentious as 'policing terror' when it comes to real or perceived erosions of civil liberties, particularly when investigations are facilitated through technology and databases which are increasingly intrusive and powerful.
3   Innes and Thiel (2008) have emphasised a cruel irony: that both the agencies charged with counter-terrorism and the terrorists themselves have a common need: to work and plan in secret for much of the time. This causes a dilemma

for government and the police and security services: how much information do we give to the public?

4   Terrorism and conventional organised crime are often strongly connected, particularly through money laundering, and this links the responses of counter-terrorist and police crime units (Ridley 2008). Counter-terrorism agencies and organised crime investigators often work together, and to work effectively they must share information. The international 'Money Trail' is particularly complex and challenging to investigate (Levitt and Jacobson 2008).

5   The counter-terrorism response of government involves many agencies and is multi-layered, although it is increasingly centralised and coordinated nationally. Figure 15.1 shows the hierarchy of terrorist-related responses: from military intervention to community action. Further details of the organisation of counter-terrorism in the UK are given by Wilkinson (2007) and Staniforth (2009).

6   Internationally sponsored terrorism that occurs in the UK cannot always be decoupled from political or military events or facilities in other parts of the world, making the task of UK agencies in reducing the threat from terrorism much harder. For example, Israeli attacks on Gaza during 2009 gave UK extremists 'ideological ammunition', and some terrorists have attended training camps in Pakistan and Afghanistan.

7   Traditional post-event police investigations into crime are often more substantive and complex than pre-arrest operations but the complexity and resource demands of post-terrorism investigations have often been eclipsed by investigative operations centred on acquiring intelligence and disrupting terrorist cells *before* any terrorist attacks occur. The prevention of terrorist acts is often given higher priority than acquiring enough information to secure a successful prosecution, with pre-emptive arrests being used to disrupt suspected terrorist attacks. Such a priority, and the complexity of such investigations, may explain why – of the 1,471 people arrested between 2001 and 2008 under s.41 of the Terrorism Act 2000 – only 340 were charged with terrorism-related offences.

8   The government response to terrorism is linked with more general arrangements to improve the resilience of the UK's infrastructure to major threats (including floods and pandemic flu). The overall National Security Strategy, subtitled 'Security in an interdependent world' (Cabinet Office 2008) summarises the world drivers of insecurity. The Civil Contingencies Act 2004 provides powers that may be used in a wide range of serious and large-scale incidents or disasters. Police forces are Category 1 Responders under the Act. Sampson and McNeill (2007), following the work of the O'Connor HMIC Report *Minding the Gap*, discuss whether or not local police forces are coordinated or organised sufficiently to protect critical national infrastructure. The key point here is that the risk of terrorism has many ramifications for all emergency services and government.

Agency		Action	Activity category
Military		War; overseas interventions; domestic interventions in civil emergencies such as freeing hostages	**'Beyond policing'** **(violent control)**
Security services: MI5, MI6, GCHQ		Intelligence collection and application; disruption	
The Special Branch and Counter-terrorism specialists		Intelligence collection and application; disruption; arrest and prosecution	
Criminal Investigation Dept (CID)		Investigation, arrest and prosecution	**'High policing'**
Uniformed policing	Response	Intelligence collection; reassurance; and arrests	**'Low policing'**
	Neighbour-hood	Community intelligence collection and reassurance; managing community tensions	
Multi-agency activity		Integration, empowerment and deradicalisation	
Civilian communities		Responsibilised empowerment; informal control, diversion and intelligence	**'Beyond policing'** **(disciplinary governance)**

Figure 15.1 The continuum of UK state counter-terrorism apparatus.

The United Kingdom's Strategy for Countering International Terrorism

The latest version of this strategy, often referred to as CONTEST 2, was published in March 2009. It reiterates the four work streams of the earlier 2006 CONTEST strategy: *Pursue* (to stop terrorist attacks), *Prevent* (to stop people supporting terrorists), *Protect* (to strengthen protective measures) and *Prepare* (to mitigate the effect of any attack). The description of the terrorism as international should be qualified: the domestic nature of the threat is very substantial.

The location, origin and nature of terrorist threats to the UK mainland has changed over the decades. In the 1970s and 1990s the greatest terrorist threat was from violent Irish Republican movements, and even in 2010 the threat of terrorist acts from small numbers of dissident republicans in Northern Ireland remains high. Nevertheless, the 2006 CONTEST strategy was unequivocal in identifying the greatest contemporary terrorist threat to the UK: 'The principal current terrorist threat is from radicalised individuals who are using a distorted and unrepresentative version of the Islamic faith to justify violence. Such people are referred to in this paper as Islamist terrorists.' 'Islamic Terrorism' is identified as a class of terrorism in the Interpol EU Terrorism and Situation Trend Report (2008), although other types of terrorism (including that based on separatism) are significant in Europe. The 2009 CONTEST 2 strategy does not use the phrase 'Islamic terrorist', preferring to use the term 'Al Qaida'. Al Qaida is not so much a simple hierarchical organisation as an international network of broad alliances, but it has been linked to many of the recent terrorist atrocities conducted on the UK mainland (see case study, 'Operation Crevice' in Box 15.8).

Box 15.8   Exercise 15F Working with the Muslim community

Name two difficulties in working with the Muslim community as part of 'PREVENT'.

CONTEST 2, including the specific PREVENT strand to specifically prevent violent extremism (Cabinet Office 2008), reflects a major governmental determination to attempt to prevent the radicalisation of young people in Muslim communities within the UK. This is now seen as the duty of many agencies, including the police, although radicalisation and the concentration of extremists in prisons also represents a considerable challenge. The role of the police service in preventing 'home-grown extremists' has been the subject of an HMIC inspection (HMIC 2009). One of the conclusions is that the police service should ensure that there are minimum levels of capability in all forces to deliver PREVENT.

However, the difficulties of forming links with the community, including the so-called 'Muslim community', should not be underestimated. While the integration of local neighbourhood policing with counter-terrorism strategies is desirable and there have been many successful local initiatives to date, there are also many obstacles. It should also be remembered that the police service cannot and does not itself engage with anyone: it is individual police officers who do this and so personal skills and relationships become critically important in the success or failure of attempts to reassure communities. Attempt the exercise in Box 15.8 before continuing.

Your answers might include:

- To whom do we speak and to whom do we not speak?
- It might be argued that there is no such thing as a 'Muslim community'. There are many sub-communities which are Muslim, reflecting different religious affiliations, interests and traditions. This means that the police service should have many ties with such communities – an expensive but arguably necessary level of provision.
- Who can represent young people within Muslim communities?

- How can we prevent the rising insecurity in communities, including that which leads to public unrest and crowd violence, as a result of police responses to terrorist outrages?

In seeking to work with communities, the police service is attempting to build trust in the police. Innes (2006) notes that 'Given the long history of difficult relations between many minority communities and the police', it is probable that only a comparatively thin form of trust can be cultivated by police. However, even an incomplete or highly qualified form of trust is valuable when terrorist threats are substantial and where the consequences of further erosions of trust are so severe. Attempt the exercise in Box 15.9 before continuing.

Box 15.9 Exercise 15G Comparison of Al Qaida and IRA

If you are unfamiliar with the history and terrorist activities of the IRA, visit the Council on Foreign Relations website (http://www.cfr.org/publication/9240/#2). An interview with Paul Arthur (University of Ulster) is also very informative (http://www.pbs.org/wgbh/pages/frontline/shows/ira/conflict/).

List four ways in which the current Al Qaida terrorist threats differ from those of the IRA in the 1970s to the 1990s.

Here are a some differences:

- Al Qaida is much more international in its origins, financing and ideological support.
- Many Al Qaida-inspired groups claim a religious justification for their actions. Although the IRA asserted that they represented Catholics in Northern Ireland, the IRA was not itself ideologically religious.
- Al Qaida is not linked to one political party internationally (as the IRA is with Sinn Fein), and within the UK it has virtually no formal political representation.
- Al Qaida has direct or indirect support from terrorist organisations in several countries but it is not widely supported within the UK, even though the UK is and has been a target for terrorist action. On the other hand, and at its peak, the IRA had significant support from parts of the population within Northern Ireland.
- Al Qaida's terrorist threat is not limited principally to one region of the UK or to major UK cities: it is international. The internet aids its communications and enhances its ability to disperse propaganda throughout the world.
- Many IRA terrorist outrages showed some degree of selectivity of target so as not to alienate its support. In contrast, recent Al Qaida-related terrorist outrages throughout the world have been largely indiscriminate.
- Al Qaida uses suicide bombers, whereas the IRA does not.

Box 15.10   Case study Operation Crevice

Operation Crevice was a coordinated police operation which resulted in raids on properties in the Crawley area of England. A total of 1,300 pounds of ammonium nitrate was also seized in West London. Five terrorists, all British citizens, were convicted in 2007 and given life sentences. The leader of the group was Omar Khayyam, then aged 24, who had visited Pakistan where it is believed he met senior members of Al Qaida.

Operation Crevice provides a glimpse of the scale, sophistication and long duration of many joint police–intelligence anti-terrorist service operations. The operation involved extensive cooperation and sharing of intelligence internationally. The operation consisted of covert and overt activities: the covert activities involved surveillance of terrorist suspects while the overt actions includes the more traditional evidence collection and investigation once arrests have been made. The timing of arrests was problematic: a balance had to be struck between the arrest of suspects so that they did not harm the public, and collecting enough information to successfully prosecute them in a court of law. This is a dilemma in many terrorist operations, although the protection of the public generally takes precedence over the likelihood of a successful prosecution.

The BBC website (http://news.bbc.co.uk/1/hi/in_depth/uk/2007/ fertiliser_bomb_plot/default.stm) contains covert film footage of some of the convicted terrorists.

The effects of counter-terrorist action, including stop and search and the arrests of suspects, may serve to heighten anxieties in the very communities that the police seek to defend. A valuable snapshot of some of the opinions of sections of London's communities, particularly of the Muslim community, is contained in the Metropolitan Police Authority's report *Counter Terrorism: The London Debate* (2007). The report illustrates the tension between police actions and priorities in response to necessarily scare intelligence, and the resentment and bewilderment at perceived stereotyping, and with police operations that often appear to be poorly communicated and heavy-handed. Many of the recommendations of the report are sensible and practical, but such reports rarely attempt to realistically balance the opposing pressures on the police. Terrorism is a cruel crime for many reasons, but the threat of terrorist acts has forced society, the police and the intelligence services to recalibrate the traditional 'proportionality' of response. No satisfactory basis for risk assessment in terrorist operations exists: the consequences of 'getting it wrong' are such that if a balance is to be struck, it will often be made in favour of ensuring that the police act precautionarily, swiftly, covertly and in overwhelming numbers in order to protect the public.

Assessing the effectiveness of counter-terrorism

Attempts to assess the success of counter-terrorism actions are complicated, not least by the paucity of information made publicly available, by the number of agencies involved, by the interrelationships between terrorism and political and military action overseas, and the degree to which agencies from other states work together.

Box 15.11 Exercise 15H Cost–benefit assessment of counter-terrorist spending

State two 'key performance indicators' that might be used to determine whether or not counter-terrorist measures are successful.

Some qualitative indication of the relative impact of events (including certain types of terrorist acts) may be obtained by examining the UK Cabinet Office's National Risk Register. This rates pandemic flu as of higher impact than terrorist attacks in crowded places or attacks on transport, yet the UK government estimates that expenditure on counter-terrorism and intelligence will rise to £3.5 billion per year by 2010 to 2011 (Cabinet Office 2008). This is likely to be very much more than is being spent by the government in preparing for a pandemic flu epidemic. Such a disparity in expenditure reflects what can be done to counter these very different types of risk, but it may also reflect political necessity and priorities. Further prioritisation is also inevitable: the current economic downturn will force the government and police service to work within reduced budgets in counteracting terrorist threats. This is a new challenge that will force great prioritisation of action.

One simple indicator of success would be the number of terrorist plots foiled by expenditure over and above (say) the expenditure on counter-terrorism by countries prior to the New York atrocities of September 2001 or since the London bombings of July 2005. We are reliant upon the security service, government or police for such information: it is also difficult to unambiguously assign a success to a particular investment in personnel or infrastructure. A Public Service Agreement (no. 26 published in 2007) exists which purports to allow measurement of the success in achieving the four streams of the CONTEST strategy but few details are available to the general public.

Stewart and Mueller (2009) prepared a Cost–Benefit Assessment of United States Homeland Security Spending. One of the metrics used was cost per life saved from conventional terrorist threats (i.e. excluding weapons of mass destruction). Since 2001 expenditure had rocketed to 2008 levels of $31 billion. The standard regulatory 'acceptable cost per life' baseline for most commercial and public purposes is quoted as $7.5 million per life saved. In other words, about 4,100 extra lives would have to be saved in order to justify the additional expenditure using the \$7.5 million baseline. It is very likely that the number of lives saved is well below 4,100: Stewart and Mueller suggest that the additional Homeland Security expenditure has saved 50 to 500 lives per year. Money cannot be spent twice and so it is sometimes the case that more lives could be saved by spending money on something else. Put another way, expenditure on Homeland Security appears very expensive for the benefits accrued. However, terrorism cannot be simply grouped in with car accidents or occupational toxicity levels for industrial chemicals. The fear caused by terrorist acts makes counter-terrorism a high political priority. Perl (2007) describes terrorist activities as occurring in 'quantum-like jumps' so that, for example, a single suicide bombing can cause an escalation of a governmental response and the justification of expenditure on a previously unprecedented scale.

References and suggested further reading

Attorney General's Office (2009) *The National Fraud Strategy – a New Approach to Combating Fraud*, Attorney General's Office, London.
Brady, H. (2008) 'Europol and the European Criminal Intelligence Model: a non-state response to organized crime', *Policing*, 2: 103–109.
Cabinet Office (2008) The National Security Strategy of the United Kingdom. Available online at http://interactive.cabinetoffice.gov.uk/documents/security/national_security_strategy.pdf. (accessed 7 March 2011)
Dean, G., Fahsing, I. and Gottschalk, X. (2010) *Organized Crime, Policing Illegal Business Entrepreneurialism*. Oxford University Press, Oxford.
Edwards, A. and Gill, P. (2003) *Transnational Organised Crime, Perspectives on Global Security*. Routledge, London.
Gilmour, S. (2008) 'Understanding organized crime: a local perspective', *Policing*, 2: 18–27.
Her Majesty's Inspectorate of Constabulary (2005) *Closing the Gap*, HMSO, London.
—— (2009) *Getting Organised*, HMSO, London.
Innes, M. (2006) 'Policing uncertainty: countering terror through community intelligence and democratic policing', *The Annals of the American Academy of Political and Social Science*, 605: 1–20. Also available online at http://www.upsi.org.uk/storage/publications/counter-terrorism/policinguncertainty.pdf (accessed 7 March 2011).
Innes, M. and Thiel, D. (2008) 'Policing terror', in Newburn, T. (ed.), *Handbook of Policing*. Willan Publishing, Cullompton, Devon.
Levy, M. (2008a) 'Policing fraud and organised crime', in Newburn, T. (ed.), *Handbook of Policing* pp. 522–553. Willan Publishing, Cullompton, Devon.
—— (2008b) *The Phantom Capitalists: The Organization and Control of Long-Firm Fraud*. Ashgate, Aldershot.
—— (2010) 'Combating the financing of terrorism', *British Journal of Criminology*, 50: 650–669.
Levitt, M. and Jacobson, M. (2008) 'The money trail, finding, following, and freezing terrorist finances', *Policy Focus 89*, the Washington Institute for Near East Policy. Also available online at http://www.washingtoninstitute.org/templateC04.php?CID=302. (accessed 7 March 2011).

Lewis, C. (2007) 'International structures and transnational crime', in Williamson, T. and Wright, A. (eds) *Handbook of Criminal Investigation*. Willan Publishing, Cullompton, Devon. (accessed 7 March 2011).

Metropolitan Police Authority (2007) 'Counter-terrorism: The London Debate. Available online at http://www.mpa.gov.uk/downloads/committees/mpa/070222-06-appendix01.pdf.

Perl, R. (2007) *Combating Terrorism: The Challenge of Measuring Effectiveness, Congressional Research Service Report* (RL33160) updated 2007. Also available online at http://www.fas.org/sgp/crs/terror/RL33160.pdf. (accessed 7 March 2011).

Ridley, N. (2008) 'Organized crime, money laundering, and terrorism', Policing, 2: 28–35.

Sampson, F. and McNeill, J. (2007) 'Redefining the gaps: connecting neighbourhood safety to national security', Policing, 1: 460–471.

Savage, S.P. (2007) *Police Reform, Forces for Change*. Oxford University Press, Oxford.

Staniforth, A. (2009) *Blackstone's Counter-terrorism Handbook*. Oxford University Press, Oxford.

Stewart, M.G. and Mueller, J. (2009) *Cost–Benefit Assessment of United States Homeland Security Spending*. Research Report 273.01.2009, University of Newcastle Australia, January. Also available online at http://hdl.handle.net/1959.13/33119.

von Lampe, K. (2006) 'The cigarette black market in Germany and in the United Kingdom', *Journal of Financial Crime*, 13(2): .235–54. Also available online at http://www.organized-crime.de/kvlCigBlackMarketGermanyUK-2006.pdf.

—— (2008) 'Organized crime in Europe: conceptions and realities', Policing, 2: 7–17.

Walker, N. (2008) 'The pattern of transnational policing', in Newburn, T. (ed.), *Handbook of Policing*. Willan Publishing, Cullompton, Devon.

Wilkinson, P. (ed.) (2007) *Homeland Security in the UK*. Routledge, London.

Wright, A. (2006) *Organised Crime*. Willan Publishing, Cullompton, Devon. The 'Ethnic Succession Thesis' is discussed in Chapter 6.

Zimmerman, D. and Wenger, A. (eds) (2006) *How States Fight Terrorism: Policy Dynamics in the West*. Lynne Rienner, London.

Useful websites

http://www.uncjin.org/Documents/Conventions/dcatoc/final_documents_2/convention_eng.pdf.

United Nations convention against transnational organised crime, including a definition of 'Organised Criminal Group' (2000).

http://www.hmic.gov.uk/SiteCollectionDocuments/Thematics/THM_20090331.pdf.

HMIC '*Getting organised': A Serious and Organised Crime Thematic Review* (2009).

http://www.opsi.gov.uk/acts/acts2005/ukpga_20050015_en_2#pt1-ch1-pb2-l1g2.

The Serious Organised Crime and Police Act 2005 which defines SOCA's role.

Various SOCA documents on organised crime and updated regularly:

http://www.soca.gov.uk/about-soca/library

http://www.unodc.org/pdf/crime/publications/Pilot_survey.pdf.

Results of a Survey of Forty Selected Organized Criminal Groups in Sixteen Countries. United Nations, Office of Drugs and Crime 2002.

http://www.organized-crime.de/.

A useful website containing many links about organised crime. It contains over 100 definitions of organised crime. Under the 'Concept and Theory of Organized Crime' tab there is a useful section on the use of models in the study of organised crime.

http://www.homeoffice.gov.uk/rds/pdfs08/horr10c.pdf.

A regional survey of business views of organised crime commissioned by the Home Office. The survey methodology used is clearly explained.

http://www.homeoffice.gov.uk/crime-victims/reducing-crime/organised-crime/.

Part of the UK Home Office site dealing with international and organised crime.

http://www.hmrc.gov.uk/mlr/.

The Money Laundering Regulations (2007) via the HM Revenue and Customs site.

http://money.howstuffworks.com/money-laundering.htm.

A clear explanation of how international money laundering works.

http://www.sfo.gov.uk/.

The Serious Fraud Office.

http://www.insurancefraudbureau.org/files/misc_pdfs/nfsa_strategy_aw_11.03@2.pdf.

The National Fraud Strategy (Attorney General's Office) 2009.

http://www.wlga.gov.uk/english/equalitypublications/hmic-closing-the-gap/.

'Closing the Gap' (2005) HMIC report on fitness for purpose of police services in England and Wales by D. O'Connor.

http://interactive.cabinetoffice.gov.uk/documents/security/national_security_strategy.pdf.

The National Security Strategy of the United Kingdom prepared by the Cabinet Office (2008).

http://www.cabinetoffice.gov.uk/ukresilience.aspx.

UK Resilience website, including reference to the Civil Contingencies Act 2004.

http://www.statewatch.org/news/2009/mar/uk-terr-strategy.pdf.

The United Kingdom's Strategy for Countering International Terrorism (2009) (big file).

http://www.official-documents.gov.uk/document/cm68/6888/6888.pdf.

Countering International Terrorism: The United Kingdom's Strategy (2006).

http://www.dcsf.gov.uk/violentextremism/downloads/Preventing%20Violent%20Extremi sm%20A%20Strategy%20for%20Delivery%203%20June%202008.pdf.

PREVENT: HM Government – Preventing Violent Extremism – a strategy for delivery (2008).

http://www.hmic.gov.uk/SiteCollectionDocuments/Thematics/THM_20090623.pdf.

HMIC report: 'Prevent – Progress and Prospects' (2009).

http://www.europol.europa.eu/publications/EU_Terrorism_Situation_and_Trend_Report_ TE-SAT/TESAT2008.pdf.

Interpol EU Terrorism and Situation Trend Report (2008).

http://www.mpa.gov.uk/downloads/committees/mpa/070222-06-appendix01.pdf.

Metropolitan Police Authority's 'Counter Terrorism: The London Debate' (2007).

http://www.hm-treasury.gov.uk/d/pbr_csr07_psa26.pdf.

Public Service Agreement 26 (2007) relating to counter-terrorism.

16   Forensic investigation and crime science

Introduction

The content of this chapter follows five main themes:

- How rapidly developing technology provides opportunities for the criminal and the criminal investigator.
- Providing an awareness of the use of statistics in forensic evidence.
- The strengths and limitations of forensic identification.
- The use of DNA profiling in criminal investigations and the controversy surrounding the DNA database.
- The 'crime science' approach to crime and crime reduction.

A basic introduction to the scope of forensic science and the duty of police officers as gatherers and preservers of forensic evidence is found elsewhere (Rogers and Lewis 2007) and this level of understanding is assumed. This chapter does not attempt to introduce the reader to the detailed scientific principles or practical procedures associated with specific forensic techniques, as these are covered by many other practical and academic texts (e.g. Beaufort-Moore 2009). Each police force has its own procedures for the submission of samples for further forensic examination, details of which may be obtained from the force's Scientific Support Department.

Introduction to forensic investigation

We shall take the term 'forensic investigation' to be the investigation of crime using scientific techniques or technology. For example:

- An unknown powder found in a suspect's garden shed, thought to be cocaine, is sent to the laboratory for analysis.
- Examination of a computer hard disc showed that it contained encrypted files conmprising pornographic images of young children.
- A suspect denies speaking to the victim immediately before he was assaulted, but an examination of the suspect's mobile phone provides contradictory evidence.

- An individual claims he was absent when a fight broke out in a pub: shards of a glass were found on his clothes.
- A suspect is eliminated from a crime because of his DNA profile, but a partial DNA match with material found at the scene suggests that the suspect's relative may have been involved.
- Paint embedded in the suspect's car does not match the victim's car paint.

Forensic investigations usually involve many agencies. Suspected arson, for example, may involve the police, the fire service, insurance companies, the Health and Safety Executive, crime scene examiners and forensic scientists. One of the tasks of the police investigating officer is to understand the contribution of other agencies and to foster good communication and cooperation between them.

Technology: the enemy and friend of the investigator

Modern technology is inextricably connected with crime. The mobile phone, for example, enables criminals to communicate with each other quickly and at great distances. On the other hand, such technology offers opportunities to investigators of crime because mobile phones send messages that pass through telecommunication networks which allows investigators to geographically locate a phone which is switched on, even if it is not being used. Confiscation of a mobile phone, or an examination of the messages that have been sent through the network provider, also provides information which may be valuable in an investigation (Box 16.1).

Box 16.1   Exercise 16A   The internet

State two advantages and two disadvantages from the criminal's viewpoint of using the internet to facilitate crime.

In answering this question, it may be helpful to think of a specific group of offences (e.g. internet-based paedophilia) and to generalise subsequently. The advantages for the criminal include not being geographically tied to a crime scene, being able to work outside of the jurisdiction of a police force in a foreign country, achieving a certain degree of anonymity in being one of billions using the internet daily and the widespread availability of technical information on the internet about security systems or procedures. The disadvantages of using the internet include traceability, the requirement to store information in some physical location (e.g. the computer's hard drive) which can be accessed later and the inability of the criminal to distinguish between genuine collaborators and police officers posing as partners in crime.

Truth as a concept

Although court proceedings can be long and complicated, the courts take a very practical approach to establishing the 'truth', and truth is commonly associated with the verdict of the court. In most criminal cases what we may call the 'judicial truth' is arrived at through a jury with the court being guided using previously agreed rules. The rules dictate which evidence is admissible and what the accepted threshold of evidence is (the 'burden of proof') for that court.

To illustrate this, consider a criminal prosecution against Jones for murder in which he is acquitted because the evidence was not strong enough to prove his guilt beyond all reasonable doubt (the burden of proof in criminal courts). How would we then answer the question 'Is it true that Jones murdered the victim?' The tradition of common law dictates that an acquittal certifies innocence; the practical consequences of an acquittal are significant, and include liberty and financial compensation. In other words, the 'judicial truth' – the outcome of the trial – depends upon the relevance and quality of evidence and the precise threshold of evidence that is dictated by the legal proceedings. This position has been summarised by Roberts (2003): that it is 'the role of the trial courts to determine whether the defendant is "legally guilty" not whether he is "factually innocent"'.

In contrast, science, through the rigorous testing of its methods by professional scientists working largely outside the court system over many years, attempts to shed light on 'universal truths' – truths which do not depend upon the rules of the criminal or civil court. Examples are: 'Does the blood found at the crime scene belong to Jones?' 'Was the spent bullet fired from Jones' revolver?' 'Are fragments of Jones' car's paint found on Parker's car?' Ideally, forensic evidence would be able to provide a 'yes or no' answer to these questions, but even if the evidence is unable to support a 'yes or no', or if statistics are used to indicate the probability that an assertion is correct, the key idea is that there is a truth which could in principle be arrived at objectively, and that such a truth is independent of the way courts work.

A consequence of scientific objectivity is that forensic science cannot make unjustified claims. While it is reasonable to ask the question 'Did the blood found at the crime scene belong to Jones?' it would be unreasonable to ask the question 'Does the blood found at the scene confirm that Jones was present at the scene?' Blood could arrive at the scene by various means (it may have been deliberately deposited there to mislead investigators), and – as we will repeatedly emphasise – the value (or otherwise) of such evidence to guilt is decided by the court itself and not by the forensic scientist.

Forensic identification

Forensic science is often introduced through the famous Locard Principle 'that every contact leaves a trace'. In practice, the question for forensic scientists is whether or not any trace is *substantial enough* to be detected, acquired and examined, and whether or not the information gleaned is selective enough to give judicially useful information. Forensic science is often concerned with the identification of individuals or of material or objects and the idea of *identity* (e.g. of a finger mark, a sample that gives rise to a DNA profile or a sample of a suspected narcotic drug) is central to the work of forensic scientists. Commonly, the crime scene gives trace evidence that is then compared to a 'control' (such as a fingerprint obtained under near-perfect conditions, the DNA profile of the suspect or the infrared spectrum of a pure sample of drug). The function of the expert is to compare the crime scene sample with the control: professional expertise and experience may then provide identification to differing degrees of certainty. The practical difficulties are often related to the poor quality of evidence at the scene (such as a smudged print of a thumb). The idea of uniqueness and identity is particularly challenging where biometric data is concerned (Meuwly 2006).

Robertson and Vignaux (1995) state that the features of an ideal forensic identification system would include:

- that it identifies features unique to the individual;
- that those features do not change over time;
- that those features are unambiguous so that two experts would describe the same feature the same way;
- that it is able to place individuals at a crime scene;
- that it is reasonably simple and cheap to operate.

Currently, no system satisfies all of these requirements (Box 16.2).

Box 16.2   Exercise 16B Searching the crime scene: reconstructing the crime scene

A crime scene investigator arrives at the scene of a burglary. How does he or she decide what to search for and where?

This may appear to be a straightforward question, but there are several judgements to be made here. The examination of a crime scene for forensic evidence inevitably involves some selectivity, since a complete examination is often impractical (Williams 2008). In other words, crime scene examiners make professional judgements about where they search and what they search for. Such judgements are formulated partly upon the information provided by any witnesses or the first police officer at the scene, but also by the examiner's understanding of 'crime reconstruction' and of how burglars are thought to work. The idea of a generic way of carrying out a burglary is useful because it allows standard methods of scene examination to be formulated and for investigators to be trained in such methods so that they work more efficiently and effectively. There is always the chance, though, that some burglars will not be so considerate as to conform to 'standard burglary practice' and, in such cases, valuable information might be missed by the scene examiner.

The idea of 'mental crime reconstruction' is central to all police investigations of crime and certain assumptions are often made about the way in which criminals act (for example, how a burglar gains access to a house). In the case of crime intelligence a related effect is noticed whereby the crime data reflect the methods used in the design of the data collection and analysis (Innes *et al.* 2005).

Box 16.3 Case study How burglars work

Nee and Meenaghan summarise previous research about decision making by burglars and report the results of a study in which 50 burglars, aged 21 to 60, were interviewed. Seventy-five per cent of burglars were motivated primarily by money, with a minority mentioning excitement or motivation by others as the primary motivation. Few of the interviewed burglars appeared to be opportunistic and most, having decided to burgle, searched a suitable area until a target presented itself.

Two-thirds of those interviewed reported using the same search pattern for every burglary. Few changed their pattern every time so as to suggest to the police that burglaries were being caused by different offenders. Many burglars followed a regular (predictable) pattern, searching the master bedroom first; then other bedrooms followed by the living rooms. Half of the sample reported searching the drawers in rooms first.

(Nee, C. and Meenaghan, A. [2006] 'Expert decision making in burglars', *British Journal of Criminology*, 46: 935–949)

The admissibility of expert evidence

> The theoretical position is that experts are expected simply to educate the jury, to pass on the relevant aspects of their knowledge and expertise so that the jury itself can properly assess the evidence to which it relates.
>
> The Law Commission Consultation Paper no. 190 (2009)

Key points relating to the admissibility of all kinds of expert evidence are:

1   If a judge or jury can form their own conclusions without the help of an expert, the opinion of an expert is unnecessary.
2   If an expert is judged as incapable of giving impartial evidence it is likely that their evidence will not be admitted by the court, since the expert's overriding duty is to the court and not to the prosecution or defence.

3. The expert must have acquired by study or experience sufficient knowledge to render their opinion of value to the court.
4. The expert witness's subject must be recognised as a sufficiently reliable body of knowledge or experience that their opinion would be valuable to the court.

The UK Law Commission Consultation Paper (no. 190) considered point 4 in detail and raised another issue (which we label as 4[b]):

> 4(b). The case-specific question whether the particular expert witness has properly drawn from 'that reliable body of knowledge' to provide a reliable opinion on the factual issue(s) the jury must resolve.

In the Sally Clark case, in which Sally Clark was accused of murdering her own children, a distinguished physician presented evidence at court, coming to the conclusion that the probability of two cot deaths occurring in the same family was only one in 73 million. It may be argued that point 4 was satisfied, since the physician's subject of expertise was generally a reliable body of knowledge and experience. However, the way that the physician drew his conclusion was subsequently shown to be flawed. If this had been realised at the time of the trial, it would be reasonable to suppose that the court would have decided that 4(b) was not satisfied and that element of the evidence of the witness would be judged inadmissible.

Point 4, recognition of an expert witness's subject, is clearly relevant to forensic science and the issue has historically been developed in detail in the US. The so-called 'Frye Test', dating back to 1923, dictates that in order to be admissible, a scientific theory underpinning an expert witness's evidence must have gained general acceptance in that field of knowledge. Partly because the Frye criteria would exclude the admission of new techniques in all circumstances, most US states have replaced Frye with the 'Daubert Test' which concentrates on the reliability of the scientific evidence being presented. One difference between the application of the Frye and Daubert tests is worth teasing out. In Frye, the court judge simply defers to the scientific community (it is therefore referred to as a 'deference test') whereas in Daubert, the reliability of a scientific technique (say) is considered in the context of its application in that case.

While the admissibility of expert evidence on the basis of relevance and reliability is enshrined in English Common Law (see case study on the court judgment in relation to Omagh Bombing in Box 16.4), there is no direct equivalent of the Daubert Test as used in US courts and the Frye test has never been part of English Law. The Law Commission, in its Consultation Paper no. 190 (2009), and in a clear move in the direction of adopting Daubert-like principles, recommended that there should be a new statutory test for courts in order to determine the admissibility of all expert evidence in criminal proceedings.

Despite the current absence of the equivalent of Daubert criteria in the English court system, Daubert criteria have evolved within forensic science itself. For example, Nic Daeid (2006) lists the Daubert Criteria in a context which is followed by many forensic scientists internationally in assessing – as a profession – the status of forensic techniques:

1. Whether the expert's technique or theory can be or has been tested – that is, whether the expert's theory can be challenged in some objective sense, or whether it is instead simply a subjective, conclusory approach that cannot reasonably be assessed for reliability.
2. Whether the technique or theory has been subject to peer review publication.
3. The known or potential rate of error[11] of the technique or theory when applied.
4. The existence and maintenance of standards and controls.
5. Whether the technique or theory has been generally accepted by the scientific community.

Note that 4 is effectively the question asked under Frye.

The idea of the reliability of scientific evidence for judicial purposes has also been discussed by Robertson and Vignaux (1995), who give the term 'reliability' at least four different meanings:

- *Sensitivity*. Can the forensic technique be used even if the amount of evidence is very small or if it is mixed into a larger matrix of background material?
- *Quality control*. Is the procedure free of contamination? Were standard methods used in any extraction of trace material or in laboratory analytical work?
- *Discriminatory power*. Can this evidence distinguish between individuals?
- *Honesty*. Has the forensic scientist told the whole truth about any tests used?

Box 16.4   Exercise 16C How does the reliability and value of trace evidence change over time?

Give two examples where the reliability of evidence changes over time.

One example is provided by the improvements in both technology and understanding associated with forensic techniques. This can work both ways. Over time, the limitations of evidence are generally better understood and this may reduce the value of trace evidence. For example, it is now understood that poorly smudged fingerprints at the crime scene (finger marks) may be of limited evidential value, despite the almost universally held belief that the fingerprints of all individuals are unique. On the other hand, the sensitivity of techniques to extract and profile DNA from the crime scene have improved greatly over the past ten years and this has made possible convictions through re-examination of crime scene evidence in so-called 'cold case review' investigations.

The Law Commission Consultation Paper No. 190 (2009) accepted that scientific developments may cause some expert testimony to be regarded as unreliable in the future. On page 6 the paper notes that

> the problems associated with expert evidence can never be entirely resolved. Scientific knowledge is continuously advancing as more empirical research is undertaken, so it is inevitable that some hypotheses will come to be modified or discarded, that expert testimony based on any such hypothesis will subsequently come to be regarded as unreliable and that this will have a bearing on the legitimacy of convictions (and, to a lesser extent, acquittals) founded on such testimony.

Case study Low template DNA profiling and the Omagh Bombing Investigation

Issues around the validation of forensic techniques surfaced during the trial of Sean Hoey in relation to the Omagh Bombing in Northern Ireland in 1998. During the trial, it was revealed that the DNA evidence against Hoey had been produced by a relatively new technique known as 'Low Template DNA' (also known as 'Low Copy Number DNA') designed to be able to detect much smaller amounts of DNA than the standard SGM+ DNA profiling kit is capable of. During the trial the way in which the Low Template DNA technique was validated was discussed in detail. Justice Weir commented: 'I am not satisfied that the publishing of two journal articles describing a process invented by the authors can be regarded, with more, as having "validated" that process for the purpose of it being confidently used for evidential processes.' Following the trial, the use of Low Template DNA was suspended for one year and its use in other trials reviewed. A scientific review of the technique (the Caddy Review) reported in 2008, concluding that 'the Low Template DNA technique was "robust" and "fit for purpose"'. The report by the Forensic Regulator (http://www.cps.gov.uk/legal/assets/uploads/files/Response%20 to%20Professor%20Caddy.pdf) supported the continued use of the technique and specifically stated that a consensus was not required before a technique could be used by the criminal justice system. The Crown Prosecution Service has since reported on additional validation procedures that have been applied to the technique (http://www.cps.gov. uk/legal/l_to_o/low_copy_number_dna_testing/). However, there have been concerns expressed at the possibility of contamination by such a sensitive technique (http://www.barristermagazine.com/articles/issue31/ Jamieson.html).

The (US) National Academy of Sciences' *Report on Forensic Sciences* (2010) is important in drawing attention to weaknesses in the way that forensic science has developed, weaknesses that have led to some subjective interpretations, exaggerated testimony and a paucity of research in certain areas. Indeed, the Honourable Harry Edwards, the report's author, states in the report that 'with the exception of nuclear DNA analysis, no forensic method has been rigorously shown to have the capacity to consistently, and with a high degree of certainty, demonstrate a connection between evidence and a specific individual or source'. The ramifications of the report to the long-term status and development of forensic science may be very substantial, but the report does not imply that forensic techniques should not be used, but that their use should not be unconditional and unquestioned. As science progresses, forensic methodologies once considered as beyond dispute are subsequently altered or rejected. The role of the courts is crucial: it is the courts that must act to protect the integrity of our legal processes by demanding higher standards for forensic evidence when it is presented in court.

Geographical context of crime

The geographical context of crime allows a simple but useful classification based upon the familiarity of the offender and victim with the crime scene (Figure 16.1). This is important in understanding the evidential value of trace evidence. For example, the presence of hair belonging to the suspect at the home of the victim is more significant than the presence of hair belonging to the suspect at the joint home of the victim and suspect.

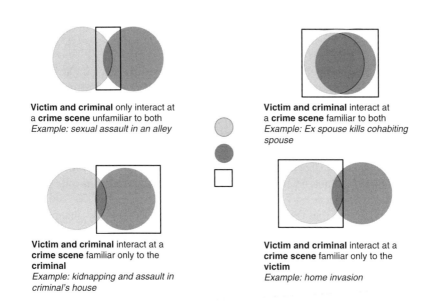

Victim and criminal only interact at a **crime scene** unfamiliar to both
Example: sexual assault in an alley

Victim and criminal interact at a **crime scene** familiar to both
Example: Ex spouse kills cohabiting spouse

Victim and criminal interact at a **crime scene** familiar only to the **criminal**
Example: kidnapping and assault in criminal's house

Victim and criminal interact at a **crime scene** familiar only to the **victim**
Example: home invasion

Figure 16.1 The context of crimes.

Forensic evidence and statistics

The statistics of criminal evidence is a subject in itself (see e.g. Aitken 2009), but the term '*likelihood ratio*' is so commonly used that we must explain it further. We will then illustrate the term using a simple example.

The likelihood ratio is a numerical ratio which indicates the relative probability of two events (1 and 2) occurring: each event represents a possible way in which the evidence in question arrived at the scene. Each event is assigned a 'match probability' p_1 and p_2: probabilities are expressed as lying between 0 and 1, with 1 being statistical certainty. The likelihood ratio is calculated as follows:

Likelihood ratio $= p_1 / p_2$.

As we shall see shortly, the events are each linked with an 'assertion' – a statement which is either true or untrue.

Consider the following scenario. A DNA profile is extracted from blood left at the scene by a burglar who was injured during an attempted robbery. A suspect, 'X', is later arrested and is forced to provide a blood sample for analysis; it is found that the DNA profile of the suspect contains several key characteristics which were found in the blood left at the scene.

One important question, of course, is 'how did this blood arrive at the scene?' We start by stating two assertions, each one linked to a scenario which explains how the DNA arrived at the scene.

1. *Assertion 1*. That the DNA evidence found at the scene originated from suspect 'X'.
2. *Assertion 2*. That the DNA evidence found at the scene originated from another person.

The match probability of assertion 1, symbolised p_1, is 1.0, since if 'X' left DNA material at the scene the probability of the DNA evidence originating from 'X' would be 1.0.

The match probability for assertion 2, symbolised at p_2, is the chance of a randomly selected individual in the population having the same DNA profile as that obtained from the crime scene. Think of this as follows. Suppose that the DNA profiles of every person in the UK are stored in a computer and one profile is selected at random. What will be the chance that the selected profile matches that found at the scene?

Suppose further that the quality of the laboratory DNA profile obtained from the crime scene stain is only fairly good (a so-called 'partial match') and that there is a one-in-a-million chance that blood from a randomly selected individual possesses the same DNA profile as that found at the scene. Accordingly, the match probability for assertion 2 is $1/1000000 = 0.000001$.

The Likelihood Ratio $= p_1 / p_2 = 1.0/0.000001 = 1$ million. In other words, the assertion that the DNA evidence originated from 'X' is 1000000 times more likely than the first assertion, that it originated from another person. Attempt the exercise in Box 16.5 before continuing.

Box 16.5   Exercise 16D DNA evidence

Does this information suggest that there is a million to one chance that the suspect 'X' is innocent?

There are two reasons why the answer is unequivocally 'no'. The first is often called the 'Prosecutor's Fallacy'. The UK's population is about 60 million so that we would expect 60 individuals to possess a DNA profile which matches that found at the scene. The chance of 'X' being responsible for the DNA profile found in the blood, in the absence of other information, is therefore 1 in 60. These are good odds against innocence, not bad odds. (The Sally Clarke case above is actually a complicated example of the Prosecutor's Fallacy.)

However, there is a more general reason why the answer is 'no'. In general, to attempt to connect innocence or guilt with likelihood ratios is frowned upon by criminal courts because it is the court itself (and not witnesses – even expert witnesses) that decides the relevance of evidence in relation to guilt or innocence. So, even if the match probability p_2 is one in a billion (which is the value commonly quoted where there are good-quality DNA profiles extracted at the scene), the expert witness cannot use statistics to assert that the suspect who has been arrested is guilty. It would be up to the court to interpret the significance of such data in relation to guilt or innocence. In exactly the same way, the relevance of an apparently positive identification of a named individual by a witness would be considered by the court and not by the witness herself.

There are two reasons why the court takes this stance. The first is that juries might be overwhelmed and blinded with statistics if the way in which scientific evidence is presented is not controlled. As Gill and Clayton (2009) note about DNA evidence: 'The assertion that any given full DNA profile is "unique", although it could well be true, is not very helpful in the courtroom context because of its emotive impact.' The second is that forensic evidence by itself does not confirm guilt or innocence. For example, consider evidence relating to a rape case. Suppose a vaginal swab yielded a DNA profile which is matched (with a high match probability) to suspect 'X'. Such evidence is highly relevant to the assertion that X's semen was found inside the victim, but even if this were true it does not mean that 'X' was guilty and it would need to be proved (beyond all reasonable doubt) that the victim did not consent to sexual intercourse. It is the court itself that must weight up these other matters before coming to a conclusion about guilt or innocence: statistics must not be allowed to cloud these issues. Attempt the exercise in Box 16.6 before continuing.

Box 16.6   Exercise 16E The expressions of opinion

A handwriting expert was asked to compare an unsigned hate letter with a letter known to be written by the suspect Jones. The question she was asked was: 'Is it likely that the hate letter was written by Jones?' Suppose that the handwriting in the letters appears very similar to Jones' handwriting. Write three sentences showing three ways in which the expert might express his or her professional opinion on this matter.

The expert might express her opinion in many ways, including the following:

'It is very likely that Jones wrote the letter.'
'There is a strong association between the two letters.'
'The evidence proves strong evidence for the view that Jones wrote the letter.'
'The handwriting in the unsigned letter is consistent with the second letter, known to have been written by Jones.'

Jackson (2009) provides a detailed discussion of the phrases that are commonly used in expressions of opinion. The variety of statements is a cause of concern because one expert may be more cautious than another: one person's strong evidence may be another person's fairly strong evidence. Thus, the judge or jury's assessment of the strength of such evidence will only be independent of the words used if there is a universal and consistent understanding of their interpretation. Even under detailed cross-examination of the expert witness, this might prove quite challenging.

The alternative would be to introduce statistics into the discussions. This brings its own challenges, but in principle it is a step in the right direction. If we stated that 'it is 90 per cent likely that the handwriting in the hate letter is the same as found in the signed letter' then we would have to be able to justify the percentage used, for example, by reference to the number of characters written in the same way in both documents. Courts do not usually demand the same statistical approach to handwriting (or to fingerprinting, or hair fibre analysis and comparison) as they do with DNA evidence. Indeed, as the following section discusses, it is not currently possible to assign reliable formal probabilities to techniques other than DNA.

Fingerprints

Fingerprints remain one of the most important, valuable and widely used techniques in the forensic armoury. The value of fingerprint evidence (essentially a comparison of *finger marks* at the scene with *fingerprints* on record) has been the subject of intense scrutiny in recent years and it is worth examining this in greater detail, as it illustrates some of the elements of reliability discussed above. As with

DNA, it is the creation of huge electronic databases that has allowed the police to pool information obtained by individual police forces. In the UK, the national fingerprint database NAFIS (National Automated Fingerprint Identification System) has now become IDENT1 which includes finger and palm print search capabilities.

Fingerprints have been studied for over 100 years and there is no evidence to suggest that the fingerprints of two individuals are identical. Criticisms of the reliability of fingerprinting centre around the uncertainty in establishing that a finger mark (which might be smudged or fragmentary) proves the identity of an individual; in other words, that the finger mark obtained at the crime scene and the fingerprint on file were produced by the same person. The extraction of finger marks from the scene is often difficult and the finger marks may be fragmentary, but where it has been subsequently proved that a fingerprint identification is itself erroneous, the error is generally considered to lie in the application of the identification procedures and protocols used: the principle of uniqueness of fingerprints itself is almost universally accepted. Despite the uncontroversial nature of most fingerprint evidence, several miscarriages of justice suggest that in practice fingerprint evidence cannot be said to be infallible, if only because the identification of finger marks retains some subjectivity since fingerprint identification cannot be fully automated. This explains (at least in part) why calculations of likelihood ratios (i.e. a numerical standard) for fingerprint evidence are rarely attempted.

The issue of subjectivity makes it questionable whether or not fingerprints conform to the Daubert Criteria. Champod and Chamberlain (2009) note that 'The present situation is that the UK courts accept the non-numerical standard and for most part do not challenge the identification', but this may change in the future and there remains a pressing need for more quality assurance in finger-printing.

The (US) National Academy of Sciences' *Report on Forensic Sciences* (Edwards Report 2010) takes a harder view and contains specific reference to fingerprints, stating: 'for years, the courts have been led to believe that disciplines such as finger-prints stand on a par with nuclear DNA analysis'. Later the report concludes:

> The Committee's Report rejects as scientifically implausible any claims that fingerprint analyses have 'zero error rates'. We also found a dearth of scientific research to establish limits of performance, to ascertain quantifiable measures of uncertainty, and to address the impact of the sources of variability and potential bias in fingerprint examinations and in other forensic disciplines that reply on subjective assessments of matching characteristics.

This was supported by Jennifer Mnookin, also quoted in the 2010 Edwards Report:

> Science deals in probabilities, not certainty. The only forensic evidence that makes regular use of formal probabilities is DNA profiling, in which experts

testify to the probability of a match. None of the rest of the traditional pattern-identification sciences – such as fingerprinting, ballistics, fibre and handwriting analysis – currently has the necessary statistical foundation to establish accurate probabilities.

Box 16.7   Case study Shirley McKie case

Perhaps the most controversial case involving fingerprint evidence in the UK in recent years has been the McKie case which is currently the subject of an enquiry ordered by the government in Scotland. Shirley McKie is a former Scottish detective constable who was accused of perjury and subsequently dismissed from her job because her thumbprint was allegedly found at a murder scene while she insisted that she had not attended the murder scene. During the court case in 1999, international defence fingerprint experts refuted the identification of the thumb mark as belonging to McKie and McKie was acquitted. The potential ramifications of this case for the reputation of the fingerprint service (and more generally the reputation of criminal justice) are extremely disturbing and criminal prosecutions against officials involved in the case cannot be ruled out.

BBC site on the McKie Case
(http://news.bbc.co.uk/1/hi/scotland/3671938.stm)
The Public Enquiry
(http://www.thefingerprintinquiryscotland.org.uk/inquiry/75.html#)

The police and forensic science

Criticisms that forensic services (particular those provided by crime scene examiners) are insufficiently integrated into police investigations or that police officers do not always understand the scope of scientific services are not new (see e.g. David Blakey's HMIC second review *Under the Microscope Revisited*, 2000). The strategic deployment of forensic science and related technology is now part of the NPIA's remit under the 'Forensics21' programme.

There have been dramatic developments in the way in which forensic science is now used. A notable example has been the application of forensic science to high-volume crime and to major crime, as described by Tilley and Townsley (2009) and Barclay (2009) respectively. The preservation of evidence has enabled 'Cold Case Reviews' of unsolved crimes to be implemented with renewed hope of success, particularly where crime scenes yield DNA profiles. More fundamentally, the value of forensic investigation to the police has changed as forensic evidence is often used to initiate lines of enquiry by police, rather than simply corroborating assertions by suspects or investigators. This has led observers to coin the phrase 'forensic intelligence' to describe the information obtained by scientists which directs subsequent police enquiries (Williams 2008).

Box 16.8   Exercise 16F Forensic intelligence

Give an example where the reverse of 'forensic intelligence' occurs and where the crime scene investigation is directed by the police.

A simple example is provided by a burglary. Police officers who are first at the scene have a duty to pass on to the crime scene investigator any information that may provide a further context for the crime. For example, they may pass on the fact that the occupants of the house do not smoke and so the smell of cigarettes at the scene may suggest that the offender paused to smoke a cigarette which might have been discarded outside the obvious site of burglary itself. This may cause the crime scene investigator to extend her examination of the house and perhaps lead to the retrieval of a cigarette butt that might provide DNA evidence which is crucial in focusing the police enquiry.

DNA evidence

DNA has assumed a special position within the forensic armoury owing to the high-profile murders that have been solved using DNA evidence. Despite the widespread achievements of the technique, its limitations (see 16.5 above) are not always understood and it appears to have acquired the status of 'a magic bullet' with which to solve crimes.

The DNA database currently contains about 4.5 million named individual profiles which are known as subject sample profiles (SSPs). Eighty per cent of SSPs are from males. Forty-one per cent of SSPs were of individuals aged 15 to 24 at the time samples were taken.

There are about 56,000 crime scene samples (CSSs) loaded on the database, including 49,000 volume crime offence profiles (including drugs and vehicle crime) and 6,000 serious crime offence profiles. Attempt the exercise in Box 16.9 before continuing.

Box 16.9   Exercise 16G Searching the database

One class of search that is carried out is that of a newly acquired subject sample against all the crime scene profiles (i.e. SSP against the CSSs). What are the two other classes of search that are possible using the DNA database?

A newly acquired crime sample might be searched against the subject profiles (CSS against SSPs). Alternatively, a newly acquired crime scene sample might be searched against all the crime scene samples (CSS against CSSs); which would indicate where unidentified individuals have been associated with repeat offences.

The controversy over the UK DNA Database

The UK National DNA Database (NDNAD) is controversial for a number of reasons:

- There are some doubts over its value for money and in particular, whether or not the expanded DNA Database has lived up to expectations. McCartney (2006), using 2004/2005 UK data, reports that '0.35 per cent of recorded crime could be claimed to have been "detected" via DNA'. Furthermore, the extent to which detections can be unambiguously attributed to DNA intelligence is unknown. This suggests that the expanded database has some way to go before it can claim to fully justify its multi-million-pound expenditure. Williams and Johnson (2008) note that 'regardless of its actual success in mundane policing (which, as we have argued, remains debateable), it is the *promise* of the database – the genetic imaginary' of automated criminal detection – which forms the basis of a government-inspired discourse about this 'weapon against crime'. However, the counter-argument is that there have been many serious offenders who would not have been convicted without DNA evidence and the application of NDNAD to solving a small number of very high-profile serious crime cases is well known.
- The proposition that eventually all active offenders will be on the NDNAD is challenged by some researchers. Pease (2008) notes that:

  > the notion that a day will dawn where all active offenders are to be found on NDNAD is naïve, despite the 2003 Home Office claim that the DNA profiles of all active offenders would be on the database by 2004. This is because of the high churn rate in active offending, with many offenders desisting, and many neophyte offenders. No more than two-thirds of active offenders will ever be found on the database, and no more than two-thirds of those on the database will be active offenders.

However, two-thirds is a very substantial part of the population and it might be argued that the investment in the DNA database might be justified for this reason alone.

- The Criminal Justice Act 2003: s.9–10 (and amending s.63 of PACE) permits the taking of fingerprints and DNA (non-intimate) samples upon arrest and without consent. In effect, this means that fingerprints and DNA samples can be taken upon 'reasonable suspicion' that an individual is responsible for an offence. It is not required that a conviction be obtained, a charge be brought against a detained individual or that the offence be considered 'serious'. Guilt or innocence is generally irrelevant and suspicion by the police, provided it is judged to be reasonable, is sufficient to require the person to provide a DNA sample. Inclusion on NDNAD may therefore be regarded as a manifestation of permanent suspicion.

- The DNA profiles of subjects are automatically retained on the database, even if the subjects are subsequently exonerated or where individuals have voluntarily provided DNA-containing samples for the purposes of eliminating themselves from a list of suspects. This has become a 'rights and freedom' issue and has been likened to 'biological tagging'. In December 2008, the European Court of Human Rights ruled that the retention of the DNA profiles of two Sheffield men who had been cleared of criminal charges breached their human rights. At the time of writing the UK government is considering its response to this ruling.
- NDNAD contains proportionately great numbers of minority ethnic subjects. This concern would disappear if it was made mandatory for the DNA profile of every UK citizen to be loaded on the database: the question for the government would then be whether or not this would be a proportionate response to the present inequality.
- There are some concerns that the DNA profiles will be used for other purposes in the future, including providing valuable information to those wishing to health-screen individuals. The use of DNA profiles are currently strictly limited to the prevention and detection of crime.
- The availability of DNA profiling may have contributed to a 'de-skilling' of police investigators who turn to DNA as a quick way of guiding or concluding their investigation. As Roach and Pease (2003) note: 'DNA science should be seen as a tool which enhances, not replaces, the skills of the detective'.

Crime science

Crime science (Smith and Tilley 2005) has been publicised as a new approach to crime reduction and investigation. It aims to pro-actively prevent crime rather than simply respond to it. The characteristics of crime science include:

- A focus on the objective of reducing crime rather than upon criminals and offender behaviour.
- A preference for simple and relatively cheap solutions which are likely to be statistically effective, including 'designing out' crime in commercial products.
- Promoting strategies which are accessible and easily understood by practitioners without formal academic or scientific training.
- Active encouragement of the involvement of the physical sciences, IT and engineering as well as the social sciences.
- An emphasis upon 'situational crime prevention' (see e.g. Groff and Birks 2008) with an assumption that a disproportionately small displacement of crime occurs in other areas.

Crime science promotes the production of crime reduction and investigative policies by any relevant and credible intellectual, theoretical or practical probe: the principles of study are not limited to those to be found in science and technology as long as the immediate objective is crime reduction and investigation. In that sense crime science subsumes conventional forensic science.

An example of crime science in action: repeat victimisation

The British Crime Survey and dedicated projects have confirmed that repeat victimisation (RV) burglary – in which targeted premises or nearby premises are re-burgled – is surprisingly widespread and victimisation is a good predictor of (future) victimisation, with repeat burglaries most likely within a short time (typically two months) of the first burglary.

RV also applies to other offences, such as school bullying, credit card fraud, assault and vandalism.

Traditionally, crime prevention and crime detection are considered separately, but for the types of crime to which RV applies there is no such distinction unless one considers one crime at a time, and so 'The attempt at detection is itself a contribution to future prevention' (Pease 1989). In ideal circumstances, police officers and crime scene investigators should work together with victims to identify likely repeat victimisations. The greater the degree of previous victimisation, the greater the need for speedy police and forensic investigation. Since a substantial number of RVs are committed by the same offenders, there are likely to be more opportunities to obtain forensic evidence about the same offender at the same crime scenes.

The influence of the natural sciences upon crime science is also evident from theoretical attempts to depict crime as following patterns observed in the life sciences. For example, the way in which some offenders select targets appears to follow the foraging behaviour of animals (Johnson *et al.* 1997; Felson 2006), with offenders minimising risk, maximising benefit and keeping the time to identify a victim to a minimum. Because burglaries are clustered in space and time, RVs can also be modelled using the epidemiological concept of 'communicability', in which premises or subjects close to the initial offence are more likely to become subject ('to catch') a subsequent offence ('disease').

References and suggested further reading

Aitken, C. (2009) 'Statistics and forensic science', in Fraser, J. and Williams, R. *Handbook of Forensic Science*. Willan Publishing, Cullompton, Devon.

Barclay, D. (2009) 'Using forensic science in major crime enquiries', in Fraser, J. and Williams, R. (eds), *Handbook of Forensic Science* 337–358. Willan Publishing, Cullompton, Devon.

Beaufort-Moore, D. (2009) *Crime Scene Management and Evidence Recovery*. Oxford University Press, Oxford.

Champod, C. and Chamberlain, P. (2009) 'Fingerprints', in Fraser, J. and Williams, R. (eds), *Handbook of Forensic Science* 57–83. Willan Publishing, Cullompton, Devon.

Daeid, N. (2006) 'Lies damn lies and statistics', Science and Justice, 46(1): 1–2.

Felson, M. (2006) *Crime and Nature*. Sage, London.

Gill, P. and Clayton, C. (2009) 'The current status of DNA profiling in the UK', in Fraser, J. and Williams, R. (eds), *Handbook of Forensic Science*. Willan Publishing, Cullompton, Devon.

Groff, E. and Birks, D. (2008) 'Simulating crime prevention strategies: a look at the possibilities', Policing, 2(2): 175–184.

Her Majesty's Inspectorate of Constabulary (HMIC) (2002) 'Under the microscope refocussed'. HMSO, London.

Innes, M., Fielding, N. and Cope, N. (2005) 'The appliance of science', British Journal of Criminology, 45: 39–57.

Jackson, G. (2009) 'Understanding forensic science opinions', in Fraser, J. and Williams, R. (eds), *Handbook of Forensic Science* 419–445. Willan Publishing, Cullompton, Devon.

Johnson, S.D., Bowers, K. and Hirschfield, A. (1997) 'New insights into the spatial and temporal distribution of repeat victimisation', *British Journal of Criminology*, 37(2): 224–244.

Lewis, R. (2007) 'Forensic support in law enforcement', in Rogers, C. and Lewis, R. (eds), *Introduction to Police Work*. Willan Publishing, Cullompton, Devon.

McCartney, C. (2009) Forensic Identification and Criminal Justice Forensic Science, Justice and Risk. Willan Publishing, Cullompton, Devon.

Meuwly, D. (2006) 'Forensic Iidividualization from biometric data', *Science and Justice*, 46: 205–213.

Pease, K. (1989) 'Repeat victimisation: taking stock', Crime Detection and Prevention Series Paper no. 90, Home Office. Also available online at: http://www.homeoffice.gov. uk/rds/prgpdfs/fcdps90.pdf (accessed 7 March 2011).

—— (2008) 'How to behave like a scientist?', *Policing*, 2(2): 154–159.

Roach, J. and Pease, K. (2006) *DNA Evidence and Police Investigations: A Health Warning*. Available: http://www.staff.Iboro.ac.uk/~ssgf/KP/2006 RoachPeaseDNA.pdf (accessed 7 March 2011).

Roberts, S. (2003) 'Unsafe convictions: defining and compensating for miscarriages of justice', *Modern Law Review*, 66: 445.

Robertson, B. and Vignaux, G.A. (1995) *Interpreting Evidence: Evaluating Forensic Science in the Courtroom*. John Wiley, Chichester, Chapter 1.

Rogers, C. and Lewis, R. (2007) *Introduction to Police Work*. Willan Publishing, Cullompton, Devon

Smith, M.J. and Tilley, N. (eds) (2005) *Crime Science – New Approaches to Preventing and Detecting Crime* 198–207. Willan Publishing, Cullompton, Devon.

Tilley, N. and Townsley, M. (2009) 'Forensic science in UK policing: strategies, tactics and effectiveness', in Fraser, J. and Williams, R. (eds), *Handbook of Forensic Science* 359–379. Willan Publishing, Cullompton, Devon.

Williams, R. (2008) 'Policing and forensic science', in Newburn, T. (ed.) *Handbook of Policing* 760–793. Willan Publishing, Cullompton, Devon.

Williams, R. and Johnson, P. (2008) 'Genetic policing: the use of DNA in criminal investigations'. Willan Publishing, Cullompton, Devon.

Useful websites

http://www.compukol.com/mendel/articles/On_Concepts_of_Law_and_Truth.pdf.
On concepts of law and truth by Mendel Sachs.

http://www.dundee.ac.uk/forensicmedicine/notes/expert.pdf.
The role of the expert (Department of Forensic Medicine, University of Dundee).

http://www.lawcom.gov.uk/docs/cp190.pdf.
Law Commission Consultation Report 190: The admissibility of expert evidence in criminal proceedings in England and Wales 2009.

http://news.bbc.co.uk/1/hi/england/2698425.stm.
The Sally Clark case (BBC News).

http://www.cadc.uscourts.gov/internet/home.nsf/AttachmentsByTitle/NAS+Report+on+Forensic+Science/$FILE/Edwards,+The+NAS+Report+on+Forensic+Science.pdf
The National Academy of Sciences Report on Forensic Sciences: What it means for the bench and the bar (Edwards Report 2010).

http://findarticles.com/p/articles/mi_hb6700/is_3_95/ai_n29204193/?tag = content;col1.
Article by Simon Cole on controversial criminal cases involving fingerprinting:

http://www.newyorker.com/archive/2002/05/27/020527fa_FACT.
Do fingerprints lie? An article in the *New Yorker* by Michael Specter.

http://www.modernmicroscopy.com/main.asp?article = 36&print = true&pix = true.
Locard Exchange: the science of forensic hair comparisons and the admissibility of hair comparison evidence: Frye and Daubert considered, by M.M. Houck, R.E. Bisbing, T.G. Watkins and R.P. Harmon. This paper considers the difficulties in calculating match probabilities for hair comparison evidence.

http://www.npia.police.uk/en/10432.htm.
Forensics21 (NPIA Forensic Programme).

http://www.npia.police.uk/en/docs/science_and_innovation.pdf.
NPIA publication: Science and innovation in the police service 2010–2013.

http://www.npia.police.uk/en/8934.htm.
NPIA: National DNA Database.

http://www.jdi.ucl.ac.uk/downloads/publications/journal_articles/RoachPease_june2006.pdf.
J. Roach and K. Pease, DNA evidence and police investigations: a health warning.

http://www.leeds.ac.uk/law/hamlyn/justice.htm.
Website on miscarriages of justice, drawn from a book edited by Professor Clive Walker.

17 Policing public disorder

Introduction

The issue of policing demonstrations and public disorder incidents is a topical one. This chapter will consider the historical context of policing such incidents, the changing role of the police when dealing with demonstrations and the impact of the police culture in such situations, and considers some strategies for maintaining public support in the face of media criticism over the handling of such demonstrations as the G20 summit.

Recent developments

The recent publication by her Majesty's Chief Inspector of Constabulary into the policing of protest in Britain (HMIC 2009) has once again focused on the way in which the police perform their duties at public protest demonstrations, particularly in the light of the recent G20 and other similar-style demonstrations in London and elsewhere. Included in the list of recommendations within this report is the adoption of a 'no surprise' communication philosophy with protesters, the wider public and the media. The report goes on to say that the public should be made aware of likely police action in order to make informed choices and decisions. In addition, it is argued, the police should engage in positive media and image activity that ensures support for their actions which should be ethical and proportionate in the circumstances. One approach – that of adopting corporate social responsibility methods – is considered in this chapter. The recent adverse incidents within policing of public demonstrations have been well publicised and reported throughout the media in the United Kingdom and across the world. Twenty-four-hour global media coverage engages, encourages and informs society on important global issues such as policing (Smith *et al.* 2001). Historically, the police have been accustomed to dealing with protests and demonstrations within the context of industrial disputes and political issues, with such public protests being based mainly upon class distinction, often attracting individuals from a particular section of society. However, recently, the police have had to deal with a plethora of protests involving people from a wide spectrum of society known as 'single-issue' protests, perhaps most notably environmental issues and the recent banking crisis (Hansen 1991). Unquestionably, such public demonstrations offer a unique challenge for today's modern police service, as it must be accountable for its tactics and actions to an increasingly informed and engaged public. The integration of issues, accompanied by the 'professionalisation of protests' and 'hybrid protestors', makes the importance of using the lawful, necessary and proportionate responses while policing demonstrations paramount (Button *et al.* 2002).

The historical context of public protests

The reason for the development of Britain's police service is a contested issue. Many commentators consider the origin of the police service to be closely associated with concerns surrounding public order and unrest (Reiner 1998; Silver 1971). Others believe the reason to be interlinked with increasing crime rates (Reith 1956). While addressing Parliament and lobbying for the creation of the police service, Sir Robert Peel made little reference to riots and focused on the growing evidence surrounding increasing levels of crime (Reiner 1998). Naturally perhaps, there are many who believed that the introduction of the police was a way of control by the state, adding another layer of bureaucracy (Hirst 1975; Monkkonen 1981), with the perception that the police are used as a mode of social control (Innes 2003). Nevertheless, public demonstrations and 'riots' have become synonymous with public order policing. Much of the industrial disputes from 1893 and into the 1980s were focused mainly on the coal industry, although there are some minor exceptions (Geary 1985). The Featherstone shootings in 1893 perhaps demonstrate the way in which such events can escalate. The Featherstone shootings were a miners' dispute which ultimately led to the killing of two people, and 14 being injured (Waddington 1992). The tactics used in this dispute by both the police and army consisted of a variety of different approaches ranging from verbal communication and escalating to the other end of the spectrum to shooting to kill (Geary 1985). Although an exception with the involvement of the armed forces, many further disputes surrounding the coal industry followed. The South Wales coal strike in 1910 to 1914, the general strike of 1926 and the miner's strike in 1984 to 1985 are some examples. Many individuals across the United Kingdom were affected in some way, either directly on the picket lines or through disruption of electricity, travel or the supply of coal. The miners' strike of 1984 is perhaps the most associated recently with industrial disputes, and is commonly referred to as 'the most important industrial conflict since 1926' (Fine and Millar 1985). The tactics and methods used while policing such events were invariably varied. Although wide-ranging in approach, the policing operation was controlled centrally through the national reporting centre. The police formulated 'riot squads', used mounted police and erected roadblocks, all in an attempt to manipulate and control the miners on the picket lines (Fine and Millar 1985). This class struggle, argue Fine and Milliar (1985), displayed the need for miners and members of the coal community to protect jobs, the industry and a way of life. Apart from industrial disorder, the police have confronted protestors on different issues, most notably through political or sporting demonstrations. Famously, the Brixton riots where the inner city unrest surrounding the stop-and-search policies of ethnic groups led to rioting (Gilligan and Pratt 2004), while the Luton vs. Millwall football match in 1985 is another example of the different issues the police have to deal with, (Giulianotti *et al.* 1994). In all demonstrations and riots, different tactics and responses have been used. Verbal communication, 'pushing and shoving', use of batons and shields, plastic rounds and ultimately the use of deadly force were some of the methods employed by the police service throughout this period.

The new age of protesting

The new age of public protesting and demonstrating brings with it a unique challenge for those responsible for maintaining public order. The balance between maintaining order, security and safety against the rights under the Human Rights Act (Home Office 2000) must be upheld and maintained. Under this legislation, freedom of expression under Article 10, freedom of assembly and association (Article 11) and freedom of thought, conscience and religion (Article 9) clearly acknowledge that individuals have a right to publicly protest and express their views on issues in a lawful manner. The unenviable task for the police service is to balance both the rights of those lawfully demonstrating against the rights of all other individuals within society. The events surrounding the G20 protests in London and Pittsburgh demonstrate perhaps the 'cross-class' type of protesting, with people lobbying on a plethora of issues, including climate change, the banking crisis, the recession, international business and capitalism (Casciani 2009). Protestors, such as climate campaigners and those lobbying for sustainable housing, a reduction in carbon emissions and other such issues were perhaps the most organised and professionally run of all the different camps involved in protesting at the summit. Employing a variety of techniques, the climate campaigners used the media to their advantage to inform and engage other like-minded individuals. Climate protesters identified that speed was paramount to their campaign when reporting events, using high-tech equipment, and the internet to blog, update videos and interview those on the 'picket line' (Lewis 2009), which in many cases was one step ahead of the official or police version of events that occurred during the demonstration.

Dynamics and realities of public order policing – role of the police

At the time of the industrial revolution, where urbanisation and industrialisation was at its pinnacle in cities such as London, new methods of social control were needed. London's and other cities' populations exploded as the forces of globalisation and industry began to influence the working class (Rawlings 2002). Sir Robert Peel, Home Secretary in 1829, following great opposition from other Members of Parliament including influential figures within society, decided to introduce a modern police service (Wright 2002). Seen by many as a method of social control in a time where there was already a great divide within the social classes, the main mandate for the constabulary was to be 'organised' and 'disciplined' and concerned with 'crime and its prevention' (Edwards 1999: 27). As the police service evolved and developed, so too did its mandate. As well as being concerned with crime and general public tranquillity, the police moved into a more diverse area of policing, which included maintenance of order (Mawby 2008). Consequently, as the police service developed, so did the whole discipline, witnessing many paradigmatic shifts through the introduction and implementation of new policing styles, technological advances and legislative changes. This has morphed and transformed the police service into the public sector organisation it is today.

Policing by consent and legitimacy

The policing policy in Britain has historically been one of mutual understanding between the police service and the public. Operating under the notion of 'policing by consent', levels of compliance from the public are relatively high compared with other countries (Waddington 1992). This has become synonymous with the British model of policing whereby the police have in the main been unarmed, 'ordinarily courteous', 'patient' and 'restrained in confrontation' (Thurmond Smith 1985: 5). Waddington (1992) also refers to the police as acting with legitimate authority, with the majority of the public accepting that the police have a right and a duty to carry out their roles within society. This consent granted by the public is not in itself given, but is gained through impartiality, and is generally accepted by each of the social classes (Waddington 1992). This method of gaining public consent means that the police do not have to enforce their will by using oppressive tactics or by carrying and using intimidating weaponry. Instead, the public simply accept the role and legitimacy of the police. Unfortunately, this was not always the case; there are many instances where simply relying on perceived public support was insufficient, resulting in the police using riot control equipment and tactics to deal with picket lines and demonstrations.

Traditional responses and paramilitary policing

The traditional response has over the decades been varied, depending on the overall policing paradigm influencing the policing landscape. Early on in the history of the modern police force, the overall arching ethos architected by Peel resulted in the police using a 'soft' approach, concluding in a typical view of the police being the quintessential British bobby on the beat, unarmed and having a harmonious rapport, thus being accepted by all classes:

> [T]hey encouraged the development of a highly disciplined force, insu-
> lated from direct political control, strictly accountable to the rule of law,
> operating primarily by preventative uniformed patrol, and performing a

variety of services to the people in need – not least in managing the problems of criminal victimisation.

(Reiner 1998: 41)

The 1950s through to the 1960s traditional response to public order and demonstrations remained 'soft', 'traditional', 'static' and 'tolerant' (Jefferson 1990). The events surrounding the civil rights movements and those opposed to the Vietnam War were relatively mild in comparison with other later public order events, with Jefferson (1990) recording only the use of defensive lines, scuffles, pushing and shoving. As the relationship between the state and society began to disintegrate around the 1970s due to political influences, so did the relationship between the police and society. The 1970s through to the 1980s imagery of policing becomes far more aggressive, being reflected in disputes and demonstrations such as the miners' strike, Notting Hill, Wapping and Brixton (Brearley and King 1996). Instead of police officers being distributed randomly along the picket line as was seen in the 1960s, the police were now fully equipped, wearing riot helmets, shields and operating in squads. This clearly demonstrates a move away from low-profile tactics to ruling with an iron fist. Further tactics have been developed which means the police using incapacitating spray, shields, 'kettling', bean bags and tear gas (Townsend 2009). 'Kettling' in particular has become associated with modern public order policing and was a tactic used while policing the G20 events in London. Essentially, 'kettling' is the containment and corralling of protestors with the use of police defensive lines to limit the movement of individuals (Donson *et al.* 2004). The associated disadvantages of this tactic are that it can often affect those not participating in the protest, and limits access to public facilities such as fresh water, food and toilets. This paramilitary style of policing has resulted in the public no longer believing that the police are divorced from the state or politics, perceiving them as being aligned with the politicians (Brewer *et al.* 1996). Subsequently, this appears to mean the police losing the understanding and sympathy of the public to enforce the law as the police are no longer impartial, with the public considering them to represent the state's method of social control. The legitimacy dependent upon community cooperation may no longer be enjoyed, and has resulted in the detachment of the police and public becoming ever more prevalent. The use of policing tactics such as these has gone some way in re-establishing the discussion concerning the police and their role when involved in class and social control. It may be argued that the public allow the police to use some tactics, such as stop and search, arrest and serving warrants, but as the nature of public order policing becomes more aggressive, society may re-evaluate its consent and may begin to question the wider role of policing within society (Uglow 1988).

Legalities and the right to protest in a democracy vs. public order policing

The balance between the 'collective right' and the 'individual right' is often difficult to gauge, especially when policing protests which attract such vast numbers from many different social classes. Public concern and apprehension has certainly grown over recent decades as the levels of violence from both protestors and the police have increased. The public are certainly becoming increasingly engaged and informed on public order events as the media continue to report (Uglow 1988). The police must balance the right to publicly demonstrate lawfully, including the right of peaceful assembly against the effect on the Queen's Peace, and take into consideration the overall public interest. The police have a variety of powers to deal with protestors given in numerous Acts of Parliament including the Public Order Act 1986 (Home Office 1986). Chief officers are now required to ensure that police officers are specifically trained in public order and have ready-to-respond squads or groups of officers to deal with conflict using quasi-militaristic methods. This public order strategy is very different from the model being used in the 1960 where police simply managed the crowds without any specialist training or equipment (Waddington 1996). Justification given by the police for the increased force whereby the police deal with public protesting is usually that the rights of a few cannot outweigh the right of society for security, order and peace. The Public Order Act 1986 enforces the right of the police to interfere and maintain the rule of law (Uglow 1988). With regard to the demands placed upon them in terms of policing disorder, it may be said that the police are in an unenviable position.

Public order and policing culture and subcultures

Within an organisation such as the police, it is inherent that a strong culture will develop. This rather nebulous subject, 'culture', develops as a result of a 'mix of informal prejudices, values, attitudes and working practises' which exists most prominently within the lower or more junior ranks of the police service (Newburn and Neyroud 2008: 203). This area has been well researched with several views and opinions published from commentators such as Ianni and Ianni (1983), Reiner (2000) and Waddington (1999). All organisations have a culture embedded within their roots, which can be defined generically within organisations as:

> The deeper level of assumptions and beliefs that are shared by members of an organisation that operates and projects unconsciously an organisation's view of itself and environment.
>
> (Grieve *et al.* 2007:116)

To comprehend police culture and especially its impact on public order policing, it is important to understand the diverse aspects that make up organisational culture, a key element of police values which is connected with moral and ethical codes forming ideas on how things should be done. Due to the working environment police officers have a sense of duty, a duty to 'fight crime' surrounded by an enhanced sense of authority (Skolnick 2005). This sense of duty has been clearly portrayed through public protests over the decades. Kiely and Peek (2002) concluded that the majority of young officers, in particular, were influenced by other police officers as they spent prolonged periods of time with each other during canteen breaks and waiting for calls in police cars. Waddington (1999) concluded that there is an apparent 'gap' between police officers' behaviour and attitudes. Observational studies by Black (1971) and Reiss (1980) found that in the privacy of a police car, station or in the canteen police officers were 'undoubtedly racist'. This may be linked back to Reiner's view that it is dependent upon how the individual officer sees the world. Mission, action, cynicism and pessimism influence police officers and in turn ensure that racism does not form part of the overall 'mission' of policing, or at least not a part of the police which the public actively experience.

Reiner (2000) identifies characteristics which help police officers identify themselves within the organisation and society. The characteristics are present in both the police culture and individual subcultures. Characteristics include:

- *Mission* – Policing is seen as a mission, to serve the public and protect the weak and vulnerable by 'locking up' the criminals to clean up the streets. This concept is closely aligned with policing values. Public order policing conforms to this sense of mission.
- *Action* – Policing is often seen as exciting, generating masses of adrenaline. Action is symbolised by the chase. This reinforces the typical view of policing and the stereotype of a police officer.
- *Cynicism* – Police officers see themselves as dealing with 'outcasts' and 'rejects' of society and this leads them to see the worst in people.
- *Pessimism* – Linked closely with cynicism as it is associated with having a negative outlook. It is easy for officers who have dealt with the unpleasant spectrum of the public to be judgemental and have preconceived beliefs.

These enable the individual to define his or her role, dealing with the bad, inhumane aspects of life:

Routine clients are drawn from the bottom layers of the social order.

(Reiner 2000: 95)

Suspicion forms a basis for cop culture and dealing with the various types of individuals involved in the criminal justice system heightens the officer's suspicion and formulates stereotypical opinions to do this. Reiner (2000) identifies that officers are in the main conservative, not only in a political sense but in their social conduct, having little tolerance for liberal behaviour. Protesters, for example, are seen as deviant. In addition to this, the police culture contains elements of machismo, being unsympathetic and heterosexual.

Routine 'sexual boasting and horseplay' often at the expense of female colleagues.

(Reiner 2000: 98)

This reinforces the view that police work is for 'the boys'. Reiner (2000) identifies isolation and solidarity formulation as a basis for this culture. This characteristic creates the idea of a 'them and us outlook' (Reiner 2000: 92), an idea of elitism and police officers 'fighting a war' and a 'tooling up' mentality against protesters. This approach becomes ever more prominent when the police encounter the same like-minded protesters such as miners or African Americas who also share a 'masculine ethos' (Waddington *et al.* 1989: 186). Ultimately Reiner looks at the effect of racial prejudice emanating from police conservatism, and its hostility and suspicion of ethnic minority groups. An example of this is the Brixton riots of 1981 and the subsequent report published by Lord Scarman (Scarman 1981). Brown (1998) illustrates how the occupational culture can develop subcultures. Subcultures form when individuals embrace different values that set them apart from the dominant culture (McLaughlin and Muncie 2006). This is partly due to differential interaction which is dependent upon the individuals' association with each other through experiences and influences. This is particularly true in militaristically structured organisations such as the police where there is a clear hierarchy through rigid rank structure, as there is a natural divide between two groups, leading to police officers at 'street level' feeling isolated from management. Ianni and Ianni (1983) highlights the differentiation between 'management cops' and 'street cops' which was recently demonstrated in the G20 events. Strategic managers made the decisions; however, it was the junior supervisor at sergeant and inspector rank who had the responsibility of enforcing implementation of the strategic initiatives. The disparity between both cultures often leads to frustration, and front-line officers disregarding policy decisions made by senior management. In the case of the G20 protests, individual police officers decided to remove identification tags and use unauthorised tactics. This may also occur in groups who communicate with each other frequently and who share experiences. This in itself can reinforce culture, as many police officers within specials teams deal with the same, often tragic or terrifying experiences. Subcultures can occur when individuals have a responsibility to perform the same tasks frequently, which results in them constructing a similar view of the outside world. Cohesion, where there is perceived performance success and specialism, can isolate individuals from other groups. This again may become apparent within specialist teams such as public order squads. Police officers dealing with public order will often have a particular outlook and view of protesters, seeing them as the 'enemy', and leading them to conclude that all protesters will riot. Similarly, personal characteristics of individuals including age, sex, education and ethnicity can result in a higher possibility that subcultural groups would be formed. Male police officers of a particular age are more likely to form a group and manifest a different culture.

Recent police strategies

The notion that the public are the 'customers' is relatively new within the policing world and there is an increasing emphasis to ensure that the police endeavour to maintain and preferably increase the public's perception of the organisation (Rogers 2008). The notion of the 'customer' is sometimes a difficult concept for the police service, as many users or 'consumers' of the service are often those deemed to be 'criminals'. The level of professionalism must be maintained when dealing with the public and its needs, and the police over recent years have relied on portraying to the public an image of an organisation attempting to improve its accountability. Police governance and local accountability have been important issues for all senior politicians and police managers alike but adverse media coverage and clever public relations (PR) work on the part of protesters appears to have negated these attempts. Accountability incorporates many factors into its definition, including 'answerability, responsiveness, openness, obedience and efficiency' (Day and Klein 1987). Many parliamentary Acts have attempted to further contextualise and solidify the ethos of accountability over past decades such as the introduction of the Police and Criminal Evidence Act 1984 (Home Office 1984), and the Serious Organised Crime and Police Act 2005 (Home Office 2005). Many argue that an effective complaints system is integral to the successful achievement, integration and implementation of a modern-day police service (Smith 2005). Since the introduction of the Independent Police Complaints Commission (IPCC), the number of complaints made against the police has increased, and in the first year the Commission recorded a 44 per cent increase, followed in subsequent years by more increases (Gleeson and Grace 2007). The IPCC has seen an increase of 8 per cent, with 31,250 complaints made in 2008 to 2009, an increase of more than 2,296 on the previous year. The total number of complaints average more that 600 per week (Crime Reduction Partnership 2009; Guardian Online 2009). The emphasis on police accountability is essential to the continuation of the modern police service due to the contract operating between the police and its customers, those who make up society. For the police service to continue to receive the public support it needs it must realign and conceivably re-enter its contract to 'police by consent'. This drive for increased professionalism and accountability has been an attempt to ensure that the contract remains intact; otherwise the risk of the licence being revoked is a realistic prospect. As complaints against the police continue to rise, correctly implementing 'corporate social responsibility' as a definitive basis for public order policing could offer a real and robust option to re-engage society and reaffirm its consent and licence to operate.

Corporate social responsibility (CSR)

Corporate social responsibility (CSR) has become an increasingly important concept across both the private and public sectors as businesses and organisations attempt to evaluate and minimise their impact upon the environment and society (Jones *et al.* 2009). Although there are many different definitions of corporate social responsibility, the one that perhaps best fits the police service incorporates the ethical and legal dimensions linked with a commitment to individuals and society. Dahlsrud provides the following definition:

> Business decision making linked to ethical values, compliance with legal requirements and respect for people, communities and the environment.
>
> (Dahlsrud 2008: 7)

Porter and Kramer (2006) notes that there are four key areas in which corporate social responsibility is closely aligned, including:

- *Moral obligation* – Being ethically and morally obliged to operate in a particular way will often drive organisations. Organisations have an obligation to be productive and act as good citizens. In addition to profiting and operating to meet the set objectives of the organisation, society expects businesses and organisations alike to solve social problems, both in the long and the short term (Holmes 1976).
- *Licence to operate* – For any business or organisation to operate, it must first gain consent, either explicitly or tacitly, from the government, society or stakeholders. This aspect is especially true for the police service, as the contract that exists through the 'policing by consent' mandate is well established. Maintaining public support and ensuring that the social contract remains intact should be of the utmost importance for today's police service. To ensure the continuation of the social contract, social expectations must be achieved and maintained (Moir 2001).
- *Sustainability* – Focusing on community and environmental stewardship, ensuring a long-term commitment and understanding. The sustainability of social contracts while carrying out everyday business activities is imperative. Ensuring that ethical codes and interactions adhere to any such contracts will increase sustainability (Dobers 2009).
- *Reputation* – Often the primary reason for implementing corporate social responsibility, reputation is concerned with improving an organisation's image, brand and relationship between itself and its customers/ users. Moir (2001) believes that 'This is a way of maintaining trust, support and legitimacy with the community, governments and employees' (Moir 2001: 17).

Following recent public order events such as the G20 and what can only be described as public relations disasters, the police service needs to further professionalise its approach in dealing with large-scale protests. Improving its image as portrayed through the media should be paramount, as will the need to realign the police and the community's goals. The corporate social responsibility approach reinforces the fact that the police service has a wider moral obligation to society that extends beyond its narrow remit of crime control, detecting and preventing crime. By addressing and robustly implementing corporate social responsibility into its corporate practises, the police service can perhaps begin to rebuild trust and reaffirm its binding contract with society. When dealing with climate protesters and other such demonstrators, the police must realise that their actions will undoubtedly come under scrutiny. By implementing the ideas of corporate social responsibility and situating them within a neighbourhood policing paradigm underscored by a consultative approach, traditional barriers will begin to break down and stimulate community re-engagement, moving away from the now traditional enforcement approach to dealing with both 'contained' and 'transgressive' groups. 'Contained' groups will include those protesters who are willing to engage with the police as opposed to 'transgressive' protesters who will attempt to antagonise and challenge any police action (Joyce 2009). Effectively managing both of these types of protesters will build legitimacy, and progress the ethical standing and moral codes, resulting in the police retraining its mandate of 'policing by consent'. Public perception and opinion will inevitably steer the policing agenda, tactics, decisions and approach when dealing with public order, and it is now up to the police service to further professionalise its approach to ethics, morality and public order policing. The current need by the police service to ensure that it wins and emerges successfully from each encounter with demonstrators clearly undermines their position. To be successful, the police must adopt a 'winning by appearing to lose' strategy on occasions which will require a complete change in direction and strategy. Adopting this strategy, combined with each element of corporate social responsibility, may at least go some way towards relegitimising the police service in the eyes of the public.

Conclusion

As with most public bodies, within the police organisation there is always the potential to improve the delivery of service to the community. Clearly there is a need to further involve the community, promoting discussion and professionalising the delivery of public order policing. While accepting that corporate social responsibility is not a panacea to all of these problems, it presents a real and robust option that must be carefully considered. In addition to these advantages, improved community cohesion, increased public confidence, organisational transparency and increased ethical standing may be enhanced. As the pressure from government, stakeholders, the media and society continues on the police organisation as a whole, meeting expectations will become increasingly difficult if the reputation of the service is not improved. It will be for police managers, planners and their partners in an ever-challenging social landscape to ensure that the organisation remains efficient, coherent and above all ethical in its public order approach so as to meet public demand. It is suggested that adopting a corporate social responsibility approach may be one way of helping to achieve this goal, as managing and rebuilding trust and legitimacy will be essential in ensuring that the police mandate of 'policing by consent' remains intact for the foreseeable future.

References and suggested further reading

Black, D. (1971) *The Social Organisation of Arrest*. Stanford Law Review, London.

Brearley, N. and King, M. (1996) 'Policing social protest: some ndicators of change', in Critcher, C. and Waddington, D. *Policing Public Order: Theoretical and Practical Issues*. Ashgate, Aldershot.

Brewer, J., Guelke, A., Hume, I., Browne, E. and Wilford, R. (1996) *The Police Public Order and the State, Policing in Great Britain, Northern Ireland, The Irish Republic, The USA, Israel, South Africa and China*, 2nd edn. Macmillan, London.

Brown, A. (1998) *Organisational Culture*, 2nd edn. Pitman Publishing, London.

Button, M., John, T. and Brearly, N. (2002) 'New challenges in public order: the professionalisation of environmental protests and the emergence of the militant environmental activist', *International Journal of the Society of Law*, 70(March): 17–31.

Casciani, D. (2009) *Eyewitness: Two Days of Protests*. Available online at: http://news.bbc.co.uk/1/hi/uk/7980400.stm (accessed 4 October 2009).

Crime Reduction Partnership (2009) *Complaints Against the Police Rise 8 Percent in 2008*. Available: http://www.crp-news.com/htm/n20090924.723735.htm (accessed 5 October 2009).

Dahlsrud, A. (2008) 'How corporate social responsibility is defined, an analysis of 37 definitions', *Corporate social responsibility and Environmental Management,* 15(1): 1–13.

Day, P. and Kilein, R. (1987) *Accountabilities*. Tavistock, London.

Dobers, P. (2009) 'Corporate social responsibility: management and methods', *Corporate Social Responsibility and Environmental Management*, 16: P185–P191.

Donson, F., Chesters, G., Welsh, I. and Tickle, A. (2004) 'Rebels with a cause, folk devils without a panic, policing tactics and anti-capitalist protests in London and Prague', *Internet Journal of Criminology*, 1–3. Available online at: http://www.internetjournalofcriminology.com/Donson%20et%20al%20-%20Folkdevils.pdf (accessed 9 October 2009.

Edwards, C. (1999) *Changing Policing Theories for 21st Century Societies*. The Federation Press, London.

Fine, B. and Millar, R. (1985) *Policing the Miners Strike*. Lawrence and Wishart, London.

Geary, R. (1985) *Policing Industrial Disputes: 1893–1985*. Cambridge University Press, Cambridge.

Gilligan, G. and Pratt, J. (2004) *Crime, Truth and Justice: Official Inquiry, Discourse and Knowledge*. Willan Publishing, Cullompton, Devon.

Giulianotti, R., Bonney, N. and Hepworth, M. (1994) *Football, Violence and Social Identity*. Routledge, New York.

Gleeson, E. and Grace, K. (2007) *Police Complaint: Statistics for England and Wales 2006/7*. Independent Police Complaints Commission, London.

Grieve, J., Harfield, C. and Macvean, A. (2007) *Policing*. Sage, London.

Guardian Online (2009) *Police Watchdog Reveals 8% Rise in Complains by Public*. Available online at: http://www.guardian.co.uk/politics/2009/sep/24/ipcc-police-complaints-rise (accessed 5 October 2009).

Hansen, A. (1991) 'The media and the social construction of the environment', *Media, Culture and Society*, 13: 443–458.

Hirst, P. (1975) 'Marx and Engels on Law', Crime and Mortality in: Taylor, I., Watton, P. and Young, J. *Critical Criminology*, Routledge and Kegan Paul, London, pp. 203–232.

HMIC (2009) *Adapting to Protest – Nurturing the British Model of Policing.* Central Office of Information, London.

Holmes, S. (1976) 'Executive perceptions of corporate social responsibility', *Business Horizons*, 19: 34–40.

Home Office (1986) *The Public Order Act 1986.* Stationery Office, London.

—— (1984) *Police and Criminal Evidence Act 1984.* Stationery Office, London.

—— (2000) *The Human Rights Act 2000.* Stationery Office, London.

—— (2005) *Serious Organised Crime and Police Act 2005.* Stationery Office, London.

Ianni, E. and Ianni, F. (1983) *Two Cultures of Policing: Street Cop Management Cop.* Transition Publishers, New York.

Innes, M. (2003) *Understanding Social Control: Deviance, Crime and Social Order.* Open University Press, Buckingham.

Jefferson, T. (1990) *The Case against Paramilitary Policing.* Open University Press, Buckingham.

Jones, P., Hillier, D., Comfort, D. and Clarke-Hill, C. (2009) 'Commercial property investment companied and corporate social responsibility', *Journal of Property Investment Finance*, 27(5): 522–533.

Joyce, P. (2009) 'The policing of protest', *Policing Today*, 15(3): 30–33.

Kiely, J. and Peek, G. (2002) 'The culture of the British police: views of police officers', *The Service Industries Journal*, 22(1): 167–183.

Lewis, P. (2009) 'Climate campers get a lesson in citizen journalism', *Guardian*, 28 August, p. 19.

Mawby, R. (2008) *Models of Policing, Handbook of Policing.* Willan Publishing, Cullompton, Devon.

McLaughlin, E. and Muncie, J. (2006) *The SAGE Dictionary of Criminology*, 2nd edn. Sage, London.

Moir, L. (2001) *What do we mean by Social Corporate Responsibility,* Corporate Governance, 1, 2: 16–22, MCB University Press.

Monkkonen, E., (1981) *Police in Urban America 1860–1920,* Cambridge, Cambridge University Press.

Newburn, T., and Neyroud, P., (2008) *Dictionary of Policing.* Willan Publishing, Cullompton, Devon.

Porter, M. and Kramer, M. (2006) 'Strategy and society: the link between competitive advantage and social responsibility', *Harvard Business Review*, 84 (12): 78–92.

Rawlings, P. (2002) *Policing: A Short History.* Willan Publishing, Cullompton, Devon.

Reiner, R. (1998) *Policing, Protests, and Disorder in Britain, in Policing Protest.* University of Minnesota Press, Minneapolis.

—— (2000) *The Politics of the Police*, 3rd edn. Oxford University Press, London.

Reiss, A. (1980) Controlling Police Use of Deadly Force. *American Academy of Political and Social Science*, issue 452: 122–134.

Reith, C. (1956) *A New Study of Police History.* Oliver and Boyd, London.

Rogers, C. (2008) *Leadership Skills in Policing.* Oxford University Press, London.

Scarman, Lord (1981) *The Brixton Disorders.* Cmnd, 8427, HMSO, London.

Silver, A. (1971) Social and ideological bases of British elite reactions to domestic crisis 1829–32. *Politics and Society*, 1: 179–201.

Skolnick, J. (2005) 'A sketch of the policeman's "working personality"', in Newburn, T. (ed.), *Policing: Key Readings.* Willan Publishing, Cullompton, Devon.

Smith, G. (2005) 'A most enduring problem: police complaints reform in England and Wales', *Journal of Social Policy*, 35(1): 121–141.

Smith, J., McCarthy, J., McPhail, C. and Augustyn, B. (2001) 'From protest to agenda building: description bias in media coverage of protest events in Washington DC', *Social Forces*, 79(4): 1397–1423. University of North Carolina Press. Chapel Hill, North Carolina.

Thurmond Smith, P. (1985) *Policing Victorian London: Political Policing, Public Order Policing and the London Metropolitan Police*. Greenwood Press, London.

Townsend, M. (2009) 'Police riot notebooks reveal brutal use of shields against G20 protesters', *Guardian*, 23 August, p. 17.

Uglow, S. (1988) *Policing Liberal Society*. Oxford University Press, Oxford.

Waddington, D. (1992) *Contemporary Issues in Public Order: A Comparative and Historical Approach*. Routledge, New York.

—— (1996) 'Key issues and controversies', in Critcher, C. and Waddington, D. (eds), *Policing Public Order: Theoretical and Practical Issues*. Ashgate, Aldershot.

Waddington, D., Jones, K. and Critcher, C. (1989) *Flashpoints: Studies in Public Disorder*. Routledge, London.

Waddington, P.A.J. (1999) *Policing Citizens: Authority and Rights*. Routledge, New York.

Wright, A. (2002) *Policing: An Introduction to Concepts and Practice*. Willan Publishing, Cullompton, Devon.

18 Future directions

Introduction

This chapter will consider the possible future directions of policing, particularly over the next five to ten years. It will in particular consider the role of policing within the wider community and how the police carry out some of their core business, particularly in investigations.

The future of policing within the 'Big Society'

The idea of promoting community agencies, groups and individuals in an attempt to encourage social interaction and thus produce a more cohesive society is not particularly new, but will gain momentum as a different philosophy to the delivery of policing starts to permeate its way into society. Previous official documents, such as Wedlock's publication on social cohesion (Home Office 2006) which promoted social cohesion and crime-resistant communities, have urged police and their partners to engage in these types of activities and this will increase. Furthermore, the importance of social capital, which has been explored in the work of Robert Putnam who considers the rise of criminal activity against a backcloth of social disengagement in the US (Putnam 2000), will also be recognised. Recent and current governmental ideas which extend this approach have been and are still being promoted by Halpern (2007, 2010) who served as an aide to the previous Labour government and now advises the present government.

It is useful to consider the concept of the Big Society against the backcloth of previous governments' activities within the field of crime and disorder reduction. The 'new' philosophy of the 'Big Society' may be seen as an extension of previous governments' attempts to relocate responsibility for crime control from purely state-owned mechanisms to the ownership of communities. Garland (2001) argues that this country has seen the development of one type of community-style programme after another since the 1960s until 'the community' has become the all-purpose solution to every criminal justice problem. Some of these have been viewed as being innovative and radical, ooolcing to respond to the concerns of citizens and enlist the help of neighbourhood residents and organisations. This ongoing attempt to extend the use of private sector and community agencies is described by Garland as a 'responsibilisation strategy', and involves a change in the manner in which governments act upon crime. Instead of addressing crime and disorder in a direct fashion by means of police and the criminal justice sanction approach, the new approach requires a new kind of indirect action. Over the past decade or so, a new kind of crime prevention approach has been developed by Western governments, especially in the UK which has seen the introduction of new strategies dependent upon such terms as partnerships, alliances, interagency cooperation, the multi-agency approach, activating citizens, etc. (Rogers 2006). This will continue. The primary object however has been to spread responsibility for crime control onto other agencies, organisations and individuals that operate outside the criminal justice system and to persuade them to act appropriately (Hughes 2007). In this sense, therefore, the idea of the big society, while projected through the lens of a different political ideology than the previous decade, may be seen as a further extension of the idea of the responsibilisation strategy employed by central government.

Police powers and individual freedom

One feature that runs through many of the chapters on investigation is the tension between the powers given to police investigators and the rights and freedoms of suspects, the accused and of the general public. In Chapter 1 these tensions were phrased in terms of the role of legislation in striking new (and changing) balances between the rights of individuals and the effectiveness of the criminal justice system. Although it may be tempting to think that the loss of rights is irreversible, several appeal cases (often to the chagrin of government) have hindered the impact of intrusive or complex legislation (Waddington 2005). For example, in July 2009, the Court of Appeal in London ruled that placing an individual on the sex register for life without the possibility of review, even if they can show that they are no longer a risk, is disproportionate. However, it is still the responsibility of Parliament to decide the threshold of evidence required to demonstrate that an individual does not constitute a risk. It is likely, then, that there are limits to the acceptance of members of the public about the precise balance between the rights of the victim and those of the suspect.

There are particular concerns over whether terrorism can be combated using the legislation framed for organised crime or through the courts, and one assumption made by investigating officers may be that 'in terrorism the rules are different because the stakes are much higher'. The emphasis upon pre-emptive action against terrorists with the reliance upon secret information sources is sometimes inconsistent with the exchange of information that necessarily accompanies even the most controlled of court proceedings. The linking of state action to suspicion without the need for charging is referred to as 'pre-crime' (McCulloch and Pickering 2009). The response of the state (including control orders and a raft of legislation aimed at criminalising intent to commit terrorist-related offences) raises the stakes for those worried about individual liberty and for the government, which is also subject to some oversight from European courts.

The move to pro-active policing and multi-agency working

Chapter 1 also emphasised the pro-active role of the criminal justice system as typified by ASBOs which shift the burden of proof to the (lower) civil court threshold. The viability of maintaining the ASBO approach is currently under review, but it is clear that the problem of antisocial behaviour will remain a priority for policing.

The police have also become increasingly pro-active in their investigations. Chapter 14 gives examples of preventive measures such as the Sex Offender Register (a form of crime reduction) while Chapter 15 reports on attempts, albeit somewhat controversial, by various agencies to reduce the radicalisation of young Muslims. All chapters emphasise the importance of multi-agency working. This has been particularly effective in dealing with sex offenders, although confidentiality often prevents the public from learning about many of the successful collaborations between the police, social workers and health professionals.

Since pro-active policing relies upon intelligence and (in various guises) the surveillance of suspects and of the public at large, there are elements of practice which remain controversial. Methods of information gathering should not be a substitute for the support of the police by the public, although if sufficiently intrusive they may undermine it. The argument that sections of the community do not always support the police and so the police must work in a 'community vacuum' is also relevant, but dependence upon remotely obtained information does not enhance community engagement and it may well make it worse. The value and intrusiveness of the information sharing between agencies (including suspicions or unfounded allegations) depends where you sit. An investigating officer may well take the view that the more information there is the better and that he or she cannot be expected (with the immediate pressure of investigations) to take the wider view on behalf of society. The impact of the Independent Safeguarding Agency in collecting and distributing information about individuals has yet to be determined and it is up to the government, Parliament and the public to assess such impacts over the coming years. However, the often stated importance of ethics in the police service poses an obligation on senior officers (in particular) to assess whether a particular law should be used for purposes for which it was not intended.

The importance of science and technology

The role of technology was discussed in Chapter 16. In one sense science and technology has revolutionised crime investigation, and the SIO's understanding of the value of forensic evidence, through appropriate training, is now much improved. DNA was one of the great hopes of the police service and is often regarded as the closest thing to an investigator's 'silver bullet'. The reality, as discussed in Chapter 16, is somewhat different. Despite its high-profile impact in serious crime and its increasing use in lower level crime, DNA evidence will not and cannot be a short cut which makes traditional investigator skills redundant. As with all science and technology, police officers must understand its limitations and strengths. Furthermore, the availability of huge databases and the maturing of DNA evidence (in particular) may well have made the investigator over-reliant on science and there is some evidence that the criminal is fighting back (e.g. by burning stolen vehicles so as to minimise the DNA-laden trace evidence left at the scene). Intelligence is, of course, much wider than DNA or fingerprints, but making links with other sections of the book, it is also unclear whether or not the police have the capability to 'feed' the voracious appetite of the National Intelligence Model, upon which many of the databases depend.

Forensic science has also become controversial. The (US) National Academy of Sciences Report on Forensic Sciences (2010) is important in drawing attention to weaknesses in the way in which forensic science has developed, weaknesses that have led to some subjective interpretations, exaggerated testimony and a paucity of research in certain areas. Its underlying theme is that the re-evaluation of previously accepted scientific methodologies is part of the evolution of all science and that honest debate about the applicability, reliability and limitations of forensic science, coupled with more rigorous testing, should be viewed as a strength and not an undermining weakness of the criminal justice system.

The question of whether or not DNA profiles should be retained from those who are subsequently found to be innocent has clearly placed the government in something of a dilemma (Chapter 16). The effects of high-profile cases such as the McKie case are also very worrying, as they serve to undermine public confidence in the objectivity of scientific evidence and in the fairness of the criminal justice system generally. It also remains to be seen whether or not the final governmental response to the McKie case strengthens or further erodes such public confidence. The (US) National Academy of Sciences Report on Forensic Sciences (2010) is important in drawing attention to weaknesses in the way in which forensic science has developed, weaknesses that have led to some subjective interpretations, exaggerated testimony and a paucity of research in certain areas.

Crime science offers a different approach to crime reduction and investigation. The opportunities presented by crime science have been slow to be accepted by the police service but in any case, in order to be effective crime science requires a wider range of sponsorship and champions. For example, crime reduction is linked to the way in which commercial products and even houses are designed and built, so that the government and the commercial world are also essential partners in promoting crime science.

Investigations are probably improving

Strenuous attempts have been made over the past ten years, through advanced training of SIOs, through the sharing of best practice and through the use of forensic science, technology and information sharing, to produce professionally run criminal investigations. Although we have no adequate basis for comparison, it is also likely that the quality of investigations has improved over the past 20 years as best practice has permeated the police service. The experience of victims and suspects has almost certainly dramatically improved as systems and legislation have been put into place to protect vulnerable witnesses and suspects, and many examples of this are to be found in Chapter 14.

For the historical reasons outlined in Chapter 14, sexual offences are often inaccurately associated with sinister strangers. The police investigation of sexual offences is particularly challenging because such allegations are often contested by the suspect and hinge on the issue of consent. The investigation of rape, discussed in Chapter 14, is a topic of intense public interest and has led to improvements in the way in which victims (who generally fall into the category of vulnerable persons) are questioned and examined so as to maximise the opportunities for reliable evidence. Internet-based sexual offences, including 'grooming' and pornography, remain challenging to investigators but non-police agencies (such as CEOP) make a major contribution to providing the police with information that informs the investigations and which protects young children.

In general, investigations are historical reconstructions of the past and are sometimes likened to locating the pieces of a giant jigsaw. The jigsaw metaphor is simplistic though, as several jigsaws may have similar pieces. In some crimes, there is simply so little evidence (so few pieces) available to distinguish between different reconstructions, and in such circumstances small pieces of evidence may, in retrospect, be given too much weighting. In particular, the effect of police objectives on the outcome of investigations has been reported to lead 'the police to interpret events in particular ways, to neglect certain lines of enquiry, and to suppress specific items of information' (Redmayne 2001: 13).

However, unlike the crime scene investigator (who may report that 'there is no trace evidence' at the scene), the police investigator of serious crime is rarely given the luxury of conceding defeat by the public, the media or their chief officer. Assessing whether or not the analysis of an investigation has remained objective is often a most difficult business but 'tunnel vision' is clearly counter-productive. As Stelfox (2009) points out, 'once we believe that we understand the truth of something we tend to stop looking at other possibilities'. The impact on criminal justice of the wrong crime reconstruction is then clear for all to see. The expectations of the public are understandably high, but open and public discussions of the complexities of serious investigations rarely surface in the media; if they do they may sometimes be misinterpreted and perceived as evidence of complacency or incompetence on the part of the police by the public themselves. The ghost of Sherlock Holmes looms large in the public imagination and it is Sherlock Holmes and his countless TV successors who have encouraged the hope that, in a technological age, crimes are always solvable and that police enquiries can reveal the culprit without substantial inconvenience to the public at large. This is far from the truth; indeed, luck is also likely to be key in determining a successful outcome.

Measures of effectiveness

The response of the police to organised crime, with its often transnational dimension, is outlined in Chapter 15. The challenges of fighting organised crime operating over different legislative frameworks, cultures and enforcement jurisdictions are enormous. Money is often laundered across many countries, and dedicated and highly trained squads of investigators are required to trace illicit funds. Organised crime challenges both the police and police structures. The perceived inadequacy of local forces in dealing with organised crime at NIM level 3 catalysed the formation of SOCA. Group-based terrorism may be regarded as the most serious form of organised crime and counter-terrorism is well resourced, although it is inevitable that controlled demand will outstrip all available resources. Particularly challenging has been the mutation of terrorism groups, as evidenced by the considerable new challenges raised by Al Qaida.

The effectiveness of policing of drug-related crime may well mirror that of other attempts to combat organised crime. Drug crime is often rooted in organised crime. The overall impact of the police service upon drug crime is uncertain, although there have been substantial and very successful individual large-scale police operations against drug crime networks. However, police successes with individual gangs or suppliers may displace crime with new dealers quickly replacing the old. Within the UK, regular assessments of the impact of SOCA and whether a gap in enforcement stills exists at regional level are highly desirable. The government is pressurising police forces to cooperate more and it is the authors' view that this will slowly move the police service towards a regional (if not a UK national) organisation and structure over the coming years.

Most organisations (whether commercial or public) attempt to assess the value for money of various strategies but the effectiveness of the collective (inter-agency) strategies for counter-terrorism, for example, would be very difficult to assess. In many ways, terrorism is a special case owing to the terror it produces in the population at large. Such terror is generally disproportionate to physical destruction because it affects workers, businesses and even world financial markets. The government responds accordingly, spending much more money on counter-terrorism than, for example, on flu pandemic preparations. However, as the public gets more used to the risk of terrorism, as the financial recession causes the government to challenge expenditure without exception, and in an era where low-level crime is probably of greater daily relevance to the population, a comparison of expenditure and benefits will inevitably occur across all budget lines, including counter-terrorism. The methodological foundation for such comparisons must be based on assessment of risk, with the usual caution: there will always be uncertainty and the risks encountered in law enforcement cannot be made truly objective. Progress in obtaining value for money has already been obtained in work transformation and modernisation and there has already been a revolution in the way in which lower paid employers (e.g. 'civilian' investigators and PCSOs) have been used effectively by the police service, and this has allowed resources to be saved so as to be used elsewhere.

Determining value for money is one thing: deciding on the priority of activities is quite another (Fleming and Grabosky 2009). The resources for criminal investigations come from the larger police pot. The prioritisation of expenditure is a 'political hot potato' in an era when organisations (particularly public ones) are very reluctant to concede that they cannot cope with all their publicly accepted responsibilities. This is a political issue and one that may be expected to unfold as cuts in public services occur, but in the long term the question 'what is it that the police should not do?' cannot be avoided if we are to retain an effective and accountable police service.

References and suggested further reading

Fleming, R. and Grabosky, initial (2009) 'Managing the demand for police services, or how to control an insatiable appetite', *Policing*, 3(3): 281–291.

Garland, D. (2001) *The Culture of Control*. Oxford University Press, Oxford.

Halpern, D. (2007) *Social Capital*. Polity Press, Cambridge.

Halpern, D. (2010) *The Hidden Wealth of Nations*. Polity Press, Cambridge.

Home Office (2006) *Crime and Cohesive Communities*. Research, Development and Statistics-Communities Group, London, Home Office. Available online at: http://rds.homeoffice.gov.uk/rds/pdfs06/rdsolr1906.pdf (accessed 23 September 2010).

Hughes, G. (2007) *The Politics of Crime and Community*. Palgrave-Macmillan, Basingstoke.

McCulloch, J. and Pickering, S. (2009) 'Pre-crime and counter-terrorism', *British Journal of Criminology*, 49(5): 628–645.

Putnam, R. D. (2000) *Bowling Alone*. Simon & Schuster, London.

Redmayne, M. (2001) *Expert Evidence and Criminal Justice*. Oxford University Press, Oxford.

Rogers, C. (2006) *Crime Reduction Partnerships*. Oxford University Press, Oxford.

Stelfox, P. (2009) *Criminal Investigation: An Introduction to Principles and Practice*. Willan Publishing, Cullompton Devon.

Waddington, P. A. J. (2005) 'Slippery slopes and civil libertarian pessimism', *Policing and Society*, 15(3): 353–375.

Notes

1   Issues around the sharing of information between partner agencies are considered in Chapter 13 (this volume).
2   Police information is defined in subsection 2.2 of the code as 'all information, including intelligence and personal data obtained and recorded for police purposes' (ACPO Centrex 2006: 70).
3   See Harfield and Harfield (2008) for a more detailed description of these exemptions.
4   There are exceptions to the general premise of the CPIA relating to intelligence derived from the interception of intelligence established under RIPA.
5   In turn, Section 26(9) of RIPA defines a covert relationship as follows:

> a relationship is used covertly, and information obtained as mentioned in subsection (8)(c) is disclosed covertly, if and only if it is used or, as the case may be, disclosed in a manner that is calculated to ensure that one of the parties to the relationship is unaware of the use or disclosure in question. It is the actions of the individual, on behalf of a law enforcement agency and in the manner described, that constitutes their status as a source that requires authorisation. Merely providing information to a law enforcement agency that is already within the individual's possession does not necessitate authorisation.
>
> (ACPO 2007: 22)

6   These hallmarks were: Empowered and Effective Leadership; Visible and Constructive Accountability; Intelligence-led Business Processes, Effective and Responsive Delivery Structures, Engaged Communities, and Appropriate Skills and Knowledge.
7   See e.g. Cope (2004).
8   Section 115 authorities include the police, police authority, local authority (including district, county, London borough, parish council, community council, county borough council), registered social landlord, local probation board, local health board (in Wales), primary care trust, strategic health authority, and fire and rescue authority.
9   Registration also applies to offenders who are: found not guilty by reason of insanity; unfit to plead but found to have committed the act charged; and those sentenced since 1991 who were, on commencement, still in contact with the criminal justice system, whether awaiting sentence, in prison, subject to supervision, serving a community sentence, detained in hospital or subject to guardianship.
10 The Sex Offender Act 1997 required offenders to register their personal details within 14 days. This was amended by the Criminal Justice and Courts Services Act 2000 which now requires registration to occur within three days. (HOC 20/2001).
11 Or contamination.

Index

Routledge
Paperbacks Direct

Bringing you the cream of our hardback publishing at paperback prices

This exciting new initiative makes the best of our hardback publishing available in paperback format for authors and individual customers.

Routledge Paperbacks Direct is an ever-evolving programme with new titles being added regularly.

To take a look at the titles available, visit our website.

www.routledgepaperbacksdirect.com

Routledge
Taylor & Francis Group